Dear Reader
This book
your mind.

MW01248784

LIVE AND LET LIVE
UNDER ONE G ˞ O ˞ D

G - GENERATOR

O - OPERATOR

D - DESTROYER

UNIVERSAL RELIGION
(A religion of Humanity and Spirituality)

by

Devidas (Dev) Tahiliani

RoseDog ❦ Books
PITTSBURGH, PENNSYLVANIA 15238

The contents of this work, including, but not limited to, the accuracy of events, people, and places depicted; opinions expressed; permission to use previously published materials included; and any advice given or actions advocated are solely the responsibility of the author, who assumes all liability for said work and indemnifies the publisher against any claims stemming from publication of the work.

All Rights Reserved
Copyright © 2016 by Devidas (Dev) Tahiliani

No part of this book may be reproduced or transmitted, downloaded, distributed, reverse engineered, or stored in or introduced into any information storage and retrieval system, in any form or by any means, including photocopying and recording, whether electronic or mechanical, now known or hereinafter invented without permission in writing from the publisher.

Rosedog Books
585 Alpha Drive
Suite 103
Pittsburgh, PA 15238
Visit our website at www.rosedogbookstore.com

ISBN: 978-1-4809-6621-5
eISBN: 978-1-4809-6598-0

THE SOURCE OF THE TRUTH:

Let us look at the cover of my book. The statue of *The Thinker*. A man sitting alone, leaning forward, elbows on his knees, his hand supporting his head (TEE BOW). There supposedly he sits in deep thought, hour after hour, day after day – just thinking!

But *The Thinker* had nothing to think from! No foundation for his thinking. No facts on which to base his conjectures. The human mind is not equipped to manufacture Truth with no basis for that Truth!

Supposedly that statue depicts the manner in which all of the Religions of the world came in to being. In each religion first came the **Philosopher**, then came **Mythologist** who built story around the philosophy, and then came the **Ritualist** who picked the good points from the story and made rituals for people to follow.

Most people accept carelessly what they are taught from childhood. And coming in to maturity, they accept that which they have repeatedly heard, read or been taught. They continue to go along, usually without question, with their peers. Most people do not realize it, but they have carelessly assumed what they believe without question or proof. Yet they will defend it vigorously and emotionally their convictions. It has become human nature for people to flow with the stream – to go along with the crowd – to believe and perform like their peers around them.

I have written this book to educate young people of the world regarding **Universal Religion (Humanity and Spirituality)**. I hope this book will appeal to the young minds in realizing as to what really the God, the Religion or the Faith is. Hope they will not follow it blindly but try to understand its deep meaning and act accordingly. It is good to have some kind of **Faith**. I wish there were 7 Billion faiths for 7 Billion people to understand and follow. But follow them with a reason.

I have put my heart in to writing this book, but I did not "invent" anything. The ideas expressed in it have been inspired by the teachings and the living example of my spiritual teachers.

I am neither the writer nor the spiritualist, so here are some ideas for leading simple and peaceful life with 'Live and Let Live' philosophy. These ideas I have collected from different books, magazines and publications, being a common prudent human being.

DONATIONS

This book is being distributed, free of cost or at nominal cost to anyone, who is interested in knowing the **cause, nature and purpose of this universe.**

This book is also being popularized on Internet as eBook, free of cost or at nominal cost to any one who is interested in knowing, Who we are? Why we are here in this world? and What is our purpose of life?

For that purpose I have started the following non-profit organization. I request the readers of this book to Donate/Pledge some offerings (if he/she wishes) for this organization, to help me fund the organization, for printing copies of this book and distribute world wide and expand it on the internet for all human beings.

"LIVE AND LET LIVE MISSION INC."
C/o Devidas (Dev) Tahiliani
13 Morgan Drive – Unit 208
Natick, MA 01760
liveandletlivemission@gmail.com

"LIVE AND LET LIVE MISSION INC." is the humanitarian mission, whose mission is to unite, all the different communities and religions of the world. The common bonds of humanity and compassion unite us together not in just face of religion fights but in understanding each other.

"LIVE AND LET LIVE MISSION INC." is registered as a 501(c)(3) non-profit organization.

Contributions to the LIVE AND LET LIVE MISSION INC. are tax-deductible to the extent permitted by law.

The LIVE AND LET LIVE MISSION INC. tax identification number is 47-1051939.

CONTENTS

PREFACE

This book is dedicated to my grandchildren and to the youth of the whole world. At the turn of the century, when my first grand child was born on **July 11, 2001**, I have been thinking as to; What gift do I or people of my generation wish to give our grandchildren and children of this 21st century, our Millennial offspring's? Do we wish to leave them a world of Pain, Violence, and War? Or do we wish for them a world of Peace, Love, and Unity? The choice is ours to make today. If we wish for their world to be better than what we have seen in the past century, then we must be willing to teach them **Love and Peace**. They will not learn it if we carry our past hatreds and prejudices into their hearts and souls. That is why I decided to write this book and distribute free to the whole world. I wish for all the 21st century children to read this book during high school or just after high school or before going to college or before entering in to this world as adults.

After more than three hundred years of British rule, India finally won back its freedom on August 15, 1947. I was seven years old at that time and was living with my parents and five siblings in the Sindh state of India. All the patriotic hearts rejoiced at seeing India becoming a sovereign nation and the triumph of hundreds and thousands of martyred souls. It was a birth of a new nation and a new beginning. **The only fact that marred the happiness was the fact that the country was divided into India and Pakistan, based on religion alone, and the violent communal riots between Muslims and Hindus took away a number of lives.** Whole state of Sindh became part of Pakistan and Extreme Muslims were chasing/killing Hindus. We being Hindus had to leave all our property (Land and Buildings) and came to India by train & ship and became refugees in 1948.

On **September 11, 2001**, around 8:55 AM while I was busy in office writing a report for one of my bridge projects, I heard my boss shouting in the hallway that the Tower One is on fire. I along with the rest of my colleagues of The Port Authority of NY & NJ (PA) followed him to the parking lot and watched the smoke coming out of the Tower One. I had just joined PA in May 2001 as project manager in the Engineering Department of PA, located in Jersey City near Holland Tunnel across the river from The World Trade Center (WTC). While we were watching the fire on Tower One, around 9:04 AM we saw a plane flew over our heads and headed towards Tower Two for the direct hit. We were all stunned as to what happened and we saw a smoke coming out of this tower too. We were shocked and we turned the car radios on to find out that this was a terrorist attack on America. We just stood there in the parking lot with our eyes and ears open. As the world watched Tower Two collapsed to the ground at about 10:00 AM, unfortunately, this horrible scene was duplicated at 10:30 AM when Tower One also crashed to the ground. We started praying for our colleagues in Tower One because PA corporate office was in that tower. PA owned and operated WTC at that time and about 43 PA police and about 43 civil employees of PA lost their lives. This terrorist attack brought about the death of approximately 3,000 men, women and children from nations around the world. My mind was very much disturbed by this incident and could not sleep during the night for quite some time and had lot of nightmares.

I became more determined to write something to educate children and create love and peace instead of hatred and violence in the minds of children.

On **January 5, 2002** around 5:00 AM, I shoveled the snow from my driveway, came up into my master bathroom to shave & shower and get ready for office. While applying the shaving cream on my face, I passed out and fell on the floor. My dear wife Ratna heard the big THUD, shouted my name but I did not respond. She got up from the bed and came into the bathroom and saw me lying unconscious on the floor. She was shocked and ran back to the bedroom and called for the ambulance. Then she came back to bathroom and saw me sitting on the floor. She asked, "Do you know what happened to you?" I responded "Nothing happened, I am just going to shave & shower and go to office". She said NO, you are not going to office today, so come and sit down on bed, ambulance is coming and we have to go to the hospital in Dover NJ. There an emergency doctor found some enzymes in my blood and said that I had heart attack and they have to do Cardiac Catheterization. I was in good spirits at that time and kept on denying that I had heart attack. Next day they transported me immediately to the St. Claire's hospital in Denville NJ, where a renowned cardiologist performed the cardiac cath. and he told us that I had 3 arteries 90% blocked and 2 arteries were 50% blocked. That means they had to do open heart triple bypass surgery. Whole family was scared of this risky procedure. After 3 days they transferred me to Morristown Memorial hospital in NJ, where heart surgeons performed the successful open heart bypass surgery. Next day surgeon came and told me that they performed quintuple bypass surgery and cleaned up all my five arteries, because he said that my pump (heart) was good and healthy but all my pipes (arteries) were clogged. We all had a big laugh.

Next day my cardiologist came and told me that there is no cure for coronary artery disease. In order to prevent the progression of heart disease and another heart attack, I must follow his advice and make necessary **lifestyle changes** — quit smoking (I was only fashion smoker in parties), lower your blood cholesterol (no more fatty food), control your diabetes (I was diagonosed for diabetes in 1997) and high blood pressure, follow an exercise plan, maintain an ideal body weight, and control stress.

After January 2002 heart attack and then quintuple bye-pass surgery at the age of 62, I felt the need to invest more time in quiet reflection and solitude. I started meditating (sit quietly in lotus form on the bed) for few minutes in the morning before leaving bed and for few minutes in the night before sleeping. I started thinking periodically the innate qualities of SOUL, revealing the mysterious entity of GOD and thinking the process of world transformation.

I became more determined to do something about the religious fights or the fights between have (rich) and have not (poor). I thought of educating children from the childhood. I started reading only religious books, magazines and religious publications.

God has given me this second chance of life, to do something for the future generation.

CHAPTER 1

WHAT IS "GOD"?

1.01 – DICTIONARY MEANING OF GOD:

GOD is the English name given to a singular being in theistic and deistic religions (and other belief systems) who is either the *sole* deity in monotheism, or a *single* deity in polytheism·

GOD is most often conceived of as the supernatural creator and overseer of the universe. Theologians have ascribed a variety of attributes to the many different conceptions of GOD. The most common among these include omniscience (infinite knowledge), omnipotence (unlimited power), omnipresence (present everywhere), omnibenevolence (perfect goodness), omnitruth (Truth in time and space), divine simplicity, eternal and necessary existence.

1.02 – COMMON CONCEPTS OF GOD:

1. The one Supreme Being, the creator and ruler of the universe. (Hindu Philosophy)
2. The Supreme Being, understood as Life, Truth, Love, Mind, Soul, Spirit, Principle. (Christian Science)
3. The Supreme Being considered with reference to a particular attribute: (the God of Islam)
4. One of several deities, especially a male deity, presiding over some portion of worldly affairs.
5. A supreme being according to some particular conception: the god of mercy.

6. An image of a deity; an idol.
7. It is Deity, Divinity, and Immortal
8. Supernatural being, who is worshipped as the controller of some part of the universe or some aspect of life in the world or is the personification of some force Related: divine
9. An image, idol, or symbolic representation of such a deity
10. Any person or thing to which excessive attention is given: money was his God
11. A man who has qualities regarded as making him superior to other men
12. It is the supernatural being conceived as the perfect and omnipotent and omniscient originator and ruler of the universe; the object of worship is monotheistic religions.
13. It is a man of such superior qualities that he seems like a deity to other people.
14. Sometimes it is a material effigy that is worshiped (like money as God).

1.03 – EXISTENCE OF GOD:

Many arguments which attempt to prove or disprove the existence of God have been proposed by philosophers, theologians, and other thinkers for many centuries.

There are many philosophical issues concerning the existence of God. Some definitions of God are sometimes nonspecific, while other definitions can be self-contradictory. Arguments for the existence of God typically include metaphysical, empirical, inductive, and subjective types, while others revolve around perceived holes in evolutionary theory and order and complexity in the world. Arguments against the existence of God typically include empirical, deductive, and inductive types. Conclusions reached include: "God does not exist" (strong atheism); "God almost certainly does not exist" (*de facto* atheism); "no one knows whether God exists" (agnosticism); "God exists, but this cannot be proven or disproven" (weak theism); and "God exists and this can be proven" (strong theism). There are numerous variations on these positions.

GOD is man made. GOD is the name people give to the reason we are here. But that reason is the laws of physics rather than some one with whom one can have a personal relationship. An impersonal GOD.

In order to offer a logical, practical and pragmatic proof of the existence of God from a purely scientific perspective, we have to assume that we exist, that there is reality, and that the matter of which we are made is real.
Some people (called atheists) have maintained that there was no beginning and the matter has always existed in the form of either matter or energy; and all that has happened is that matter has been changed from form to form. They think that matter is self-existing and not created. This assertion that matter/energy is eternal is scientifically wrong. How is it possible that from empty space with no force, no matter, no energy and no intelligence, matter would have to become existent? In order for matter to come out of nothing, all of our scientific laws dealing with the conservation of matter/energy would have to be wrong, invalidating all of chemistry. All of our laws of conservation of angular momentum would have to be wrong, invalidating all of physics.

Therefore the biblical assertion that there was a beginning is scientifically correct. In the beginning GOD created the heaven and the earth and he did so with planning and reason and logic. This GOD's creation has been explored in many different ways. For most of us, simply looking at our newborn child is enough to rule out chances.

In order to offer a logical, practical and pragmatic proof of the existence of GOD from a purely scientific perspective, we have to assume that we exist, that there is reality, and that the matter of which we are made is real.

1.04 - MY IDEA OF GOD:
Sometimes I wonder, what was it that created this world. The "Big Bang Effect"!! Sure sure....if it was that then would have to be something that created that, and so on and so forth. I then participate in the so-called "faculty of wonder", and realize, there is more to it than that. Unexplained events are as much a part of our lives, as the creation of this world. Setbacks come and go,

providing a passage to the next phase of our lives. The wheels keep turning, the music keeps playing, and life goes on. As we are caught up in this ride and rhythm of life, we don't take time to "think', thinking we will miss too much if we do.

But the power is there, the one force that keeps everything in motion. That I believe is GOD. NATURE AND SOUL IS MY GOD.

G - O – D (These are just three forms of the same GOD)

(G) GOD as the Creator or Generator:
Reason tells me that spiritual and material energy in the form of souls and matter didn't just suddenly appear out of nothing.

1. The first law of thermodynamics states that energy cannot be either created or destroyed. Matter itself is a form of condensed energy. Souls are also conscious points of energy. Both are uncreated and therefore eternal.

2. The second law of thermodynamics shows us that energy, when in use, moves from a potential state, in which energy is available, to spent state in which it is no longer available.

Putting both laws together we have what appears to be a system in which the basic components have neither beginning nor end. They move towards a state of energy exhaustion (**Entropy**).

If, as has been shown above, GOD's presence, power and knowledge are purely spiritual, then creation has to be a spiritual act and not a physical one. Creation can be understood as the regeneration or reshaping of what is already there.

(O) GOD as the Sustainer or Operator:
We may think that GOD is the sustainer in the sense that he gives us our goods, wealth, health, food, water, air and so on. But that is not so. Whatever fruits one earns are the results of his/her own efforts, but GOD fills us with His Power, Virtues and Knowledge to help us in our spiritual endeavor and does not put bread on our tables.

(D) GOD as Destroyer:
God is destroyer of Evil and the creator of Virtue.

Prayers to GOD: -
O GOD, thou are the giver of life, the remover of pain and sorrow, the bestower of happiness; O creator of the universe, may we receive thy supreme, sin destroying light; may thee guide our intellect in the right direction.

1.05 - GOD REALIZATION:[2]
There are many ways to reach **God within you**, just as there are many ways to take any journey. Some are easy and some are difficult and take a long time to accomplish. **Yoga** is a Hindu theistic philosophy teaching the suppression of all activity of body, mind, and soul, in order that the self may realize its distinction from them and attain liberation. A path is designed for each of the four personality types.

1. **Jnana (Knowledge) Yoga**
   It is for those people who are reflective and seek knowledge, find their own divinity through rationality and spirituality.

2. **Bhakati (Devotion) Yoga**
   It is the path of God through love and devoted service.

3. **Karma (Work) Yoga**
   It is the path to God through work. Be productive and strive to work towards noble goals and work unselfishly.

4. **Raja (Self-Searching) Yoga**
   It is a way to God through psychophysical experiments. Self-Searching could be one way to describe Raja Yoga. Looking inwards to distinguish between humanness from goodness and bringing them together. It involves meditation and Self-Discipline.

1.06 - THE NATURE IS OUR GOD

The concept of GOD is fundamental element in the human constitution. It is by its nature the essence of knowledge and the essence of Bliss. It is man's ceaseless Endeavour to become free from laws of nature. Science has been struggling for thousands of years in its attempt to gain freedom and yet will not believe that we are under laws of nature. Hence the **NATURE is our GOD.**

We humans are living beings. In the living there is **FREEDOM**, there is **INTELLIGENCE**; in the dead all is bound and no freedom is possible, because there is no intelligence. This freedom that distinguishes us from mere machines is what we are all striving for. We have been stifling that inner voice, seeking to follow law and suppress our true nature, but there is that human instinct to rebel against nature's laws. To be free is the goal of all our efforts; for only in perfect freedom can there be perfection. This effort to attain freedom underlies all forms of worship.

Humans are born slave of nature, but there is a BEING who is not bound by nature. He is free and master of nature. The conception of GOD is as essential and as fundamental a part of the mind as is the idea of bondage. Both are outcome of the idea of the freedom. The idea of nature's controlling every step onward overrules the idea of freedom. The embodiment of Freedom, the Master of Nature, is what we call GOD.

The whole of nature is worship of GOD. Wherever there is life there is this search for freedom, and that freedom is the same as GOD. Freedom gives mastery over all nature and is impossible without knowledge. Mastery alone makes us strong. That BEING who is entirely Free and is master of Nature, that BEING must have a perfect knowledge of Nature, must be Omniscient, omnipotent, omnipresent, omnibenevolent, and Omni truth. Only that BEING who has acquired these will be beyond Nature and that is GOD.

GOD is always established upon his own majestic changeless SELF. You and I try to be one with him, but find us diverted by nature, by the trifles of daily life, by money, by fame, by human love, and all these changing forms, which make for bondage. When nature shines, it depends upon GOD and not upon the sun or the moon or the stars. Whenever anything shines, whether it is the light in the sun or in our own consciousness, it is HE THE GOD.

If we are ever to gain freedom, it must be by conquering nature, never by running away. We have to fight fear and troubles and ignorance, if we expect them to flee before us. Unless a man passes through pleasure and pain he is not free. We must learn how to worship and love him in the thunderbolt, in shame, in sorrow and in sin. There is only ONE GOD of virtue and of sin. **Until we see GOD everywhere and in everyone, unity will not exist for us. We have to see GOD in every person – working through all hands, walking through all feet, and eating through every mouth. When we shall feel that ONENESS, we shall be immortal.**

1.07 - GOD IS UNIVERSE:

The effect is the cause in another form. How this universe was created. It could not have risen out of nothing. Out of seed the big tree grows; the tree is the seed plus the air and water that are taken in. So the cause is seed plus air plus water and the effect is the tree. Therefore effect is the cause in another form. Therefore we conclude that GOD has changed its form to make this UNIVERSE. So GOD is the UNIVERSE because we have to see it through **Time, Space and Causation.** Actually the GOD has not changed at all, it is just the perception. For example in the darkness of night, someone waiting for his companion looks upon a stump of tree as a ghost by a superstitious person or as a policeman by a robber, or as a friend. In all these cases the stump of the tree did not change, but there were apparent changes as perceived by different people. This world is admitted as an apparent world, bound by the laws of time, space and causation, GOD does not change.

God is eternal spirit. God is formless, all effulgence, all consciousness, all love, all light and sound, all peace and all bliss. Each religion recognizes one GOD as the creator of all. The word or name used for GOD may differ from one religion or one culture to another.

It is easier to have faith in the Personal God than in the impersonal. God dons the earthly cloak. He bodies forth the creation of His own time, and casts a far-flung glance into the yet unborn to bring it into existence. He reveals Himself to each individual according to his power of receptivity.

It is a sad fact that often the disciples of various paths misinterpret the teachings of their masters to the extent of claiming theirs as the only Master. In doing so, they bring their teachers down to the level of ordinary men. An aspirant, they claim, in spite of high achievements, counts for nothing unless and until he is prepared to give all credit to their master. What blind ignorance! If the master were an ear-witness of his disciple's utterance, he would burn with shame.

1.08 - WHY DID THE SUFFERING START?

Since GOD purposed or humans to have such a marvelous future, why did he permit suffering to start?

When GOD created Adam and Eve, he made them perfect in body and mind. He put them in paradise garden and gave them satisfying work to do. God implanted in Adam and Eve the **wonderful gift of free will** as part of human make up. They were not to be mindless robots. However their continued happiness depend upon their using free will in the right way – to obey God's laws. Misuse of free will would result in catastrophe, since humans were not created to be independent of GOD. Sadly, our first parents felt that they could be independent of God and still be successful. But when they pulled away from God's ruler ship, he no longer sustained them in perfection. So they began to degenerate until finally they got old and died.

The main issue – Sovereignty?

Why did God not destroy Adam and Eve and start over with another human pair? Because God's universal sovereignty, that is, his right to rule, had been challenged. The question was who has the right to rule, and whose rule is right? By extension, could humans do better if not ruled by God? In allowing them enough time to experiment with total freedom, God would establish once and for all whether they are better off under his rule or their own. The time allowed had been long enough for humans to try all types of political, social, economic, and religious systems apart from God's guidance. The result is the current human condition at present as the Bible foretold for our times.

Suffering is near its end?

All the evidence shows that we are nearing the end of man's tragic experiment in independence from God. It has been clearly demonstrated that ruler ship by humans apart from God can never succeed. Only God's ruler ship can bring peace, happiness, perfect health and everlasting life.

God and Potato Chips
(a fictitious story to explain the existence of God)

A little boy wanted to meet God. He knew it was a long trip to where God lived, so he packed his suitcase with a bag of potato chips and a six-pack of root beer and started his journey.

When he had gone about three blocks, he met an old man. He was sitting in the park, just staring at some pigeons. The boy sat down next to him and opened his suitcase. He was about to take a drink from his root beer when he noticed that the old man looked hungry, so he offered him some chips. He gratefully accepted it and smiled at him.

His smile was so pretty that the boy wanted to see it again, so he offered him a root beer. Again, he smiled at him. The boy was delighted!

They sat there all afternoon eating and smiling, but they never said a word.

As twilight approached, the boy realized how tired he was and he got up to leave; but before he had gone more than a few steps, he turned around, ran back to the old man, and gave him a hug. He gave him his biggest smile ever.

When the boy opened the door to his own house a short time later, his mother was surprised by the look of joy on his face. She asked him, "What did you do today that made you so happy?"

He replied, "I had lunch with God." But before his mother could respond, he added, "You know - what? He's got the most beautiful smile I've ever seen!"

Meanwhile, the old man, also radiant with joy, returned to his home. His son was stunned by the look of peace on his face and he asked, "Dad, what did you do today that made you so happy?"

He replied "I ate potato chips in the park with God." However, before his son responded, he added, "You know, he's much younger than I expected."

Too often we underestimate the power of a touch, a smile, a kind word, a listening ear, an honest compliment, or the smallest act of caring, all of which have the potential to turn a life around. People come into our lives for a reason, a season, or a lifetime! Embrace all equally!

1.09 - ORIGIN OF GOD - GOD IS SOMEBODY TO LEAN ON: -
There is a theory that God is man made for selfish reasons. Because **man** needs somebody to lean on, needs somebody to blame, needs somebody to ask for and needs somebody to thank for everything.

Yes it is true, we human-beings need somebody to lean on in times of sorrow, some body to give thanks in times of happiness, some body to curse or blame in case of failures and somebody to be grateful in case of success. That somebody was created or imagined by learned people to be GOD.

Why does man, in every nation, in every state of society, want a perfect ideal somewhere, either in man or in God or elsewhere? Because the ideal is within you. It was your own heart beating and you did not know that it is God within you that is impelling you to seek him, to realize him. After long searches here and there, in temples and churches, on earth and in Heaven, at last you come back to your own Soul. You find that whom you have been seeking all over the world, for whom you have been weeping and praying in churches and temples, on whom you were looking as the mystery of all mysteries, shrouded in the clouds, is the nearest of the near, is your own self, the reality of your life, body, and Soul. The infinite self is the real nature of every man.

The vast majority of our quarrels with one another arise simply from this one cause: that we are always trying to judge others' Gods by our Gods, other's ideals by our ideals, and other's motives by our motives.

As the tangible man is only an appearance, a partial manifestation of the Real man, so the idea we form of God is a creation of the mind, only a partial manifestation. Behind that is the real God, who never changes the ever pure, the immutable. But the manifestation is always changing, revealing more and more the Reality behind. When it reveals the more of the fact behind, it is called progression; when it hides more of the fact behind, it is called retrogression. Thus as we grow, so the Gods grow. In simple way, just as we reveal ourselves, as we evolve, so the Gods reveal themselves.

If the virtues of God increased in arithmetical progression, the difficulty and doubt increased in geometrical progression.

Why under the reign of an Almighty and All-loving God of the universe, should diabolical things be allowed to remain? Why so much more misery than happiness and so much more wickedness than good?

We must direct our energies towards the truth, and fulfill the truth that exists, not try to make new truths. Thus instead of denouncing these old ideas of God as unfit for modern times, the ancient sages began to seek out the reality that was in them. From the old deities and from the monotheistic God, the ruler of universe, they ascended to yet higher and higher ideas. And the highest of them all they called Impersonal Absolute, in which they beheld the oneness of the Universe. He who sees in this world of manifoldness that One running through all; in this world of death, he who finds that One Infinite Life; and in this world of insentience and ignorance, he who finds that One Light and Knowledge – unto him belongs eternal peace.

The God of heaven becomes the God in nature and God in nature becomes the God who is Nature, and the God who is nature becomes the

God within this temple of the Body, and the God dwelling in the temple of body at last becomes the temple itself, becomes the Soul and Man.

What is the origin of GOD?

If God created matter/energy, and designed the system that has propelled matter in to its present arrangement, who or what accomplished that for God? Why is it anymore reasonable to believe that God has always "been' than is to say that matter has always "been". The problem here is that many people have a mistaken concept of God. If we conceive of God as physical, anthropomorphic (like man) being, the question of God's origin is valid, but in reality God is a Spiritual entity. He exists outside of the three-dimensional, physical world we live in. Not only is God described as being outside space, but he is also described as being outside of time. If God exists outside of time and space and if he is the creator of time and space, He obviously was not created! God began the beginning.

1.10 - GOD IS ABSOLUTE: - [2]

Only when something has become limited by our mind do we know it; when it is beyond our mind it is not known. Now if the Absolute becomes limited by the mind, it is no more Absolute; it has become finite. Everything limited by the mind becomes finite. Therefore to know the Absolute is again a contradiction in terms. That is why this question has never been answered; because if it were answered there would no more be an Absolute. A God known would no more be God: He would have become finite like one of us. He cannot be known; he is always the unknown one.

The whole universe is a peculiar form of Absolute. Consider that Absolute is the Ocean, while you and I, and sun and stars, and everything else are the waves of the ocean. And **what makes the waves different? Only the Form – and that Form is nothing but Time, Space and Causation, which again, are all entirely dependent on the wave.**

God is our real self

God is neither knowable nor unknowable, but something infinitely higher than either. He is one with us; and that which is one with us is neither knowable nor unknowable, like our own self. You can not know your own self, you can not move it out and make it an object to look at, because you are that and can not separate yourself from it. Neither it is unknowable; for what is better known than your self. It is really the center of our knowledge. In exactly the same sense, God is neither unknowable nor known, but infinitely higher than both; for He is our real self.

Seek Refuge in GOD:
To seek refuge is to trust in the Lord. – Fully, completely and entirely. He is the one light that shines and shines and ever shines. Though the storms howl and darkness grows deeper, his light shines on! He is the creator and the nourisher of all that is. He is the deliverer from whom all evils flee. He is nearer to us than our heartbeats and closer than our breathing. He is the all-powerful. He knows what can be known, but not one knows him.

Fear:
We live in fear, we walk in fear, and we talk in fear.

We are afraid of the future, afraid of poverty, afraid of unemployment, afraid of dishonor and disgrace, afraid of disease and death.

Fear is a child of Faith, **he who lives in fear does not truly believe in God.**

Forgiveness:
To walk the way of forgiveness, one has to pass through 4 stages.
1. The first is the stage of **Hurt**.
2. Hurt leads to **hate** which idles the second stage.
3. Then comes the third stage, it is the stage of **Healing**.
4. The fourth is the stage of **Coming-Together**.

Like Lotus Flower:
The boat must stay on the waters. But the waters must not be allowed to enter the boat, else the boat will sink and we will drown.

Likewise, the boats of our lives must float on the waters of worldliness. We have to live in the world and perform our duties, but we must not let the waters of worldliness enter our boats.

GOD'S WILL:

We do not want to do God's will. We want God to do our will. The more we strive for our will to be done, the more restless we become, and consequently, more unhappy and miserable. It is only God's will that can restore harmony and order.

1.11 - BELIEF IN GOD: - [4]

Progressive people say that fundamentalism is growing rapidly and non-belief is defamed. The world is polarized over religion. **It is getting both more religious and less religious at the same time.** We have "Neither" the staunch Hinduism, western Christendom, real Sufism of Islam, as in the past "Nor" the secular, religion-less society that was predicted for the future. Because doubt and belief are each on the rise, our political and public discourse on matters of faith and morality has become deadlocked and deeply divided. **The cultural wars are taking a toll.** Emotions and rhetoric are intense, even hysterical. Those who believe in God are out to impose their belief on the rest of us and turn back the clock to a less enlightened time. Those who don't believe are "enemies of truth". But even as believers should learn to look for reasons behind their faith, skeptics must learn to look for a type of faith hidden within their reasoning.

Religion generally speaking, tends to create a slippery slope in the heart. There is a call to outlaw religion, condemn religion, or at least to radically privatize it. The 20th century gave rise to one of the greatest and most distressing paradoxes of human history; that the greatest intolerance and violence of that century were practiced by those who believed that religion caused intolerance and violence. Going hand in hand with such efforts was a widespread belief that religion would weaken and die out as the human race became more technologically advanced.

If we believe in God, then the Big Bang is not mysterious, nor the fine-tuning of the universe, nor the regularities of nature. All the things that we see make perfect sense. Also, if God exists, our intuitions about the meaningfulness of beauty and love are so expected.

God's miracles vs. Science: -

There has been some studies done to prove that the more intelligent, rational, and scientifically minded you are, the less you will be able to believe in God. It is one thing to say that science is only equipped to test for natural causes and cannot speak to any others. It is quite another to insist that science proves that no other causes could possibly exist. Science proceeds on the assumption that whatever events occur in the world can be accounted for in terms of other events. No supernatural cause (Miracle) for any natural phenomenon is possible. Miracles cannot happen. There can't be a God who does miracles. To be sure that miracles cannot occur one would have to be sure beyond a doubt that God did not exist, and that is an article of faith. The existence of God can be neither demonstrably proven nor disproven.

Evolutionary science assumes that more complex life forms evolved from less complex forms through a process of natural selection. Many religions believe that God brought about life this way. Each side has brought in to the warfare model of the relationship of science to faith. Many scientists see no incompatibility between faith in God and their work. Scientists are asked if they believe in a God who personally communicates with humanity. The response from the members of National Academy of Sciences (NAS) was 50-50. Many complex factors lead a person to belief or disbelief in God. Some are personal experiences, some are intellectual, and some are social. A majority of scientists consider themselves deeply or moderately religious – and those numbers have increased in recent decades. There is no necessary disjunction between science and devout faith.

God's Clues: -

If one puts aside the existence of God and the survival after life as too doubtful, one has to make up one's mind as to the use of life. If death ends all, if I have neither to hope for good nor to fear evil, I must ask myself what I am here for, and how in these circumstances I must conduct myself. Now the answer is plain, but so unpalatable that most will not face it. There is no meaning for life, and thus life has no meaning.

Do you think that we appeared by chance; do we exist like a plant, an animal, or a microbe. No, some supernatural power gave us the power to think, eat and drink to preserve our precious existence. **That supernatural power I call GOD.**

Big Bang Theory: -

Almost everyone now believes that the universe, and time itself, had the beginning at the big bang. We have this very solid conclusion that the universe had an origin, the big bang. Fifteen billion years ago, the universe began with an unimaginably bright flash of energy from an infinitesimally small point. That implies that before that, there was nothing. I can't imagine that how nature, in this case the universe, could have created itself. And the very fact that the universe had a beginning implies that some one was able to begin it. And it seems to me that had to be outside nature. What could that be but something outside of nature, a supernatural, non-contingent being that exists from itself. We should accept that our universe simply had to be created by an intelligent being; this would suggest that this being is the GOD.

For organic life to exist, the fundamental regularities and constants of physics – the speed of light, the gravitational constant, the strength of the weak and strong nuclear forces – must all have values that together fall in to an extremely narrow range. The probability of this perfect calibration happening by chance (like big bang) is so tiny as to be statistically negligible. Matter would not have able to amalgamate; there would have been no galaxy, stars, planets or people. The odds against universe like ours emerging out of something like the Big Bang are enormous, there seems to be clear religious implications. This has been called the **"Fine Tuning Argument"** or the **"Anthropic Principle"** namely that the universe was prepared for human beings. Though one could not prove that the fine-tuning of the universe was due to some sort of design, it would be unreasonable to draw the conclusion that it wasn't.
That intelligence designer we call GOD.

Is there a God?

If there is no God, there can be no good reason to be kind, to be loving, or to work for peace. We will not be better than animals. Either God exists or He does not, but if he does not, nothing and no one else can take his place. The fact is that if there is no God, then all moral statements are arbitrary, all moral valuations are subjective and internal, and there can be no external moral standard which judges a person's feelings and values.

Is Nature our God?

We have to realize that nature is completely ruled by one central principle – violence by the strong against the weak.

There is no basis for moral obligation unless we argue that nature is in some parts unnatural. We can not know that nature is broken in some way unless there is some SUPERNATURAL standard of normalcy apart from nature by which we can judge right and wrong. That means there would have to be GOD or some kind of divine order outside of nature in order to make the judgment.

If God of peace, justice, and love made the world, then that is why we know that violence, repression, and hate are wrong. If the world is fallen, broken, and needs to be redeemed, that explains the violence and disorder we see.

If you believe human rights are a reality, then it makes much more sense that God exists than that he does not. If you insist on secular view of the world and yet you continue to pronounce some things right and some things wrong, then I hope you see the deep disharmony between the world your intellect has devised and the real world and The God, that your heart knows exists.

We all live as if it is better to seek peace instead of war, to tell the truth instead of lying, to care and nurture rather than to destroy. We believe that these choices are not pointless, that it matters which way we choose to live. Yet if the Cosmic Bench is truly empty, then who says that one choice is better than the other.

A cynic might say that this is a way of "having one's cake and eating it too." That is, you get the benefit of God without the cost of following him. But there is no integrity in that. The other option is to recognize that you do know there is God. You could accept the fact that you live as if beauty and love have meaning, as if there is meaning in life, as if human beings have inherent dignity – all because you know that God exists. It is dishonest to live as if he is there and yet fail to acknowledge the one who has given you all these gifts.

Self-Existence: -
Every person must find someway to justify his or her existence. In more traditional cultures, the sense of worth and identity comes from fulfilling duties to family and giving service to society. In our contemporary individualistic culture, we tend to look at our achievements, our social status, our talents, or our love relationships. There are an infinite variety of identity basis. Some get their sense of "Self" from gaining and wielding power, others from human approval,

and others from self-discipline and control. But everyone is building his or her identity on something.

If we take our meaning in life from our family, our work, as cause, or some achievement other than God, they enslave us. Human beings are so integral to the fabric of things that when human beings turned from God, the entire warp and woof of the world unraveled. Disease, genetic disorders, famine, natural disasters, aging and death itself are as much the result of sin as are oppression, war, crime, and violence.

GOD is Everything: -
There is a philosophy, which says, "If there are no devotees, there is no God". Until human beings came on this planet, there was no God. That means animals, and birds and beasts and insects – they don't know what God is. It's like a person who's never married saying, "I'm waiting for my wife." You can't have wife; there are billions of women all over the world, but you have a wife only when you are married. Similarly, you have a God only when you recognize his presence in your life. Not as some fictitious presence somewhere in some god-forsaken heaven, which doesn't exist.

1.12 - FACE TO FACE WITH GOD: -
To be in tune with yourself, go beyond the sound of thoughts, the sound of feelings and especially beyond the sound of **What, Why, Who, Where, When.**

What is God after all?

The Divine, Supreme, Infinite, Mind, Spirit, Soul, Principle, Life, Truth, Love, Peace – that is God.

GOD IS BEING-CONSCIOUSNESS-BLISS
GOD is described as having two aspects.
Under one aspect we should know him as **NATURE**
Under other aspect we should know him as **SOUL**
NATURE is described as the cause in the creation of effects from causes

SOUL is described as the cause of experiencing the pleasure and pain.

LIFE is pursuit of **HAPPINESS**

HAPPINESS is based upon **HOPE & FEAR**

The idea of God incarnating Himself in flesh, it seems, is equally unacceptable, if not outright repugnant, to the intellect of many behavioral scientists. Add to this the resistance many have to spirituality in general, specially at a time when we have been duped by large number of charismatic spiritual figures from both East and West.

Why is there God?

God is beyond human comprehension, but He is a living reality. He is no metaphysical abstraction. The existence of God cannot be proved through scientific experimentation. The Absolute baffles the mind of even the greatest scholar. It eludes the grasp of even the mightiest intellect. It is experienced as pure consciousness, where intellect dies, scholarship perishes and the entire being itself is completely lost in it.

The proof of God lies in man's need for God. Ever since the pre-historic ages when the primitive homo-sapiens invoked spirits to ward off natural calamities and later learnt to worship their own pantheon of Gods and demigods, man has been intuitively aware of the fundamental fact that there is a power which dictates all events and phenomena in this world and regulates the course of cosmic destiny. The belief that there is a constant, changeless entity at the core of this transitory and ever-changing existence is seated deep inside the heart of every human, perhaps every being. In other words, man's faith is itself enough evidence of the existence of the Almighty.

Who is God?

God is totality of all that exists, animate and inanimate, sentient and insentient. He is free from all ills and limitations. He is omniscient, omnipotent, omnipresent, omnibenevolent, and Omni truth. He has no beginning, middle or end. He is the indweller in all beings. He controls from within. God is all in all. God is the only reality in this universe. The existence of things is by the light of God. God is ever living. All depends on him. He is not dependent on anyone. He is the truth. God is the end or goal of all spiritual exercise. He is the center towards which all things strive. He is the highest purpose or highest good of the world.

Where is God?

There is no place where he is not. Just as one thread penetrates all the flowers in the garden, so also one Self penetrates all the living beings. He is hidden in all beings and all forms, like oil in seed, butter in milk and mind in brain, fetus in the womb, sun behind the clouds, fire in the wood, fragrance in flowers, gold in quartz, microbes in blood and life in the body. He is not very far, but is nearer to us than we are to ourselves.

Close your eyes, withdraw your senses from your sensual objects. Search him in the heart with one-pointed mind, devotion and pure love. You will surely find him.

When is God?

God is Supreme Being, the creator and ruler of the universe.

His attributes are: infinite power, limitless wisdom, boundless love, inexhaustible goodness, interminable justice, and absolute truth. Its glory, majesty, sovereignty is unparalleled. God's will expresses itself everywhere as law. The laws of gravitation, cohesion, relativity, cause and effect, so also nature as a whole must be explained. It must have some cause. This cause must be different from the effect. It must be some supernatural entity i.e. GOD.

Nature is not a mere chance, collection of events, mere jumble of accidents, but an orderly affair. The planets move regularly in their orbits, seeds grow in to trees regularly, the seasons succeed each other in order. It requires the existence of an intelligent being – GOD – who is responsible for it. Even Einstein, the greatest scientist, was strongly convinced of the creation of the universe by a Supreme Intelligence.

Through out the ages, sages and seers all over the world have testified by their personal experience that it is impossible for any blissful till he has sought – and got – the experience of God-Realization or Self-Realization. Each man must and will one day come to grips with realization that there is something deep within him that mocks at all the sensual and material pleasures that this phenomenal world can offer – that the highest form of pleasure is obtained only from the serene and incessant contemplation of the Highest Self.

To the ordinary man, reluctant to reach beyond the routine of eating, drinking and sleeping, the lord bestows the 'so called' 'Troubles', which make him (probably for the first time in his career) look to God as well as within himself. If the troubles remind one of the sources, they are disguised boons. The trouble that initiates the process of conquering all troubles once for all should be viewed as the quest for happiness and everlasting peace and welcomed as such. True devotion shakes the kingdom of the almighty at the very base and makes life a veritable communion with the Divine.

1.13 - IS GOD IN OUR GENES?

Ask true believers of any faith to describe the most important thing that derives their devotion and they will tell you that it is not a thing at all but a sense – a feeling of a higher power far beyond us.

There have always been other, more utilitarian reasons to get religion. Chief among them is the survival. The structure that religion provides our lives helps preserve both mind and body. But that in turn has raised a provocative question, which came first, the GOD or the need for GOD? In other words, did human create religion from signals sent from above, or did evolution instill in us the sense of the divine so that we would gather in to the communities essential to keeping the species going.

Even among people who regard spiritual life as wishful hocus-pocus, there is a growing sense that humans may not be able to survive without it. It's hard enough getting by in a fang-and-claw world in which killing, thieving, and cheating pay such rich dividends. Far from being an evolutionary luxury, the need for GOD may be a crucial trait stamped deeper and deeper in to our genome with every passing generation. Molecular biologist Dean Hammer claims that human spirituality is an adoptive characteristic, but he also says that he has located one of the genes responsible, a gene that happens to also code for the production of the neurotransmitters that regulate our moods. Hammer believes that every thought we think and every feeling we feel is the result of the activity in the brain. He also thinks that humans follow the basic law of nature, which is that we are a bunch of chemical reaction running around in a bag. Brain chemicals, including Sertorius, norepinephrine, and dopamine, that regulate such fundamental functions as mood and motor control.

Spirituality is a feeling or a state of mind; religion is the way that state gets codified into law. Our genes don't get directly involved in writing legislation. Perhaps understanding a little bit the emotional connection many have to their religions.

Spirituality is intensely personal, religion is institutional: -
For one thing, GOD is a concept that appears in human cultures all over the globe, regardless of how geographically isolated they are. When tribes living in remote areas come up with a concept of GOD as readily as nation living shoulder to shoulder, it is a fairly strong indication that the idea is preloaded in the genome rather than picked up on the fly. If that's the case it's an equally strong indication that there are very good reasons that it's there. But the most important survival role religion may serve is, as the mortar holds the bricks together, **worshiping GOD does not have to be a collective, it can be done in isolation, disconnected from any organized religion**. The overwhelming majority of people, however, congregate to pray, observing the same rituals and heeding the same creeds. Once that congregation is in place, it is only a small step to using the common system of beliefs and practices as the basis for all the secular laws that keeps the group functioning. In order to survive, you have to organize yourselves in to a culture.

The downside to this is that often-religious groups gather not in to congregation but in to camps – and sometimes they are armed camps. In a culture of crusades, holocausts and Jihads, where in the world is the survival advantage of the religious wars or terrorism? One facile explanation has always been herd culling – an adaptive way of keeping populations down so that resources are not depleted. But there is little revolutionary upside to wiping out an entire population of breeding age males, as countries are trying to recover from wars. Why do we then often let the sweetness of religion curdle in to combat? The simple answer might be that just because we are given a gift, we don't necessarily always use it wisely.

Value of Doubt: - [27]
A decade after mother Teresa's death, her secret letters show that she spent almost 50 years without sensing the presence of God in her life.

She condemned abortion and bemoaned the youthful drug addiction in the west. She suggested that upcoming Christmas holidays should remind the world " that radiating joy is real" because Christ is everywhere" – "Christ is in our hearts, Christ in the poor we meet, Christ in the smile we give and in the smile that we receive."

Yet she wrote in her secret letters "I am ready never to consider again any of those strange thoughts which have been coming continually." Those thoughts were of her doubts in God, because once she wrote that 'She regrets the dryness, darkness, loneliness and torture she is undergoing". She compares her experience of working with poor in Calcutta, India; to hell and at one point says, "It has driven her to doubt the existence of heaven and even of God."

"Come be my light" is that rear thing, a posthumous autobiography of Mother Teresa, which raise questions about God and Faith, the engine behind great achievement and the persistence of love divine and human.

Once she wrote " The more I want him – the less I am wanted – such deep longing for God, and ... repulsed – empty – no faith – no love – no zeal – souls hold no attraction – heaven means nothing – pray for me please that I keep smiling at him in spite of everything." And then again she wrote, "What do I labor for? If there be no God – there can be no soul – if there is no soul then Jesus – you are also not true."

Mother Teresa knew that what she was doing made sense. She once wrote "I can not express in words – the gratitude I owe you for your kindness to me - for the first time in ... years – I have come to love the darkness – for I believe now that it is a part of very small part of Jesus – darkness and pain on earth. You have taught me to accept it as a spiritual side of your work – today really I felt a deep joy- that Jesus can not go anywhere through the agony – but that he wants to go through me."

One powerful instance of this may have occurred very early on. In 1968 a British writer-turned filmmaker Malcolm Muggeridge visited Teresa. Muggeridge had been an outspoken Agnostic, but by the time he arrived with a film crew in Calcutta he was in full spiritual search mode. Beyond impressing him with her work and her holiness, she wrote a letter to him in 1970 that addressed his doubts full-bore. "Your longing for God is so deep and yet he keeps him away from you. He must be forcing himself to do so – because he loves you so much – the personal love Christ has for you is infinite – The small difficulty you have in overcoming the finite with the infinite. Muggeridge apparently did. He became an outspoken Christian apologist and converted to Catholicism in 1982.

He will use her extraordinary faith in the face of overwhelming silence to illustrate how doubt is a natural part of everyone's life, be it an average believer's or a world famous saint's. The particularly holy are no less prone than the rest of us to misjudge the workings of history – or if you will, of God's providence. Teresa considered the perceived absence of God in her life as her most shameful secret but eventually learned that it could be seen as a gift assisting her work.

Faith in God

Forget it. It says even more emphatically, if you do not realize that He is here, you are not going to find him anywhere. I don't believe in faith. What is faith? Oh! I have faith that God exists. But you don't show it in your way of life. If you had faith that God exist, you would not be a liar and thief and a murderer, criminal and a black money maker and a Do-gooder. Would you? We are all liars. No body has faith in God. We know that he doesn't exist. Therefore, with impunity we are cheating, murdering, robbing.

Making money from others, evading taxes. Our way of life proves that we are sure there is no God. So have faith that God is inside you, and do the right thing by adopting the policy of Live and Let Live.

Let God

Whether you believe in God or not is not important. Belief can be an obstacle to experience. The main thing is to keep an open mind, and be willing to start the conversation. The experience of so many people is that when they engage in a mental conversation, whether it's with a question or simply sharing what is in their heart, they get a reply. This is God as a personal experience, not just a voice in your head. Not your higher self. But the presence of the Source in your life. God is not a concept, or a belief. You cannot have a conversation with a concept. You cannot have a meaningful relationship with a belief. Worth a try? Dear God.

God is everywhere

Two men went to a Master to ask for initiation. He examined both of them and gave them one pigeon each, saying "Kill it where nobody can see you." So one went out, he was very clever; he went behind a wall, shot the bird, and brought it back in no time. The other was running about, tossing here, there, from morning till night; he could not find any place where he could kill the bird where nobody could see him. He came back at night, "I have not found any place." "Why not?" asked the Master. "Because I could always see the pigeon and furthermore, the pigeon could see me." "All right, you are fit for initiation." When you see He sees every action of yours, you cannot conceal anything. That's the greatest thing that appeals to God.

How to Find God

"It is said that God wanted to hide the treasure of spirituality so that no one would find it… In all His wisdom, God said, 'Hide it in the one place where no one will ever look. That place is within themselves.' Thus, God hid the greatest treasure, which is spirituality, inside people, the last place one would ever look."

We can reach Him only when our desire is so intense that all conflicting desires disappear. It is when we seek God above everything else that worldly attachments fall away.

SPIRIT

We are spirit, an atom of the Ocean of All consciousness we call God. What gives comfort to the body does not necessarily give peace and comfort to this atom of the Ocean of Consciousness.

1.14 - GOD VS. SCIENCE: -

There are two great debates under the broad heading of the God vs. Science. Can Darwin evolution withstand the criticism of Christians who believe that it contradicts the creation account in the book of Genesis? In recent years creationism took on new currency as the spiritual originator of "intelligent design " (ID), a scientifically worded attempt to show that blanks in the evolutionary narrative are more meaningful than its very convincing totality.

Science and religion, far from being complementary responses to the unknown, are at utter odds.

We humans want to cheer on science's strides and still humble ourselves on the faith. We want access to both MRIs and miracles. We want debates about issues like stem cells without conceding that the positions are so intrinsically hostile as to make discussions fruitless. We seek those who possess religious conviction but also scientific achievements to credibly argue the widespread hope that science and God are in harmony – that indeed **Science is of God**.

The question of whether there exists a supernatural creator, a GOD, is one of the most important that we have to answer. God cannot be completely contained within nature, and therefore God's existence is outside of science's ability to really weigh in. For centuries the most powerful argument for God's existence from the physical world was the so-called argument from design: living things are so beautiful and elegant and so apparently purposeful, an intelligent designer could only have made them. But the Darwin provided a simpler explanation. His way is gradual incremental improvement starting from very simple beginnings and working up step by tiny incremental step to more complexity, more elegance, and more adaptive perfection. By being outside of nature, God is also outside of space and time. Hence at the moment of creation of the universe, God could also have activated evolution, with full knowledge of how it would turn out.

The gravitational constant, if it were off by one parting a hundred million, then the expansion of the universe after the big bang would not have occurred in the fashion that was necessary for life to occur. When one looks at that evidence, it is very difficult to adopt that view that this was just a chance. But if one is willing to consider the possibility of a designer, this becomes a rather plausible explanation for what is otherwise an exceedingly improbable event – namely our existence. God is the answer to all of those "How it must have come to be" questions. We humans can ask, such as "Why am I here? "What happens after we die?" "Is there a God?" If you refuse to acknowledge their appropriateness, you end up with a zero probability of God after examining the natural world because it does not convince one on the proof basis. But if your mind is open about whether God might exist, one can point to aspects of the universe that are consistent with that conclusion.

To a medieval peasant, a radio would have seemed like a miracle. All kinds of things may happen, which we by the lights of today's science would classify as miracle just as medieval science might think of a Boeing 747. From the perspective of believer, once you buy in to the position of faith, then suddenly you find yourself losing all of your natural skepticism and your scientific credibility. The scientific instincts of some scientists are less rigorous than others. The difference is that for some scientists the presumption of the possibility of God and therefore the supernatural is not zero. **Faith is not the opposite of reason.** Faith rests squarely upon reason, but with the added component of revelation. There are answers that science is not able to provide about the natural world – the questions about why instead of the questions about how. We find many of these answers in the spiritual realm. If there is God, it's going to be a whole lot bigger and a whole lot more incomprehensible than anything that any theologian of any religion has ever proposed.

While physics and mathematics may tell us how the universe began, they are not much use in predicting human behavior because there are far too many equations to solve.

1.15 - FINALLY THE GOD

The God watch over us and guide our destinies, many human cultures teach; other entities, more malicious, are responsible for the existence of evil. Both classes of beings, whether considered as natural or supernatural, real or imaginary, serve human needs. Even if they are wholly fanciful, people feel better believing in them. So in an age when traditional religions have been under withering fire from science, is it not natural to wrap up the old Gods and Demons in scientific raiment and call them aliens.

For we wrestle not against flesh and blood but against principalities, against powers, against the rulers of the darkness of this world, against spiritual wickedness in high places.

GOD – A Being conceived as the perfect, omniscient, omnipotent, omnipresent, omnibenevolent, and Omni truth, originator and ruler of the universe, the principal object of faith and worship in monotheistic religions. A being of Supernatural powers, believed in and worshiped or idealized by people.

DEMON – means "Knowledge" in Greek. They can assume any form, and know many things. An evil supernatural being, A Devil, A persistently tormenting person, force, or passion. One who is extremely zealous or diligent?

SCIENCE – means "Knowledge" in Latin. The observation, identification, description, experimental investigation, and theoretical explanation of the phenomena. The methodological activity, discipline, or study. An activity regarded as requiring study and method. Knowledge gained through experience.

Science may have evicted Ghosts and witches from our beliefs, but it just as quickly filled the vacancy with aliens having the same functions. Only the extraterrestrial outer trappings are new. All the fear and psychological dramas for dealing with it seem simply to have found their way home again, where it is business as usual in the legend realm where things go bump in the night.

Perhaps when everyone knows that GOD comes down to earth, we hallucinate GOD; when all of us are familiar with demons, it's incubi and succubae; when fairies are widely accepted, we see fairies; in an age of spiritualism, we encounter spirits; and when the old myths fade and we begin thinking that extraterrestrial beings are plausible, then that's where our hypnogogic imagery tends.

Therefore mankind has to realize that God is in everything. In life and in death, in happiness and in misery, the God is equally present. The whole world is full of the God. Open your eyes and see him. If you put your God in every movement, in your conversation, in your form, in everything, the whole scene will change, and the world, instead of appearing as one of woe and misery, will become a heaven.

1   God is not about fear guilt and Condemnation.
2   God is Wisdom, Love and Logic.
3   God does not have favorites and does not discriminate on the basis of nationality, gender, race or class.
4   God treats humans with dignity and respect.
5   God is not a slave master, or despot, among his serfs.
6   God is man's Soul Mate and Partner.

7   God is not Jealous, Wrathful or Vengeful.

8   Man is not sinful, fallen or depraved.

9   God has no opponent and heaven & hell are states of mind and being.

CHAPTER 2

WHAT IS "RELIGION"?

A Universal Religion: Good Thoughts, Good Words, Good Deeds (NO religion can have a monopoly on GOD)

2.01 – THE RELIGION: -

The word religion comes from the prefix *re* and the Latin word *ligare*, meaning to relink. That means religion seeks to reconnect us with our origin, our source of life.   .

All religions seem different because each religion was formed in a different time, in a different place, with different language, and under different conditions.

Three religions, which are from prehistoric time, are Zoroastrianism, Judaism, and Hinduism.

Zoroastrianism: - The religion known in the west as Zoroastrianism, is the 'Religion of Good Conscience', has laid claim to being the first Monotheist religion, the first Universal religion and the root of much of Jewish, Christian and Islamic doctrine and belief. Zarathustra's is a message about a spirituality that progresses towards self-realization, fulfillment and completeness, as a good creation of a totally good GOD. It is a message of freedom - freedom to choose, freedom from fear, freedom from guilt, freedom from sin, freedom from stultifying rituals, superstitious practices, fake spirituality and ceremonials. The God of Zarathustra is not a God of **"Thou shall"** and **"Thou shall not"**. God in Zoroastrianism does not care what you wear, what and when you eat or where and when you worship. **God instead cares how righteous, progressive and**

good you are. The Zoroastrian Religion pictures humanity as the growing and evolving creation of a God that respects it, and wants it to collaborate in the task of **preserving, nourishing, fostering** and **refreshing** this Living World of ours. A Zoroastrian is supposed to progress towards God by **his own choices**. Choosing to do well, and to avoid choosing to do wrong or evil. Zoroastrianism is thus the first truly ethical religion of mankind and teaches that mortals achieve their goal of god-likeness and spiritual completeness by fighting evil through **good thoughts, words and deeds.** It teaches the equality of all mortals before their Wise creator God; who only sees a difference in righteousness among mortals. Thus there is equality of race, nation, gender and social position.

Judaism: - Jewish history extends back through the ancient Israelite and Hebrew people to Abraham. As the timeline of Judaism shows, through centuries and millenniums of suffering, persecution, dispersion, and victory, Judaism continues to exert a profound influence around the world. The basic facts of Judaism are found in its beliefs, history, and practices. **Jewish beliefs begin with the conviction that there is only one God.** This important truth is revealed through the sacred writings of men like Moses and the prophets, the most important of which is Torah. In Judaism, religion is not one aspect of life, but it is Life. There are holidays and celebrations year round, like Passover and Bar mitzvahs, to commemorate what God has done in the past and is doing in people's lives today.

Hinduism: - Hindus have received their religion through revelation about 5000 years ago through **The Vedas.** Vedas mean the accumulated treasure of spiritual laws discovered by different persons in different times. Hindus believe that he is a spirit or the **Soul**. The Soul is not bound by the conditions of matter; it is free, unbounded, holy, pure, and perfect. Human Soul is eternal and immortal, perfect and infinite, and death means only a change of center from one body in to another. The present is determined by our past actions, and the future by the present. The soul will go on evolving up or reverting back, from birth to birth and death to death.

2.02 - THE MESSAGE OF ZARATHUSTRA

Zarathustra was the founder of the first religion on record in the western world. He was the first to preach Monotheism. He was the first to proclaim a message for all mortals - **a universal message.** He was the first to preach equality of all regardless of race, gender, class or nationality. At a time when mankind was barely out of the Stone Age, when might was right, he proclaimed that a leader must be "chosen" thereby for the very first time in history, sowing the seeds of democracy.

Zarathustra claimed to have received a vision from God, a God he called **Mazda Azhura,** the Wise God. His God is one who cherishes all his living creation and wishes to promote its freshness and preservation. He wants that mortals actively aid him and work as His co-workers in this task of promotion and preservation of His "Good Creation". This "Mantra" was thus the first to introduce us to the concept of "ecology" some 3700 years ago!

The Gathas. Zarathustra's sublime message to mankind is so simple that it is contained in a small book of 17 songs called **"The Gathas of Zarathustra"**. The word "Gatha" means songs or hymns. Yet this small book contains many profound and unique truths and to comprehend which it is important to understand certain Gothic concepts.

2.03 - WHAT IS RELIGION?

1. A set of beliefs concerning the cause, nature, and purpose of the universe, especially when considered as the creation of a superhuman agency or agencies, usually involving devotional and ritual observances, and often containing a moral code governing the conduct of human affairs.

2. A specific fundamental set of beliefs and practices generally agreed upon by a number of persons or sects: the Christian religion; the Buddhist religion; etc.

3. The body of persons adhering to a particular set of beliefs and practices: a world council of religions.

4. The life or state of a monk, nun, etc.: to enter religion.

5. The practice of religious beliefs; ritual observance of faith.

6. Something one believes in and follows devotedly; a point or matter of ethics or conscience; to make a religion of fighting prejudice.

7. Belief in, worship of, or obedience to a supernatural power or powers considered to be divine or to have control of human destiny.

8. Any formal or institutionalized expression of such belief.

9. The attitude and feeling of one who believes in a transcendent controlling power or powers.

10. The way of life determined by the vows of poverty, chastity, and obedience entered upon the monks, friars, and nuns; to enter religion.

11. Something of overwhelming importance to a person: football is his religion.

12. Archaic (Ancient)
    a. The practice of sacred ritual observances
    b. Sacred rites and ceremonies

2.04 - DEFINITION OF RELIGION: -

Religion as it is generally taught allover the world, is found to be based upon faith and belief and in most cases consists only of different sets of theories; that is why we find religions quarreling with each other. These theories are again based upon belief. If you analyze the various religions of the world, you will find that they are divided in to two classes; those with a book and those without a book. Those with book are stronger and have large number of followers. Those without book have mostly died out or have very few followers. Yet in all of them we find one consensus of opinion: that the truth they teach are the results of the experiences of particular persons. At the present time these experiences have become obsolete, and therefore we have to take these religions on faith.

From childhood onwards we have been taught to pay attention only to things external, but never to things internal; hence most of us have nearly lost the faculty of observing the internal mechanism. The goal of all the teachings is to show how to concentrate the mind; then how to discover the innermost recesses of our own minds; then how to generalize its contents and form our own conclusions from them.

Of all the forces that have worked and are still working to mold the destinies of the human race, none, is more potent than that whose manifestation we call religion. All social organizations have a background, somewhere, the workings of that particular force and the greatest cohesive ever brought in to play among human units has been derived from this power. It is obvious to all of us that in very many cases the bonds of religion have proved stronger than the bonds of race or region or even of descent. It is well known fact that persons worshipping the same God, believing in the same religion, have stood by each other with much greater strength and constancy than people of merely the same descent or even than brothers.

Religion has strength through Discipline
Religion has strength through Community
Religion has strength through Action

Three Theories:
1. Spirit theory of religion - Ancestor worship – the idea of double.
2. Evolution of the idea of the infinite – Which the religion originates in the personification of the powers of nature.
3. Human struggle to transcend the limitations of the senses.

None of us has yet seen an ideal human being, and yet we are told to believe in him. None of us has yet seen an ideally perfect man and yet without that ideal we cannot progress. Thus one fact stands out from all these different religions; that there is an ideal abstract unity, which is put before us in the form of either of a person, or of an impersonal being or of a law or of a presence or of an essence. We are always struggling to raise ourselves up to that ideal.

The lowest types of humanity in all nations find pleasure in the senses, while the cultured and the educated find it in the thought, in philosophy, in the arts and sciences.

Thus religion as study seems to be absolutely necessary. It is the greatest motive power that moves the human mind. No other ideal can put into us the same mass of energy that the spiritual can.

Religion must be studied on a broader basis than formerly. All narrow limited fighting ideas of religions have to go. All sectarian ideas and tribal or national ideas of religion must be given up. That each tribe or nation should have its own particular God is a superstition that should belong to the past. As the human mind broadens, its spirituals ideas broaden too. The time has already come when a man can not record a thought without its reaching to all corners of the earth, by merely physical means of computer we can come in touch with the whole world.

So the future religions of the world have to become universal and wide.

Religions must also be inclusive and not look down with contempt upon one an other because their particular ideals of God are different. The idea of personal God, the Impersonal, the Infinite, the Moral Law, and the Ideal man – these all have to come under the definition of religion. Religious ideas will have to become universal, vast and infinite. The power of religion broadened and purified is going to penetrate every part of human life

What is needed is a fellow feeling between different types of religion. To bring about this harmony, both will have to make concessions, sometimes very large, sometimes painful, but each will find itself the better for the sacrifice and more advanced in truth. And in the end the knowledge which is confined within the domain of time and space will meet and become one with that which is beyond them both, where mind and senses can not reach – the Absolute, the Infinite, the One without a second.

Humans listen to the Lord when everything seems to be lost, and hope has fled, when one's dependence on his own strength has been crushed down, and everything seems to melt away between his fingers and life is a hopeless ruin. **This is called Religion.**

Death is better than a vegetating ignorant life; it is better to die on the battle-field than to live life of defeat. **This is the basis of Religion.**

All the various manifestations of Religion, in whatever shape or form they have come to mankind, have one common, central basis, it is the preaching of freedom, the way out of this world. In spite of the almost hopeless contradictions of the different systems, we find the Golden Thread of unity running through them all. This Golden Thread has been traced, revealed little by little to our view, through the knowledge that we are all advancing towards Freedom.

The questions raised are " What is this Universe?' "From what does it arise?" and "Where does it go?" – Answers are "In Freedom it rises, in Freedom it rests and into Freedom it melts away.

2.05 - FREEDOM: -

It indicates that freedom is Human being's goal. He/she seeks it ever and its whole life is a struggle after it. This longing for freedom produces the idea of a Being who is absolutely free. The concept of GOD is fundamental element in the human constitution. It is by its nature the essence of the Knowledge and the essence of the Bliss. It is man's ceaseless endeavor to become free from laws of nature. Science has been struggling for thousands of years in its attempt to gain freedom and yet will not believe that we are under laws of nature.

We cannot deny that bodies acquire certain tendencies from heredity, but those tendencies only mean the physical configuration through which a peculiar mind alone can act in a peculiar way. There are other tendencies peculiar to a Soul caused by his past actions. And a Soul with a certain tendency would, by the laws of affinity, take birth in a body, which is the fittest instrument for the display of that tendency. This is in accord with science, for science wants to explain everything by habit, and habit is got through repetitions. So repetitions are necessary to explain the natural habits of a newborn soul. And since they were not obtained in this present life, they must have come down from past lives.

The Hindu believes that he is a Spirit/Soul. Him the sword cannot pierce - Him the fire cannot burn - Him the water cannot melt - Him the air cannot dry. The Hindu believes that every Soul is a circle whose circumference is nowhere but whose center is located in the body, and that death means the change of the center from body to body. Nor is the Soul bound by the conditions of matter.

Well, then, the human Soul is eternal and immortal, perfect and infinite, and death means only a change of center from one body to another. The present is determined by our past actions, and the future by the present. The soul will go on evolving up or reverting back from birth to birth and death to death.

God is everywhere, the pure and formless. He is the Almighty and the All Merciful. 'Thou art our father, Thou art our mother, Thou art our beloved friend, Thou art the source of all strength; give us strength. Thou art He that beareth the burdens of the universe; help me bear the little burden of this life.'

Buddha taught that a man ought to live in this world like a lotus leaf, which grows in water but is never moistened by water; so a man ought to live in the world - his heart to God and his hands to work.

And what becomes of a man when he attains perfection? He lives a life of bliss infinite. He enjoys infinite and perfect bliss, having obtained the only thing in which man ought to have pleasure, namely God, and enjoys the bliss with God. The perfection is absolute, and the absolute cannot be two or three. It cannot have any qualities. It cannot be an individual. And so when a Soul becomes perfect and absolute, it must become one with Brahman (Generator), and it would only realize the Lord as the perfection, the reality, of its own nature and existence, the existence absolute, knowledge absolute, and bliss absolute. We have often and often read this called the losing of individuality and becoming a stock or a stone.

Superstition: - is a great enemy of man, but bigotry is worse. Why does a Christian go to church? Why is the cross holy? Why is the face turned toward the sky in prayer? Why are there so many images in the Catholic Church? Why are there so many images in the minds of Protestants when they pray? We can no more think about anything without a mental image than we can live without breathing. By the law of association the material image calls up the mental idea and vice versa. This is why the Hindu uses an external symbol when he worships. He will tell you. It helps to keep his mind fixed on the Being to whom he prays. He knows as well as you do that the image is not God, is not omnipresent. How much does omnipresence mean to almost the whole world? It stands merely as a word, a symbol. Has God superficial area? If not, when we repeat that word 'omnipresent', we think of the extended sky or of space - that is all.

Self Realization: - As we find that somehow or other, by the laws of our mental constitution, we have to associate our ideas of infinity with the image of the blue sky, or of the sea, so we naturally connect our idea of holiness with the image of a church, a mosque, or a cross. The Hindus have associated the ideas of holiness, purity, truth, omnipresence, and such other ideas with different images and forms. But with this difference that while some people devote their whole lives to their idol of a church and never rise higher, because with them religion means an intellectual assent to certain doctrines and doing good to their fellows, the whole religion of the Hindu is centered in realization. Man is to become divine by realizing the divine. Idols or temples or churches or books are only the supports, the helps, of his spiritual childhood; but on and on he must progress.

To the Hindu, then, the whole world of religions is only a travelling, a coming up, of different men and women, through various conditions and circumstances, to the same goal. Every religion is only evolving a God out of the material man, and the same God is the inspirer of all of them. Why, then, are there so many contradictions? The contradictions come from the same truth adapting itself to the varying circumstances of different natures.

The Buddhists or the Jains do not depend upon God; but the whole force of their religion is directed to the great central truth in every religion, to evolve a God out of man.

Living and Dead and Freedom: - In the living there is freedom, there is intelligence; whereas in the dead all is bound and no freedom is possible, because there is no intelligence. This freedom that distinguishes us from mere machines is what we are all striving for. To be more free is the goal of all our efforts; for only in perfect freedom can there be perfection. This effort to attain freedom underlies all form of worship - As an example consider a huge locomotive rushes down the tracks, and a small worm that has been creeping upon one of the rails saves its life by crawling out of the path of the locomotive because it is a living being and has some intelligence and wants to be free, whereas the locomotive is a dead machine.

2.06 - PRACTICE OF THE RELIGION: -

Religion is the belief in and worship of a superhuman controlling power. Religion is a collection of cultural systems or beliefs that relate humanity to spirituality (moral values).

Many religions have narratives, symbols, traditions and sacred histories that are intended to give meaning of life.

Most religions have organized behaviors, including clerical hierarchies, a definition of what constitutes adherence or membership, congregations of worshipers, regular meetings or services for the purposes of worship of a deity or for prayer, holy places (either natural or architectural), and/or scriptures. The practice of a religion may also include sermons, commemoration of the activities of a God or Gods, sacrifices, festivals, feasts, dreams, initiations, funerary services, matrimonial services, meditation, music, art, dance, public service, or other aspects of human culture.

It seems apparent that one thing religion or belief helps us to do is deal with problems of human life that are significant, persistent, and intolerable. One important way in which religious beliefs accomplish this is by providing a set of ideas about how and why the world is put together that allows people to accommodate anxieties and deal with misfortune.

Many of the great world religions appear to have begun as revitalization movements of some sort, as the vision of a charismatic prophet fires the imaginations of people seeking a more comprehensive answer to their problems than they feel is provided by everyday beliefs. **Charismatic individuals have emerged at many times and places in the world**. It seems that the key to long-term success- and many movements come and go with little long-term effect – has relatively little to do with the prophets, who appear with surprising regularity, but more to do with the development of a group of supporters who are able to institutionalize the movement. The four largest religious groups by population, estimated to account for between 5 and 7 billion people, are Christianity, Islam, Buddhism, and Hinduism.

Some scholars classify religions as either *universal religions* that seek worldwide acceptance and actively look for new converts, or *ethnic religions* that are identified with a particular ethnic group and do not seek converts. Others reject the distinction, pointing out that all religious practices, whatever their philosophical origin, are ethnic because they come from a particular culture. Because religion continues to be recognized in Western thought as a universal impulse, many religious practitioners have aimed to band together in interfaith dialogue, cooperation, and religious peacebuilding.

The terms "atheist" (lack of belief in any gods) and "agnostic" (belief in the unknowability of the existence of gods), though specifically contrary to theistic (e.g. Christian, Jewish, and Muslim) religious teachings, do not by definition mean the opposite of "religious". There are religions (including Buddhism and Taoism), in fact, that classify some of their followers as agnostic, atheistic, or nontheistic. The true opposite of "religious" is the word "irreligious". Irreligion describes an absence of any religion; antireligion describes an active opposition or aversion toward religions in general.

Religion as Myth: -

The term "myth" can be used disapprovingly by both religious and non-religious people. By defining another person's religious stories and beliefs as mythology, one implies that they are less real or true than one's own religious stories and beliefs. Joseph Campbell (author of the power of myth) remarked, "Mythology is often thought of as *other people's* religions, and religion can be defined as mis-interpreted mythology."

In sociology, however, the term *myth* has a negative meaning. There, *myth* is defined as a story that is important for the group whether or not it is objectively or provably true. Examples include the death and resurrection of Jesus, which, to Christians, explains the means by which they are freed from sin and is also apparently a historical event. But from a mythological outlook, whether or not the event actually occurred is unimportant. Instead, the symbolism of the death of an old "life" and the start of a new "life" is what is most significant. Religious believers may or may not accept such symbolic interpretations.

Religion and Health: -
Impacts of religion on health
Mayo Clinic researchers examined the association between religious involvement and spirituality, and physical health, mental health, health-related quality
of life, and other health outcomes. The authors reported that: "Most studies
have shown that religious involvement and spirituality are associated with better health outcomes, including greater longevity, coping skills, and health-related quality of life (even during terminal illness) and less anxiety, depression,
and suicide."

Religion and Violence: -
Charles Selengut (author of Sacred Fury: understanding religious violence)
characterizes the phrase "religion and violence" as "jarring", asserting that "religion is thought to be opposed to violence and a force for peace and reconciliation. He acknowledges, however, that "the history and scriptures of the world's
religions tell stories of violence and war as they speak of peace and love."
Hector Avalos (Biblical scholar) argues that, because religions claim divine
favor for themselves, over and against other groups, this sense of righteousness
leads to violence because conflicting claims to superiority, based on unverifi-
able appeals to God, cannot be arbitrated objectively.

Critics of religion Christopher Hitchens and Richard Dawkins (author of The
God Delusion) go further and argue that to **Religions do tremendous harm
to society by using violence to promote their goals, in ways that are endorsed and exploited by their leaders.**

Regina Schwartz (teacher seventeenth-century literature) argues that all
monotheistic religions are inherently violent because of an exclusivism that inevitably fosters violence against those that are considered outsiders. Lawrence
Wechsler (auther) asserts that Schwartz isn't just arguing that Abrahamic religions have a violent legacy, but that the legacy is actually genocidal in nature.
Critics consider religion to be outdated, harmful to the individual (such as brain-
washing of children, faith healing, circumcision), harmful to society (such as holy
wars, terrorism, wasteful distribution of resources), to impede the progress of
science, and to encourage immoral acts (such as blood sacrifice, discrimination
against homosexuals and women). But this is all due to ignorance and illitracy.

2.07 - DIFFERENT RELIGIOUS PERSPECTIVES: - [10]

The religious perspectives on the meaning of life are those ideologies which explain life in terms of an implicit purpose not defined by humans.

WESTERN AND MIDDLE EASTERN RELIGIONS
Zoroastrianism:

Zoroastrianism is the religion and philosophy named after its prophet Zoroaster, which is believed to have influenced the beliefs of Judaism and its descendant religions. Zoroastrians believe in a universe created by a transcendental God, Azhura Mazda, to whom all worship is ultimately directed. Azhura Mazda's creation is truth and order, and it is in conflict with its antithesis, falsehood and disorder.

Since humanity possesses free will, people must be responsible for their moral choices. By using free will, people must take an active role in the universal conflict, with good thoughts, good words and good deeds to ensure happiness and to keep chaos at bay.

Judaism:

In the Judaic world view, the meaning of life is to elevate life, both in this world ('Olam HaZeh) and in the world to come ('Olam HaBa). The most important way to elevate life is through the observance of "mitzvot" (divine commandments in the Torah), of which the most significant are to serve the One God of Israel and to prepare for the world to come. In Judaism God is not affected or benefited through worship, but a person benefits when drawing close to God through prayer and service of the heart, by bringing out their own intrinsic holiness and divine nature. Among other crucial values in the Torah is pursuit of justice, compassion, peace, kindness, hard work, prosperity, humility, and education. The "Olam Haba" thought is about elevating oneself spiritually, connecting to God in preparing for "Olam Haba"; Jewish thought is to use "Olam Hazeh" (this world) to elevate oneself. "Al shlosha devarim," a well-known Mishnah from Pirkei Avot, relates to one of the first scholars of the Oral Law, Simeon the Righteous, the saying that "the world stands on three things: on torah, on worship, and on acts of loving kindness." This concept further explains the Jewish mentality towards the meaning of it all.

Judaism's most important feature is the worship of a single, incomprehensible, transcendent, one, indivisible, Being of absolute existence, who created the universe and governs it. Closeness with the one God of Israel, and adherence to the laws revealed in the Torah for the benefit of the world, is the central concept of Judaism. Per traditional Judaism, God established a covenant with the Jewish people, at Mount Sinai, revealing his laws and commandments in the Torah. In Rabbinic Judaism, the Torah comprises the written Pentateuch (Torah) and the oral law tradition (later transcribed as sacred writing).

Kabbalistically, the meaning of life is to connect with the One God. Kaballah theorizes that there only God exists, though "Klipot" (shells) separate the holiness of God, therefore, the meaning of life is to remove those shells and connect to God.

CHRISTIANITY:

Though Christianity has its roots in Judaism, and shares much of the latter faith's ontology, its central beliefs derive from the teachings of Jesus Christ, as presented in the New Testament. Life's purpose in Christianity is to seek divine salvation through the grace of God and intercession of Christ. The New Testament speaks of God wanting to have a relationship with humans both in this life and the life to come, which can happen only if one's sins are forgiven.

In the Christian view, humankind was made in the Image of God and perfect, but the Fall of Man caused the issue of the first Parents to inherit Original Sin. The sacrifice of Christ's passion, death and resurrection provide the means for transcending (surpassing) that impure state. The means for doing so varies between different groups of Christians, but all rely on belief in Jesus, his work on the cross and his resurrection as the fundamental starting point for a relationship with God. For by grace you have been saved through faith; and that not of yourselves, it is the gift of God; not as a result of works, that no one should boast. People are justified by belief in the propitiatory sacrifice of Jesus' death on the cross. The Gospel maintains that through this belief, the barrier that sin has created between man and God is destroyed, and allows God to change people and instill in them a new heart after his own will, and the ability to do it. This is what the terms "reborn" or "saved" almost always refer to.

Islam:

In Islam, man's ultimate life objective is to worship the creator Allah by abiding by the Divine guidelines revealed in the Qur'an and the Tradition of the

Prophet. Earthly life is merely a test, determining one's afterlife, either in *Jannat* (Paradise) or in *Jahannam* (Hell).

For Allah's satisfaction, via the Qur'an, all Muslims must believe in God, his revelations, his angels, his messengers, and in the "Day of Judgment". The Qur'an describes the purpose of creation as follows: "Blessed be he in whose hand is the kingdom, he is powerful over all things, who created death and life that he might examine which of you is best in deeds, and he is the almighty, the forgiving" and "And I (Allâh) created the mankind that they should be obedient (to Allah)." Obedience testifies to the oneness of God in his lordship, his names, and his attributes. Terrenal life is a test; how one *acts* (behaves) determines whether one's soul goes to Jannat (Heaven) or to Jahannam (Hell).

The Five Pillars of Islam are duties incumbent to every Muslim; they are: Shahadah (profession of faith); Salah (ritual prayer); Zakah (charity); Sawm (fasting during Ramadan), and Hajj (pilgrimage to Mecca). They derive from the Hadith works, notably of Sahih Al-Bukhari and Sahih Muslim.

Beliefs differ among the Kalam. The Sunni concept of pre-destination is divine decree; likewise, the Shi'a concept of pre-destination is divine justice; in the esoteric view of the Sufis, the universe exists only for God's pleasure; Creation is a grand game, wherein Allah is the greatest prize.

Bahá'í Faith:
The Bahá'í Faith emphasizes the unity of humanity. To Bahá'ís, the purpose of life is focused on spiritual growth and service to humanity. Human beings are viewed as intrinsically spiritual beings. People's lives in this material world provide extended opportunities to grow, to develop divine qualities and virtues, and the prophets were sent by God to facilitate this.

SOUTH ASIAN RELIGIONS
Hindu philosophies:
Hinduism is a religious category including many beliefs and traditions. Since Hinduism was the way of expressed meaningful living for quite a long time immemorial, when there was no need for naming this as a separate religion, Hindu doctrines are supplementary and complementary in nature, generally non-exclusive, suggestive and tolerant in content. Most believe that the tman (spirit, soul)—the person's true *self*—is eternal. In part, this stems from Hindu

beliefs that spiritual development occurs across many lifetimes, and goals should match the state of development of the individual. There are four possible aims to human life, known as the *purusharthas* (ordered from least to greatest): 1.*K ma* (wish, desire, love and sensual pleasure), 2.*Artha* (wealth, prosperity, glory), 3.*Dharma* (righteousness, duty, morality, virtue, ethics, encompassing notions such as *ahimsa* (non-violence) and satya (truth)) and 4.*Moksha* (liberation, the cycle of reincarnation).

In all schools of Hinduism, the meaning of life is tied up in the concepts of karma (causal action), sansara (the cycle of birth and rebirth), and moksha (liberation). Existence is conceived as the progression of the tman (similar to the western concept of a soul) across numerous lifetimes, and its ultimate progression towards liberation from karma. Particular goals for life are generally subsumed under broader yogas (practices) or dharma (correct living) which are intended to create more favorable reincarnations, though they are generally positive acts in this life as well. Traditional schools of Hinduism often worship Devas which are manifestations of Ishvara (a personal or chosen God); these Devas are taken as ideal forms to be identified with, as a form of spiritual improvement.

Advaita and Dvaita Hinduism:
In monist i.e Advaita Vedanta, tman (Soul) is ultimately indistinguishable from Brahman (Generator or God)), and the goal of life is to know or realize that one's tman (soul) is identical to Brahman. Whoever becomes fully aware of the tman, as one's core of self, realizes identity with Brahman, and, thereby, achieves Moksha (liberation, freedom).

Dualist i.e. Dvaita Vedanta and other prayer schools have a dualist interpretation. Brahman is seen as a supreme being with a personality and manifest qualities. The tman depends upon Brahman for its existence; the meaning of life is achieving Moksha (ultimate freedom) through love of God and upon His grace.

Vaishnavism:
Vaishnavism is a branch of Hinduism in which the principal belief is the identification of Vishnu or Narayana as the one supreme God. This belief contrasts with the Krishna-centered traditions, such as Vallabha, Nimbaraka and Gaudiya, in which Krishna is considered to be the One and only Supreme God and the source of all avataras.

Vaishnava theology includes the central beliefs of Hinduism such as monotheism, reincarnation, sansara, karma, and the various Yoga systems, but with a particular emphasis on devotion (prayer) to Vishnu through the process of Bhakti (prayer) yoga, often including singing Vishnu's name's (bhajan or religious songs)), meditating upon his form and performing deity worship.

Jainism:
The Jainist Vow of Ahinsa (non-violence). The dharmachakra (wheel) is the resolve to halt the cycle of reincarnation via truth and non-violence.

Jainism is a religion originating in ancient India, its ethical system promotes self-discipline above all else. Through following the ascetic teachings of Jiva(Eternal Soul)), a human achieves enlightenment (perfect knowledge). Jainism divides the universe into living and non-living beings. Only when the non-living become attached to the living does suffering result. Therefore, happiness is the result of self-conquest and freedom from external objects. The meaning of life may then be said to be to use the physical body to achieve self-realization and bliss.

Jains believe that every human is responsible for his or her actions and all living beings have an eternal soul, *jiva*. Jains believe all souls are equal because they all possess the potential of being liberated and attaining Moksha (ultimate freedom). The Jain view of karma is that every action, every word, every thought produces, besides its visible, an invisible, transcendental effect on the soul.

Jainism includes strict adherence to ahinsa, a form of nonviolence that goes far beyond vegetarianism. Jains refuse food obtained with unnecessary cruelty. Many practice a lifestyle similar to veganism due to the violence of modern dairy farms, and others exclude root vegetables from their diets in order to preserve the lives of the plants from which they eat.

Buddhism:
Buddhists believe that life is inherent with suffering or frustration. This does not imply that there is no pleasure in life, but rather that pleasure alone does not lend itself to lasting happiness. True suffering is caused by attachment to objects material or non-material, which in turn causes one to be born again and again in the cycle of existence. The Buddhist s tras and tantras (Budhist hyms and rituals) do not speak about "the meaning of life" or "the purpose of

life", but about the potential of human life to end suffering through detaching oneself from cravings and conceptual attachments. Suffering can be overcome through human activity, simply by removing the cause of suffering. Attaining and perfecting dispassion is a process of many levels that ultimately results in the state of Nirvana (Nirvana means freedom from both suffering and rebirth). Theravada Buddhism is generally considered to be close to the early Buddhist practice. It promotes the concept of Vibhajjavada (Pali), literally "Teaching of Analysis", which says that **Insight must come from the aspirant's experience, critical investigation, and reasoning instead of by blind faith**. However, the Theravadin tradition also emphasizes heeding the advice of the wise, considering such advice and evaluation of one's own experiences to be the two tests by which practices should be judged. The Theravadin goal is liberation (or freedom) from suffering. This is attained in the achievement of Nirvana, or Unbinding which also ends the repeated cycle of birth, old age, sickness and death.

Mahayana Buddhist schools de-emphasize the traditional view (still practiced in Theravada) of the release from individual Suffering (Dukkha) and attainment of Awakening (Nirvana). In Mahayana, the Buddha is seen as an eternal, immutable, inconceivable, omnipresent being. The fundamental principles of Mahayana doctrine are based on the possibility of universal liberation from suffering for all beings, and the existence of the transcendent **Buddha-Nature**, which is the eternal Buddha essence present, but hidden and unrecognised, in all living beings.

Sikhism:

The monotheistic Sikh religion was founded by Guru Nanak Dev, the term "sikh" means student, which denotes that followers will lead their lives forever learning. This system of religious philosophy and expression has been traditionally known as the Gurmat (literally "the counsel of the gurus") or the Sikh Dharma. The followers of Sikhism are ordained to follow the teachings of the ten Sikh Gurus, or enlightened leaders, as well as the holy scripture entitled the *Gur Granth S hib*, which includes selected works of many philosophers from diverse socio-economic and religious backgrounds.

The Sikh Gurus say that salvation can be obtained by following various spiritual paths, so Sikhs do not have a monopoly on salvation: "The Lord dwells in every heart, and every heart has its own way to reach Him." Sikhs believe that all people are equally important before God. Sikhs balance their moral and spiritual values with the quest for knowledge, and they aim to promote a life of peace and equality but also of positive action.

A key distinctive feature of Sikhism is a non-anthropomorphic concept of God, to the extent that one can interpret God as the Universe itself (pantheism). Sikhism thus sees life as an opportunity to understand this God as well as to discover the divinity which lies in each individual. While a full understanding of God is beyond human beings, Nanak described God as not wholly unknowable, and stressed that God must be seen from "the inward eye", or the "heart", of a human being: devotees must meditate to progress towards enlightenment. Nanak emphasized the revelation through meditation, as its rigorous application permits the existence of communication between God and human beings.

EAST ASIAN RELIGIONS
Taoism:
Taoist cosmogony emphasizes the need for all sentient beings and all man to return to the *primordial* or to rejoin with the *Oneness* of the Universe by way of self cultivation and self realization. All adherents should understand and be in tune with the ultimate truth.

Taoists believe all things were originally from Taiji and Tao, and the meaning in life for the adherents is to realize the temporal nature of the existence. "Only introspection can then help us to find our innermost reasons for living ... the simple answer is here within ourselves."

Shinto:
Shinto is the native religion of Japan. Shinto means "the path of the kami", but more specifically, it can be taken to mean "the divine crossroad where the kami chooses his way". The "divine" crossroad signifies that all the universe is divine spirit. This foundation of free will, choosing one's way, means that life is a creative process.

Shinto wants life to live, not to die. Shinto sees death as pollution and regards life as the realm where the divine spirit seeks to purify itself by rightful self-development. Shinto wants individual human life to be prolonged forever on earth as a victory of the divine spirit in preserving its objective personality in its highest forms. The presence of evil in the world, as conceived by Shinto, does not humiliate the divine nature by imposing on divinity responsibility for being able to relieve human suffering while refusing to do so. The sufferings of life are the sufferings of the divine spirit in search of progress in the objective world.

New religions:
There are many new religious movements in East Asia, and some with millions of followers: Chondogyo, Tenrikyo, Cao ài, and Seicho-No-Ie. New religions typically have unique explanations for the meaning of life. For example, in Tenrikyo, one is expected to live a Joyous Life by participating in practices that create happiness for oneself and others.

For Seven Billion people on earth, let there be Seven Billion religions or faiths.

2.08 - KEEPING THE FAITH: -
What is going on in our world today emphasizes the tragedy of a world dominated by religions that require blind faith and obedience. We will continue to abuse each other until man understands that spirituality is the power within each of us to intellectually understand that we all share responsibility for ourselves and for each other. This spirituality and power is called humanism.

The key to finding the balance of Truth found in all spiritual paths and that accommodates varying religious beliefs is the recognition that each religion contains elements of Truth. By accepting this principle, we are then free to view each religion as the spiritual path to the infinite, eternal, and omnipotent divine source of all things. We can each follow our own path; share our faith with others without hatred, scorn, or violence; and accept other paths as equally valid to our own.

2.09 - GOOD REASON TO BELIEVE IN RELIGION: -

The Hindus say we must not do this and must do that because the Vedas say so; The Christians say you must do this and not that because Bible says so; Same way Mohemmedans would say; and same way Buddhists will say. Therefore religion must become broad enough to include these minds. Everything any religion claims must be judged from the standpoint of **GOOD REASON**. We should therefore follow reason and also we should sympathize with those who, following reason, do not come to any sort of belief.

For it is better that mankind should become atheists by following reason than blindly believe in two hundred millions of Gods on the authority of somebody. What we want is progress, development, and realization. No theories ever made men higher. No amount of books can help us to become purer. **The only power is in realization, and that lies in us and comes from thinking. Let men think.** A clod of earth never thinks; but it remains only a clod of earth. The glory of man is that he is a thinking being. It is the nature of man to think, and therein he differs from animals. I believe in Reason and follow reason, having seen enough of the evils of authority.

We not only believe in universal toleration, but we accept all religions as true.

As the different streams, having their sources in different places, all mingle their water in the sea, same way the different paths which men take through different tendencies, various though they appear, crooked or straight, all lead to GOD.

2.10 - THE UNIVERSAL RELIGION [2]

Religion expresses itself at three levels, the philosophical, the mythological or historical, and the ritualistic. Each of these three levels is marked by the same conflict of opposites, often taking positions of violent extremes. The greatest harm comes from the fanatic. We may not doubt the sincerity of the fanatic but often he has the irresponsibility of a lunatic. The fanatic is the greatest enemy of mankind.

Is the idea of the universal religion realistic or just idealistic?

But behind all these differences, we must recognize a deeper level of common-ality that suggests that the universal religion already exists, and is constantly evolving and taking clearer shape. No two persons are exactly alike, yet, despite these differences, there is a common thread of humanity.

"If I am sure of anything, it is this humanity, which is common to all.... So it is with the universal religion, which runs through all the various religions of the world in the form of GOD; it must and does exist through eternity. 'I am the thread that runs through all these pearls... ' (Gita) and each pearl is a religion or even a sect thereof, only the majority of mankind is entirely unconscious of it..."

While the human mind and inclination occur in an innumerable variety, four broad types of humans may be recognized for practical purposes: the person of action, the person of emotion, the mystic or person of spirit, and the philosopher or person of intellect. Religion must offer a path for each type to follow, suited to the nature of each type.

"But is there any way of practically working out this harmony in religions?

Radical or Revolutionary religions do no good to this world... Secondly, take a person where he stands, and from there give him a lift. If it were true that God is at the center of all religions, and that each of us is moving along one of these radii, then it is certain that all of us must reach that center. At the center, where all radii meet, all our differences will cease; but until we reach there, differences there must be ... "

Religion is realization, not talk, nor doctrine, nor theories, however beautiful they may be. It is being and becoming, not hearing or acknowledging; it is the whole soul becoming changed into what it believes. That is religion.

If there is ever to be a universal religion, it must be one which will have no lo-cation in place or time; which will be infinite like the God it will preach, and whose sun will shine upon the followers of Krishna and of Christ, on saints and sinners alike; which will not be Brahmanism or Buddhist, Christian or Mohammedan, but the sum total of all these, and still have infinite space for development; which in its catholicity will embrace in infinite arms, and find a place for, every human being from the lowest groveling savage, not far re-moved from the brute, to the highest man towering by the virtues of his head and heart almost above humanity, making society stand in awe of him and doubt his human nature. It will be a religion which will have no place for persecution or intolerance in its society, which will recognize divinity in every man and woman, and whose whole scope, whose whole force, will be centered in aiding humanity to realize its own true, divine nature.

May He who is the Brahman of the Hindus, the Azhura-Mazda of the Zoroastrians, the Buddha of the Buddhists, the Jehovah of the Jews, the Father in Heaven of the Christians, give strength to you to carry out your noble idea and make it Universal.

UNIVERSAL RELIGION AND ITS' REALIZATION:

Universal religion must be one which will have no location in place or time; which will be infinite, and whose sun will shine upon all saints and sinners alike, and still will have infinite space for development, which will embrace in infinite arms and find a place for every human being, from the lowest groveling savage, not far removed from the brute, to the highest man, towering by the virtues, of his head and heart almost above humanity. It will be a religion which will have no place for persecution or intolerance in its society, which will recognize divinity in every human being and whose whole scope and force will be centered in aiding humanity to realize its own true, divine nature.

The seed is put in the ground; earth, air and water are supplied to it. The seed does not become the earth or the air or the water but it becomes a plant. It develops after the law of its own growth, assimilates the air, the earth and the water, converts them to plant substance and grows in to a plant. Thus also it is with religion. The Christians not to become a Hindu or a Buddhist, nor is a Hindu or Buddhist to become a Christian. But each must assimilate the spirit of others and yet preserve his individuality and grow according to his own law of growth.

The way to the realization of the universal religion:

No study has taken so much human energy, whether in times past or present, as the study of the SOUL, of GOD, and of HUMAN DESTINY. Humans have always wanted to look beyond, wanted to expand himself; and all that we call progress, evolution, has always been measured by that one search, the search for human destiny, the search for GOD.

As our social struggles are represented, among different nations, by different social organizations, so man's spiritual struggles are represented by various religions. And as different social organizations are constantly quarrelling, are constantly at war with each other, so these spiritual organizations have been constantly at war with each other, constantly quarreling. And thus we find that though nothing has brought man more blessings than religion, yet at the same time there is nothing that has brought him more horror than religion. Nothing has made more for peace and love than religion; nothing has endangered fiercer hatred than religion. Nothing has made the brotherhood of man more tangible than religion; nothing has bred more bitter enmity between man and man than religion. Nothing has built more charitable institutions, more hospitals for men and even for animals, than religion; nothing has deluged the world with more blood than religion.

We must remember that all the great religions of the world are very ancient – not one has been formed at the present time – and that every religion of the world had its origin in the region between the Ganges and the Euphrates. Not one great religion has arisen in Europe, not one in America. Every religion is of Asiatic origin and belongs to that part of the world. The western people are grand in organizations, social institutions, armies, governments and so forth, but when it comes to preaching religion they cannot come near the Asiatic. In every country you would find that the religions sometimes progress and sometimes go back. Sects are multiplying all the time. If the claim of any one religion that it has all the truth and that God has given all the truth in certain book, why then there are so many sects. Take the bible for instance, and all the sects that exist among the Christians. Each one puts its own interpretation upon the same text and each says that it alone understands that text and all the rest are wrong. So is with every religion. There are many sects among the Mohammedans and among the Buddhists, and hundreds among the Hindus. You see that happening all the time. You cannot make all conform to the same ideas and that in fact is good. I am glad that sects exist and wish they might go on multiplying more and more. Seven billion people of the world should have Seven billion ways of realizing God. If all the people of the world were to think exactly the same thoughts, there would be no thought for us to think. We know that two or more forces must come into collision in order to produce motion. It is the clash of thought, the differentiation of thought that awakens thought. Variation is the sign of life and it must be there.

Now how can all this variety be true? How can contradictory opinions be true at the same time? This reminds me of the following childhood story.

"Once upon a time, six blind men happened to come near a standing elephant. They felt with their hands, different parts of the huge animal, and began disputing about its nature. One caught the end of the tail, and said it was a broom or brush. Another felt the trunk and declared it was a huge python. A third found an ear, and affirmed that it was a large winnowing fan. A fourth found the abdomen and maintained it was a vast drum. A fifth stroked a leg, and asserted it was a thick column. A sixth grasped a tusk, and was sure it was a very large pestle (grinder or crusher). They argued over their positions. A seventh person happened to pass, and saw them disputing. He had eyes, was a man of vision, a man of wisdom. He explained to them what it was; a compound of all their opinions. Each blind man was right, but he only explored one facet of the whole elephant."

In the same way, we are all looking at the truth from different standpoints, which vary according to our birth, education, surroundings, and so on. We are viewing Truth, getting as much of it as these circumstances will permit, coloring it with our own feelings, understanding with our own intellect, grasping it with our own minds. We can feel only as much of truth as is related to us, as much of it as we are able to receive. This makes the difference between humans and sometimes-even occasions contradictory ideas. Yet we all belong to the same great, **Universal Truth.**

Just think of Islam: - Islam makes all its followers **EQUAL** that is the peculiar excellence of Mohammedanism. In many places in Koran you find very sensual ideals of life. What Mohammedanism comes to preach to the world is this **practical brotherhood** of all belongings to their faith. That is the essential part of the Mohammedan religion, and all other ideas, about heaven and life and so forth, are not real Mohammedanism. They are accretions.

With the Hindus: - There is one great idea: **SPIRITUALITY.** The spirit must be divine and spirit as such must not be identified with the physical world. The idea of unity, of the realization of GOD, the omniscient, the omnipotent, the Omnipresent, the omnibenevolent, and the Omni truth is preached throughout. All the heavens that ever existed are here in this world. Humans have to only realize it. Renunciation and Spirituality are the two great ideas of Hindus.

With the Christians: - The central idea that has been preached by them is **"Watch and Pray, for the kingdom of heaven is at hand."** Which means- purify your mind and be ready. Christians have always tried to prepare them- selves for the coming of the Lord by trying to help others, building hospitals and so on.

Therefore all these religions are different forces in the economy of GOD, working for the good of mankind, and not one can be ignored. The ideal, which every religion represents, is never lost, and so every religion is intelli- gently on the march. **The UNIVERSAL RELIGION** about which philoso- phers and others have dreamt in every country already exists. As the universal brotherhood of people already exists, so also does the universal religion. Only there are number of persons who fail to see this and upset it by crying for new brotherhoods. The Universal religion too already exists.

If the priests and other people who have taken upon themselves the task of preaching different religions simply cease preaching for a few mo- ments, we shall see that Universal Religion is there. They are disturbing it all the time, because it is to their interest. Not only must they have the spiritual ideas, they also must come to you according your own method. They must speak your own language, the language of your soul, and then alone will they satisfy you. When the person comes who speaks my language and gives me the truth in my language, I at once understand it and receive it forever. This is a great fact.

Religion of the Universe: -
Like the Bee, gathering honey from different flowers, the wise man accepts the essence of different scriptures and sees only the good in all religions.

There is only one religion, though there are hundred versions of it.

All mystics speak the same language, for they come from the same country.

Every prophet and every saint hath a way, but it leads to GOD; all the ways are really one.

There are so many who can believe one thing at a time. I am so made as to re- joice in the many and behold the beauty of the one in the many. Hence my natural affinity to many religions; in them all I see revelation of the one spirit. And deep in my heart is the conviction that I am a servant of all prophets.

Following are the three forms of the Universal GOD:

G - Generator – We are all given life by our Generator called GOD
O – Operator – All our lives are being sustained by one Operator called GOD
D – Destroyer – All our lives are destroyed in the end by one Destroyer called GOD

Why there is rivalry in religion?
Rivalry in religion is meaningless. There can be no rivalry in true religion. Rivalry is due to two things – want of knowledge and lack of sympathy. Sometimes there is lack of sympathy and often there is lack of both. Religion, which was meant to be bond of union, has become a source of sectarian strife's.

Why have so many lost faiths in religion, today?
People have lost faith in religion because religion has been separated from life. Religion will come in to existence when people will learn to live amicably and helpfully with their fellow men. Civilization is sinking, for there is lack of unity in our lives. Civilization may be saved if life is built in the vision of the One-in-all.

2.11 - SCIENCE AND SPIRITUALITY: -
Science without religion is lame, religion without science is blind.

Spirituality is a science and it concerns the discovery of the one self in all, whereas physical science is discovery of the laws of nature.

People are awed by the miracles of science as much as they are fascinated by the powers of spirituality.

There is an interaction and a unity between spirituality and science. Number of scientists has said that we are busy studying the electrons – what if the electron was to turn around and ask, "Who is this entity trying to study us?" This takes us to the fundamental question, what is Human? What am I? This makes many of us feel that science is now only one step away from spirituality. When scientists are able to answer this question, there will be total integration between science and spirituality.

It cannot be denied that modern medicines are amazing. The miracles of healing performed by modern medicine are astounding. But the modern medicine treats only the body, neglecting link the dimensions of human-being. Modern medicine considers body as a machine, which can be repaired when it goes out of order. But human-being is a composite being built out of body, mind and soul. The body is only a garment we have worn. The mind is an instrument we have brought with ourselves to do our work on the physical plane. Essentially we are the SOUL. If the soul were sick, do whatever you will with the body, it will keep on moving from one sickness to the other.

2.12 - SEVEN DIMENSIONS OF RELIGION: - [10, 28]
These seven dimensions of religion help to characterize religions, as they exist in the world. The point of the list is so that we can give a balanced description of the movements, which have animated the human spirit and taken a place in the shaping of society, without neglecting either ideas or practices.

1. The Doctrinal and Philosophical dimension:
    During Roman philosophical and intellectual heritage it became necessary to face questions about the ultimate meaning of creation, the inner nature of God, the notion of grace, the analysis of how Christ could be God and human being, and so on. These concerns led to the elaboration of Christian doctrine. In the case of Buddhism, the doctrinal ideas were more crucial right from the start, for the Buddha himself presented a philosophical vision of the world which itself was an aid to salvation.

    In any event, doctrines come to play a significant part in all the major religions, partly because sooner or later a faith has to adapt to social reality and so to the fact that much of the leadership is well educated and seeks some kind of intellectual statement of the basis of the faith.

2. The narrative or Mythic dimension:
    It is the story side of religion. It is typical of all faiths to hand down vital stories; some historical; some about that mysterious primordial time when the world was in its timeless dawn; some about things to come at end of the time; some about great heroes and saints; some about great founders such as Moses, the Buddha, Jesus, Mohammad, Rama and Krishna; some about assaults by the evil one; some parables and edifying tales; some about the adventures of Gods; and so on. These stories are often called myths. The term may be a misleading, for in the context of the modern study of religion there is no implication that a myth is a false.

3. The practical and Ritual dimension.
    Every tradition has some practices to which it adheres – for instance regular worship, preaching, prayers, and so on. They are often known as rituals (though they may well be more informal than this word implies). This practical and ritual dimension is especially important with faiths of a strongly sacramental kind.

4. The experiential and Emotional dimension.
    We only have to glance at the religious history to see the enormous vitality and significance of experience in the formation and development of religious traditions. Consider the visions of the Prophet Mohammad, the conversion of Paul, the enlightenment of Buddha.

    So it is important in understanding a tradition to try to enter in to feelings which it generates – to feel the sacred awe, the calm peace, the rousing inner dynamism, the perception of brilliant emptiness within, the outpouring of love, the sensation of hope, the gratitude for favors which have been received.

5. The Ethical and Legal dimension.
    The law, which a tradition or a sub tradition incorporates in to its fabric, can be called the ethical dimension of religion.

6. The social and institutional dimension.
    To understand faith we need to see how it works among people. Sometimes the social aspect of the worldview is simply identical with society itself, as in small-scale groups such as tribes. It is not however the formal officials of a religion who may in the long run turn out to be the most

important person in the tradition. For there are Charismatic or sacred personages, whose spiritual power glows through their demeanor and actions, and who animate the faith of most ordinary folk – saintly people, gurus, mystics and prophets, whose words and examples stir up spiritual enthusiasm of the masses and who lend depth and meaning to the rituals and values of tradition.

7.   The material dimension.
     This social or institutional dimension of religion almost inevitably becomes incarnate in a different way, in material form, as buildings, works of art, and other creations.

2.13 - RELIGIOUS AND SPIRITUAL BELIEFS: -

In this world there are so many different people, so many different dispositions. There are seven billion human beings and we need seven billion different religions, because there is such large variety of dispositions. Each individual should embark upon a spiritual path that is best suited to his or her mental disposition, natural inclination, temperament, belief, family, and cultural background. Therefore, we must respect and appreciate the value of all the different major world religious traditions. One reason to respect these other traditions is that all of these traditions can provide an ethical framework, which can govern one's behavior and have positive effect on his way of life. There are many reasons to respect other religious traditions because all major religions have provided tremendous benefit for millions of human beings throughout many centuries in the past, present and in future also, these different religious traditions will give inspiration to millions of coming generations.

One way of strengthening that mutual respect is through closer contact between those of different religious faiths. It is essential that we develop closer bonds among the various religions; through this we can make a common effort for the benefit of humanity. There are so many things that divide humanity, so many problems in the world. Religion should be a remedy to help reduce the conflict and suffering in the world not another source of conflict. We often hear people say that all human beings are equal. By this we mean that everyone has the obvious desire of happiness. Everybody has the right to be a happy person. And everyone has the right to overcome suffering. So if some one is deriving happiness or benefit from a particular religious tradition, it becomes important to respect the rights of others, thus we must learn to respect all these major religious traditions.

True meaning of spiritual practices: -
It has to do with the development and training of your mental state, attitudes, and psychological and emotional state and well-being. True spirituality is a mental attitude that you can practice at any time. For example, if you find yourself in a situation in which you might be tempted to insult some one, and then you immediately take precautions and restrain yourself from doing that. Similarly, if you encounter a situation in which you may loose your temper, immediately you are mindful and say, 'No, this is not the appropriate way'. That actually is a spiritual practice.

All Religions are same: -
All major religions are equally valid and basically teach the same thing.

All human beings should be convinced that whatever their religious beliefs, each religion or faith is just of many equally valid paths to God and ways to live in the world. The doctrinal differences between Judaism, Islam, Christianity, Buddhism, and Hinduism are superficial and insignificant, that they all believe in the same God, which is all loving spirit in the universe.

Different doctrines of each religion are also important because each religion sees part of spiritual truth, but none can see the whole truth.

Sometimes this point is illustrated with the story of the blind men and the elephant. Several blind men were walking along and came upon an elephant that allowed them to touch and feel it. "This creature is long and flexible like a snake" said the first blind man, holding the elephant's trunk. "Not at all – it is thick and round like a tree trunk, " said the second blind man, feeling the elephant's leg. "No, it is large and flat," said the third blind man, touching the elephant's side. Each blind man could feel only part of the elephant – none could envision the entire elephant. In the same way it is argued, the religions of the world each have a grasp on part of the truth about spiritual reality, but none can see the whole elephant or claim to have a comprehensive vision of the truth.

Religious belief is too culturally and historically conditioned to be **"Truth"**.

Without reference to any divine revelation or confessional tradition, we should work together on the great problems of our time – such as Aids, Poverty, Education and so on. We should keep our religious views to ourselves and unite around policies that "work" best for the most people.

2.14 - SCIENCE AND RELIGION: -

Science: – The purpose of science is to study our world – the physical universe, the human experience, and all of nature – and provide conclusions that add meaning to our lives and help us make decisions. Science is insatiable; once a particular conclusion is reached, it is time to move to next. It seems almost inevitable that someday science will start to tackle the spiritual questions of life. One could argue that science will never really achieve its ultimate purpose until it starts to tackle the questions of GOD, the existence of SOUL, and other spiritual matters.

Religion: - Among all religions there is one common mystical idea that what we call "Reality" is actually an "Illusion". The mystical sects of all religions tell us that our five senses only give us a limited view of a greater infinite Reality. It is the reality of our Inner Self, our true self that is eternal and presents everywhere. The SOUL does not die, and is therefore much more "Real" than the body, which is just a temporary vehicle for the Soul. It is the common belief among the mystics that both time and space are part of the illusion, the veil that covers the truth.

2.15 – LOVE FOR RELIGION IS THE ULTIMATE FREEDOM: –

Love is the most liberating freedom-loss of all. One of the principles of love- either love for a friend or a romantic love- is that you have to loose independence to attain greater intimacy. If you want the freedom of love – the fulfillment, security, and sense of worth that it brings – you must limit your freedom in many ways. You cannot enter in to deep relationship and still make unilateral decisions or allow your friend or lover to say no to how you live your life. To experience the joy and freedom of love, you must give up your personal autonomy.

Freedom, then, is not the absence of limitations and constraints but it is finding the right ones, those that fit our nature and liberate us. For a love relationship to be healthy, there must be a mutual loss of independence. If only one party does all the sacrificing and giving, and the other does all the ordering and taking, the relationship will be exploitative and will oppress and distort the lives of both people.

At first sight, then, a relationship with God seems inherently dehumanizing. Surely it will have to be "one way" God's way. God, the divine being, has all the power. We must adjust to GOD – there is no way that God could adjust to and serve us. When you fall deeply in love, you want to please the beloved.

Sin and Solution: -
There is a profound and fundamental difference between the ways the other religions tell us to seek salvation and the way described in the gospel of Jesus. All other major faiths have founders who are teachers that show the way to salvation. Only Jesus claimed to actually be the way of salvation himself.

Egotism: -
An enormous capacity for egotism, self-absorption, and regard for your own interest over those of all others, and self-aggrandizement (exaggeration or overdoing) is the foundation of the so much of the misery of the world. It is the reason that the powerful and rich are indifferent to the plight of the poor. It is the reason for most of the violence, crime, and warfare in the world. It is at the heart of most cases of family disintegration. We hide from ourselves, and our self-centered capacity for acts of evil, but situation arise that act as a 'potion (medicine)', and out they come.

Sin and evil are self-centeredness and pride that lead to oppression (Domination) against others, but there are two forms of this. One form is being very bad and breaking all the rules, and the other form is being very good and keeping all the rules and becoming self-righteous.

2.16 – ABRAHAM: - [29]

Imagine a world saturated with ignorance and hatred, a lonely, brutish place, without any hope of redemption. Now picture a man – Abram, the bible calls him – who hears a command from God: Leave behind the life you know, and I will one day bless the entire world through you. How this will happen, and why, is a mystery to this man, but he sets out. In time God gives him a new name: Abraham. In time he will become the patriarch of three monotheistic faiths – Judaism, Christianity, and Islam. And history will be transformed by his story.

Was there ever, thousands of years ago a personage named Abraham whom more than three billion people – more than half of humanity –venerate as the father, patriarch, and spiritual ancestor of their faiths. Two billion of them are Christians, 1.2 billion are Muslims and close to 15 million are Jews. And had Abraham verily spoken with God and celebrated with him covenants that became the foundation of these three religions. The outlines of Abraham's life appear first and most fully in genesis, the first book of the holy scriptures of Judaism and the Christian bible's old testament. Abraham also makes frequent appearances in other Jewish and Christian writings, including the Talmud and the New Testament, and he is mentioned time and again in the Koran, the holy book of Islam.

Abraham is philosophy, Abraham is culture, and Abraham may or may not be historical. Abraham is a message of loving-kindness. Abraham is an idea. Abraham is everything. We don't need flesh and blood.

What makes anyone think that Christians, Muslims and Jews can unite behind any man, when they cannot live in peace under the one true God they all believe in?

The search for peace through Abraham will lead only along the path we have already traveled – to disagreements, discord and strife. The sole solution is for people of the three faiths to live together as children of one GOD.

It is misleading to think the current conflict in the Holy Land is a continuation of the mythic struggle between Abraham's sons. There is nothing holy about savage bloodshed that has destroyed generations of innocent lives for the sole purpose of maintaining political power and control of land and power.

When Jews, Christians and Muslims shed their exclusive claims on Abraham and recognize that he is the patriarch of all three faiths, may be these cousins can co-exist in peace. But that requires courage and compassion.

2.17 - BUDDHISM: - [30]

The origins of the SGI-USA (SOKA GAKKAI International-USA) worldview can be traced to the teachings of the historical Buddha Shakyamuni, who lived some 2,500 years ago in what is modern-day Nepal. Born Gautama Siddhartha, he abandoned his sheltered, princely life and sought instead to understand the inescapable sufferings of every human being—birth, aging, sickness and death—and the means by which these sufferings could be overcome.

Following his enlightenment at age 30, he traveled throughout India for some 50 years, sharing the wisdom he had discovered. The term *Buddha*, or "enlightened one," is applied to any human being who realizes the eternity of life and the operation of cause and effect throughout the three existences of past, present and future.

Throughout Shakyamuni Buddha's life, he expounded many sutras, or teachings, the highest and most comprehensive being the **Lotus Sutra**. Shakyamuni stated that all of his teachings prior to the Lotus Sutra should be regarded as provisional; these teachings strove to awaken people to the impermanence of all phenomena in order to free them from the sufferings that arise from egoistic attachment to things that the passage of time will destroy or render meaningless.

As his essential teaching, revealed in the last eight years of his life, **the Lotus Sutra teaches the existence of an innate and universal truth known as the Buddha Nature**, the manifestation of which enables one to enjoy absolute happiness and to act with boundless compassion. Rather than stressing impermanence and the consequent need to eliminate earthly desires and attachments, the Lotus Sutra asserts the ultimate reality of the Buddha nature inherent in all life. It is therefore a teaching, which profoundly affirms the realities of daily life, and which naturally, encourages an active engagement with others and with the whole of human society.

The Lotus Sutra is also unique among the teachings of Shakyamuni in that it makes the attainment of enlightenment a possibility open to all people—without distinction based on gender, race, social standing or education.

Nichiren Daishonin:

After Shakyamuni's passing, his teachings became splintered and increasingly misunderstood as they spread throughout Asia and beyond. In the 13th century, a Japanese Buddhist reformer, Nichiren Daishonin, declared the Lotus Sutra, taught during the final eight years of Shakyamuni's life, to be the highest and ultimate teaching of Buddhism. The Lotus Sutra most clearly shows Buddhism as a powerful, life-affirming, egalitarian and humanistic teaching.

Born the son of a fisherman in a time of social unrest and natural catastrophe, Nichiren became a religious aid and after a period of intensive study came to realize that the **Lotus Sutra constitutes the heart of Buddhist teachings.** His great gift to humanity was in giving concrete expression to this life-affirming philosophy by creating a simple yet profound daily practice accessible to all people. Nichiren first chanted the title of the Lotus Sutra Nam-myoho-renge-kyo on April 28, 1253, and later inscribed the mandala of the Gohonzon (the physical object of devotion for all humanity). It is the philosophy taught by Nichiren that forms the foundation of the Buddhism.

Nam-myoho-renge-kyo

Nichiren taught that all the benefits of the wisdom contained in the Lotus Sutra can be realized by chanting its title Nam Myoho-renge-kyo. The universal law of life is expressed as Nam-myoho-renge-kyo; reciting this allows each individual to tap into the wisdom of his or her life to reveal his or her Buddha Nature. Chanting these words and excerpts from the Lotus Sutra is the core of this Buddhist practice, supported by study and helping others reveal their own Buddhahood. Faith, practice and study are the basics of Buddhist practice, pursuing activities for one and activities for the sake of others.

This is the mystic law, the natural principle governing the workings of life in the universe, the law to which all Buddha's are enlightened and the true aspect of our own lives. Using our voices to express and convey the state of our inner life – whether that is one of joy, gratitude, despair or determination – is central to our identity as humans. The voice serve as the vital link between ourselves, our fellow humans and a universe that is itself vibrant with the rhythms of life and death.

What, then, does **Nam-myoho-renge-kyo** mean? The phrase can be literally translated as "I devote myself to the Lotus Sutra of the wonderful Law".

Nam: - derives from Sanskrit and means to venerate or dedicate oneself. It is often translated as "Hail" or "Take Refuge In"

Myoho: - corresponds to Saddharna and may be translated as "wonderful or mystic law". The great power of mystic law embraces everything, brings out the positive possibilities of all situations, transforming everything toward the good, reviving and giving new life to all experiences.

Myo and Ho are also identified by Nichiren as corresponding to Life and Death, which Buddhism regards as two aspects- one active and manifests, the other latent and unseen – of deeper life continuum. This continuum is permeated and shaped by the law of causality, or cause and effect, which Nicheren identifies with **renge,** the lotus flower.

Renge: - The Lotus Flower – Specifically the fact that the lotus flower already contains seeds when it opens, symbolizes the principle of the simultaneity of cause and effect, the idea that causes we make are engraved in the deepest, most essential realms of life, and on this plane we immediately experience the effects of our thoughts, words and deeds. In terms of Buddhist practice that means that " Anyone who practices this law will obtain both the cause and effect of Buddha hood simultaneously." The fact that lotus flower sends forth pure white blossoms from roots sunk deep in muddy water expresses the idea that our highest nature is brought forth through committed engagement with the often difficult or disagreeable realities of life and society.

KYO: - signifies the Sutra, the voiced and transmitted teachings of the Buddha. Kyo represents the words and voices of all living beings...KYO may also be defined as that which is constant and unchanging in the three existences of the past, present and future.

Elsewhere Nichiren associates each of the characters of Nam-myoho-Renge-Kyo with parts of the human body: head, throat, chest, abdomen and legs, respectively. This may be understood as indicating that the mystic principle or law that guides and governs the living cosmos is in no way separate from the concrete realities of our lives.

By invoking the mystic law and bringing forth our highest, most enlightened nature, we naturally inspire those around us to strive toward the highest, most creative and compassionate way of life.

Quotations: -

Buddha was asked, "What have you gained from meditation?"

He replied "Nothing"!

However Buddha said, let me tell you, what I lost;

Anger
Anxiety
Depression
Insecurity
Fear of old Age
And
Fear of Death

2.18 - POWER OF HEALING: - [31]
Religious people have healthy life style:

I am sure you'll agree that the world's major religions encourage healthy living. Some even mandate abstention or moderation as basic doctrine. Devout Hindus are strict vegetarians, as are many traditional Buddhists. The dietary laws of Judaism, kashrut, date from the earliest books of the Bible. Few pious Muslims drink alcohol. Mormons and Seven Adventists practice healthy temperance in their daily lives. All established religions discourage drunkenness, risky sexual behavior, and any habit or activity harmful to the human body, which has traditionally been viewed as sacred, created in the image of God.

1. A growing array of research is charting the benefits to physical health that religious people often enjoy. I'm particularly impressed by studies showing that adolescents from strong religious backgrounds who frequently attend worship service, pray, and read scripture are far less likely to drink alcohol, smoke tobacco, or experiment with illegal drugs than their nonreligious peers.

2. Research also indicates premarital sexual intercourse is far less common among religious adolescents than among less religious teenagers.

3. And there's convincing evidence that the shield of religious moderation continue into adulthood.

4. These lifestyle attitudes are the basis of the much lower rates of alcohol- and tobacco-related afflictions and sexually transmitted diseases among the religious when compared with their secular peers.

2.19 – FINALLY WHAT IS RELIGION?

Some say it is a form of belief in God. But that would not fit Buddhism, which does not believe in God at all.

Some say it is a belief in the supernatural power. But that does not fit Hinduism, which does not believe in supernatural realm beyond the material world, but only a spiritual reality within the empirical.

Some say it is set of beliefs that explain what is life all about, who we are, and the most important things that human beings should spend their time doing.

For example, some think that this material world is all there is, that we are here by accident and when we die we just rot, and therefore the important thing is to choose to do what makes you happy and not let others impose their beliefs on you. Notice that though this is not an explicit "organized" religion, it contains a master narrative, an account about the meaning of life along with a recommendation for how to live based on that account of things. Some call this a" worldview' while others call it a "narrative Identity'. In either case it is a set of faith assumptions about the nature of things. It is an implicit religion.

Human communities should not be completely inclusive, but should be open to all on the basis of our common humanity. The idea of totally inclusive community is, therefore an illusion. Every human community holds in common some beliefs that necessarily create boundaries, including some people and excluding others from its circle. Each community should have beliefs that lead its members to treat persons in other communities with love and respect – to serve them and meet their needs.

Freedom of Religion: -
Christianity, Judaism and Islamic religions are supposedly a limit to personal growth and potential because it constraints our freedom to choose our own beliefs and practices. The present day enlightened human beings trusts in their own power of thinking, rather than in authority or tradition. This resistance to authority in moral matters is now a deep current in our culture.

Freedom to determine our own moral standards is considered a necessity for being fully human.

In many areas of life, freedom is not so much the absence of restrictions as finding the right ones, the liberating restrictions. If we only grow intellectually, vocationally, and physically through judicious constraints – why would it not also be true for spiritual and moral growth? Instead of insisting on freedom to create spiritual reality, shouldn't we be seeking to discover it and disciplining ourselves to live according to it?

CHAPTER 3

WHAT IS "MIND POWER"?

3.01 - POWER OF MIND: - [32]

In every country, you will find individuals of extraordinary mental or psychic powers, bordering on the miraculous.

Beyond mental or intellectual power lies another distinct dimension that gives extraordinary power to individuals to influence people. This can be simply stated as power of the personality.

Compare the great leaders of religion with the great philosophers. The philosophers scarcely influenced anyone's inner man, and yet they wrote most marvelous books. The religious teachers on the other hand, moved countries in their lifetime. In the one case ... it is a flash of light ... In the other, it is like a torch that goes around quickly, lighting up the others"

The science of Yoga (Body and Mind control) addresses the laws and methods, which help man to grow and strengthen his personality. These laws indicate that behind the gross level of power that we can physically sense, lie sources of power of increasing subtlety, the ultimate one being the spirit. Man, both as an individual and as a race, is progressing, not only towards acquiring these deeper powers, but also to an ideal beyond.

The mind plays an important role in achieving every kind of success and goal, minor everyday goals or major goals.

With minor or day-to-day goals, one usually knows what he or she wants to do or get, but when it comes to major goals, most people don't know what they really desire. They desire to do something big, but they don't know what. They might have a vague idea, but this is not enough.

To accomplish anything, and to use your mind power, you have to know exactly what it is you want to do. To focus your mind power on a goal, you need to have a clear and well-defined goal. How do you go about that?

You have first to think or meditate, to find out what is it that you want to accomplish or gain. This might not be a simple step, and requires deep thinking, investigation and time.

After discovering what you really want to accomplish, you need to come up with a plan for action. You need to know what you have to do first and how to proceed. All of this requires planning, which means using the power of the mind.

After deciding on a goal and coming up with a plan, you need to hold in your mind a clear mental image of your goal. You need to see it accomplished. This step requires that you use your imagination, which is another power of the mind. Not everyone can visualize clear mental images, but regular training of the imagination can do wonders. You may, for example, look at photos of what you want to achieve, and then close your eyes, and try to see it in your imagination. This will enhance your ability to visualize.

At this point you have to display patience, self-discipline and the power to persist in your efforts. This requires a one pointed mind.

Three Powers of Mind
1. **Affirmations** are another useful mental tool for achieving success. What you affirm sinks into the subconscious mind, becomes part of the subconscious mind, and consequently affects your behavior and actions. If your affirmations are positive, they lead you to success.

2. Another important power of the mind is **thought transference**. You need to be able to transmit your thoughts to other people, who would aid you with your plans. Often, you have to persuade others to invest in your plans or to help you in other ways. It is not enough just to talk

with them, you need to believe in what you are saying; you need to be enthusiastic and persuasive, otherwise they won't listen and won't care. You need to be able to reject your and their doubts. To be able to do so, you need concentration, control over your thoughts, willpower, self-discipline and patience. All these are mental tools and skills.

3. **Motivation** is another mental and emotional power that you require for achieving success. How can you achieve anything if you are not motivated enough? To increase your motivation and enthusiasm, think often of your goal, about its advantages and benefits, and how it will change your life. Doing so, will strengthen your motivation.

Your thoughts, which are part of your mind, possess power. The thoughts that you most often think tend to come true. If you pour your mental energy into the same thoughts or mental images day after day, they will become stronger and stronger, and would consequently affect your attitude, expectations, behavior and actions. Other people, who would then offer you help or opportunities, can even subconsciously perceive these thoughts and mental images. Your thoughts can also create what is usually termed as coincidence. They can attract into your life corresponding events, situations and opportunities.

Not every thought turns into reality. A thought has to be repeated often, and be tinged with desire, in order to come true. Doubts, fears and worries tend to destroy what you build with the power of your mind. This means that you need to clear your mind of negative thoughts and doubts.

Use your mind power to achieve your goals: -
Understanding the mind power you have and using it can bring you everything you want. Increasing mind power is something anyone can do. Your mind is your most precious asset yet most people treat it like it doesn't matter. Don't you make the same mistake?

Most don't even understand that the conscious mind and subconscious mind are two different things and the two don't always want the same things or even work together.

If you can learn to understand how hypnosis works in your subconscious mind, it's like having an owner's manual for your own mind and you will be better able to use or increase your own mental power. You can easily learn this.

Scientists and Doctors say we only use nine to eleven percent of our brains or mental power. Just think how much better your life could be if you learned to use just five percent more of your mental faculties.

Human brains are wonderful things and our subconscious has much more power than most of us believe. We have all kinds of capabilities that go largely unused due to our disbelief that they can even happen. Science is proving more and more often that things we thought the mind could never do are now very possible.

3.02 - MATTER AND ENERGY

The whole universe is resolved in two components, **matter and energy**. Both can be resolved still in higher entity called Mind, the thought power. Thought is the finer manifestation than matter or energy. It is thought that splits itself in to these two. By combination of these two the whole universe has been produced.

Human body has five senses: -
Each sense has an instrument and each instrument has an organ (nerves). Organ then transfers the news to the mind. The state of mind, which reacts, is called the **Intellect.** There is something upon which the mind is painted all these pictures, this something upon which our sensations, carried by the mind and intellect, are placed and grouped and formed in to unity, is what is called the **Soul** of man. In the universe, behind the universal mind, there is also a SOUL, **and it is called God.**

We are Body and Mind only, not Soul - Why?
Buddhists deny the whole theory of Soul. They say, why there be not a soul as substratum, a something that is neither mind nor body but stands as background for both mind and body. Let there be only mind and body. Body is the name of the stream of matter continuously changing. Mind is the name of the

stream of consciousness or thought similarly changing. But the SOUL is the supreme commander of both body and mind, which never changes.

Now how does one explain the unity of body and mind?
This unity really does not exist. Take for instance, a lighted torch. If you whirl it rapidly, you see a circle of light. The circle does not really exist, but because the torch is continually moving, it creates the appearance of a circle, so there is no unity in its body, it is mass of matter continually rushing on, and this stream of matter you may call one unity. Similarly in mind each thought is separate from every other thought, it is only rushing current that leaves behind the illusion of unity; there is no need of the third substance called Soul. This universal phenomenon of body and mind all that really is, do not post something behind it.

But this is not true; SOUL is the binding power of body and mind.

3.03 - HOW HUMAN MIND WORKS: -
Many passages of scriptures show that there is a *spirit* in the man. A Spirit is not matter, and man is matter. To distinguish from God's Holy Spirit, let us designate it as " Human Spirit". Nevertheless, it is spirit and not matter.

This human spirit imparts the power of intellect to the human physical brain. The spirit cannot see, hear, taste, smell or feel. The brain sees through the eye, hears through the ear, etc. The human spirit cannot of itself think. The physical brain thinks.

What then is the function of this human spirit? – It is the SOUL, and 1) it imparts the power of intellect-of thinking, and of mind power, to the human brain; and 2) It is the very means God has instilled, making possible a personal relationship between Human Man and Divine God.

3.04 - MEDITATION ON THE NATURE OF MIND: - [17]

The purpose of the meditation is to begin to recognize and get a feel for the nature of our mind. When we refer to our mind, we are talking about an abstract concept, without having a direct experience of our mind. If we are asked to identify the mind, we may be compelled to merely point to the brain. If we were asked to define mind, we may say it is something that has the capacity to 'know', something that is 'clear', and 'cognitive'. But without having directly grasped the mind through meditative practices, these definitions are just words. It is important to be able to identify the mind through direct experience, not just an abstract concept. So the purpose of the meditation is to be able to directly feel or grasp the conventional nature of the mind, so when you say the mind has the qualities of 'Clarity' and 'cognition', you will be able to identify it through experience, not just as an abstract concept.

Meditation helps you to deliberately stop the discursive thoughts and gradually remain in that state for longer and longer duration. As you practice meditation, eventually you get to a feeling as if there is nothing there, a sense of vacuity. But if you go further, you eventually begin to recognize the underlying nature of the mind, the qualities of 'Clarity' and 'knowing'. It is similar to having pure crystal glass full of water. If the water is pure, you can see the bottom of the glass, but you still recognize that the water is there.

Generally speaking, our mind is predominantly directed towards external objects. Our attention follows after the sense experiences. It remains at a predominantly sensory and conceptual level. In other words normally our awareness is directed towards physical sensory experiences and mental concepts. But in meditation, what you should do is to withdraw your mind inwards, don't let it chase after or pay attention to sensory objects. At the same time, don't allow it to be totally withdrawn that there is kind of dullness or lack of mindfulness. One should maintain a very full state of alertness and mindfulness, and then try to see the natural state of your consciousness – a state in which your consciousness is not afflicted by thoughts of the past, the things that have happened, your memories and remembrances, nor is it afflicted by thoughts of the future, like your future plans, anticipations, fears, and hopes. But rather try to remain in a natural and neutral state. When you are able to stop your mind from chasing sensory objects and thinking about the past and future and so on, and when you can free your mind from being totally 'blanked out', then you will begin to see underneath this turbulence of the thought process. There is an underlying stillness, an underlying clarity of the mind. One should try to observe or experience this.

Fill every thought with determination, every step with courage and every word with love by meditation.

Learn Meditation:
Why has meditation been the core practice of all wisdom paths for over two thousand years? Because it is the most effective method to access your innate wisdom, rediscover inner peace and enhance your creative ability. Meditation restores well-being, and once you're being is well again, all that you do will be successful and fulfilling. But maybe you think you are OK as you are. Perhaps you feel your being is well. But is it. Do you feel tense, worried, hopeless, mentally tired, emotionally upset...ever? Then your being is not well. Your body may be OK but you, the being, are unwell. Medication is for the body, and meditation is for the soul, that's you, and for your mind. Learning how to meditate is one of the greatest gifts you can give to yourself. Practicing meditation says you care about yourself. Being in meditation can touch the minds and hearts of others a thousand miles away. It actually says that you care about others too.

Real Renunciation: -
On the path mapped out by the true spiritual philosophers and pioneers, there is great emphasis placed on the idea and need for renunciation. It is seen as the way to enlightenment, and freedom from the attachments, which we misuse as sources of limited happiness and contentment. Renunciation does not mean giving everything away, shaving our heads, saying farewell to family and friends and finding a Himalayan mountaintop. It means seeing our attachments and dependencies, our weaknesses and our evasions, and consciously giving them up. There is no sense of loss. The material necessities still come to us, paradoxically more will come. And when we renounce our own weaknesses and dependencies there is always strength and a new freedom to be found hiding underneath. Renunciation is a pathway to a simpler life and a highway to spiritual freedom - one of spirit's deepest yearnings in 'the age of accumulation'.

OWN POWER:
Power is within you, energy is within you, and all you have to do is to unfold it.

Krishna said – I am seated in the hearts of all, in hearts of every one of us, call it by whatever name it is, all the powers are within you.

Bible also says: - Man is made in the image of God. Image of God is shrined in everyone.

Sink deeper in to yourself:
Say I am not the Body, I am the Soul, and I am one eternal spirit.

Body – Meta physics – Needs material values – Got to work, consider it as a duty for 3 essentials – Food, Shelter and clothing – Become a Karma Yogi.

Soul – non-metaphysics – Needs spiritual values – Got to pray God or do good deeds or help others.

3.05 – KNOW LOVE

We seek it here, we seek it there, and we look for love everywhere! We expect it to come to us, usually through another person. All our conditioning says it is something that happens to us. The mythology of our stories, legends and modern day entertainment industries say it is something we 'fall into'. And yet...and yet real love cannot be acquired, possessed or accumulated. It cannot be known when we think it comes from outside ourselves. The ultimate paradox is we are it. We are love. Each one of us is a source of love that has forgotten that 'love is what I am'. Say it now "I am love". Doesn't feel right does it? That's because it's been so long since we knew and experienced ourselves in this true way. And yet we all know that the deepest trust and the purest love is known and experienced only when we give it, not take it. As we give love in whatever way is appropriate, we are the ones to experience it first, on the way out. Falling in love is impossible. It is only infatuation, obsession with an external object, which appears to fill a gap in us. As soon as the object or person is remembered when they are not present and when they do not need to be remembered, it is simply attachment, which, if sustained, will become a dependency. And attachment and dependency are not love. But you already know that...don't you?

Open Heart: - [12]

The Heart is like a flower – unless it is open it cannot release its fragrance in to the world. The fragrance of the heart is made up of the qualities and virtues of our spirit. Most of us have learnt how to keep our heart closed in a world that would trample all over us if we let it.

Being open hearted today seems to require tremendous courage. It is a courage, which comes only when we realize that no one can hurt us, no matter what they say or do. They may hurt our body, but if we have realized we are spirit, nothing outside can touch us, if we so decide.

Little by little, practices opening your heart to those you think have hurt you. Realize it was not them that hurt you, it was yourself. And it taught you not to trust and you closed your heart. A closed heart is in need of opening. And when you do, you will have begun to heal yourself.

3.06 - SPIRITUALITY

Spirituality is the art of balancing your responsibility to yourself, your family and to the whole world. The basis for this is a deep understanding of the SELF, GOD and the law of CAUSE AND EFFECT.

Knowing the SELF enables you to be detached from physical factors and their limitations. Knowing GOD enables you to create a deep link of love and draw into yourself all attributes, virtues and powers, from the Source. Understanding the deep philosophy of 'karma' motivates you to settle debts of the past and perform elevated actions now. Anyone can fall victim to the suffering of a 1.Poor state of mind, 2.Ill health, 3.Loss of wealth or 4.Unhappy relationships. Human life depends on these four factors and yet each of them has become so fragile and unreliable.

God's power restores tolerance and the ability to face anything. An understanding of the deep philosophy of **karma** reveals how elevated thoughts, pure feelings and good actions can resolve all difficulties for the self and for the world.

Spirituality says, dear friends, live in the present, forget heaven, forget hell, neither exists, if it exists, it is right where you are. You don't have to go to it; it is there in you right now. Then what are you looking for? What are you searching for? Realize it, turn inside, and see that divine abode of God.

Let Go:
Just as the bird has to find the courage to let go of the branch in order to fly, so we also must let go of our branches if we are to know the exhilaration of soaring to the highest potential of our life. The branches we hold to are our inner attachments - our beliefs, ideas and memories. And then there are the outer attachments - People, Possessions, Positions and Privileges are a few. But as long as we hold on to them we will live in fear (of letting go and loss) and we will never be free. And just watch those birds, by letting go of one branch they are able to spend the rest of their life alighting on a million other branches, and they enjoy the view from each. Are you flying and soaring in your life, or are you stuck on one branch, cursing others as they fly past. Go on, try it ...let go!

Powers in the world:
Gentleness, love, humility, forgiveness are the greatest powers in the world.

Golden Rule:
Pharmaceutical companies are working on drugs that mimic the anti-aging effects of caloric restriction. But for the moment the best antidote for aging may just be the golden rule - **do unto others, as you would have them do unto you.** In fact, several recent and long-standing studies demonstrate a connection between longevity and the affected states of being selfless, generous and forgiving.

They improve their mental health, physical well-being. Scientist have concluded that People who reported helping others - even if it was just giving emotional support to a spouse - were only about half as likely to die as those who did not.

To be sure, more research about the cause and effect is required. But for his part, seniors who want to live longer might embrace the internal approach to prolongevity rather than wait on the external or biotechnological approach to longer lives.

NAIL IN THE FENCE (Anger in story form):
There once was a little boy who had a bad temper. His Father gave him a bag of nails and told him that every time! He lost his temper; he must hammer a nail into the back of the fence.

The first day the boy had driven 37 nails into the fence. Over the next few weeks, as he learned to control his anger, the number of nails hammered daily gradually dwindled down. He discovered it was easier to hold his temper than to drive those nails into the fence.

Finally the day came when the boy didn't lose his temper at all. He told his father about it and the father suggested that the boy now pull out one nail for each day that he was able to hold his temper.

The days passed and the young boy was finally able to tell his father that all the nails were gone.

The father took his son by the hand and led him to the fence. He said, "You have done well, my son, but look at the holes in the fence. The fence will never be the same. When you say things in anger, they leave a scar just like this one.

You can put a knife in a man and draw it out. It won't matter how many times you say I'm sorry, the wound is still there. " **A verbal wound is as bad as a physical one.**

Friends are very rare jewels, indeed. They make you smile and encourage you to succeed. They lend an ear, they share words of praise and they always want to open their hearts to us."

Introspection (Contemplation): -
Introspection is the attitude of going inside (self examination or meditation) when it's necessary. It is especially applicable before a task or a busy day. The result of going inside is peace and calmness, which gives clarity to the intellect for making right decisions. Introspection does not mean avoiding the world, it means going inside and getting empowered to act along with others.

Peace of Mind

Peace of mind comes not from wanting to change others, but by simply accepting them as they are. Peace consists of pure thoughts, pure feelings and pure wishes. When the energy of thought, word and action is balanced and stable, the individual is at peace with the self, in relationships and the world. To exercise the power of peace look inward (self examination or meditation) in order to look outward with courage, purpose and meaning.

3.07 - WORDS (Sparks of purity): -

Words! They are all around me! I see them. I use them. Harsh words, soothing words, biting words; words that give pain and sorrow; words that give joy and pleasure. They are vital to communication.

When words are spoken there are reactions, negative or positive. Either thoughts are triggered or emotions fired or actions performed. Words color our behavior. And how lovely it is to hear words that are calm and free from resentment and aggression. To hear words that lifts the soul and leaves it with renewed vigor. Such words are the sparks of purity.
It is important to remember that our speech indicates what is in our mind. As the thinking, so the words uttered. Mental calmness makes our words calm. A pure mind makes for pure words. It is said that speech may exalt someone to kingship or send him to the gallows (cross beams). I should never let myself indulge in false, bitter and vicious speech. My words should reflect my true, inner nature, that of purity and peace. Words, once spoken, can never be recalled. They reverberate all around, beyond our control.

Today, as I utter words, what effect will they have on those who hear them? Will they be the words that are poisonous and cause pain? Or will my tongue be like that of the nightingale, sweet and so, so very soothing and lovely to the ear?

Calmness & Silence:

Calmness increases efficiency. Silence increases effectiveness.

Help Yourself

Unfortunately these two words tend to describe the generally selfish and materialistic culture in which most of us live. They result not in self-help but in dependency. Our education and our role models do not encourage us to help ourselves to grow, change and expand our capacities as human beings. Real self-help means recognizing that no one else is responsible for our thoughts and feelings, and that we are only ever victims because we choose to be. Our destiny is always and only in our own hands - despite all apparent evidence, which may indicate otherwise. Learning to help us is also a prerequisite to extending a hand of assistance to others. We all need a leg up from time to time, but once there, we are always on our own.

3.08 - RESOURCE FULL: -

We each have the three energies we need to learn to manage - **Body, Mind and Spirit**. All three need a good diet - body needs pure food, your mind needs positive ideas and images, and the spirit that you are needs time in silence and stillness to refresh and renew. These are our resources, and each one needs topping up, otherwise we run on empty and disease comes to visit. But diet is just the beginning, next comes exercise and meditation.

Open Mind

The mind is like a parachute - it works best when it is open. How quickly we make assumptions, jump to conclusions and close our mind. How easily we form and hold fast to our opinions and then close our mind. How fast do we make a judgment, slap on a label and then close our mind? A closed mind never knows the delight of playing with possibilities, being enlightened by others point of view or enjoying the diversity of human life. An open and understanding mind never assumes, doesn't jump to conclusions and won't hold fast to any opinion. Perhaps it is no wonder, a closed mind is not a very relaxed mind.

Banish Worry:

Worry is otherwise known as 'fantasized catastrophsizing' where we create an image of the future and use it to frighten ourselves! Be aware that you are doing it, and then stop doing it; otherwise the image will become a self-fulfilling prophecy. Imagine only the brightest future, and so it will be. Besides there is nothing to worry about... unless you are under the illusion that you're well being and security are dependent on material things. If they are, then you will have many ways in which you can create worry. Possible loss, damage, separation, uncertainty are but a few. Look, you're killing yourself with worry, all because of the misuse of your imagination. Don't do it.

3.09 - MIND MATTERS: -

The most important part of you is your mind (not your brain - the brain is the hardware and the mind creates the software). Care for your mind, make friends with it, always feed it healthy food, engage it in positive activity, and exercise it with knowledge and wisdom. Like a garden returns fragrance and beauty according to the care invested, so your mind will repay you with thoughts, ideas and visions of great beauty when tended and invested with care. Your mind is not made of matter but it does matter what you give it and what you create with it. Where your mind goes, you go. What your mind creates becomes your destiny.

Calming The Mind:

Don't give your mind permission to get disturbed. A disturbed mind is easily influenced. This will cost you your peace. Learn to maintain your peace by freeing yourself from attachments. Competing or comparing yourself with others will not allow you to focus inwards. An inner focus allows you to keep your eye on your higher self. Remember your original nature. It allows you to forge a link with the Divine. Then it becomes easy to recognize useless thoughts and replace them with a spiritual perspective. A calm mind is not just peaceful; it is focused, self-directing and divine.

Heal Yourself:

The deepest wounds we all carry are locked in our subconscious (out of our awareness). Deep memories and subtle impressions, from unfinished experience, rooted in the past. The pain from those wounds comes to revisit, to block and paralyze us in the moment called now. We all know it comes without warning - "Why am I feeling this way, I didn't mean to do that, I don't know what made me say that." Healing does not mean finding and treating every single inner scar, which send it message to haunt us. It means going even deeper, past those wounds, beyond those distant memories and recording of unfinished business, to the core of our self, to the heart of our spirit, where we find the light and warmth of our own core qualities of love and peace. They are eternally present within us they are what we need to heal all our inner wounds. **That's why this kind of deep healing is called spirituality and not therapy.**

Perceive Positively:
True self-awareness, plus the ability to choose our perceptions of life, the universe and everything, is the basis of free will. Every situation and scene in front of us has so many possibilities in terms of how we perceive and interpret. If someone is 10% selfish and 90% generous what should we focus on, what should we perceive first within them? Most of us are now well trained to perceive and focus on the negative, the selfishness in others, and to follow it quickly with accusation and judgment. We forget that what we perceive is what we empower within another and, more importantly what we perceive is what we empower within ourselves in that moment. And what we choose to see is usually what we get. So how important is it that we choose to perceive only the best, the highest, the greatest in another, even if it's only a half a percent? Bosses and parents - take note!! Don't forget - your perception is your reality. Your perception is what you project. And what you project is what comes back!

Power On:
Each day we all need to recharge our spiritual battery, otherwise the light of our consciousness becomes dim, thoughts become fuzzy, and decisions are impregnated with doubt. Power is available inside and outside. Inside us we have a **spiritual center**, at the core of our consciousness, pure radiant spiritual light. This is what we are. However it is now blocked by our attachments, the record of all our life experiences and many learned beliefs and perceptions. Outside us we have the sun of spirit, the source, invisible to our physical eyes but only one second away when we are able to be quiet and focus our mind. Meditation connects us to both sources of power - that's why meditation is the way to access the real vitamins and the minerals that spirit craves. The vitamin of pure love and the minerals of truth and wisdom. Take time to empower yourself today. Sit quietly and connect your mind to each source and allow yourself to recharge and renew.

Procrastination:
Procrastination is not only the thief of time; it is the creator of subtle inner tension. You know you are cheating yourself. There are three secrets to overcoming procrastination.

1. Don't wait till you feel like doing it – the feeling will come when you start doing it.
2. List all the things you have to do and then prioritize the list.
3. Create a vision of the result and be motivated by the vision of the outcome, not the thought of the process.

Mindful Moments:
Most of us are of sound mind, but many of us have trouble maintaining a note of harmony and peace. Most of us know how to think, but few of us are able to control our thoughts. We all have the capacity to be creative, to image new ideas, but few of us are able to do it together and co-create in harmony with each other. We could all do with some mental training so that we may use the most powerful energy in the universe, **The Mind,** which is always at our instant disposal. We can begin with mindfulness. It's a simple way to gently help our mind go where it is best to go, do what is the best thing to do. It begins by simply being fully aware of what you are doing. Mostly we are not fully aware, as our minds wander into the past and then into possible futures. We spend most of our time watching others and so rarely fully focus on what we are actually doing ourselves. Next time you sit down to a meal, watch your self. Be aware of only what you are eating. Every time your mind wants to wander, bring it gently and lovingly back to the action and sensation of eating. Then do the same when cleaning, when writing, when working. The more you do it stronger and more focused and more rational will be your concentration, the more natural will be your actions, the more peaceful you will feel, and the more relaxed you will be, no matter what you are doing.

Mind Based Stress Reduction (MBSR):
It was developed in 1979 by Jon Kabat-Zinn, an MIT educated scientist. Mindfulness techniques associated with the philosophy are intended to help practitioners quiet a busy mind, becoming more aware of the present moment and less caught up in what happened earlier or what is to come. If distraction is the pre-eminent condition of our age, then mindfulness, in the eyes of its enthusiasts, is the most logical response. Researchers have found that multi-tasking leads to lower overall productivity. Students and workers who constantly and rapidly switch between tasks have less ability to filter out irrelevant information and they make more mistakes. The technology has gone beyond what we are capable of handling. There is nothing bad or harmful about the smartphone if we have the awareness of how to use it in the right way.

Solution: - Scientist have been able to prove that meditation and rigorous mindfulness training can lower blood pressure, increase immune response and possibly even affect gene expression. Scientific study is also showing that meditation can have an impact on the structure of the brain itself. Educators are also turning to mindfulness with increasing frequency – perhaps a good thing, considering how digital technology is splitting kids' attention spans too. (The average American teen sends and receives more than 3,000 text messages a month.)

3.10 – TRUE PEACE: -

True peace can be experienced only when we stop giving and taking sorrow. In order not to give sorrow we need a clear heart that has no ill feelings and for not taking sorrow we need a big heart that can tolerate and help other souls to get over their weaknesses.

Contentment:

The more positive the thoughts flowing through one's mind, the more contented one will feel. It is easy to feel contented when we are praised and appreciated but to remain contented when we are being criticized and rejected is the mark of real spiritual strength. The way to develop this level of strength is to learn about God's way of loving. Only when I am in deep contemplation can I see God showing me the kind of love I need to express so that I myself never reject or criticize and always generate good wishes for others. Then I will feel satisfied no matter what life throws at me.

Anger is weakness, Tolerance is bravery and Humility makes you strong.
Anger

If even one person in a house has anger, there is a battle. An angry person makes a household very sorrowful. Anger is a very bitter enemy. Where there is anger and sorrow that is called hell. Do not make others unhappy due to your anger.

Change:

It is wise to bend rather than to break. Those who change will get spiritual wisdom. Conversely, those who have wisdom will decide to change. Change is the first law of Nature.

Thoughts are like seeds:

When you sow a thought you reap an action, when you sow an action you reap a habit, when you sow a habit you reap a character and when you sow a character you reap a destiny. Thoughts are like seeds. You cannot sow the seed of one plant and get another: thistles will never produce daffodils! When your thoughts are positive, powerful and constructive, your life will reflect this.

Emotions:

"When you blame other people for your reactions, when you believe they are responsible for your feelings, you relinquish control over your life. You allow others to take charge of your life. Be a master of your emotions!"

Senses:

Senses are connected to the mind; so let me maintain peace of mind by using my eyes, ears and mouth with utmost care.

Power To Tolerate:

You have the power to tolerate anyone and any situation. But tolerance is not just suffering in silence. It means going beyond any personal discomfort you may feel, and giving a gift to whom ever you would tolerate. Give your time, attention, understanding, compassion, care - all are gifts, which paradoxically, you also receive in the process of giving. And, as you do, you will experience your own self-esteem and inner strength grow. In this way you can turn tolerance into strength.

The Power of Thoughts:

Thoughts are more powerful than actions because they are the creators of actions. You have to keep in mind that the thought-waves of your good wishes and pure feelings, your vibrations of peace and love, can once again bring harmony in nature and happiness in the world.

Self-Manage:

There is a huge hole in the heart of all our educations. It is where the skills and abilities of self-management should be. No one teaches us how to manage our thoughts, feelings, attitudes and behavior, so we find it hard to manage the four Rs; Relationships, Roles, Responsibilities and Resources. So let's get started. Consciously choose the quality of your thoughts today – accentuate the positive, eliminate the negative and clean up the waste. Everything, which means everything in your life, begins with your thoughts.

Self-Control:
When things go wrong, our first thought is often about controlling the situations or people involved. But since neither the situations nor people are in our hands, there is no success guaranteed with this way of thinking, which only increases the negativity. Instead of trying to control something one has no control upon, one need to start with one-self. The more one is able to control one-self with constant attention, checking and changing, the more one will have everything under control.

CHAPTER 4

WHAT IS "BIRTH"?

4.01 – BIRTH: -
Birth is the act or process of bearing or bringing forth offspring. The offspring is brought forth from the mother. The time of human birth is defined as the time at which the fetus comes out of the mother's womb into the world.

Definitions:
It is still a challenge for scientists and philosophers to define life in unequivocal terms· Defining life is difficult—in part—because life is a process, not a pure substance. Any definition must be sufficiently broad to encompass all life with which we are familiar, and it should be sufficiently general that, with it, scientists would not miss life that may be fundamentally different from life on Earth.

Biology:
Since there is no unequivocal definition of life, the current understanding is descriptive, where life is a characteristic of organisms that exhibit all or most of the following phenomena·

1. **Homeostasis**: Regulation of the internal environment to maintain a constant state; for example, electrolyte concentration or sweating to reduce temperature.

2. **Organization**: Being structurally composed of one or more cells, which are the basic units of life.

3. **Metabolism**: Transformation of energy by converting chemicals and energy into cellular components (anabolism) and decomposing organic

matter (catabolism). Living things require energy to maintain internal organization (homeostasis) and to produce the other phenomena associated with life.

4. **Growth**: Maintenance of a higher rate of anabolism than catabolism. A growing organism increases in size in all of its parts, rather than simply accumulating matter.

5. **Adaptation**: The ability to change over a period of time in response to the environment. This ability is fundamental to the process of evolution and is determined by the organism's heredity as well as the composition of metabolized substances, and external factors present.

6. **Response to stimuli**: A response can take many forms, from the contraction of a unicellular organism to external chemicals, to complex reactions involving all the senses of multicellular organisms. A response is often expressed by motion, for example, the leaves of a plant turning toward the sun (phototropism) and by chemotaxis.

7. **Reproduction**: The ability to produce new individual organisms, either asexually from a single parent organism, or sexually from two parent organisms.

4.02 - LIVING SYSTEM THEORIES: -

Some scientists have proposed in the last few decades that a general living systems theory is required to explain the nature of life. Such a general theory, arising out of the ecological and biological sciences, attempts to map general principles for how all living systems work. Instead of examining phenomena by attempting to break things down into component parts, a general living systems theory explores phenomena in terms of dynamic patterns of the relationships of organisms with their environment.

Recent experiments have demonstrated true Darwinian evolution of unique RNA enzymes called ribozymes are made up of two separate catalytic components that replicate each other *in vitro*. In describing this work from his laboratory, Gerald Joyce stated: "This is the first example, outside of biology, of evolutionary adaptation in a molecular genetic system." Such experiments make the possibility of a primordial RNA World even more attractive to many scientists.

Recent findings by NASA, based on studies with meteorites found on Earth, suggests DNA (DeoxyriboNucleic Acid) and RNA (RiboNucleic Acid) components (adenine, guanine and related organic molecules) may also be formed extraterrestrially in outer space.

Earth is the only planet known to harbor life. The Drake equation, which relates the number of extraterrestrial civilizations in our galaxy with which we might come in contact, has been used to discuss the probability of life elsewhere, but scientists disagree on many of the values of variables in this equation. Depending on those values, the equation may either suggest that life arises frequently or infrequently.

Spiritual meanings:
- **Astrology** is based upon the belief that an individual's life is influenced by the geocentric positions of the Sun, Moon, and planets in the sky or below the horizon at the moment of birth; a natal chart is calculated using the exact time, date, and place of birth to try to interpret these cyclical influences on a person's life.

- **Born again**, a term used primarily in Protestant Christianity, is associated with salvation, conversion, and spiritual rebirth.

- **Rebirth** is a belief that a person is born again after their death based on the karma of their previous births.

- **Virgin birth of Jesus** is the Christian doctrine that asserts that Jesus Christ was born to a virgin, and thus his conception was carried out without an earthly father.

Legal meanings:
- **Birth certificate** is a legal document describing details of a person's birth.

- **Birthday** is a day to celebrate that the person has lived a certain number of years. It is an annual event based either on the anniversary of a person's date of birth, or on astrological birthtime calculations.

- **A nuclear family** comprising the father, mother, brother or sister, is an institution where the members are related by birth.

In some countries a person is considered of **illegitimate birth** if the child is born of parents not legally married to one another.

Hylomorphism:
Hylomorphism is the theory (originating with Aristotle (322 BC)) that all things are a combination of **matter and form**. Aristotle was one of the first ancient writers to approach the subject of life in a scientific way. Biology was one of his main interests, and there is extensive biological material in his extant writings. According to him, all things in the material universe have both matter and form. The form of a living thing is its **SOUL** (Greek *psyche*, Latin *anima*). There are three kinds of souls: the "**vegetative soul**" of plants, which causes them to grow and decay and nourish themselves, but does not cause motion and sensation; the "**animal soul**" which causes animals to move and feel; and the "**rational soul**" **which is the source of consciousness and reasoning** which (Aristotle believed) is found only in humans. Each higher soul has all the attributes of the lower one. Aristotle believed that while matter can exist without form, form cannot exist without matter, and therefore the soul cannot exist without the body.

Consistent with this account is a **teleological explanation of life**. A teleological explanation accounts for phenomena in terms of their purpose or goal-directedness. Thus, the whiteness of the polar bear's coat is explained by its *purpose* of camouflage. The direction of causality is the other way round from materialistic science, which explains the consequence in terms of a prior cause. Modern biologists now reject this functional view in terms of a material and causal one: biological features are to be explained not by looking forward to future optimal results, but by looking backwards to the past evolutionary history of a species, which led to the natural selection of the features in question.

4.03 - SECULAR HUMANISM:

Per secular humanism, the human race came to be by reproducing in a progression of unguided evolution as an integral part of nature, which is self-existing. Knowledge does not come from supernatural sources, but from human observation, experimentation, and rational analysis (the scientific method): the nature of the universe is what people discern it to be. Likewise, "values and realities" are determined "by means of intelligent inquiry" and "are derived from human need and interest as tested by experience", that is, by critical intelligence "As far as we know, the total personality is [a function] of the biological organism transacting in a social and cultural context."

People determine human purpose, without supernatural influence; it is the human personality (general sense) that is the purpose of a human being's life; humanism seeks to develop and fulfill: "Humanism affirms our ability, and responsibility, to lead ethical lives of personal fulfillment that aspire to the greater good of humanity". Humanism aims to promote enlightened self-interest and the common good for all people. It is based on the premises that the happiness of the individual person is inextricably linked to the well-being of humanity, as a whole, in part, because humans are social animals, who find meaning in personal relations, and because cultural progress benefits everybody living in the culture.

The philosophical sub-genres posthumanism and transhumanism (sometimes used synonymously) are extensions of humanistic values. One should seek the advancement of humanity and of all life to the greatest degree feasible, to reconcile Renaissance humanism with the 21st century's technoscientific culture, thus, **every living creature has the right to determine its personal and social "meaning of life" in its own unique way.**

From a humanistic-psychotherapeutic point of view, the question of the meaning of life could also be reinterpreted as "What is the meaning of my life?" Instead of becoming focused on cosmic or religious questions about overarching purpose, this approach suggests that the question is intensely personal. There are many therapeutic responses to this question, for example Viktor Frankl argues for "Dereflection", which largely translates as ceasing to endlessly reflect on the self, instead of engaging in life. On the whole, the therapeutic response is that the question of meaning of life evaporates if one is fully engaged in life. The question then transforms into more specific worries such as "What delusions am I under?", "What is blocking my ability to enjoy things?", "Why do I neglect loved-ones?".

4.04 - LOGICAL POSITIVISM:

Logical positivists ask: "What is the meaning of life?", "What is the meaning in asking?" and "If there are no objective values, then, is life meaningless?" Ludwig Wittgenstein and the logical positivists said: "Expressed in language, the question is meaningless"; because, in life the statement the "meaning of x", usually denotes the consequences of x, or the significance of x, or what is notable about x, etc., thus, when the meaning of life concept equals "x", in the statement the "meaning of x", the statement becomes recursive, and, therefore, nonsensical, or it might refer to the fact that biological life is essential to having a meaning in life.

The things (people, events) in the life of a person can have meaning (importance) as parts of a whole, but a discrete meaning of (the) life, itself, aside from those things, cannot be discerned. A person's life has meaning (for himself, others) as the life events resulting from his achievements, legacy, family, etc., but, to say that life, itself, has meaning, is a misuse of language, since any note of significance, or of consequence, is relevant only in life (to the living), so rendering the statement erroneous. Bertrand Russell wrote that although he found that his distaste for torture was not like his distaste for broccoli, he found no satisfactory, empirical method of proving this:

When we try to be definite, as to what we mean when we say that this or that is "the Good," we find ourselves involved in very great difficulties. Bentham's creed, that pleasure is the Good, roused furious opposition, and was said to be a pig's philosophy. Neither he nor his opponents could advance any argument. In a scientific question, evidence can be presented on both sides, and, in the end, one side is seen to have the better case — or, if this does not happen, the question is left undecided. But in a question, as to whether this, or that, is the ultimate Good, there is no evidence, either way; each disputant can only appeal to his own emotions, and employ such rhetorical devices as shall rouse similar emotions in others ... Questions as to "values" — that is to say, as to what is good or bad on its own account, independently of its effects — lie outside the domain of science, as the defenders of religion emphatically assert. I think that, in this, they are right, but, I draw the further conclusion, which they do not draw, that questions as to "values" lie wholly outside the domain of knowledge. That is to say, when we assert that this, or that, has "value", we are giving expression to our own emotions, not to a fact, which would still be true if our personal feelings were different.

4.05 – ORIGIN AND NATURE OF BIOLOGICAL LIFE:

The exact mechanisms of abiogenesis are unknown: notable theories include the RNA (RiboNucleic Acid) world hypothesis (RNA-based replicators) and the iron-sulfur world theory (metabolism without genetics). The Darwin theory of evolution does not attempt to explain the origin of life but the process by which different lifeforms have developed throughout history via genetic mutation and natural selection. At the end of the 20th century, based upon insight gleaned from the gene-centered view of evolution, biologists George C. Williams, Richard Dawkins, David Haig, among others, conclude that if there is a primary function to life, it is the replication of DNA (DeoxyriboNucleic Acid) and the survival of one's genes.

However, though scientists have intensively studied life on Earth, defining life in unequivocal terms is still a challenge. Physically, one may say that life "feeds on negative entropy which refers to the process by which living entities decrease their internal entropy at the expense of some form of energy taken in from the environment. Biologists generally agree that lifeforms are self-organizing systems regulating the internal environment as to maintain this organized state, metabolism serves to provide energy, and reproduction causes life to continue over a span of multiple generations. Typically, organisms are responsive to stimuli and genetic information tends to change from generation to generation resulting in adaptation through evolution, these characteristics optimizing the chances of survival for the individual organism and its descendants respectively.

Non-cellular replicating agents, notably viruses, are generally not considered to be organisms because they are incapable of "independent" reproduction or metabolism. This controversy is problematic, though, since some parasites and endosymbionts are also incapable of independent life. Astrobiology studies the possibility of different forms of life on other worlds, such as replicating structures made from materials other than DNA.

Though the Big Bang model was met with much skepticism when first introduced, it has become well-supported by several independent observations. However, current physics can only describe the early universe from 10^{-43} seconds after the Big Bang (where zero time corresponds to infinite temperature); a theory of quantum gravity would be required to go further back in time. Nevertheless, many physicists have speculated about what would have preceded this limit, and how the universe came into being. Some physicists think that the Big Bang occurred coincidentally, and when considering the anthropic principle, it is sometimes interpreted as implying the existence of a multiverse.

CHAPTER 5

WHAT IS "LIFE"?

5.01 - DEFINITIONS OF LIFE: -
It is still a challenge for scientists and philosophers to define life in unequivocal terms. Defining life is difficult—in part—because life is a process, not a pure substance. Any definition must be sufficiently broad to encompass all life with which we are familiar, and it should be sufficiently general that, with it, scientists would not miss life that may be fundamentally different from life on Earth. **Life** is a characteristic that distinguishes objects that have signaling and self-sustaining processes (i.e., living organisms) from those that do not, either because such functions have ceased (death), or else because they lack such functions and are classified as inanimate. Biology is the science concerned with the study of life.

Living organisms undergo metabolism, maintain homeostasis, possess a capacity to grow, respond to stimuli, reproduce and, through natural selection, adapt to their environment in successive generations. More complex living organisms can communicate through various means. A diverse array of living organisms (life forms, approximtely 8.4 million forms of life) can be found in the biosphere on Earth, and the properties common to these organisms—plants, animals, fungi, protists, archaea, and bacteria—are a carbon- and water-based cellular form with complex organization and heritable genetic information.
In philosophy and religion, the conception of life and its nature varies. Both offer interpretations as to how life relates to existence and consciousness, and both touch on many related issues, including life stance, purpose, conception of a God or Gods, a Soul or an afterlife.

Hylomorphism:

Hylomorphism is the theory (originating with Aristotle (322 BC)) that all things are a combination of matter and form. Aristotle was one of the first ancient writers to approach the subject of life in a scientific way. Biology was one of his main interests, and there is extensive biological material in his extant writings. According to him, all things in the material universe have both matter and form. The form of a living thing is its **Soul** (Greek *psyche*, Latin *anima*). There are three kinds of Souls: the **"vegetative soul"** of plants, which causes them to grow and decay and nourish themselves, but does not cause motion and sensation; the **"animal soul"** which causes animals to move and feel; and the **"rational soul"** which is the source of consciousness and reasoning which (Aristotle believed) is found only in humans. Each higher soul has all the attributes of the lower one. Aristotle believed that while matter can exist without form, form cannot exist without matter, and therefore the soul cannot exist without the body.

Vitalism:

Vitalism is the belief that the life-principle is essentially immaterial. This originated with Stahl (17th century), and held sway until the middle of the 19th century. It appealed to philosophers such as Henri Bergson, Nietzsche, Wilhelm Dilthey, anatomists like Bichat, and chemists like Liebig.

Vitalism underpinned the idea of a fundamental separation of organic and inorganic material, and the belief that organic material can only be derived from living things. This was disproved in 1828 when Friedrich Wöhler prepared urea from inorganic materials. This so-called Wöhler synthesis is considered the starting point of modern organic chemistry. It is of historical significance because for the first time an organic compound was produced from inorganic reactants.

Later, Helmholtz, anticipated by Mayer, demonstrated that no energy is lost in muscle movement, suggesting that there were no *vital forces* necessary to move a muscle. These empirical results led to the abandonment of scientific interest in vitalistic theories, although the belief lingered on in non-scientific theories such as homeopathy, which interprets diseases and sickness as caused by disturbances in a hypothetical vital force or life force.

5.02 - ORIGIN OF LIFE: -

Evidence suggests that life on Earth has existed for about 3.7 billion years, with the oldest traces of life found in fossils dating back 3.4 billion years. All known life forms share fundamental molecular mechanisms, and based on these observations, theories on the origin of life attempt to find a mechanism explaining the formation of a primordial single cell organism from which all life originates. There are many different hypotheses regarding the path that might have been taken from simple organic molecules via pre-cellular life to protocells and metabolism. Many models fall into the "genes-first" category or the "metabolism-first" category, but a recent trend is the emergence of hybrid models that combine both categories.

There is no scientific consensus as to how life originated and all proposed theories are highly speculative. However, most currently accepted scientific models build in one way or another on the following hypotheses:

Life as we know it today synthesizes proteins, which are polymers of amino acids using instructions encoded by cellular genes—which are polymers of deoxyribonucleic acid (DNA). Protein synthesis also entails intermediary ribonucleic acid (RNA) polymers. One possibility is that genes came first and then proteins. Another possibility is that proteins came first and then genes. However, because genes are required to make proteins, and proteins are required to make genes, the problem of considering which came first is like that of the chicken or the egg. Most scientists have adopted the hypothesis that because DNA and proteins function together so intimately, it's unlikely that they arose independently. Therefore, many scientists consider the possibility, apparently first suggested by Francis Crick that the first life was based on the DNA-protein intermediary: RNA. In fact, RNA has the DNA-like properties of information storage and replication and the catalytic properties of some proteins. Crick and others actually favored the RNA-first hypothesis even before the catalytic properties of RNA had been demonstrated by Thomas Cech.

Recent experiments have demonstrated true Darwinian evolution of unique RNA enzymes (ribozymes) made up of two separate catalytic components that replicate each other in vitro. In describing this work from his laboratory, Gerald Joyce stated: "This is the first example, outside of biology, of evolutionary adaptation in a molecular genetic system." Such experiments make the possibility of a primordial *RNA World* even more attractive to many scientists.

Recent findings by NASA, based on studies with meteorites found on Earth, suggests DNA and RNA components (adenine, guanine and related organic molecules) may also be formed extraterrestrially in outer space.

5.03 - MEANING OF LIFE: -

The **meaning of life** is a concept that provides an answer to the philosophical question concerning the purpose and significance of life or existence in general. It can be expressed through answering a variety of related questions, such as **"Why are we here?" "What is life all about?" and "What is the meaning of it all?"** It has been the subject of much philosophical, scientific, and theological speculation throughout history. There have been a large number of theories to these questions from many different cultural and ideological backgrounds. Even so, the meaning of life could manifest that question itself: "what is the meaning of life," or life seeking the meaning of itself.

The meaning of life is deeply entrenched in the philosophical and religious conceptions of existence, social ties, consciousness, and happiness, and borders on many other issues, such as symbolic meaning, ontology, value, purpose, ethics, good and evil, free will, conceptions of God, the existence of God, the soul, and the afterlife. Scientific contributions focus primarily on describing related empirical facts about the universe, exploring the context and parameters concerning the 'how' of life. Science also provides its own recommendations for the pursuit of well-being and a related conception of morality. An alternative, humanistic approach poses the question **"What is the meaning of my life?"** The value of the question pertaining to the purpose of life may coincide with the achievement of ultimate reality, or a feeling of oneness, or even a feeling of sacredness.

Questions about the meaning of life have been expressed in a broad variety of ways, including the following:
- *What is the meaning of life? What's it all about? Who are we?*
- *Why are we here? What are we here for?*
- *What is the origin of life?*
- *What is the nature of life? What is the nature of reality?*
- *What is the purpose of life? What is the purpose of one's life?*

- *What is the significance of life?*
- *What is meaningful and valuable in life?*
- *What is the value of life?*
- *What is the reason to live? What are we living for?*

The answers to these questions have resulted in a wide range of competing answers and arguments, from scientific theories, to philosophical, theological, and spiritual explanations.

WESTERN PHILOSOPHICAL PERSPECTIVES OF LIFE: -
The philosophical perspectives on the meaning of life are those ideologies which explain life in terms of ideals or abstractions defined by humans.

Platonism:
Plato was one of the earliest, most influential philosophers - mostly for idealism - a belief in the existence of universals. In the Theory of Forms, universals do not physically exist, like objects, but as ghostly, heavenly forms. In *The Republic*, the Socrates character's dialogue describes the Form of the Good.

In Platonism, the meaning of life is in attaining the highest form of knowledge, which is the Idea (Form) of the Good, from which all good and just things derive utility and value. Human beings are duty-bound to pursue the good.

Aristotelianism:
Aristotle, an apprentice of Plato, was another early and influential philosopher, who argued that ethical knowledge is not *certain* knowledge (such as metaphysics and epistemology), but is *general* knowledge. Because it is not a theoretical discipline, a person had to study and practice in order to become "good"; thus if the person were to become virtuous, he could not simply study what virtue *is*, he had to *be* virtuous, via virtuous activities. To do this, Aristotle established what is virtuous:

Every skill and every inquiry, and similarly, every action and choice of action, is thought to have some good as its object. This is why the good has rightly been defined as the object of all endeavor. Everything is done with a goal, and that goal is "good".

Yet, if action A is done towards achieving goal B, then goal B also would have a goal, goal C, and goal C also would have a goal, and so would continue this pattern, until something stopped its infinite regression. Aristotle's solution is the *Highest Good*, which is desirable for its own sake, it is its own goal. The Highest Good is not desirable for the sake of achieving some other good, and all other "goods" desirable for its sake. This involves achieving *eudaemonia*, usually translated as "happiness", "well-being", "flourishing", and "excellence". What is the highest good in all matters of action? To the name, there is almost complete agreement; for uneducated and educated alike call it happiness, and make happiness identical with the good life and successful living. They disagree, however, about the meaning of happiness.

Enlightenment philosophy:
The Enlightenment and the colonial era both changed the nature of European philosophy and exported it worldwide. Devotion and subservience to God were largely replaced by notions of inalienable natural rights and the potentialities of reason, and universal ideals of love and compassion gave way to civic notions of freedom, equality, and citizenship. The meaning of life changed as well, focusing less on humankind's relationship to God and more on the relationship between individuals and their society. This era is filled with theories that equate meaningful existence with the social order.

Classical liberalism:
Classical liberalism is a set of ideas that arose in the 17th and 18th centuries, out of conflicts between a growing, wealthy, propertied class and the established aristocratic and religious orders that dominated Europe. Liberalism cast humans as beings with inalienable natural rights (including the right to retain the wealth generated by one's own work), and sought out means to balance rights across society. Broadly speaking, it considers individual liberty to be the most important goal, because only through ensured liberty are the other inherent rights protected.

Pragmatism:
Pragmatism, originated in the late-19th-century U.S., to concern itself (mostly) with truth, positing that "only in struggling with the environment" do data, and derived theories, have meaning, and that *consequences*, like utility and practicality, are also components of truth. Moreover, pragmatism suggests that *anything* useful and practical is not always true, arguing that what most

contributes to the most human good in the long course is true. In practice, theoretical claims must be *practically verifiable*, i.e. one should be able to predict and test claims, and, that, ultimately, the needs of mankind should guide human intellectual inquiry.

Pragmatic philosophers suggest that the practical, useful understanding of life is more important than searching for an impractical abstract truth about life. William James argued that **truth could be made, but not sought**. To a pragmatist, the meaning of life is discoverable only via experience.

20th century philosophy:
The current era has seen radical changes in conceptions of human nature. Modern science has effectively rewritten the relationship of humankind to the natural world, advances in medicine and technology have freed us from some of the limitations and ailments of previous eras, and philosophy—particularly following the linguistic turn—altered how the relationships people have with themselves and each other is conceived. Questions about the meaning of life have seen equally radical changes, from attempts to reevaluate human existence in biological and scientific terms (as in pragmatism and logical positivism), to efforts to meta-theorize about meaning-making as an activity (existentialism, secular humanism).

Existentialism:
Each man and each woman creates the essence (meaning) of his and her life; life is not determined by a supernatural God or an earthly authority, one is free. As such, one's ethical prime directives are *action, freedom,* **and** *decision*, thus, existentialism opposes rationalism and positivism. In seeking meaning to life, the existentialist looks to where people find meaning in life, in course of which using only reason as a source of meaning is insufficient; the insufficiency gives rise to the emotions of anxiety and dread, felt in facing one's radical freedom, and the concomitant awareness of death. **To the existentialist, existence precedes essence; the (essence) of one's life arises *only* after one comes to existence.**

Naturalistic pantheism:
According to naturalistic pantheism (a doctrine that equates GOD with the forces and laws of the universe), the meaning of life is to care for and look after NATURE (the environment) and SOUL of all living creatures. This is my religion.

EAST ASIAN PHILOSOPHY OF LIFE: -
Mohism:
The Mohist philosophers believed that the purpose of life was universal, impartial love. Mohism promoted a philosophy of impartial caring - a person should care equally for all other individuals, regardless of their actual relationship to him or her. The expression of this indiscriminate caring is what makes human a righteous being in Mohist thought. This advocacy of impartiality was a target of attack by the other Chinese philosophical schools, most notably the Confucians who believed that while love should be unconditional, it should not be indiscriminate. For example, children should hold a greater love for their parents than for random strangers.

Confucianism:
Confucianism recognizes human nature in accordance with the need for discipline and education. Because mankind is driven by both positive and negative influences, Confucianists see a goal in achieving virtue through strong relationships and reasoning as well as minimizing the negative. This emphasis on normal living is seen in the Confucianist scholar Tu Wei-Ming's quote, "we can realize the ultimate meaning of life in ordinary human existence."

Legalism:
The Legalists believed that finding the purpose of life was a meaningless effort. To the Legalists, only practical knowledge was valuable, especially as it related to the function and performance of the state.

SCIENTIFIC INQUIRY AND PERSPECTIVES: -
DNA, is the substance containing the genetic instructions for the development and functioning of all known living organisms. Members of the scientific community and philosophy-of-science communities believe that science may be able to provide some context, and set some parameters for conversations on topics related to meaning in life. This includes offering insights from the science of happiness or studies of death anxiety. This also means providing context for, and understanding of life itself through explorations of the theories related to the big bang, abiogenesis and evolution.

Psychological significance and value in life:
Science may or may not be able to tell us what is of essential value in life (and various materialist philosophies such as dialectical materialism challenge the

very idea of an absolute value or meaning of life), but some studies definitely bear on aspects of the question: researchers in positive psychology (and, earlier and less rigorously, in humanistic psychology) study factors that lead to life satisfaction, full engagement in activities, making a fuller contribution by utilizing one's personal strengths, and meaning based on investing in something larger than the self.

One value system suggested by social psychologists, broadly called Terror Management Theory, states that all human meaning is derived out of a fundamental fear of death, whereby values are selected when they allow us to escape the mental reminder of death.

Neuroscience has produced theories of reward, pleasure, and motivation in terms of physical entities such as neurotransmitter activity, especially in the limbic system and the ventral tegmental area in particular. If one believes that the meaning of life is to maximize pleasure, then these theories give normative predictions about how to act to achieve this. Likewise, some ethical naturalists advocate a science of morality - the empirical pursuit of flourishing for all conscious creatures.

Sociology examines value at a social level using theoretical constructs such as value theory, norms, anomie, etc.

5.04 - WHAT IS LIFE?
Life is a Challenging Journey:

Challenge of course we have to meet and journey we have to complete.
We all must travel in our own unique way
Memories behind us and dreams ahead
And a new beginning each day.
May you always find new paths to travel?
New horizons to explore and
New dreams to call your own.

A perfect life is a contradiction in terms. Life itself is a state of continuous struggle between us and everything outside. Every moment we are actually fighting with external nature, and if we are defeated our life must go. There is for instance, a continual struggle for food, water and air. If food, water or air falls we die. Life is not a simple and smooth flowing thing; it is complex affair. **This struggle between something inside and the external world is what we call life.** So it is clear that when this struggle ceases there will be an end of life. What is meant by ideal happiness is this: the cessation of struggle. But then life too will cease, for the struggle can cease only when life itself has ceased.

Laws of nature are a method, the manner, in which our mind grasps a series of phenomena; it is all in the mind. Certain phenomena, happening one after another, or together, and followed by the conviction of the regularity of their recurrence, thus enabling our mind to grasp the method of the whole series, are explained by what we call **natural law.**

Life is but momentary, whether you are a toiler in the streets or an emperor ruling millions. Life is but momentary, whether you have the best of health or the worst. **There is but one solution of life and that solution is SELF RE-ALIZATION.** If God and Religion are real, then life becomes explained, life becomes bearable and life becomes enjoyable. We have to see God to be convinced that there is God. Nothing but our own realization can make religion real to us.

AGNOSTIC:
All these questions – whether there is immortal SOUL, whether there is GOD, whether there is any Supreme Intelligence guiding this universe, or not – are beyond the field of reason. Reason can never answer these questions. What does reason say? It says, "I am an Agnostic; I do not know either yea or nay." Yet these questions are very important to us. Without a proper answer to them human life will be purposeless.

The human mind has a higher state of existence, beyond reason, a super-conscious state, and that when mind rises to that state, then this knowledge, which is beyond reason, comes – **metaphysical and transcendental knowledge** comes to that man. So this explains why an inspiration, or transcendental knowledge, may be the same in different countries, but in one country it seems to come through an Angel, and in another through a Deva, and third through God. It means that mind brought out the knowledge from within itself and that the manner of finding it was interpreted according to the beliefs and education of the person through whom it came.

Life:
If we have to renounce the results, why we have to work (mentally and physically) for the results?

Work is not an end itself, it is only means. Work is a means to self-purification and self-discipline and self-realization. That self purification will come about only if I work and accept whatever result the super power sends me.

What is truly successful and fulfilled life?
Success is very often confounded with making money – plenty of money and with gaining prestige and reputation. True success does not lie in these things. True success is freedom and fulfillment. If you have freedom, if you have fulfillment, you have truly succeeded. True success belongs to a person who completely dedicates himself to the Lord, who works on this earth plane only as an instrument of the Lord, instrument of His mercy in this world of suffering and pain.

5.05 - WHY DO WE SUFFER SO MUCH?
We suffer so much because we have not yet realized our true identity. We have to transcend both the body and the mind, and then there is no suffering at all. It is the mind that creates the suffering. If only one transcends the mind there is no suffering at all. But to learn this lesson of transcendence, each one of us has to ultimately transcend our senses. To learn this we have to pass through many painful experiences. And without pain we cannot gain anything. This mind can convert this pain in to a joy, into a source of happiness.

For me personally, the suffering is a very special experience. It's humbling to feel the strength of Mother Nature and battle the elements.

The root of suffering is the attachment: -
You have created a space in your mind that holds a person or object as part of you. When that person or object is criticized, neglected or not with you, you feel pain in your mind and you experience a sense of loss.

Why it is that bad things happen to good people, while so many who are evil, have the best of life?

Bad things happen to good people that they may grow better, nobler, and purer. Even as gold is burnt in the crucible to be cleansed of its dross, even so the good people are burnt in to fire of suffering, and so become pure as thrice burnished gold.

Wealth and pleasures and power and honor are not as good as they seem to be. In many cases, they degrade man and make him corrupt. Whatever be the condition in which you find yourself, whatever be the suffering through which you pass, keep on thanking the Lord all the time. When you do so, your heart expands and you become receptive to the helpful and healing forces of GOD.

What is Real Sense of Life?

Life is but a stage,
And we all have part to play.

Life is but a journey,
And we go through ups and downs together.

Life is but a dream,
And when we finally wake up, it might be over.

Life is but a game,
And yet we take it so seriously.

Life is but a comedy,
And yet we cry with all our mighty.

Life is but a love song,
And yet we close our ears to its lyrics.

Life is but a paradise
And yet we choose not to see its beauty.

Life is Love,
Life is beauty,
Life is opportunity,
But only to those who choose to see it that way.

FEAR: -
Why does one feel fear?

How do we overcome it?

Fear is felt when anticipated. Anticipation is again an instrument we handle ourselves.

There is nothing to fear but fear itself.

Values and Education: -
Values are inherited through tradition, upbringing and personal development. All these factors, along with the education we receive from institutions, are what we symbolize a person's character.

Shadows of Life: -
We run after money, fame and joy, to attain happiness, to be at peace with ourselves. Yet when we attain them, the satisfaction is temporary. And there is no peace.

5.06 - OH GOD MY LIFE: -

Unraveling life's "mysteries" and discovering life's "Secrets" (which are in fact neither mysteries nor secretive) may take the courage and determination found only in a self-motivated pursuit.
Only the curious will learn and only the resolute overcome the obstacles to learning. The quest quotient has always excited me more than the intelligent quotient.

The more we learn, the more we can do. The more we do, the more we can learn. But in all this doing and learning, let's not forget one of the most important lessons of all – enjoyment.

How good is man's life, the mere living! How fit to employ all the heart and the soul and the senses forever in joy!

Learn to enjoy the process of learning.
Enjoy your ice cream while it's on your plate.

It doesn't take much inner listening to know that "in there" are many voices: speaking, singing, shouting, and whispering.
What the inner voice says will not disappoint the hoping soul.

Do you think we're all "old enough" to set aside the source, history and trappings of certain techniques and ask of them a simple question: Do they work? (Do they produce the desired result? Do they get you what you want and need?)
My religion consists of a humble admiration of the illimitable superior spirit who reveals him in the slight details we are able to perceive with our frail and feeble mind.

Unfortunately, our senses are limited; therefore our view of the world is limited.
Some problems are just too complicated for rational, logical solutions. They admit of insights, not answers.

If you think you are fooling people with your act of goodness, and that you think you aren't all that good, maybe the one you're fooling is yourself.
The only good is knowledge and the only evil is ignorance.

Whatever we find "True" about the people and the things around us, is also true about ourselves.
When we see men of a contrary character, we should turn inwards and examine ourselves.

The next time you think about someone " I hate you, " ask yourself, "what is it this person is reminding me about myself that I hate?" And the next time you think about another, " I love you, " ask yourself, "What is it I love about myself that I see in this person too?"
The best mirror is an old friend.

There are three distinct, yet overlapping, phases of recovery. We go through each phase no matter what the loss. The only difference is the intensity of feeling, and duration. The first stage is shock/denial/numbness. The second stage is Fear/anger/Depression. The third stage is understanding/acceptance/moving on.

In the darkest hour the soul is replenished and given strength to continue and endure.

Mistakes, obviously, show us what needs improving. Without mistakes, how would we know what we had to work on?

Mistakes are the portals of discovery.

Pain (any pain-emotional, physical, mental) has a message. Once we get the pain's message, and follow its advice, the pain goes away.

If I had a formula for bypassing trouble, I would not pass it around. Trouble creates a capacity to handle it.

The simple solution for common depression: Get up and get moving. Physically move. Do something. Anything. Act. Get going.

Perhaps the most valuable result of all education is the ability to make yourself do the thing you have to do when it ought to be done, whether you like it or not; it is the first lesson that ought to be learned; and however early a man's training begins, it is probably the last lesson that he learns thoroughly.

What is your purpose in life? A purpose is something you discover. It's already there. It's always been there. You have lived your life by it, perhaps without fully realizing it. It's your bellwether, your personal inner divining rod of truth. It tells you, in any given moment, whether you are living your life "on purpose" or not.

My function in life was to render clear what was already blindingly conspicuous.

The house, car, better body, career or money you want – yes, even a romantic relationship, religion or spiritual path – is simply a method or behavior to get something else, something inner, something experiential (security, fun, energy, satisfaction, love, knowledge of God, inner peace)

You must first be who you really are, then you do what you need to do, in order to have what you want.

Successful achievement requires the use and coordination of three things – Thoughts, Feelings and Actions. Thoughts spark the process, get it going. Feelings keep the thoughts alive, encourage more thoughts and get the body moving. Action is important to accomplish the physical tasks necessary for achievement.

To change one's life; Start immediately. Do it flamboyantly. No exceptions.

Life naturally contains negative thoughts. No big deal. Really. Let them drift through your mind like leaves on the patio. There is no need to resist them, hold on to any of them, or entertain them.

Nobody, as long as he moves about among the chaotic currents of life, is without trouble.

Affirmations usually begin with "I am…." "I am a healthy, wealthy and happy person. " "I am joyful no matter what is happening around me." " I am loving and kind."

The words "I am…." Are potent words; be careful what you hitch them to. The thing you are claiming has a way of reaching back and claiming you.

Health is more than just the absence of illness. Health is the presence of aliveness, energy, and joy.

Health is the state about which medicine has nothing to say.

Forgiving means "for Giving" – for, in favor of; giving, to give.

Of course God will forgive me; that's his business.

After you have forgiven, there is only one thing to do; forget it. Whatever "protection" you think you may gain from remembering past grievances are far less important than the balm of forgetting.

Education is what survives, when what has been learned has been forgotten.

Unlike money, wealth is not just what you have, wealth is what you can do without.

To live content with small means; to seek elegance rather than luxury, and refinement rather than fashion; to be worthy, not respectable, and wealthy, not rich; to study hard, think quietly, talk gently; act frankly, to listen to stars and birds, to babes and sages, with open heart; to bear all cheerfully, do all bravely, await occasions, hurry never. In a word, to let the spiritual, unbidden and unconscious, grow up through the common. This is to be my symphony.

We have so many conflicting beliefs about money in our culture. Some are uplifting; some are "down pushing". It's little wonder, and then, that the way most people feel about money is simply confused.
From birth to age 18, a girl/boy needs good parents, from 18 to 35 she/he needs good looks, from 35 to 55 she/he needs a good personality, and from 55 on she/he needs cash.

Learn to sacrifice. The things we think you'd be better off sacrificing, are things such as Desire, Anger, Greed, Attachment and Ego. You don't need them anymore.
Don't go to piano bars where young, unemployed actors get up and sing. Definitely don't be young, unemployed actors who get up and sing.

You might like to try any number of meditative and contemplative techniques available – or you might just want to sit quietly and relax.
This art of resting the mind and the power of dismissing from it all care and worry is probably one of the secrets of energy in our great men.

Some people think meditation takes time away from physical accomplishment. Taken to extremes, of course, that's true. Most people, however, found that meditation creates more time than it takes.
Your vision will become clear, only when you can look in to your own heart. Who looks outside, a dream; that looks inside, awakes.

Peace is the cessation of being against. If you want peace, stop fighting. When you're not against yourself or others, you are at peace. Peace. Be still.
First keep the peace within yourself, and then you can also bring peace to others.

Love is a thing. Loving is an action. ("The difference between love and loving is the difference between fish and fishing," We like loving – the moving, growing, changing, active, dynamic interplay (inner play) between self and others, and between self and self.
Joe never feels guilty about having warm human feelings toward anyone.

When we give ourselves the loving we need (and it takes so little time when we actually do it!), our time with others tend to be joyful, graceful, playful, touching and – in each moment – complete.

Life is a play. It's not its length, but its performance that counts.

5.07 - BALANCED LIFE: - [17]

A balanced and skillful approach to life, **taking care to avoid extremes** becomes a very important factor in conducting one's everyday existence. It is important in all aspects of life. For instance, in planting a sapling of a plant or tree, at its very early stage you have to be very skillful and gentle. Too much moisture will destroy it, too much sunlight will destroy it, too little will also destroy it. So what you need is a very balanced environment where the sapling can have a healthy growth. Or for a person's physical health, too much or too little of any one thing can have destructive effects. For example, too much protein is bad and too little is bad.

This gentle and skillful approach, taking care to avoid extremes, applies to healthy mental and emotional growth as well. For instance if we find ourselves becoming arrogant, being puffed up by self importance based on one's supposed or actual achievements or qualities, then the antidote is to think more about one's own problems and suffering, contemplating the unsatisfactory aspects of existence. This will assist you in bringing down the level of your heightened state of mind, bringing you more down to earth. And on the contrary if you find that reflecting on the unsatisfactory nature of existence, suffering and pain and so forth, makes you feel like overwhelmed by the whole thing, then again there is a danger of going to the other extreme. In that case you might become totally discouraged, helpless and depressed, thinking that "Oh, I can not do anything, I am worthless etc. So under such circumstances, it is important to be able to uplift your mind by reflecting on your achievements, the progress you have made so far, and your other positive qualities, so that you can uplift your mind and get out of that discouraged or demoralized state of mind. So what is required here is a kind of very balanced and skillful approach.

Materialistic Balance: -

One needs to understand the source or basis of extreme behavior. Consider the pursuit of material goods – shelter, clothing, food etc. On one hand poverty can be seen as sort of extreme and we have every right to strive to overcome this and assure our physical comfort. On the other hand, too much luxury, pursuing excessive wealth is another extreme. Our ultimate aim in seeking more wealth is a sense of satisfaction, of happiness. But the very basis of seeking more is a feeling of not having enough, a feeling of discontentment. That feeling of discontentment, of wanting more and more and more, does not arise from the inherent desirability of the objects we are seeking but rather from our mental state.

Spiritual balance: -

Not only the balanced life approach is helpful for one's physical and emotional health, but it applies to spiritual growth as well. For spiritual balance there are many different techniques and practices. But it is very important to be very skillful in one's application of various techniques and not to be too extreme. One needs a balanced and skillful approach here too. It is important to have a coordinated approach, combining studying and learning with the practices of contemplation and meditation. This is important that there will not be any imbalances between academic or intellectual learning and practical implementation.

5.08 - POSITIVE CHANGES IN LIFE: -

What would be the approach to overcoming negative behaviors and making positive changes in one's life?

1. The first step involves **Learning and Education -** The systematic training of mind. By selecting and focusing on positive mental states and challenging negative mental states. Learning and education are important because they help one to develop conviction of the need to change and help increase one's commitment. Therefore learning and education is the first step in bringing about internal transformation, rather than more transcendental or mystical spiritual practices. In trying to determine the reasons for these beneficial effects of education, scientists have reasoned that better educated individuals are more aware of health risks factors, are better to implement healthier life style choices, feel a greater sense of empowerment and self esteem, have greater problem solving skills and more effective coping strategies – all factors that contribute to a happier, healthier life.

2. The next step is **Developing Conviction (confidence)** - This conviction to change then develops in to determination.

3. **Determination and Enthusiasm** - This determination transforms in to action. This step is also widely accepted by the cotemporary Western Science as an important factor in achieving one's goals. In certain studies psychologists have examined the lives of some America's most accomplished artists, athletes, and scientists and have discovered that drive and determination, not great natural talent, led to their success in their respective fields. As in any other field, one could assume that this principle would equally apply to the art of achieving happiness. Behavioral scientists have extensively researched the mechanism that initiates, sustains and directs our activities and that mechanism is called 'Human Motivation'.

4. **Human Motivation** - Psychologists have identified three principle types of motives –- a) Primary motives - are drives based on our biological needs that must be met for survival. This would include for example, needs for food, water, and air. — B) Stimulation and information. – This is an innate need required for proper maturation, development and functioning of nervous system. - c) secondary motives – these are motives based on learned needs and drives. Many secondary motives are related to required needs for success, power, status or achievement. However these motives generated are not used only in the pursuit of worldly success but develops as one gains a clearer understanding of the factors that lead to true happiness and are used in the pursuit of higher goals, such as kindness, compassion, and spiritual development.

5. **Action** – The strong determination to change enables one to make a sustained effort to implement the actual changes.

6. **Effort** – The final factor of effort is critical. This is the final factor in bringing about change. The effort is the necessary factoring establishing new conditioning. Through new conditioning we can change our negative behavior and thoughts.

7. **Genetic, Social and Cultural Forces;** - While science has recently revealed that one's genetic predisposition (one's nature) clearly plays a role in an individual's characteristic way of responding to the world. But most social scientists and psychologists feel that a large measure of the way we behave, think and feel is determined by learning and conditioning (one's nurture), which comes about as a result of our upbringing and the social and cultural forces around us. And since it is believed that behaviors are established by conditioning and reinforced and amplified by 'habituation', this opens up the possibility of extinguishing harmful or negative conditioning and replacing it with helpful, life-enhancing conditioning.

Negative Emotions in Life: -
It is a fact that ultimate happiness depends on eliminating our negative behaviors **like Desire, Anger, Greed, Attachments and Ego.**

But these kinds of emotions seem to be a natural part of our psychological make up. All human beings seem to experience these darker emotions to one degree or another. It seems impractical and even unnatural to try to completely eradicate something that is integral part of our natural make up. Among humans these emotions vary according the degree of emotions.

But above thinking is wrong. For example all of us are born in an ignorant state. In this sense ignorance is also quite natural. When we are young we are quite ignorant, but as we grow day-by-day through education and learning we can acquire knowledge and dispel ignorance. So if we leave ourselves in a 'natural state' without making an effort to dispel these negative emotions, then these negative emotions will overpower your education, learning and training; whereas we should gradually reduce our negative emotions to a lesser and lesser degree and increase positive state of mind such as **Love, Compassion, and Forgiveness.**

There are three methods of over-powering negative emotions:

1. **Valid Foundation** - These two kinds of emotions (positive and negative emotions) are basically two states of mind. One way of categorizing these emotions is in terms of understanding that the positive emotions are those, which can be justified, and negative

emotions are those, which cannot be justified. For instance there can be positive desire and negative desire. Desire for one's basic needs to be met is a positive kind of desire. It is justifiable. It is based on the fact that we all exist and have the right to survive. And in order to survive there are certain things we require, certain needs that have to be met. So that kind of desire has valid foundation. Excessive desire and greed are negative desires. Those kinds of desires are not based on valid reasons and often create trouble and complicate one's life. **So we can say that positive emotions have a firm and valid foundation, and the negative emotions lack this valid foundation.**

2. **Wisdom Factor** - Our positive state of mind can act as antidote to our negative tendencies and delusory state of mind. The cultivation of certain specific positive mental qualities such **as Patience, Tolerance, kindness and so on** can act as specific antidotes to negative states of mind such as anger, hatred and attachment. Applying antidotes such as love and compassion can significantly reduce the degree or influence of mental and emotional afflictions. In order to fully overcome all of these negative tendencies, one must apply the antidote to ignorance – **'Wisdom Factor'**. The wisdom factor involves generating insight in to the true nature of reality.

3. **Meditation** - Mind of clear light – Essential nature of mind is pure. It is based on the belief that the underlying basic subtle consciousness is untainted by the negative emotions. This is achieved through **Meditation**.

Therefore by these three methods mental and emotional afflictions ultimately can be eliminated through deliberately cultivating antidotal forces like love, compassion, tolerance and forgiveness, and through various practices such as meditation.

LOVE THY LIFE: -
We have a longing for joy, love, and beauty that no amount or quality of food, sex, friendship, or success can satisfy. We want something that nothing in this world can fulfill. Isn't that at least a clue that this "Something" that we want exists. This unfulfilling longing, then, qualifies as deep, innate human desire,

and that makes it a major clue that there is GOD, who operates our life. Some people believe that beauty and love are just biochemical responses, in the presence of great art and beauty we inescapably feel that there is real meaning in life, there is the TRUTH and JUSTICE that will never let us down, and love means everything.

5.09 - SELF REALIZATION: - [9]

Man is not at peace with himself till he has become like unto God. The endeavor to reach this state is supreme, the only ambition worth having. AND THIS IS THE SELF REALIZATION.

How can the body be made temple of God? In other words how can one be free from action i.e. from the taint of sin?

By desire less action, by renouncing the fruits of actions, by dedicating all activities to God i.e. surrendering one self to him body and soul.

He is the devotee who is jealous of none, who is a fount of mercy, who is without egotism, who is selfless, who is ever forgiving, who is always contented, whose resolutions are firm, who has dedicated mind and soul to God, who causes no dread, who is not afraid of others, who is free from exultation, sorrow and fear, who is pure, who is versed in action, and yet remains unaffected by it, who renounces all fruit, good or bad, who treat as friends and foe alike, who is untouched by respect or disrespect, who is not putted by the praise, who does not go under when people speak ill of him, who loves silence and solitude, who has a disciplined reason.

One can attain self-realization only if one sheds his attachment to the Ego. We can follow truth only in the measure that we shed our attachment to the Ego.

According to Hindu Vedas: - Sattva, Rajas and Tamas are the qualities sprung from Nature. Satva attaches man to happiness, Rajas to action, Tamas to heedlessness.

Sattva – Goodness mode - bind the bond of happiness and the bond of knowledge. Those persons whose food, recreation and thoughts are Satvic are healthy. Victuals (Foods) that add to one's year's vitality, strength, health, happiness and appetite, and are savory, rich, substantial and inviting are dear to the Satvic. (Goodness mode)

Rajas – Passion mode - is of the nature of passion, the source of thirst and attachment. It keeps man bound with bond of action. Rajas are associated with desire, this means either that it has its source in, or that it is the cause of desire. Victuals (foods) that are bitter, sour, salty, over hot, spicy, dry, burning, and causing pain, bitterness and disease are dear to the Rajas. (Passion mode)

Tamas – Darkness mode - is born of ignorance, of mortal man's delusion; it keeps him bound with heedlessness, sloth and slumber. Food, which has become cold, insipid, putrid, stale, discarded and unfit for sacrifice, is dear to the Tamas. (Darkness mode)

How to achieve Self Realization?
Go confidently in the direction of your dreams. Live the life you have imagined.

Life is made up of our memories and moments that have shaped us in to who we are.

There is crack in everything, that's how the light gets in.

You must be the change; you wish to see in the world.

The future is with fate, the present is our own.

Watch your thoughts, because they become words.
Watch your words, because they become actions.
Watch your actions, because they become habits.
Watch your habits, because they become your character.
Watch your character, because it becomes your destiny.

What we think or what we know or what we believe is in the end of little consequence. The only consequence is what we do.

Hope is the thing with feathers that perches in the soul, and sings the tune – without the words. And never stops at all.

Love begins at home, and it is not how much we do... but how much love and how much we put in that action.

We think sometimes that poverty is only being hungry, naked and homeless. The poverty of being unwanted, unloved and uncared for is the greatest poverty. We must start in our own homes to remedy this kind of poverty.

5.10 - THE OPTIMISM BIAS:
The belief that future will be much better than the past and present is known as the optimism bias. It abides in every race, region and socioeconomic bracket.

The **optimism bias** (also known as **unrealistic** or **comparative optimism**) is a bias that causes a person to believe that they are less at risk of experiencing a negative event compared to others. There are four factors that cause a person to be optimistically biased: 1. Their desired end state, 2. Their cognitive mechanisms, 3. The information they have about themselves versus others, and 4. Overall mood.

We like to think of ourselves as rational creatures. We watch our backs, weigh the odds, and pack an umbrella. But both neuroscience and social science suggest that we are more optimistic than realistic. On average we expect the things to turn out better than they wind up being. People hugely under estimate their chances of getting divorced, losing their job or being diagnosed with cancer; expect their children to be extraordinarily gifted; envision themselves achieving more than their peers; and overestimate their likely lifespan (sometimes by 20 years or more.)

Schoolchildren are rampant optimists, but so are grown ups. A 2005 study found that adults over 60 are just as likely to see the glass half full as young adults. Overly positive assumptions can lead to disastrous miscalculations. But the Bias also protects and inspires us. It keeps us moving forward rather than the nearest high raise ledge. Without optimism our ancestors might never have ventured far from their tribes and we might all be cave dwellers.

To make progress we need to be able to imagine alternative realities – better ones – and we need to believe that we can achieve them. Such faith motivates us to pursue our goals. Hope keeps our minds at ease, lowers stress and improves physical health. Researchers studying the heart disease patients found that optimists were more likely than non-optimistic patients to take vitamins, eat low fat diets and exercise, thereby reducing the overall coronary risk.

Hardwired for Hope:

A growing body of scientific evidence points to the conclusion that optimism may be hard wired by evolution in to the human brain. Memory also ends up being a reconstructive process, and occasionally, details are deleted and others inserted.

Optimism starts with what may be the most extraordinary of human talents; mental time travel, the ability to move back and forth through time and space in one's mind. Although most of us take this ability for granted, our capacity to envision a different time and place is in fact critical to our survival. While mental time travel has clear arrival advantage, conscious foresight came to humans at an enormous price – the understanding that somewhere in the future, death awaits. Knowledge of death has to emerge side by side with the persistent ability to picture a bright future.

The human time machine:

The capacity to envision the future lies partly on the **Hippocampus,** a brain structure that is crucial to memory. Patients with damage to hippocampus are unable to recollect the past, but they are also unable to construct detailed images of future scenarios. They appear to be stuck in time, where as the rest of us constantly move back and forth in time.

But the brain does not move in a random fashion. It tends to engage in specific types of thoughts, positive and negative. The research shows that most of us spend less time in mulling about negative outcomes than we do over positive ones. Findings from some studies suggest that directing our thoughts of future toward the positive is the result of our **Frontal Cortex's** communicating with **sub cortical regions** deep in our brain.

5.11 - The Mayonnaise Jar & Coffee
(Explaining the priorities of Life & Make good use of time)

When things in your life seem, almost too much to handle,
When 24 Hours in a day is not enough,
Remember the mayonnaise jar and 2 cups of coffee.

A professor stood before his philosophy class
And had some items in front of him.
When the class began, wordlessly,
He picked up a very large and empty mayonnaise jar
And proceeded to fill it with golf balls.

He then asked the students, if the jar was full.
They agreed that it was.

The professor then picked up a box of pebbles and poured
Them into the jar. He shook the jar lightly.
The pebbles rolled into the open Areas between the golf balls.

He then asked the students again if the jar was full. They agreed it was.

The professor next picked up a box of sand and poured it into the jar.
Of course, the sand filled up everything else.
He asked once more if the jar was full. The students responded with a unanimous 'yes.'

The professor then produced two cups of coffee from under the table and
poured the entire contents into the jar, effectively
Filling the empty space between the sand. The students laughed.

'Now,' said the professor, as the laughter subsided,
I want you to recognize that this jar represents your life.

The golf balls are the important things - family,
Children, health, Friends, and Favorite passions -
Now suppose that if everything else was lost and only they remained, your life
would still be full.

The pebbles are the other things that matter like your job, house, and car.

The sand is everything else —The small stuff.

'If you put the sand into the jar first,' He continued,
There is no room for the pebbles or the golf balls.
The same goes for life.

If you spend all your time and energy on the small stuff,
You will never have room for the things that are important to you.

So...

Pay attention to the things that are critical to your happiness.
Play With your children.
Take time to get medical checkups.
Take your partner out to dinner.

There will always be time to clean the house and fix the disposal.

'Take care of the golf balls first and then pebbles second —
The things that really matter.
Set your priorities. The rest is just sand.'

One of the students raised her hand and inquired what the coffee represented.

The professor smiled.
'I'm glad you asked'.

It just goes to show you that no matter how full your life may seem,
There's always room for a couple of cups of coffee with a friend.'

5.12 - TEN COMMANDMENTS OF LIFE: -
1. Keep your mind alert (e.g. learn new things)
2. Think positive – one can always catch the train by running

3. Give 110% of yourself to the task at hand
4. Forgive, Forgive, Forgive – but may be hard to forget
5. Meditate or spend 10 minutes each day in introspection.
6. Take vitamin W – Water and Walk
7. Laugh, Laugh, Laugh – Laughter is the best medicine
8. Do not spill your "beans" – it is potent
9. Eat 'Satvik' food and do not fly in to a rage ever.
10. Give, Give, Give – do not give blindly

5.13 - BE IN THE PRESENT: -

When we are young, we had the enthusiasm of youth, and enthusiasm for the future, it may be education, it may be just sports, it may be carrier or it may be marriage. Now a days we are talking about nothing else but our future, saving money for future, postponing our enjoyment for future, buying books for reading tomorrow or the day-after - but nothing to be done in the present.

Today we are doing a lot of space travel. We are travelling in airplanes, in cars, in faster trains etc., but getting nowhere. The same grind, round and round and monotonous. Soul killing. Then what is this future that we are thinking of, when we do not have even the present in our grip. If I am not alive in the present then what am I going to do in future, I will be dead.

Even the religion does not point in the right direction. It is pointing somewhere or at least we imagine that it is pointing somewhere up, far away in the Christian heaven, the Nirvana of the Buddhists, the heaven of Islam. But if it is there, then what are we doing here. So Spirituality seeks to prove to you by experience that, this wonderful abode of the divine, where neither the sun shines nor the moon, nor the wind blows, where there is neither light nor darkness, where there is no day no night, there **HE (GOD)** exists. **That must be the only place inside you, your heart and your soul.**

SPIRITUALITY says, dear friends live in the present, forget heaven, forget hell – neither exists. If it exists, it is right where you are; you don't have to go to it. It is there in you right now. Then what are you looking for? What are you searching for? Realize it, turn inside, and see that divine abode of GOD. Again to repeat, there is no sun, no moon, no wind, no shine, no light, no darkness, no day and no night. What can it be? **EXPERIENCE IT INSIDE YOU,** but you do not feel it, because you are trying to see something you like, but you cannot see.

All we have to give up is our obsession with our **desires**, whether it is for fame or name or possession of wealth or even to do good to the others. Because there is rarely a person, who wants to do good to others for the sake of the one for whom he is doing the good. They always do well for themselves. A person is charitable because one expects to go to heaven. If you tell that charitable person that you are going to hell, he would run away from the charity. Some wise man has said, "Not for the sake of the other am I good, but for the sake of myself". They imagine that they are doing good to others in the desperate hope of doing something good to themselves, because they don't know any other way of doing good to themselves.

COSMIC CONUNDRUM: -

Given that we haven't found any life beyond earth yet, "Remarkably hospitable' may sound a bit strong, though it is true. Many of the most fundamental characteristics of our cosmos – the relative strengths of gravity, electromagnetism, and the forces that operate inside atomic nuclei as well as the masses and relative abundance of different particles – are so finely tuned that if just one of them were even slightly different, life as we know it couldn't exist. The proposition that the cosmos is – against all odds – perfectly tuned for life is known as the **anthropic principle.**

A vocal sector of the religious community, on the other hand, has seized on the **anthropic principle** as further evidence that GOD created the universe just for us. – Adding intellectual support to the so-called intelligent design movement, which believes that the staggering complexity of nature can be explained only by assuming that some higher intelligence had a hand in designing it. Over the past several years pitched battles have been fought in school boards in United states over whether to give intelligent design and Darwin's theory equal time in classrooms.

It does not matter whether the **anthropic principle** makes us happy. What matters is whether it is true – that is, whether cosmic numbers really are as arbitrary as they seem. If they are not; physics may eventually succeed in explaining many features of our world that seem so puzzling today. And if the anthropic principle is true? Well, then the universe will seem even more energetic and decorative than before.

Over and over in our history, natural phenomena – lightning, the changing of the seasons, the nature of the sun and moon – have been explained simply by saying GOD did it, only to have that explanation fall away as science provided a more satisfying answer. May be we have really reached the limits of intellectual understanding, but few scientists are willing to give up quite yet, even on seemingly intractable problems. To Einstein's celebrated thinking about whether GOD had choice in creating the universe, the answer seems to be a resounding Yes; all sorts of universes are possible. Belief in multiple universes is just as much a matter of faith as any other religious belief. On belief's that seem to imply we are special – that we at the center of the solar system or the center of the galaxy, or that the Milky Way is the only galaxy in the universe. Every time it turned out that we were not special after all. We just did not have enough knowledge.

5.14 - BODY AND MIND: -
To what extent are we the master of our fate?
To what extent do we make our lives? And
To what extent do forces beyond our control make our lives for us?

I think that the thing that has shifted in the modern era that the balance of those two elements (BODY AND MIND) has been weighted more heavily on the side of loss of control. Our characters are no longer entirely our destinies. When those planes ran in to those buildings of World Trade Center on 9/11/2001, it did not matter what the character of the people inside was.

After watching the show **"survival"** on CBS, where 18 people are put on an island with nothing to eat, sleep or live on – I realized that that – Life is survival. For 4 days they had practically nothing to eat and very less sleep. Their body was deteriorated and mind could not think. Some were becoming insane. That is where I realized that for our survival **BODY & MIND** has to be in healthy condition and higher intelligence comes from healthy body. Our body is made of trillions of cells. These cells generate and degenerate by itself. Active cells can only regenerate and depends upon our intake (food), surroundings, circumstances, nature and trillions of other outside factors (forces), but most of all it depends on mind (Thinking Power). Therefore Mind and Body go hand in hand and they are interdependent.

Survival is the game of life – Life changes every moment, every minute, every Hour, every Day, every week, every month & every year.

Life is a chance, like lottery, like stock market or like anything happening in the world is BY CHANCE. There are billions of factors (called **Super Natural Powers**) responsible for what happens to each individual or group of people or to a village or to a city or to a country or to the world.

Never fight, nothing is worth fighting for. Wisdom never fights; it waits patiently, speaks positively, releases easily, sees benefit in everything and envisions a future of abundance. Knowing that all needs will be met at the right moment, in the right way. If you think life is a struggle, you will always be struggling. If you think life is a breeze, your attitudes and actions will convey lightness and easiness. And that's what attracts everything you need, and much more. Make today a breeze not a battle.

The root of suffering is the attachment: -
You have created a space in your mind that holds a person or object as part of you. When that person or object is criticized, neglected or not with you, you feel pain in your mind and you experience a sense of loss.

An angel is some one who stays above the negative influences of the world and sees only the goodness in others.

Peace is more than just being quiet. It is a state of complete contentment, and inner stability achieved with a deep understanding and acceptance of the self.

We can only give what we have, and can only do what we know, so to spend time to help you is the only way to help others.

Every addition to True Knowledge is an addition to Human Power.

Honesty is the best policy: -
Being open and sharing with others can bring a new vision of situations, which lets us let go of any limited ideas we may be holding on to.

Forget the past, it is gone.
Don't worry about the future, you do not know.
Learn to live in the present and discover how full it is of peaceful moments.

Humility: -
The best ornament is humility
The richest wealth is wisdom.
The strongest weapon is patience
The best security is faith
The best tonic is laughter.

As you awaken, the first thought is your foundation for the rest of the day.

When you open your eyes, sit for a moment and appreciate the gift of new day.
Create a peaceful thought and enjoy some moments of silence.

Impossible becomes possible with power of determination.

To forgive and forget is to reflect love. Many are slaves of the past. Situations pass, they cease to exist, but they continue to be alive in the mind. Open your heart and be generous, free yourself from that sorrow. Forgive and forget and you will live every moment in peace.

Mingle in life: -
The meaning of life will not be revealed by mere contemplation.
Mingling with life is necessary.
Fellowship with the poor is essential to spiritual progress.

5.15 - PRACTICAL WAYS TO MAKE IMPOSSIBLE TO POSSIBLE:
Always expect the best. Strength, Victory, Success and not failure, disease or death. Always positive in statements and no negative thoughts.

Person who wishes to make Impossible to possible will not be afraid of taking risks. Shakespeare had said, "Life is a Play – All world is the stage – And you are the Star."

You must go and do the things you are afraid to do. – Fear will vanish.

You must learn to accept every stopping stone as a stepping-stone – every obstacle is truly an opportunity.

You must learn to think for yourself, on your own, have courage to stand for your own convictions, be on drivers seat and not be driven.

Never say about a thing, it is impossible unless you give it a chance. – Be problem solution oriented and not problem creator.

Remember what is impossible to man is possible to GOD.

Five Principles to govern relationship:
  1. Mutual Respect
  2. Mutual non-aggression
  3. Mutual non-interference
  4. Equality and cooperation for mutual benefits
  5. Peaceful coexistence

Handle **ADVERSITY** very carefully, do not try to change others but change yourself. ———- Read the story below:

ADVERSITY

A daughter complained to her father about her life and how things were so hard for her. She did not know how she was going to make it and wanted to give up. She was tired of fighting and struggling. It seemed as one problem was solved, a new one arose.

Her father, a chef, took her to the kitchen. He filled three pots with water and placed each on high fire. Soon the pots came to a boil. In one he placed carrots, in the second he placed eggs, and the last he placed ground coffee beans. He let them sit and boil without saying a word.

The daughter sucked her teeth and impatiently waited, wondering what he was doing. In about twenty minutes he turned off the burners. He fished the carrots out and placed them in a bowl. He pulled the eggs out and placed them in a bowl. Then he ladled the coffee out and placed it in a bowl.

Turning to her he asked. "Darling, what do you see. "? "Carrots, Eggs, and Coffee" she replied.

He brought her closer and asked her to feel the carrots. She did and noted that they were soft. He then asked her to take an egg and break it. After pulling off the shell, she observed the hard-boiled egg. Finally, he asked her to sip the coffee. She smiled, as she tasted its rich aroma.

She humbly asked, "What does it mean father?"

He explained that each of them had faced the same adversity, boiling water, but each reacted differently.

The carrot went in strong, hard and unrelenting. But after being subjected to the boiling water, it softened and became weak.

The egg had been fragile. Its thin outer shell had protected its liquid interior. But after sitting through the boiling water, its inside became hardened.

The ground coffee beans were unique however. After they were in the boiling water, they had changed the water.

"Which are you?" he asked his daughter, "when adversity knocks on your door, how do you respond? Are you a carrot, an egg, or a coffee bean?"

How about you?

Are you the carrot that seems hard, but with pain and adversity do you wilt and become soft and loose your strength?

Are you the egg, which starts off with a malleable heart? Were you a fluid spirit, but after a death, a breakup, or a layoff have you become hardened and stiff. Your shell looks the same, but are you bitter and tough with a stiff spirit and heart?

Or are you like the coffee bean? The bean changes the hot water; the thing that is bringing the pain, to its peak flavor reaches 212 degrees Fahrenheit. When the water gets the hottest, it just tastes better and makes things better around you.

How do you handle adversity? Are you a carrot, an egg, or a coffee bean?

5.16 – WHAT IS LOVE: - (in a story form)

> A woman came out of her house and saw 3 old men with long white beards sitting in her front yard. She did not recognize them. She said, "I don't think I know you, but you must be hungry. Please come in and have something to eat."
>
> "Is the man of the house home?" they asked.
>
> "No", she replied. "He's out."
>
> "Then we cannot come in", they replied.
>
> In the evening when her husband came home, she told him what had happened.
>
> "Go tell them I am home and invite them in!" The woman went out and invited the men in.
>
> "We do not go into a House together," they replied.
>
> "Why is that?" she asked.
>
> One of the old men explained: "His name is Wealth," he said pointing to one of his friends, and said pointing to another one, "He is Success, and I am Love." Then he added, "Now go in and discuss with your husband which one of us you want in your home."

The woman went in and told her husband what was said. Her husband was overjoyed. "How nice!!" he said. "Since that is the case, let us invite Wealth. Let him come and fill our home with wealth!"

His wife disagreed. "My dear, why don't we invite Success?"

Their daughter-in-law was listening from the other corner of the house. She jumped in with her own suggestion: "Would it not be better to invite Love? Our home will then be filled with love!"

"Let us heed our daughter-in-law's advice," said the husband to his wife. "Go out and invite Love to be our guest."

The woman went out and asked the 3 old men, "Which one of you is Love? Please come in and be our guest."

Love got up and started walking toward the house. The other 2 also got up and followed him.

Surprised, the lady asked Wealth and Success: "I only invited Love, Why are you coming in?"

The old men replied together: "If you had invited Wealth or Success, thE other two of us would've stayed out, but since you invited Love, wherever He goes, we go with him. **Wherever there is Love, there is also Wealth and Success!"**

Therefore Love is the strength that gives you life.

When you receive love you loose fear and you can give the best in you. The practical form of love is respect. Respect means acceptance of the fact that we are all different and unique and at the same time, we all have something important and valuable to share.

The power of love is the greatest power on earth. When you open your heart with sincerity, anyone with you will be moved to a level of feeling, much deeper and purer than the level of thinking.

GOD'S WISH FOR YOU...
-Where there is pain; GOD wish you peace and mercy.

-Where there is self-doubting, GOD wishes you a renewed confidence in your ability to work through it.

-Where there is tiredness, or exhaustion, GOD wishes you understanding, patience, and renewed strength.

-Where there is fear, GOD wishes you love, and courage.

5.17 - SELF-AWARENESS: - [14]
Life is a Challenging Journey. So Challenge we must meet and Journey we must complete. Every time a challenge comes in one's life, whether it is about family, job, friends, personal relationships etc., one has to be aware of the following stages of awareness.

Stage 1. AWARENESS OF HOPE AND FEAR:
Your desires are dissatisfied; something you want is meeting with opposition. There is underlying hope and fear. Your mind does not know what action to take. Every action has its consequences good or bad. There is big confusion in the mind. One gets frustrated and sometimes anger takes charge. Lot of energy is lost in thoughtlessness and one gets exhausted. The more one struggles to get free of a problem, the more he/she is trapped in to it.

Stage 2. AWARENESS OF MID WAY BETWEEN HOPE AND FEAR:
Now one is tired, taken deep breath, sitting down calmly and started rationalizing the ideas of hope and fear. Your vision extends beyond the conflict, giving you more clarity. With clear vision, you no longer feel confused. The need to struggle begins to diminish. You start to let go. You approach decisions with confidence. You meet fear realistically and it starts to lessen. You can tell that you have reached this level of awareness when you no longer feel stuck. A process has begun. With greater expansion, unforeseen forces come to your

aid. You move forward according to what you desire from your life. If one rationalizes the situation further, he/she will find that following questions come in to one's mind.

1. Why do I perceive the whole situation in negative way?
2. Why do I assume certain things and do not look in to facts?
3. Why do I expect certain things from other people? One should know that positive expectations are ruled by hope and negative expectations are ruled by fear.
4. Why do I disguise my feelings? Being emotional is equated with being out of control; which itself is an undesirable feeling.

Stage 3. SELF-AWARENESS:
This is the stage where no problem exists. Every challenge is a creative opportunity. You feel completely aligned with the forces of nature. The outer world reflects what is happening in your inner world. You feel completely safe and at home in the universe. This is the spiritual level. Now is the time to take some positive action.

5.18 - WHAT IS LIFE AFTERALL?
KISS THY LIFE – (KISS = Keep It Simple & Sweet)

Keep It Simple and Sweet - Simplifying our activities does not mean sinking in to laziness; on the contrary, it means acquiring a growing freedom and counteracting the subtlest aspect of inertia. To simplify our speech is to curtail the stream of pointless talk that continuously flows from our mouths.

Having a simple mind is not the same thing as being simple minded. On the contrary, simplicity of mind is reflected in clarity of thought. Like clear water that lets us see all the way to the lake bottom, simplicity reveals the nature of the mind behind the veil of restless thought.

If you analyze each chapter of Gita (Hindu Bible), following is the nutshell meaning of **life.**

1. Life is a Challenge	Meet it
2. Life is a Gift	Accept it
3. Life is an Adventure	Dare it
4. Life is a Sorrow	Overcome it
5. Life is a Tragedy	Face it
6. Life is a Duty	Perform it
7. Life is a Game	Play it
8. Life is a Mystery	Unfold it
9. Life is a Song	Sing it
10. Life is an Opportunity	Take it
11. Life is a Journey	Complete it
12. Life is a Promise	Fulfill it
13. Life is a Love	Enjoy it
14. Life is a beauty	Praise it
15. Life is a Spirit	Realize it
16. Life is a Struggle	Fight it
17. Life is a Puzzle	Solve it
18. Life is a Goal	Achieve it

Life is a game of forgetting and remembering.

You are losing the game when you... forget who you are and what you are doing here, and remember the false things of the past and what they did to you.

You are winning the game when you... remember your true identity of peace, and remember GOD who is always peaceful and has unconditional love for you, forget troubles of the past and move forward with the lessons learned. Observe what you remember during the day and what you forget during the day.

SIX PRINCIPLES OF LIFE: -
1. No point using limited life to chase unlimited money.
2. No point in earning so much money that you cannot live to spend it.
3. Money is not yours until you spend it.
4. When you are young, you use your health to chase the wealth; when you are old, you use your wealth to buy back your health; difference is that it is too late.
5. How happy a man is, it is not how much one has but how little one needs.

6. No point working so hard to provide for the people you have no time to spend with.

LIFE CHOICES: -
Life is all about choices. When you cut away
all the junk, every situation is a choice.
You choose how you react to situations.
You choose how people affect your mood.
You choose to be in a good mood or bad mood.
The bottom line: It's your choice how you live life.

What I am experiencing at this moment is the result of choices and decisions made in the past; what I will experience in the future depends on choices and decisions I make now.

Think Simply: -
With so many choices and decisions, so many demands from people and events, in our modern fast changing world, it's a real challenge to 'keep it simple'. Making it simple means making things easy and clear. The magic wand to wave over your life is 'planning and prioritizing'. Make plans, long and short term and then prioritize. Then practice taking one thing at a time, so you can have one thought at a time, with some space before you have to have your next thought. But don't get attached to your plans or priorities. Be flexible (easy) and yet focused (clear) and in this way you can teach yourself to think simply and act simply. One thought at a time. At your own pace. In your own space. A simple life is a contented life.

Life of Peace: -
Ignorance makes you believe that life functions haphazardly. Wisdom teaches you that everything that happens in this theatre of life has profound significance. What you see today is not the fruit of chance but a fruit from seeds planted in the past. Plant seeds of peace now and you will create a life of peace in the future.

Live purposefully: -
If you do not live life on purpose you live life by accident. Why do some days feel like a motorway pile up? It is because you haven't sorted out your purpose yet. The highest purpose is always giving, or serving others, without wanting anything

in return. This is why relaxation is always impossible if we are always ' on the take'. There is an overall purpose for your life, and each of the many scenes, which fill your day, is opportunity to serve your purpose. Take time to think deeply, listen to your intuition, and with patience, the reason why you are here, and what you uniquely have to give, will occur to you. Then you can live your life 'on purpose'.

Quality of Life is to OBSERVE: -
It is far better to observe than to absorb every word, feeling and attitude, to get over-involved, or react too much. Observing gives us the patience and clarity to think and act appropriately. Observing creates an inner focus that allows us to see reality.

Use. These. In. life

Talk————Softly
Walk————Humbly
Eat————-Sensibly
Breathe————Deeply
Sleep————Sufficiently
Dress————-Smartly
Act————-Fearlessly
Work————-Patiently
Think————-Truthfully
Believe————Correctly
Behave————-Decently
Learn————-Practically
Plan————-Orderly
Earn————Honestly
Save————Regularly
Spend————Intelligently
Love————-Passionately
ENJOY ————COMPLETELY

Making a Life: -
We make a living by what we get, but we make a life by what we give.

A Long And Healthy Life: -
There are three ingredients for a long and healthy life:
1. Live with attention but without worry,

2. Use time in a worthwhile way,
3. Keep your thoughts pure, positive and filled with strength.

Transform Obstacles: -
Is life an obstacle course? Sometimes it may feel like it. If you join the military you will be sent around an obstacle course of increasing degrees of difficulty. Why? To increase your strength and stamina and expand your creative capacity under strain. So it is on the course called 'life' - you can choose to perceive people, situations or events as obstacles, or you can choose to use these things to strengthen and expand your capacity to be creative and to find ways round, under, over. The choice lies in your perception. Obstacles are never ever 'out there'; they are always in our own minds.

Work: -
Work without happiness is like a burden that you have to endure, but when you are internally happy it becomes a game, and you're just having fun.

Pure Living: -
When we look around to examine the state of our environment, which is what we leave behind after developing and exploiting the resources of the planet, many are quick to see pollution and waste. We are not slow in pointing out the damage and the impurities, which will be our legacy for the future generations. We are not so quick to spot the impurities, which we have allowed to develop and accumulate in our own personal lives. At the level of our thoughts, is every thought a pure and benevolent one, which carries the best wishes for our fellow travellers. Unlikely, as we mostly learn to criticize and complain, attack and blame. At the level of our intentions do we always mean well and want the best for others, or are our intentions sometimes colored by selfishness or greed? At the level of outcomes do we celebrate the achievements of others as they grow to be all that they can be, or do we stand back in envy or jealousy? Our lives all begin within our own consciousness. The lakes and the landscapes of our mind and intellect are where we all live the most. Do we keep them clean and pure and unspoiled? Can beauty and harmony be found within? No! Then perhaps we need to clean up inside before we condemn others on the outside. Because what is out there is simply a reflection of what is in here! And we are all in it together. Perhaps that is why no one is to blame but we are all responsible.

Barriers to Love: -

Whatever is in your heart that is not clean, not true, will ultimately begin to act like a wall, obstructing the natural flow of love. This wall is blocking people, who say that there is no love in their life. Actually there is love, but they just can't accept it. Ego is the clearest example of this. Ego limits the flow of love by placing conditions on the love you give and receive. Ego uses love to satisfy its own needs and desires. It produces a love, which is deceptive, one which brings only temporary satisfaction. Ego does not allow you to experience true love or share it. If fact, ego is capable of destroying your ability to feel love altogether.

FOOD: -

The food we eat not only has an effect upon our physical, emotional, and mental makeup, but on our spiritual consciousness.

Balance In Life: -

The indication of balance in life is a sense of well-being, optimism and a clear conscience. The foundation for achieving this is to look after one's spiritually - making one's mind peaceful, loving and thoughtful at all times. Then one will instinctively know how much time to spend on his/her own well-being and how much on fulfilling other responsibilities. One can only give its best to others when one itself is at his/her best.

Give Up the Habit of Worrying: -

As one grows in strength in his/her spiritual life, one gives up the habit of worrying. It serves no purpose other than to make him/her feel tense and miserable. When one stops worrying about things that are beyond one's control and focus instead on generating optimistic and kind thoughts, his/her life can begin to flow in ever more positive directions. Such a light and easy approach to life enables one to take everything in stride.

Self-Manage: -

There is a huge hole in the heart of all our educations. It is where the skills and abilities of self-management should be. No one teaches us how to manage our thoughts, feelings, attitudes and behavior, so we find it hard to manage the **Four Rs – Relationships, Roles, Responsibilities and Resources.** So let's get started. Consciously choose the quality of your thoughts today – emphasize the positive, eliminate the negative and clean up the waste. Everything, which means everything in your life, begins with your thoughts.

Harmony: -

Love dissolves hate. Kindness melts cruelty. Compassion calms passion. Co-operation evokes love and when we bow, others bend. This creates harmony.

Relationships: -

Good feelings for others are like ointments that heal wounds and re-establish friendship and relationships. Good feelings are generated in the mind, are transmitted through your attitude and are reflected through your eyes and smile. Smiling opens the heart and a glance can make miracles happen.

Never Battle: -

Never fight. Nothing is worth fighting for. Wisdom never fights, it waits patiently, speaks positively, releases easily, sees benefit in everything and envisions a future of abundance...knowing that all needs will be met at the right moment, in the right way. If you think life is a struggle you will always be struggling, if you think life is a breeze, your attitudes and actions will convey lightness and easiness. And that's what attracts everything you need, and much more. Make today a breeze not a battle.

Observe and Reflect in Silence: -

Many times with the good intention of solving a problem you become part of the problem. In order to accept the problem it is more practical firstly to remain silent and serene. It is not necessary to understand the causes but to find solutions. Observe and reflect in silence and then make a decision.

CHAPTER 6

WHAT IS "DEATH"?

6.01 – CONCEPTS OF DEATH: -

Death is the term used to describe the cessation of all biological functions that sustain a living organism. Phenomena which commonly bring about death include old age, predation, malnutrition, disease, and accidents or trauma resulting in terminal injury. All known organisms inevitably experience death. Bodies of living organisms begin to decompose shortly after death.

In human societies, the nature of death has for millennia been a concern of the world's religious traditions and of philosophical enquiry. This may include a belief in some kind of resurrection (common in Abrahamic religions), reincarnation (common in Dharmic religions) or that consciousness ceases to exist (common among atheists).

Commemoration ceremonies after death may include various mourning or funeral practices. The physical remains of a person, commonly known as a *corpse body*, are usually interred whole or cremated, though among the world's cultures there are a variety of other methods of mortuary disposal.

The concept of death:

It is a key to human understanding of the phenomenon. There are many scientific approaches to the concept. For example, brain death, as practiced in medical science, defines death as a point in time at which brain activity ceases. One of the challenges in defining death is in distinguishing it from life. As a point in time, death would seem to refer to the moment at which life ends. However, determining when death has occurred requires drawing precise conceptual boundaries between life and death. This is problematic because there is little consensus over how to define life. It is possible to define life in terms of consciousness. When consciousness ceases, a living organism can be said to have died. One of the notable flaws in this approach, however, is that there are many organisms which are alive but probably not conscious (for example, single-celled organisms). Another problem with this approach is in defining consciousness, which has many different definitions given by modern scientists, psychologists and philosophers. This general problem of defining death applies to the particular challenge of defining death in the context of medicine.

Definitions of Death:
All definitions for death focus on the character of cessation of something. In this context "death" describes merely the state where something has ceased, for example, Life. Thus, the definition of "LIFE" simultaneously defines death.

When the Soul leaves the body, it is not just the body that dies but it's as if all the connections with the world of that individual are simply switched off. Not only the relationships but all specific plans, projects and desires suddenly have no further means through which they could be expressed or cultivated. The faculties of thinking, deciding, and personality traits connected with the life that is being left behind, stop and go in to a momentary state of latency.

It is interesting to note that even when the body is sick, it can only be treated when the Soul is still present. If we take out the Soul, no one remains to take care of the body. Body is truly marvelous vehicle for the Soul to express it through. No manufactured machine could compete with it. Research has shown that just in one day, the brain is able to complete a hundred times more connections than the entire telecommunication system on the planet, or the human eye with any manufactured camera or the heart with any manufactured pump.

Brain is essentially a computer and consciousness is like a computer program. It will cease to run when the computer is turned off. Theoretically it could be recreated on a neutral network, but that would be very difficult, as it would require all one's memories.

Death never takes wise man by surprise; he is always ready to go.
Everyone knows he must die, but no one believes it.

Death is like sunset, which is only an appearance. For what is sunset here is sunrise elsewhere. In reality the sun never sets. Likewise there is no death. Death is only an illusion, an appearance. **For death there is birth elsewhere.**

Death and Science:
Those people maintaining that only the neo-cortex of the brain is necessary for consciousness sometimes argue that only electrical activity should be considered when defining death. Eventually it is possible that the criterion for death will be the permanent and irreversible loss of cognitive function, as evidenced by the death of the cerebral cortex. All hope of recovering human thought and personality is then gone given current and foreseeable medical technology. However, at present, in most places the more conservative definition of death – irreversible cessation of electrical activity in the whole brain, as opposed to just in the neo-cortex – has been adopted (for example the Uniform Determination Of Death Act in the United States). In 2005, the Terri Schiavo case brought the question of brain death and artificial sustenance to the front of American politics.

In certain cultures, death is more of a process than a single event. It implies a slow shift from one spiritual state to another.

The leading cause of death in developing countries is infectious disease. The leading causes of death in developed countries are atherosclerosis (heart disease and stroke), cancer, and other diseases related to obesity and aging. These conditions cause loss of homeostasis, leading to cardiac arrest, causing loss of oxygen and nutrient supply, causing irreversible deterioration of the brain and other tissues. Of the roughly 150,000 people who die each day across the globe, about two thirds die of age-related causes. In industrialized nations, the proportion is much higher, reaching 90%. With improved medical capability, dying has become a condition to be managed. Home deaths, once commonplace, are now rare in the developed world.

Autopsy:
An autopsy, also known as a *postmortem examination* or an *obduction*, is a medical procedure that consists of a thorough examination of a human corpse to determine the cause and manner of a person's death and to evaluate any disease or injury that may be present. It is usually performed by a specialized medical doctor called a pathologist.

Autopsies are either performed for legal or medical purposes. A forensic autopsy is carried out when the cause of death may be a criminal matter, while a clinical or academic autopsy is performed to find the medical cause of death and is used in cases of unknown or uncertain death, or for research purposes. Autopsies can be further classified into cases where external examination suffices, and those where the body is dissected and an internal examination is conducted. Permission from next of kin may be required for internal autopsy in some cases. Once an internal autopsy is complete the body is generally reconstituted by sewing it back together. Autopsy is important in a medical environment and may shed light on mistakes and help improve practices.

A "necropsy" is an older term for a postmortem examination, unregulated, and not always a medical procedure. In modern times the term is more often used in the postmortem examination of the corpses of animals.

6.02 – EVOLUTION OF AGING: -

Inquiry into the evolution of aging aims to explain why so many living things and the vast majority of animals weaken and die with age (a notable exception being **Hydra,** which may be biologically immortal). The evolutionary origin of senescence (the state of being old) remains one of the fundamental puzzles of biology. Gerontology specializes in the science of human aging processes.

Hydra is a genus of simple fresh-water animal possessing radial symmetry. They can be found in most unpolluted fresh-water ponds, lakes, and streams in the temperate and tropical regions and can be found by gently sweeping a collecting net through weedy areas. They are multicellular organisms which are usually a few millimetres long and are best studied with a microscope. Biologists are especially interested in hydras due to their regenerative ability; and that they appear not to age or die of old age.

Distinction between Living and Dead:
Living = Freedom + Intelligence
Child cries in protest for Bondage i.e. Is God's concept for freedom.

Dead = No Freedom + No Intelligence.
It is completely bound.

Extinction:
Extinction is the gradual process by which a group of taxa or species dies out, reducing biodiversity. The moment of extinction is generally considered to be the death of the last individual of that species. Because a species' potential range may be very large, determining this moment is difficult, and is usually done retrospectively after a period of apparent absence. Species become extinct when they are no longer able to survive in changing habitat or against superior competition. Over the history of the Earth, over 99% of all the species that have ever lived have gone extinct; however, mass extinctions may have accelerated evolution by providing opportunities for new groups of organisms to diversify.

Fossils:
Fossils are the preserved remains or traces of animals, plants, and other organisms from the remote past. The totality of fossils, both discovered and undiscovered, and their placement in fossil-containing rock formations and sedimentary layers (strata) is known as the *fossil record*. Such a preserved specimen is called a "fossil" if it is older than the arbitrary date of 10,000 years ago. Hence, fossils range in age from the youngest at the start of the Holocene Epoch to the oldest from the Archaean Eon, up to 3.4 billion years old.

Suicide:
- Suicide (or, "escaping existence"): a solution in which a person simply ends one's own life.
- Religious belief in a transcendent realm or being: a solution in which one believes in the existence of a reality that is beyond the Absurd, and, as such, has meaning. Kierkegaard (a philasopher) stated that a belief in anything beyond the Absurd requires a non-rational but perhaps necessary religious acceptance in such an intangible and empirically unprovable thing (now commonly referred to as a "leap of faith"). However, Camus (a philosopher) regarded this solution as "philosophical suicide".
- Acceptance of the Absurd: a solution in which one accepts and even embraces the Absurd and continues to live in spite of it. Camus endorsed this solution, while Kierkegaard regarded this solution as "de-

moniac madness": *"He rages most of all at the thought that eternity might get it into its head to take his misery from him!"*

Absurdism:

In absurdist philosophy, the Absurd arises out of the fundamental disharmony between the individual's search for meaning and the apparent meaninglessness of the universe. As beings looking for meaning in a meaningless world, humans have three ways of resolving the dilemma. Kierkegaard and Camus describe the solutions in their works, *The Sickness Unto Death* (1849) and *The Myth of Sisyphus* (1942):

The ultimate fate of the universe, and implicitly humanity, is hypothesized as one in which biological life will eventually become unsustainable, be it through a Big Freeze, Big Rip, or Big Crunch. However, there are conceivable ways in which these fates can be avoided, as it may be possible given sufficiently advanced technology to survive indefinitely by directing the flow of energy on a cosmic scale and altering the fate of the universe.

Die Alive:

To the unenlightened, death comes but once a lifetime. To those who have chosen to become enlightened there are a thousand chosen deaths before it's time to leave the body and move on. **This kind of death is the releasing off all our attachments, from false identity to opinions, from people to possessions.** Cutting the subtle threads of attachment frees the spirit from fear, and when the time comes to move on, it's like 'shooting the breeze'. Dying alive is simply letting go of all you hold fast to in your mind. It doesn't actually mean losing anything, simply changing your relationship with the things in your life today. The greatest pleasure for every soul is the result of choosing the living death called detachment. Why? Because attachment is a form of slavery, and it all takes place in our own minds. **And the result of detachment? Real freedom.**

6.03 - DEATH IS CERTAIN BUT CLINGING TO LIFE IS MAYA (Illusion):

There is tremendous fact about Death. The whole world is going towards death. Everything dies. All our progress, our vanities, our reforms, our luxuries, our wealth, our knowledge, has that one end – **DEATH**. That is all that is certain.

Cities come and go, empires rise and fall, planets break in to pieces and crumble in to dust, to be blown about by the atmospheres of other planets. Thus it has been going on from time without beginning. Death is the end of everything. Death is the end of life, of beauty, of wealth, of power, of virtue too. Saints die and sinners die, kings die and beggars die. They are all going to death. And yet this tremendous clinging to life exists. Somehow, we do not know why, we cling to life; we cannot give it up. And this is **MAYA**. (Read para 11.06 for further definition of MAYA)

There comes a time in the lives of individuals and of races when involuntarily they ask, "Is this real". "What becomes of this? What is real?"

"Is death the end of all these things to which we are clinging, as if they are the most real of realities, the most substantial of all substances?" The world vanishes in a moment and is gone.

The hopes of lifetime, built up little by little with all the energies of a great mind, vanish in a second. Are they real?

Then again, there is a desire to be happy. We run after everything to make ourselves happy; we pursue our mad career in the external world of the senses. Every sense activity results in a reaction. Everything is evanescent. Enjoyment, Misery, Luxury, Wealth, Power and Poverty – even life itself – **all are evanescent**.

Two positions remain to mankind:
1. If we believe that destruction of political and social institutions is necessary, then we can never know anything about the future, the past or even the present.

2. To seek for an explanation, to seek for the real, to discover in the mist of this eternally changing evanescent world whatever is real. In this body, which is an aggregate of molecules of matter, is there anything, which is real. This has been the search throughout the history of the human mind.

What happens after human body dies?
The knowing SELF (SOUL) never dies; is never born. It arises from nothing, and nothing arises from it. Unborn, eternal, everlasting, this **SELF (SOUL)** can never be destroyed with the destruction of the body.

6.04 - NATURE - CAUSE AND EFFECT: -
(LIFE CYCLE)

The whole mass of existence, which we call **Nature**, has been acting on the human mind from time immemorial. It has been acting on the thought of humans, and as its reaction has come the question: " What are these? What is its source?"

The mountain comes from sand and goes back to sand; the river comes out of vapor and goes back to vapor; plant life comes from the seed and goes back to the seed; human life comes out of the human germ and goes back to the germ. The universe with its stars and planets has come out of the nebulous (unclear) state and must go back to it. And what do we learn from this? That the manifested or grosser state is the **Effect**, and the finer state, the **Cause**.

When humans die their body goes back to the elements, which gave them their body; if the earth dies it will go back to its cause. Therefore we learn that the effect is the same as the cause, not different. It is only in another form. **Therefore Effect is reproduction of the Cause in a grosser form.**

This universe must be resolved in to its causes, the sun, moon, stars and earth, the body and mind and everything in this universe, must return in to their finer causes, disappear, be destroyed as were. But they will live in causes in finer forms. Out of these finer forms they will emerge again as new earths, suns, moons, and stars. **This is called Life Cycle.**

Involution and Evolution:
Every involution is preceded by an evolution and vice versa. The seed is the father of the tree, but another tree was itself the father of the seed. Like chicken and egg, egg comes out of chicken and chicken lays eggs. Same way the little cell that afterwards becomes the human is simply the human involved and becomes evolved as a man. Involution and evolution are going on throughout whole of nature.

The self of man (**SOUL**), being beyond the law of causation, is not a compound. It is ever free and is the ruler of everything that is within law. It will never die, because death means going back to the component parts, and that, which was never a compound, can never die. If anything is beyond death, naturally it must also be beyond life. The soul of man is part of the cosmic energy, which is **GOD. There is only one being (GOD), one existence – the ever Blessed, the omniscient, the omnipotent, the omnipresent, the omnibenevolent, the birth-less, the death-less, and the Omni truth.**

6.05 - DELIVERANCE FROM DEATH: -
What is the way that can lead us to deliverance from Death?

We must make note of three truths:

1. **Know: that transient is all earthly things and forms**. All that you see around you will, one day, perish. Everything carries within it the seed of decay. Such is the life. A man lives 100 years or longer, yet must he, one day depart. The rich and the poor, the young and the old, the wise and unwise – are subject to death.

2. **Know: that there is no escape from death**. When the hour arrives, not all the armies of kings and conquerors can save you from death. So it is that while friends and relatives helplessly look on and shed tears, their dearly loved ones are snatched away by death.

3. **Know: that the wise do not grieve over the dead.** Grief and lamentation do not bring the dead to life. Rather they add to our suffering and rob us of our richest treasure – peace of mind. Wise men accept whatever comes – discomfort, disease, and death – and so overcome suffering and sorrow.

Body made by the Intelligent Designer: -
Physical body is an electro-biochemical mechanism of truly magnificent conception and design. It has evolved over the many millions of years since life first came a shore from the primordial seas. Think of its many "systems": the skeleton, the blood circulation system, the nerves, etc. Think also of its many important organs such as the brain, heart, lungs, pancreas, kidneys, liver, genitals, large and small intestines, etc., the two to three square yards of skin, which make up the body's all-enclosing envelope, and the organs,

which provide our five senses. Individually, all of these are fantastically complex and protected to an awesome degree. And, unlike any man-made mechanism or machine that must go in to the repair shop even for a minor malfunction, its intelligent creator has endowed the electro-biochemical mechanism, which is the physical body, with a built-in capability to maintain and even repair itself.

6.06 - BODY, MIND, and SPIRIT (SOUL): -
Senses: -
Most of what we know about our surroundings is a result of the working of man's five senses – touch, taste, smell, sight and hearing. In fact almost everything we think we know about our world and the universe has come to us through one or more of these sense organs. We feel quite content in our belief that we can rely on these sense organs to give us a completely factual, dependable, and highly accurate picture of the universe in which we are each immersed. But this is a false belief.

Consider the sense of sight. Our eyes can see only the fraction of what is going on all around us. They can detect only matter, which reflects light in the very narrow band of wavelengths we call the visible spectrum. Laboratory research has shown that there is much going on all around us in wavelengths that our limited sense organs cannot detect.

Everything in our world, this universe and the cosmos, results from **ENERGY**, and ENERGY manifests as vibration at some specific frequency. All of the scientific knowledge like Supersensible Sight and Supersensible Hearing teaches us that we know very little about important aspects of our Body, Mind and Spirit (Soul). Our ignorance of what we know about the "solid", everyday "material" world can be described in one word "Colossal". The normally invisible sights and unheard sounds have a most important **bearing on the question of Life after Death.**

How much does a Soul weigh: -
Since we would like to identify that portion of the individual person, which survives death of the physical body, it would seem we could narrow our search.

Obviously the water portion will evaporate during the days, weeks and months after death. Yet there is a solid proof that the essence – that is the mind, personality and soul – depart the physical body within a period of minutes to a maximum of three days. Moreover there seems to be a possibility that the surviving mind, personality and soul may be "contained" in a very small and perhaps almost weightless "package', because by scientific research it has been found that the instantaneous weight loss at death varied between ½ and ¾ ounce.

Your Brain is not your mind: -
Certainly one of the greatest blocks modern man has in understanding life after death seems from having been told that brain and mind are synonymous. However, a different picture emerges for those serious researchers in to the nature of man who can look beyond conventional notions. For such scientists it has become increasingly obvious that the brain and mind is not the same thing. Neither the psychologists could identify the site of brain, for **conscious, subconscious, or super-conscious states of mind.** Yet concepts attributing the three levels or aspects to the human mind existed hundreds of years before psychiatry and psychology came in to existence. For example, both the native peoples have the Pacific and American plains Indians recognized three levels of mind, and represented them in their tribal Totem Poles. Only in the last few years it has been discovered that most of the many millions of cells in the physical body have what the scientist call "communication capability". This means that cells can receive and send messages. We are also learning that cells go beyond this function and it is almost as though each cell has a mind of its own. Now we can begin to understand that not only is "the brain not the mind' but that the mind function extends throughout the entire body.

We know that the brain controls all aspects of the body, which it serves. We can say that the body, the "bio-electrical mechanism', is controlled by its computer, the brain. We can go further and say that the brain is infinitely more sophisticated than the most advanced computer yet built by man. But we also must say that the brain, like even the most fancy computer, is totally useless unless there is a programmer – some intelligence separate and distinct from the computer itself. It is only in the last three decades – that science has given us a valuable tool which enables us to understand that the **Mind** is the programmer, how it can penetrate the 'empty space' in our wet, squishy physical body, and how it can control every single action of the more than 60 trillion cells which make up the physical body. What is this magic and mysterious tool called **Mind?**

Following are the proofs of Mind and Spirit (Soul): -
- **Deathbed, Near Death and Out-of-Body Experiences: -** Careful research has clearly established that people in various cultures and totally different religious backgrounds "SEE" loved ones and/or helpers coming to help them make the transition from their dying physical body in to their new state of existence. Research has also clearly documented that the real you can leave the body and travel; and that this same "Spirit Body" carries you into your next state of existence.

- **Communication through individual Mediumistic Persons: -** From the earliest Bible days down to the present moment, there have been and are persons who have the ability to "Live in two worlds at the same time" and thereby bring through communications from persons who have passed into the world of spirit.

- **Apparitions, Hauntings and Ghosts: -** Encounters with Ghosts over 4000 years in all parts of the world indicate that something survives death of the physical body.

- **Obsessing Spirits; -** Obsessing spirits are still a reality today. They may be elementals, thought forms or spirits or souls of people who have departed their physical bodies and who, due to their baser habits of thought and behavior, are very much confused and in darkness. Still being attracted to the earth plane from which they have only recently departed, they attach themselves to the magnetic auras of living persons. They actually affect the thoughts, emotions and actions of the obsessed person.

- **Spirit Doctors: -** Very careful research by medical doctors, psychiatrists, psychical researchers and others suggests that healers in various parts of the world do, in fact, get help from dedicated medical doctors who themselves now live in the worlds of spirit. These doctors desire to continue their ministrations to ailing humanity. From their present vantage point they know far more about cause and cure of physical and mental illness than they ever did when occupying their physical bodies.

- **Spirit Photographs:** - Dozens of photographers in many countries, using many kinds of cameras and films, with many types of lighting conditions (including total darkness) have obtained photographs of persons known to have died and whose bodies were buried or cremated. While this phenomenon is easy to duplicate by fraudulent means, there is solid evidence and there are fully documented cases of the genuine thing.

- **Materialization:** - From Biblical times down to the present, competent witnesses have observed, touched, examined and even weighed bodies of persons and animals known to have died and been buried or cremated. Our present day studies of the phenomenon and rapid expansion in our knowledge regarding the physical universe and its interpenetrating non-physical universe at last makes it possible to begin to understand the natural laws behind this 'miracle'.

- **Reincarnation:** - Reincarnation is a belief that:
  a. Each person has a soul.
  b. The soul survives the death of physical body.
  c. The soul then spends time in other realms of existence.
  d. Next the soul is reborn in to a new physical body for the purpose of further mental and spiritual growth.
  e. The cycle is repeated until the soul reaches a high state of development and reunites in full consciousness with God.
  f. Although more than half the population of the world accepts reincarnation, it is strongly resisted in Christendom. Most Christians believe in a, b, and c, but relatively few believe in d and e. The current scientific research suggests that the individual soul survives the death of the physical body and may, under certain circumstances inhabit a new human physical body.

- **Space-Time Relationships;** - The mind, personality and soul already exist in a separate and interpenetrating space-time system. This same interpenetrating space-time system is where we continue to live when we cast off our physical body.

- **Conservation of Matter and Energy:** - We have seen that science now accepts as one of its basic tenets that matter-energy can neither be created nor destroyed. The higher, finer matter that is our spiritual body continues to exist after the grosser physical body decays and returns to nature as gas, water vapor, and particulate matter ("DUST")

6.07 - FACING THE REALITIES OF LIFE:
A. FEAR OF DEATH

Death is an inescapable and inevitable reality. To ignore it is utter foolishness. To attempt to avoid it is impossible. To hope for physical immorality is absurd. The suggested exhortations are the following:

1. **Make death a part of life by understanding that life without death is incomplete and never possible.**

   As soon as we are born, we begin to die. Life is sacred so we cannot afford to squander it in daydreams, fantasies, and false hopes. Life without death, pleasure without pain, light without darkness, and good without evil, are never possible. We must either accept both or rise above both, by overcoming embodiment through the knowledge of self.

2. **Develop immunity against death by practicing meditation and dispassion.**

   In meditation we try to reach our true identity, the deathless self, by crossing over the three states of consciousness – waking, dreaming, and deep sleeping. We partially and temporarily die in our physical and mental existence. With meditation, practice dispassion, which is knowing that nothing material will accompany us when we leave this earth and nothing in this world can be of any help to us to overcome death.

3. **Build your own raft to cross the ocean of mortality.**

   Life is a journey toward our true self, the realization of which alone can give us immortality. But the raft for this journey is not given to us. Each person must build his or her own raft by the practice of self-awareness through meditation on the self and self-analysis. No practice of this self-awareness is ever lost. As we go on with our practices, all our experiences of self-awareness join together and grow in to a mass, which is called the raft on which a mortal crosses the ocean of mortality.

4. **Free yourself from all attachments.** Our attachments and desires keep us tied to our physical existence. We often hope for the impossible and want to achieve the unachievable. To free ourselves from these attachments and desires, we need to cleanse ourselves. Just as we cleanse our body with soap and water, so do we cleanse our mind with self-awareness?

B. AFTER LIFE: -

Medicine and religion share at least one trait – both can be seen as responses to the prospect of death. But while science is quiet on a possible afterlife, following religious practices are shaped by their conception of their undiscovered country.

Judaism: - Jewish texts have little to say about a possible afterlife, placing more focus on the proper actions in this life, not the one to come.

Christianity: - The vast majority of Christians believe in heaven and hell – and that your destination depends on your deeds and faith during this life.

Islam: - Similar to Christians, Muslims believe in a day of judgment in the afterlife, when the dead will be divided between paradise and damnation.

Buddhism: - Though specific beliefs vary by sect, Buddhist hold fast to the doctrine of reincarnation, ending only in the final liberation known as Nirvana.

Hinduism: - Like Buddhists, Hindus believe in reincarnation and Karma, with the status of your next life depending on your actions in this life.

Taoism: - Life and death are flip sides of the Tao, and death is a transformation from being to nonbeing, with no heaven or hell.

6.08 - LIFE AFTER DEATH: -

Human life is animal existence but with human spirit empowering the brain with intellect. The human spirit in man makes possible the union with the Holy Spirit and mind and immortality of God. When mortal man dies, the body reverts to dust, and the spirit returns to God. The departed human spirit at death is in fact a spiritual mold, of itself unconscious, yet in the resurrection bringing in to the resurrected body all the memory, knowledge and character as well as form and shape of the person before death. The human spirit of itself cannot see, hear, think or know. The only real Life, inherent and self-containing, lies in the holy spirit of God, united with the human spirit. The value of the human life lies in the human spirit and its potential of being united with God's Spirit – which is God Mind and God –life.

6.09 – THE PROBLEM OF HUMAN SUFFERING: -

One of the great problems and one of the great mysteries of life is the problem of human suffering and the problem of death.

According to the bible when man was put upon earth he was told to be fruitful, to replenish the earth, to subdue it. His first responsibility upon earth was to take care of the garden i.e. earth. To make sure that earth was properly nurtured and properly supervised. The essence of that command still exists. Much of the suffering and tragedy man experiences is because he has not discharged this responsibility.

Man's persistence in polluting the water, for example, has caused disease and other problems, which in some cases have been tragic. Man's unwise use of the land has caused floods and tornadoes that have brought great tragedy and great suffering upon man. When we violate the natural environment that God has given us, we can not expect God to allow the consequences of this violation to occur. Another aspect of the problem of suffering is seen when we fail to heed the warnings of nature and thus reap the consequences.

Indeed this physical body that we live in, ugly as it may be from outside, is a marvelous machine and if properly cared for might run as long as hundred years without a valve job or a new transmission or even a change in oil. Some of us may sometimes feel like we need a new transmission, but the fact of matter is that we are fearfully and wonderfully made. Physical pain is that which protects us and enables us to survive in the environment in which we live.

Emotions: -
Same type of thing is true in the emotional sense. Human beings have to experience guilt and sympathy and compassion and should be able to relate to the needs of fellow human beings. One of the greatest tragedies of our society today is the fact that somehow we have equated the ability to be sympathetic, the ability to be compassionate, the ability to relate to the needs of our fellow human beings as weakness – when in fact it is sign of strength.

Ignorance: -
One of our great problems in the area of pain and suffering and death is brought on by ignorance. And that this is true of death more than anything else. Ignorance has caused us to throw away one of the great blessings that we are human beings. In fact is it not a marvelous thing that when those we love are no longer able to exist realistically in a physical way that they do not have to go on suffering. God has provided us means by which the spirit can be separated from the body and the physical pain that we endure now fades in to insignificance. Ignorance is one of the great curses of man. Ignorance of death is one of the great curses of the human beings.

Pain and Suffering: -
No one would want to bring the pain and suffering in to a man's life, but the fact of the matter is that sometimes it takes pain, sometimes it takes suffering, sometimes it takes a tragedy to make us realize that we need God. Pain humbles us. Somebody has said, "Humility is a funny thing, just when you think you have it, you've lost it. Sometimes it takes a tragedy to make us realize that we are not self-sufficient. Sometimes it takes a disease to make us realize that no matter how much money we have, no matter how much vocal we are, no matter how many friends we have, no matter what our situation in life might be, that sometimes there is no one who can help us but God.

Time of Death: -
When we keep putting off our spiritual life to tomorrow, we end up copping out every single day. Death draws near, with every step we take, every tick and

every tock of the clock. It could strike any moment and we can't do a thing about it. While death is certain, its moment of arrival is unpredictable.

There are two types of lunatics, those who don't know that they must die, and those who have forgotten that they are alive.

Death seems to be so distant, yet it is always so near. Distant because we always imagine it at some time yet to come; near because it can strike at any moment. While our death is certain, its hour is unpredictable. When it comes, no eloquence can persuade it to wait, no power can stop it, no wealth can buy it off, no beauty can seduce it.

Life and Death: -
We cannot live fully by excluding death from life, but by welcoming death in to our lives, we grow and enrich our lives. The way we think about death has a considerable impact on our quality of life. Some people are terrified of it; others prefer to ignore it, yet others contemplate it so as to better appreciate every passing moment and to recognize what is worth living for. Accepting death as part of life serves as a spur to diligence and saves us from wasting our time on vain distractions. While we are all equal in having to meet death, each of us prepares for it in his own way.

At the start we should fear death like a stag trying to escape from the trap. At midway we have nothing to regret, like a peasant who have carefully tended to his field. At the end, we should be happy, like some one who has accomplished a great task.

It is better to learn how to profit from fear of death than to ignore it. We need not live haunted by death, but we must remain aware of the fragility of existence. This understanding will help us appreciate fully the time we have left to live. Death often strikes without warning. We may be in good health, enjoying a fine meal with our friends, and yet be living out our final moments. **We may blame ourselves only for what we have neglected to do. Someone who has used every second of his life to become a better person and to contribute to others, happiness can die in peace.**

So death the most frightening of bad things, is nothing to us; since when we exist, death is not yet present and when death is present, then we do not exist.

Death represent the ultimate and inevitable destruction of that to which we are most attached which is ourselves. Clearly therefore the teachings on non-ego and nature of the mind can be of enormous help. As death draws near, then it is best to adopt a serene, selfish, and detached attitude. In that way death need be neither a mental torment nor a physical ordeal.

Now a day people are too ready to avert their eyes from death. It is disguised, covered up, sanitized. Since there is no material way to avert it, we prefer to remove death altogether from our consciousness. When it does come along, it is all the more shocking, because we are unprepared for it. Meanwhile life has been slipping away day after day, and if we have not learned to find meaning in its every passing moment, all it has meant to us is wasted time.

The wise man enjoys a very special kind of freedom: prepared for death, he appreciates every moment of life's bounty. He lives each day as if it were his only one. That day naturally becomes the most precious of his existence. When he looks at the sunset, he wonders: "Will I see the sunrise again tomorrow morning? He knows that he has no time to lose, that time is precious, and that is foolish to waste it in idleness. When death finally comes for him, he dies tranquilly, without sadness or regret, without attachment or regret, without attachment to what he is leaving behind.

CONDOLENCES: -
Dear ——————:

We all here in this part of the world remember our dear ———- and pray for his/her soul to rest in peace. We human beings cannot do anything in this re-gard; we are all transient & mortal beings in this world. One philosopher had said "Death is only a movement from one room to another. It is very much like sunset. The sun appears to set, but you know that sun never sets. What is sunset here, is sunrise elsewhere. What is death here, is birth elsewhere."

God will give enough courage to all of you to bear this loss, and help your brothers/sisters in such a way that they do not feel lonely anytime.

With God's Blessings and loves for all

yours truly

6.10 - DEATH IS FINAL: -

Death is the most fearful prospect of all.

The last frontier to be conquered by self-awareness is Death. This is inevitable, given that almost everyone avoids thinking about death. But at deeper level, dying would seem to be immune to consciousness. The most pervasive influence on your whole life begins with how you feel about life and death. It is undeniable that being afraid of death will make you feel unsafe in the world, constantly being vigilant about threats and holding the death to be more powerful than life.

Solution is to transcend that is to go beyond an ordinary waking state. You already do that through fantasy, daydreams, and visions of the future, imagination, and curiosity about the unknown. Taking the process a step further through meditation, contemplation, and self-reflection, you can expand your awareness to reach an experience of pure awareness (spiritual awareness). When you are established there, fear of death is replaced by knowing the state of immortality.

CHAPTER 7

WHAT IS "THE SOUL"?

7.01 – THE SOUL: -

THE SOUL – in certain spiritual, philosophical, and psychological traditions – is the incorporeal essence of a person, living thing, or object. Many philosophical and spiritual systems teach that only humans have souls, while others teach that all living things, and even inanimate objects (such as rivers), have souls. The latter belief is commonly called animism (attribution of conscious life)· SOUL can function as a synonym for *spirit, mind* or *self* Scientific works, in particular, often consider 'SOULI' as a synonym for 'mind'.

Plato, drawing on the words of his teacher Socrates, considered the SOUL the essence of a person, being that which decides how we behave. He considered this essence to be an incorporeal, eternal occupant of our being. As bodies die, the SOUL is continually reborn in subsequent bodies. The Platonic SOUL comprises three parts:

1. **the logos**, or logistikon (mind, nous, or reason)
2. **the thymos**, or thumetikon (emotion, or spiritedness, or masculine)
3. **the eros**, or epithumetikon (appetitive, or desire, or feminine)

Each of these has a function in a balanced, level and peaceful soul.

Aristotle defined the SOUL or *psyche* as the *first actuality* of a naturally organized body, but argued against its having a separate existence from the physical body. In Aristotle's view, the primary activity of a living thing constitutes its soul; for example, the soul of an eye, if it were an independent organism, would be seeing (its purpose or final cause).

The various faculties of the SOUL or psyche, such as nutrition, sensation, movement, and so forth, when exercised, constitute the "second" actuality, or fulfillment, of the capacity to be alive. A good example is someone who falls asleep, as opposed to someone who falls dead; the former actuality *can* wake up and go about their life, while the second actuality can no longer do so. Aristotle identified three hierarchical levels of living things: **plants, animals, and people**, for which groups he identified three corresponding levels of SOUL, or biological activity: The form of a living thing is its **SOUL** (Greek *psyche*, Latin *anima*). There are three kinds of souls: the "**vegetative soul**" of plants, which causes them to grow and decay and nourish themselves, but does not cause motion and sensation; the "**animal soul**" which causes animals to move and feel; and the "**rational soul**" **which is the source of consciousness and reasoning** which (Aristotle believed) is found only in humans. Each higher soul has all the attributes of the lower one. Aristotle believed that while matter can exist without form, form cannot exist without matter, and therefore the SOUL cannot exist without the body.

Philosophy of mind:

For a contemporary understanding of the SOUL/MIND and the problem concerning its connection to the brain/body, consider the advances, which have been made in neuroscience and which are steadily uncovering the truth/falsity of the concept of an independent soul/mind. The philosophies of mind and of personal identity also contribute to a contemporary understanding of the mind. The contemporary approach does not so much attack the existence of an independent soul as render the concept less relevant. The advances in neuroscience mainly serve to support the mind/brain identity hypothesis, showing the extent of the correlation between mental states and physical-brain states. The notion of soul has less explanatory power in a western world-view which prefers the empirical explanations involving observable and locatable elements of the brain. Even so, there remain considerable objections to simple-identity theory. Notably, philosophers such as Thomas Nagel and David Chalmers have argued that the correlation between physical-brain states and mental states is not strong enough to support identity theory. Nagel (1974) argues that no amount of physical data is sufficient to provide the "what it is like" of first-person experience, and Chalmers (1996) argues for an "explanatory gap" between functions of the brain and phenomenal experience. On the whole, brain/mind identity theory does poorly in accounting for mental phenomena of intentionality. While neuroscience has done much to illuminate the functioning of the brain, much of subjective experience remains mysterious.

7.02 - RELIGIOUS VIEWS OF SOUL: -
Judaism:
In modern Judaism the soul is believed to be given by God to a person by his/her first breath, as mentioned in Genesis, "And the LORD (GOD) formed man [of] the dust of the ground, and breathed into his nostrils the breath of life; and man became a living being." From this statement, the rabbinical interpretation is often that human embryos do not have souls, though the orthodox often oppose abortion as a form of birth control. Judaism relates the quality of one's SOUL to one's performance of mitzvot and reaching higher levels of understanding, and thus closeness to GOD. A person with such closeness is called a tzadik. Judaism also has a concept of purity of body and soul, which requires avoidance of "unclean" things. Such practices mentioned in the Torah include the keeping of kashrut and daily bathing (tevilah) in a mikveh. In biblical times, it was believed that "impurity" was something that could be spread by touching, and unclean people were temporarily separated from the group. Though Jewish theology does not agree on the nature of an afterlife, the soul is said to "return to God" after death.

Christianity:
Most Christians understand the SOUL as an reality distinct from, yet integrally connected with, the body. Its characteristics are described in moral, spiritual, and philosophical terms. According to a common Christian, when people die, their souls will be judged by GOD and determined to spend an eternity in Heaven or in Hell. Though all branches of Christianity –Catholics, Eastern Orthodox and Oriental Orthodox, Evangelical or mainline Protestants – teach that Jesus Christ plays a decisive role in the salvation process, the specifics of that role and the part played by individual persons or religious rituals and relationships, is a matter of wide diversity in official church teaching, theological speculation and popular practice. Some Christians believe that if one has not repented of one's sins and trusted in Jesus Christ as Lord and Saviour, one will go to Hell and suffer eternal damnation or eternal separation from God. Variations also exist on this theme, e.g. some which hold

that the unrighteous soul will be destroyed instead of suffering eternally. Believers will inherit eternal life in Heaven and enjoy eternal fellowship with God. There is also a belief that babies (including the unborn) and those with cognitive or mental impairments who have died will be received into Heaven on the basis of God's grace through the sacrifice of Jesus.

Soul at inception of life:- Among Christians, there is uncertainty regarding whether human embryos have souls, and at what point between conception and birth the fetus acquires a soul and consciousness. This uncertainty is the general reasoning behind many Christians' belief that abortion should not be legal·

Roman Catholic beliefs:
The present Catechism of the Catholic Church defines the soul as "the innermost aspect of humans, that which is of greatest value in them, that by which they are most especially in God's image: **'SOUL' signifies the *spiritual principle* in man."** All SOULS living and dead will be Judged by Jesus Christ when he comes back to earth. The souls of those who die unrepentant of serious sins, or in conscious rejection of God, will at judgment day may be forever in a state called Hell. The Catholic Church teaches that the existence of each individual soul is dependent wholly upon God: "The doctrine of the faith affirms that the spiritual and immortal soul is created immediately by God."

Orthodox Christian beliefs:
Eastern Orthodox and Oriental Orthodox views are somewhat similar, in essence, to Roman Catholic views although different in specifics. Orthodox Christians believe that after death, the SOUL is judged individually by God, and then sent to either Abraham's Bosom (temporary paradise) or Hades/Hell (temporary torture). At the Last Judgment, God judges all people who have ever lived. Those that know the Spirit of God, because of the sacrifice of Jesus, go to Heaven (permanent paradise) whilst the damned experience the Lake of Fire (permanent torture). The Orthodox Church does not teach that Purgatory exists.

Protestant beliefs:
Protestants generally believe in the SOUL's existence, but fall into two major camps about what this means in terms of an afterlife. Some, following Calvin believe in the immortality of the SOUL and conscious existence after death,

while others, following Luther believe in the mortality of the SOUL and unconscious "sleep" until the resurrection of the dead·

Other Christians reject the idea of the immortality of the SOUL, citing the Apostles' Creed's reference to the "resurrection of the body". They consider the SOUL to be the life force, which ends in death and will be restored in the resurrection. Theologian Frederick Buechner sums up this position in his 1973 book *Whistling in the Dark*: "...we go to our graves as dead as a doornail and are given our lives back again by God (i.e., resurrected) just as we were given them by God in the first place."

Islam:
According to the Quran, Ruh (SOUL) is a command from Allah (GOD). And they ask you (O Muhammad SAW) concerning the Rûh (the Spirit); Say: "The Rûh (the Spirit): is one of the things, the knowledge of which is only with my Lord. And of knowledge, you (mankind) have been given only a little."

Buddhism:
Buddhism teaches that all things are in a constant state of flux: all is changing, and no permanent state exists by itself. This applies to human beings as much as to anything else in the cosmos. Thus, a human being has no permanent self. According to this doctrine of *anatta* (P li; Sanskrit: *an tman*) – "no-self" or "NO SOUL" – the words "I" or "me" do not refer to any fixed thing. They are simply convenient terms that allow us to refer to an ever-changing entity.

The *anatta* doctrine is not a kind of materialism. Buddhism does not deny the existence of "immaterial" entities, and it (at least traditionally) distinguishes bodily states from mental states. Thus, the conventional translation of *anatta* as "NO-SOUL" can be confusing. If the word "SOUL" simply refers to an incorporeal component in living things that can continue after death, then Buddhism does not deny the existence of the SOUL. Instead, Buddhism denies the existence of a permanent entity that remains constant behind the changing corporeal and incorporeal components of a living being. Just as the body changes from moment to moment, so thoughts come and go. And there is no permanent, underlying mind that experiences these thoughts, as in Cartesianism; rather, conscious mental states simply arise and perish with no "thinker" behind them. When the body dies, the incorporeal mental processes continue and are reborn in a new body. Because the mental processes are constantly changing, the being that is reborn is neither entirely different than, nor exactly the same as, the being that died. However, the new being is *continuous* with the being that died – in the same way that the "you" of this moment is continuous with the "you" of a moment before, despite the fact that you are constantly changing.

Buddhist teaching holds that a notion of a permanent, abiding self is a delusion that is one of the causes of human conflict on the emotional, social, and political levels. They add that an understanding of *anatta* provides an accurate description of the human condition, and that this understanding allows us to pacify our mundane desires.

Various schools of Buddhism have differing ideas about what continues after death. The Yogacara school in Mahayana Buddhism said there are Store consciousness which continue to exist after death. In some schools, particularly Tibetan Buddhism, the view is that there are three minds: **very subtle mind**, which does not disintegrate in death; **subtle mind**, which disintegrates in death and which is "dreaming mind" or "unconscious mind"; and **gross mind**, which does not exist when one is *sleeping*. Therefore, *gross mind* less permanent than *subtle mind*, which does not exist in death. *Very subtle mind*, however, does continue, and when it "catches on", or coincides with phenomena, again, a new *subtle mind* emerges, with its own personality/assumptions/habits, and *that* entity experiences **karma** in the current continuum.

Plants were said to be non-sentient but Buddhist monks should avoid cutting or burning trees, because some sentient beings rely on them. Some Mahayana monks said non-sentient beings such as plants and stones have buddha-nature· Some buddhists said about plants or divisible consciousnesses·

Certain modern Buddhists, particularly in Western countries, reject—or at least take an agnostic stance toward—the concept of rebirth or reincarnation, which they view as incompatible with the concept of *anatta*. Stephen Batchelor discusses this issue in his book, *Buddhism Without Beliefs*. Others point to research that has been conducted at the University of Virginia as proof that some people are reborn.

Hinduism:
In Hinduism, the Sanskrit words most closely corresponding to soul are "Jeev", "Aatma" and "Purusha", meaning the individual Self. The term "SOUL" is

misleading as it implies an object possessed, whereas Self signifies the subject which perceives all objects. This Self is held to be distinct from the various mental faculties such as desires, thinking, understanding, reasoning and self-image (ego), all of which are considered to be part of Prakriti (Nature).

All the three major schools of Hindu philosophy agree, on the basis of the Vedic revelation, that the Aatma or jeevaatma(individual Self) is related to Brahman or the Supreme Self of the Universe (ParamAatma). But they differ in the nature of this relationship. In Advaita Vedanta (non-dualism) the Individual Self (jee-vaatma) and the Supreme Self (paramaatman) are one and the same. Dvaita or dualistic rejects this concept of identity, instead identifying the Self as separate but similar part of supreme Self (God), but it never lose its individual identity. Visishtadvaita or Qualified Non-dualism takes a middle path and accepts the jeevatman as a "mode" [prakara] or attribute of the Brahman.

The jeevatman becomes involved in the process of becoming and transmigrating through cycles of birth and death because of ignorance of its own true nature. The spiritual path consists of Self-realization – a process in which one acquires the knowledge of the SELF and through this knowledge applied through meditation and realization one then returns to the Source which is Brahman.

The qualities which are common to both Brahman and jeevaatma are: **being (sat), consciousness (chit), and bliss/love (ananda).** Liberation or Moksha (final release) is liberation from all limiting adjuncts and the unification with Brahman.

The Mandukya Upanishad verse 7 describes the Aatma (SOUL) in the following way:-
"Not inwardly cognitive, not outwardly cognitive, not both-wise cognitive, not a cognition-mass, not cognitive, not non-cognitive, unseen, with which there can be no dealing, ungraspable, having no distinctive mark, non-thinkable, that cannot be designated, the essence of the assurance of which is the state of being one with the Self, the cessation of development, tranquil, benign, without a second (a-dvaita)—[such] they think is the fourth. That is the SELF. That should be discerned."

In Bhagavad – Gita Lord Krishna describes the 'SOUL' in the following way:
"For the SOUL there is neither birth nor death at any time. He has not come

into being, does not come into being, and will not come into being. He is unborn, eternal, ever – existing and primeval. He is not slain when the body is slain."

Srila Prabhupada, a great Vaishnava saint of the modern time further explains: The SOUL does not take birth there, and the SOUL does not die...And because the SOUL has no birth, he therefore has no past, present or future. He is eternal, ever-existing and primeval – that is, there is no trace in history of his coming into being.

Since the quality of Aatma (SOUL is primarily consciousness, all sentient and insentient beings are pervaded by Aatma, including plants, animals, humans and gods. The difference between them is the contracted or expanded state of that consciousness. For example, animals and humans share in common the desire to live, fear of death, desire to procreate and to protect their families and territory and the need for sleep, but animals' consciousness is more contracted and has less possibility to expand than does human consciousness.

When the Aatma becomes embodied it is called birth, when the Aatma leaves a body it is called death. The Aatma transmigrates from one body to another body based on karmic [performed deeds] reactions.

In Hinduism, the Sanskrit word most closely corresponding to soul is **"Aatma"**, which can mean **SOUL** or even **GOD**. It is seen as the portion of Brahman within us. Hinduism contains many variant beliefs on the origin, purpose, and fate of the soul. For example, advaita or non-dualistic conception of the soul accords it's union with Brahman, the absolute uncreated (roughly, the Godhead), in eventuality or in pre-existing fact. Dvaita or dualistic concepts reject this, instead identifying the SOUL as a different and incompatible substance

Bahá'í Faith:
The Bahá'í Faith affirms that "the SOUL is a sign of GOD, a heavenly gem whose reality the most learned of men hath failed to grasp, and whose mystery no mind, however acute, can ever hope to unravel. Bahá'u'lláh stated that the SOUL not only continues to live after the physical death of the human body, but is, in fact, immortal. Heaven can be seen partly as the SOUL's state of nearness to GOD; and hell as a state of remoteness from GOD. Each state follows as a natural consequence of individual efforts, or the lack thereof, to develop spiritually. Bahá'u'lláh taught that individuals have no existence prior to their

life here on earth and the SOUL's evolution is always towards GOD and away from the material world.

Brahma Kumaris:
In Brahma Kumaris, SOULs, called Atmas, are believed to be an infinitesimal point of spiritual light residing in the forehead of the bodies they occupy.

Jainism:
In Jainism SOUL exists too, having a separate existence from the body that houses it. Every living being from a plant or a bacterium to human, has a SOUL. The SOUL (Jiva) is differentiated from non-soul or non-living reality (ajiva) that consists of: matter, time, space, medium of motion and medium of rest.

Sikhism:
Sikhism considers SOUL (Atma) to be part of GOD (Waheguru). Various hymns are cited from the holy book "Sri Guru Granth Sahib" (SGGS) that suggests this belief. "GOD is in the SOUL and the SOUL is in the GOD." The same concept is repeated at various pages of the SGGS. For example: "The soul is divine; divine is the soul. Worship Him with love." and "The soul is the Lord, and the Lord is the soul; contemplating the Shabad, the Lord is found." The "ATMA" or "SOUL" according to Sikhism is an entity or "spiritual spark" or "light" in our body because of which the body can sustain life. On the departure of this entity from the body, the body becomes lifeless – No amount of manipulations to the body can make the person make any physical actions. **The SOUL is the 'driver' in the body.** It is the 'roohu' or spirit or atma, the presence of which makes the physical body alive. Many religious and philosophical traditions, support the view that the soul is the ethereal substance – a spirit; a non material spark – particular to a unique living being. Such traditions often consider the SOUL both immortal and innately aware of its immortal nature, as well as the true basis for sentience in each living being. The concept of the SOUL has strong links with notions of an afterlife, but opinions may vary wildly even within a given religion as to what happens to the SOUL after death. Many within these religions and philosophies see the SOUL as immaterial, while others consider it possibly material.

Taoism:
According to Chinese traditions, every person has two types of SOUL called **hun** and **po**, which are respectively yang and yin. Taoism believes in ten

SOULs, "three *hun* and seven *po*". The pò is linked to the dead body and the grave, whereas the hún is linked to the ancestral tablet. A living being that loses any of them is said to have mental illness or unconsciousness, while a dead SOUL may reincarnate to a disability, lower desire realms or may even be unable to reincarnate. Also, Journeys to the Under-World said there can be hundreds of divisible SOULs.

Science:
Science and medicine seek naturalistic accounts of the observable natural world. This stance is known as methodological naturalism. Much of the scientific study relating to the SOUL has involved investigating the SOUL as an object of human belief, or as a concept that shapes cognition and an understanding of the world, rather than as an entity in and of itself.

When modern scientists speak of the SOUL outside of this cultural and psychological context, they generally treat *SOUL* **as a poetic synonym for** *MIND*. Francis Crick's book, *The Astonishing Hypothesis*, for example, has the subtitle, "The scientific search for the soul". Crick held the position that one can learn everything knowable about the human SOUL by studying the workings of the human brain. Depending on one's belief regarding the relationship between the SOUL and the mind, then, the findings of neuroscience may be relevant to one's understanding of the soul. Skeptic Robert T. Carroll suggests that the concept of a non-substantial substance is an oxymoron, and that the scholarship done by philosophers and psychologists based on the assumption of a non-physical entity has not furthered scientific understanding of the working of the mind.

Daniel Dennett has championed the idea that the human survival strategy depends heavily on adoption of the intentional stance, a behavioral strategy that predicts the actions of others based on the expectation that they have a mind like one's own (see theory of mind). Mirror neurons in brain regions such as Broca's area may facilitate this behavioral strategy. The intentional stance, Dennett suggests, has proven so successful that people tend to apply it to all aspects of human experience, thus leading to animism and to other conceptualizations of soul.

7.03 – COMMON DEFINITIONS OF SOUL: -

1. The immaterial essence, animating principle, or actuating cause of an individual life.

2. a) the spiritual principle embodied in human beings, all rational and spiritual beings, or the universe. b) *Capitalized Christian Science*: GOD.

3. A person's total SELF.

4. *a*: an active or essential part, *b*: a moving spirit, c: leader

5. *a*: the moral and emotional nature of human beings, *b* : the quality that arouses emotion and sentiment, *c* : spiritual or moral force: fervor

6. Person <not a *soul* in sight>

7. Personification <she is the *soul* of integrity>

8. *a*: a strong positive feeling (as of intense sensitivity and emotional fervor) conveyed especially by black American performers, *b* : negritude *c* : soul music *d* : soul food *e* : soul brother

9. An immaterial force within a human being thought to give the body life, energy, and power <many religions teach that the *soul* is immortal>

10. A member of the human race <I promise I won't tell another *soul*>

11. The quality or qualities that make a thing what it is <a kind act that was the very *soul* of charity>

12. The seat of one's deepest thoughts and emotions <knew in her *soul* that it was true>

7.04 - WHAT IS BODY AND SOUL?

Human body has five senses, (vision, hearing, smelling, taste and touch). Consider one of the senses say vision, for vision you need 1. **Instrument**, the eyes. 2. **Organ**, the nerve center in the brain. 3. **Mind,** if the mind is not joined to the organ, the organ may take the impression and yet we may not be conscious of it. 4. **Intellect,** the intellect is the determinative faculty and decides upon what is brought to it. 5. **Soul,** the king on the throne, from him comes the order as to what to do or what not to do; and the order goes down in the same sequence, Soul to the intellect, to the mind, to the organs, and the organs convey it to instrument and perception is complete.

Therefore the human being is composed first of this external covering, the body, secondly, of the fine body, consisting of mind, intellect, and ego. Behind them is the real soul of man. When the soul reflects its powers on the mind and the mind thinks, and then time appears. How can the soul, therefore be said to be existing in time, when time itself exists in soul. It has neither birth nor death.

The SOUL is not bound by the conditions of the matter. In its very essence it is free, unbounded, holy, pure and perfect.

Science is nothing but the finding of the unity. As soon as science reaches perfect unity, it will stop from further progress, because it would have reached its goal. Similarly the science of religion will become perfect when it discovers him, who is the one life in universe of death, who is the constant basis of the ever changing world, one who is the only SOUL, of whom all Souls are but delusive manifestations.

Aggregate of materials, we call the body is the cause of the manifestation of the force we call the SOUL/THOUGHT or whether it is thought that manifests the body. The religions of the world say that the force called Thought manifests the body and not reverse. It is more logical to say that the force, which takes up the matter and forms, the body is the same, which is manifested through the body.

What is the force, which manifests itself through the body? Whatever the force be, that is something, which takes particles up as it were and creates forms out of them – Human Bodies. Soul is that force which is now working through us.

The SOUL is of the same essence as of the GOD. The soul enlivens every living being. Its essence is eternal, all consciousness, all love, all light and sound, all peace and all bliss. Human beings can realize their Soul and realize God while in the human body. **Within the SOUL is the source of wisdom from which all knowledge flows.** A love far greater and fulfilling than any we can know in the outer world is waiting to embrace us with open arms within. At our center is the strength and power that can enable us to overcome any fear. The highest aim of human life is to attain self-knowledge (first hand knowledge of the soul) and God realization. The SOUL resides in the human body and can be realized through the process of inversion or meditation. Meditation ultimately gives us spiritual consciousness. **Spiritual consciousness means becoming aware of the SOUL and GOD within us.** Most of us are aware of our body, of the thoughts passing through our mind, and of the world around us. This is called body or physical consciousness. But human beings are more than a body and mind. We are actually SOUL, a conscious entity that inhibits the body.

Second definition of Soul is "Thoughts":
Every human being has MIND & BODY. Mind thinks and Body takes action. What we are at present depends upon our thoughts and actions of the past in this life.

What we will be in future depends upon our Thoughts and Actions of the present time in this life. Therefore we make our own destiny.

Your thoughts guide you to your destiny. If you always think the same, you will always get to the same place. Think in a new way and you will be a new person. Give happiness to all and you will live in peace. Create peace in your mind and you will create a world of peace around you.

The events of the world are not in my hands, therefore I cannot change them, but if I choose not to let my thoughts and feelings be dependent on external factors, I can be in control of myself and therefore help to shape the world I live in.

Therefore SOUL is the living and intelligent inner being that inhibit and gives life to the body.

SOUL is Immortal, Eternal (no beginning or end), Metaphysical, Unlimited, Pure conscience energy.

Body is mortal, is born and dies, Physical, Limited, Made up of matter.

If every physical part of the body is an instrument, who or what is it that is using it.

It is I, the Self, The Soul.

The SOUL uses the word I for itself and the word my when referring to the body, my hand, my mouth, my brain, and so on. I am different from my body. When I assume my true identity as a spiritual being, then I also immediately have access to the love, peace, happiness and power that are part of me.

7.05 - WHAT IS MIND AND SOUL?

The mind is an instrument of cognition, of knowing things, knowing the material world. The SOUL is a ray of GOD, that which you essentially are. The mind is an instrument with which we know. We try to understand things. The SOULl is immortal, the mind is mortal. The Mind is discursive (conversational), the SOUL is synergic (conditions such that the total effect is greater than the sum of the individual effects). The SOUL integrates everything but the mind analyzes. We need the help of mind in doing our work on the physical plane. That is why we have brought ourselves the instrument of the mind. **Out of GOD emanate many rays, every ray is a SOUL**. That is what makes all of us one. **The soul is universal**. The mind is individual. The mind individualizes but the Soul unites.

Spirituality

The term spirituality has nothing to do with religion. Actually spirituality begins where religion ends. Religion enforces an externalization of the mind in one's search for God, whereas spirituality internalizes the search and directs the mind to the heart of man. **God is inside us.** Being within us, such a being is not always accessible, but readily reachable and all that spirituality requires of us to achieve the sense of oneness with God, is to focus the mind inwards and approach him with love.

The average human being of today gives a great deal of thought, and applies a great amount of energy, to attain high levels of material welfare. But not withstanding even success in this endeavor, there is yet much happiness, discontent and misery pervading the lives of the people. Why is this? It is the result of unbalanced application of effort. The human existence consists of two planes of existence, the **material and spiritual**, and both these are important and essential for the harmonious well being of the individual. As a bird needs two wings of existence, the spiritual and the material. If either is neglected for the other, such a life becomes unnatural. Neglect of the material existence results in poverty and in sickness, and the neglect of the spiritual, which is the case with most of us, results in horrors of man-made diseases and sufferings. To correct this sorry state of affairs, we have to bring back balance into our lives.

7.06 - OUR SOUL: - [2]

The differences between human beings and between all things in the whole creation are not in kind but only in degree. There is same SOUL in the saint and the sinner, in the happy and the miserable, in the beautiful and the ugly, in humans and animals. The differences are caused by the **degree of expression**. In some it is expressed more and in others less, but those differences have no effect on the SOUL. If one person's dress shows more of his/her body than others, it does not make difference in their bodies, the difference is in their dress.

Men of childish intellect, ignorant persons, run after desires, which are external, and enter the trap of far-reaching death; but the wise, understanding immortality, never seek the Eternal in this life of finite things. Similarly in this external world, which is full of finite things, it is impossible to see and find the infinite. The infinite must be sought in that alone which is infinite and the only thing infinite about us is that which is within us, our own SOUL.

He is in the all moves; he is in all that is pure. He fills the universe. He is in the sacrifice, he is the guest in the house, he is in man, in water, in animals and in truth; He is great one. As fire coming in to this world manifests itself in various forms, even so this one SOUL of the universe manifests himself in various forms, even though the one SOUL of all SOULs, of all beings, manifests itself in all forms.

Happiness is not in this heaven or in that heaven; it is in the SOUL. The highest heaven is in our SOUL, the greatest temple of worship is the human SOUL, greater than all heavens; for in no heaven, anywhere, can we understand Reality as distinctly and clearly as in this life, in our own SOUL.

The SOUL is one with Freedom, and the SOUL is one with Existence, and the SOUL is one with Knowledge. **SATCHITANANDA, Existence-Knowledge-Bliss.** Absolute, is the nature, the birthright, of the Soul, and all the manifestations are its expressions. Birth and Death, Life and Decay, Degeneration and Regeneration are all manifestations of Oneness. It is the universal idea working through all religions.

Philosophical Definition of SOUL:
The different philosophies seems to agree that this SOUL, whatever it may be, has neither form nor shape and that which has neither form nor shape must be omnipresent. Time, space and causation are in the mind and as this SOUL is beyond the mind and formless, it must be beyond time, space and causation, so it must be infinite. Then comes the highest speculation in our philosophy. The infinite cannot be two; therefore there is only one SOUL. Therefore the various ideas of different SOULs in different bodies are not real. The Real Man therefore is one and Infinite, the Omnipresent Spirit. And the Apparent Man (we the individuals) is only limitation of that real man. The Real Man, the spirit being beyond cause and effect, not bound by time and space must be free. This is the reality behind our SOULs, this omnipresence, this spiritual nature, this infinity. Therefore there is no question of birth and death.

The human body is not the real man, neither is the mind; for the mind waxes and wanes, one moment it is happy, another moment unhappy; one moment strong, another weak. Thus the body and mind are continually changing. So that cannot be SPIRIT/SOUL, which is Infinite, Unchangeable, Immovable, and Absolute.

Soul is Absolute:
The whole universe is Absolute, the Unchangeable, and the feeling thereof constitutes the phenomenon. Every phenomenon that we can see, feel, or think is finite, limited by our knowledge. And the personal God as we perceive of him is in fact a phenomenon. This phenomenal universe, as we have seen, is the same Impersonal Being felt by our Intellect. Whatever is real in this uni-

verse is that Impersonal Being and the forms and names are given by our intellects. The personal God and all that exists in this universe are the same Impersonal Being felt through our minds. When we get rid of our minds, our little personalities, we shall become one with it. This is what is meant by "Thou art That". We must know our true nature, the ABSOLUTE SOUL.

The gigantic intellect lies coiled up in the protoplasmic cell; each one of us comes out of a protoplasmic cell and all the powers we posses are coiled up there. The energy is in the cell potentially no doubt, but still there. So the infinite power is in the SOUL of man. Its manifestation is only a question of being Conscious of it and is conscious of its powers. **That power is the power of SELF-Realization and that is ABSOLUTE SOUL.**

SOUL and ATOM: -
Material world we see around us as a variety of forms and colors, light and heat, is formed of physical energy. The most beautiful scene in nature is merely a pattern of energy waves and vibrations. The atom is seen to be the point source of energy, and different energy levels and vibrations between neighboring atoms gives the appearance of form, color and heat.

The sense organs select the vibrations and relay a message to the mind where all images are formed. The eyes see some of the patterns as light forms and colors, the nose receives odors, and tastes and sensations are detected and transmitted to the mind. The human body is complex pattern of physical energies. Atoms come together to form the organic structure and inorganic minerals, which perform the body's chemical interactions, thus forming the basis of the hormonal and nervous control of the body.

One of the basic differences between SOULs and ATOMs is that while Souls can exercise choice of their movements, where as Atom cannot exercise such choice of movement. In a way **Soul is a point source of spiritual energy** that has awareness of its own existence and **Atom is point- source of physical energy**.

SOUL and its Position, Form and Attributes: -

Position: - The sentient functions are controlled and monitored through the nervous and hormonal systems from a particular point in the area of the brain housing the Thalamus, Hypothalamus, Pituitary and Pineal glands. This region is known as the seat of the **SOUL** or **THIRD EYE**. The connection between the physical and non-physical is by the medium of thought energy. When viewed from front, this region appears to be between and slightly above the line of the eyebrows. – As the brain is the control center for all of the various processes of the body – metabolism, the nervous endocrine, immunology and lymphatic systems – **it makes sense that the inner person (SOUL) be located somewhere in the brain.**

Form: - All of the characters present in the SOUL are subtle or non-dimensional in nature – Thoughts, Feelings, Emotions, Decision making power, personality traits and so on. If they are all without size, then it is reasonable to conclude that the conscious energy from which they emerge is also size less and therefore eternal. Just as the sun is in one place and yet its light radiates throughout the solar system, the SOUL is in one place and its energy permeates the whole body. Something, which has no physical dimension, is called point. **The SOUL therefore is an infinitesimal point of conscientious light.**

Attributes: - Qualities of SOUL are Love, Patience, Tolerance, Understanding, Empathy, and so on. These are all in a latent state and do not translate very easily in to action. They need to be empowered. One of the most immediate benefits of the practice of Meditation is to improve the functioning of this inner ruler. My innate qualities are just waiting for a chance to manifest them. Like a light bulb without a current, they need to be connected to a source of power. This is what exactly meditation brings.

The innate qualities of Soul are the following:
Patience – Peace, Purity, Love, and Power
Courage – Power and Truth
Discernment – Truth, Peace, Happiness and Balance

The inner faculties of SOUL: - (State of Consciousness)
Mind – Thoughts, Desires, Feelings or attachments, Anger, Greed, Vanity, sensation, emotions, experience, etc.

Intellect – Willpower, it discerns or discriminates and judges (decision making), reasoning power, the ability to remember, Associate and identify, ability to understand, recognize and know, etc.

Sub-consciousness or Un-consciousness – Personality traits, Habits, Tendencies, Memories, Values, Beliefs, Learning, Talents, Instincts, etc.

7.07 - MEDITATION: -

Meditation is a way to eliminate the lack of balance caused by the mental stresses of life. By spending time in meditation, we create a calm haven in which we restore equilibrium and peace to our mental functioning. Researchers have recorded that the brain activity in people who meditate functions at 4-10 hertz, a state of deep relaxation. Their mind becomes calm, and it also calms the body. If we could spend some time each day in meditation, we would find our stress levels would be reduced."

Definition of Meditation: -

The present meaning of the word MEDITATION is to 'REFLECT' or 'TO PONDER' i.e. to Weigh or Measure and 'TO GIVE CLOSE ATTENTION'. Similarly the Sanskrit word for MEDITATION is DHYANA, is closely related to DHYATI, meaning to REFLECT. Therefore to Meditate means to Ponder, to Reflect, while giving close attention to what is actually going on as one does so.

Without attempting to probe in to this deeper meaning of meditation, one can however say that meditation can bring order to our overall mental activity and this may be a key factor in bringing about an end to the sorrow, the misery, the chaos and confusion, that have, over the ages, been the lot of mankind, and that are still generally continuing without visible prospect of fundamental change, for the foreseeable future.

Meditation works entirely on the level of Mind, Intellect, and sub-conscious, rather focusing on the bodily forms, postures or rituals. The first stage of meditation is to stabilize the self in the pure experience of the inner tranquility of the Soul. At first the distracting thoughts may come to the mind. One has to train oneself to get involved in a struggle to contain or eradicate them. One has to learn to step away and become an observer as soon as one becomes aware of them.

Through meditation the accuracy of this role is heightened so that positive qualities are permitted entry and continuity while negative ones are weakened and transformed. Meditation can bring real and permanent peace of mind by filling the Intellect with strength and wisdom and purifying the sub conscience. After some practice, one can have the intellectual power the sub-conscience mind at any time. In a situation which would lead most people to experience negative moods or emotions such as fear, depression, anxiety, boredom, fatigue, hatred or aggression, one can become detached and access innate qualities.

Meditation involves the development and refinement of the so-called **Third Eye**, so that one does not see spirituality only but also understand and adjust to it in the most natural way possible.

4 steps in Meditation Practice: –
1. Detach the Self from negative, wasteful and mundane thinking.
2. Create pure or elevated thoughts about your original state and about your original home.
3. Visualize yourself as a point of conscious light energy directly in front of GOD in his radiant form of light.
4. Open yourself to receiving God's love.

Easy way of exercising and meditating for BODY and MIND for 16 minutes daily to reduce stress and increase the focus: -

Get up early in the morning about 16 minutes earlier than your regular time. Perform the following steps after your morning ablutions and before the breakfast.

1. Stand straight on the floor with feet about 6 inches apart. Keep your body straight, Close your eyes, and take a deep breath (inhale) while raising your arms straight up.

2. While exhaling, drop your arms slowly down, bend you body by squeezing the stomach, do not bend the knees, and try to touch your feet and the floor. This should take about 10 seconds. Hold your breath in that position for next 10 seconds. Focus on the sensation of the air moving out of your lungs. (As thoughts come into your mind and distract you from exhaling, acknowledge these thoughts-permit

positive thoughts and try to weaken negative thoughts-and then return to focusing on your exhaling and counting.)

3. While taking a deep breath and inhaling air, raise your body and arms
    up slowly. This should take about 10 seconds. Hold the breath for next
    10 seconds. Focus on the sensation of the air moving into your lungs.
    (As thoughts come into your mind and distract you from breathing,
    acknowledge these thoughts-again permit positive thoughts and try to
    weaken negative thoughts-and then return to focusing on your inhal-
    ing and counting.)

4. Repeat the steps 2 & 3 for 25 times, which should take you about 16
    minutes.

5. Don't judge yourself or try to ignore distractions. Your job is simply
    to notice that your mind has wandered and to bring your attention
    back to your inhaling and exhaling and counting.

The benefits of Meditation: -
1. Transformation of the negative personality traits

2. Obtaining power of self control

3. Improvement of the vision one has of the self and others

4. Inner emotional fulfillment through each of the relationships

5. Replacement of lost or spent spiritual and mental energy

6. Don't do in excess. Too much of anything is not good.

7.08 - BODY-CONSCIOUSNESS – The origin of negativity: [11] & SOUL-CONSCIOUSNESS – The origin of positivity: [11]

In Body Consciousness, Vices are just virtues that have lost their direction
and power.

When I have inner strength, my tendencies and talents are reflected in the form of virtues. If the self is weak, those same tendencies emerge as vices.

In the state of spiritual insecurity the following five main negative forces or vices or emotions are born:

1. **Desire or Lust** – The urge towards sense satisfaction as a means of fulfillment.

2. **Anger** – the feeling of animosity when any of other vices are threatened.

3. **Greed** – The attempt to find fulfillment through the acquisition of material goods, position or status, or through the physical senses as with food.

4. **Attachment** – the attempt to find security through developing relationships of ownership or possessiveness with people and objects.

5. **Ego or Vanity** – The cultivation of a self-image that is false, temporary or unreal.

The basis of sexual, social, racial and religious prejudice that one may have is in the vision and classification of others as their respective bodies, cultures or social customs. It is the ignorance of our true nature that breeds prejudice, that generated conflict, that gives rise to war and hatred and so on. The so-called vicious cycle continues until the seed of ignorance is removed.

We all human beings have these five vices, but these vary in the form of degree or extent. This degree varies from person to person in the range of 25% to 90%. No one is perfect.

Body-consciousness is basically attachment to one's physical self-image. One becomes trapped in the world of name and forms and limit oneself to the condition of the Place, Time, and circumstances that are surrounding him/her.

In Soul Consciousness, Soul is one's Consciousness:
How one sees others is definitely based on the consciousness with which one views him/her. So many possibilities of perception arise when one has to deal

with others. Many times one does not see others, as they really are, but merely as part of their national, cultural or social background. Age, sex, profession, social status and degree of beauty add to the compartments that become subtle or obvious barriers in our relationship with them. They camouflage our own self-identity and tint the glasses through which we observe and therefore react to others.

If we replace all of these categories with the vision of the soul as a tiny dot of conscious energy as distinct from the physical body and all its identifying attributes, it brings a great sense of freedom. One can move away from all the prejudice in a very effective way. Different results are attained according to the level of awareness.

Following is the example of the boss towards his/her employees.

	BODY-CONSCIOUSNESS	SOUL-CONSCIOUSNESS
AWARENESS	I am the boss here; I know more than everyone here. After all, that is why I am the boss.	I am a spiritual being; I have to play out a role of responsibility. Each of my employees has his/her own specific role.
THOUGHT	They should listen to me. After all I am the one who pays their salaries.	Let me listen to their suggestions. Perhaps we can improve something.
DECISION	I will show them who is the boss here.	Let me understand each of their specialties.
ACTION	The boss shouts and argues with them	A two-way dialogue ensues.
RESULT	Ill-feeling between boss and employees	Respect and a climate of trust are maintained.

Consciousness at last:

There is no such thing as unconsciousness, because who is unconscious has no way of knowing that he is unconscious. It is your thinking that makes you feel that you are alive, that you are conscious. That is possible only when the knowledge you have about things is in operation. You become conscious only through the help of thought.

Body Consciousness –Desire, Anger, Greed, Attachment, Ego, = **Sorrow**

Soul Consciousness – Peace, Knowledge, Love, Purity, Bliss, = **Happiness**

7.09 - WE CREATE OUR OWN DESTINY: -

The steps of my journey towards higher consciousness are what I actually do and not just think or speak.

If a man speaks or acts with an evil thought, sorrow will follow him as the cart goes after the ox.

What I create is what is going to happen, if I choose to exchange love and peace in my interaction with others, I create relationship based on those qualities.

The idea of God as the pusher does not fit in with a God of love, mercy and compassion.

I am the architect of my own destiny. Fate or destiny is just the effect of my own acts.

Whatever I sow, I reap in all three ways; Thoughts, Words and Actions.

I am the master of my fate: I am the captain of my soul.

The five types of thoughts are created in our minds: -

1. **Waste Thoughts** – Those that have nothing to do with reality. This includes doubts, excuses, the creation and continuance of unrealistic

fantasies (building castles in the air), worry about trivialities, confusion, misunderstandings and paranoia.

2. **Negative Thoughts** – Those that have origin in the vices such as desire, anger, greed, attachments, and ego.

3. **Necessary Thoughts** – Those connected with the activities of one's family, professional, social or other responsibilities. This includes looking after one's own health and hygiene.

4. **Ordinary Thoughts** – Those associated with mundane matters, news and views about situations.

5. **Elevated Thoughts** – Those related to meditative introspection, the contemplation of aspects of spiritual knowledge or self-development and spiritual service for others – real creative thinking.

7.10 - GOD, THE MISSING CONNECTION: -

If I have been searching for a **LOVE** that never lets me down, a **TRUTH** that is unshakeable, and a **BEAUTY** that goes beyond the superficial, I have indeed been searching for **GOD**. – Perhaps without even knowing it.

If a survey were to be done among believers throughout the world as to the **identity and attributes of GOD**, answers will be following:

The Creative Principle
All-Powerful
All loving, all knowing
Absolute Truth
Supreme parent (Mother / Father)
Some form of superior non-physical energy.
GOD is one, morally perfect and absolute just
GOD is the supreme benefactor
Finally GOD is Omniscient, Omnipotent, Omnipresent, Omnibenevolent, and Omni truth.

On the basis of our similarities of form and abode, I learn from God of my own original attributes of Peace, Purity, Love, Truth, Power, Happiness, and Balance.

GOD as the Mother and Father and other relationships

In the perfect personality of the supreme there is the feminine principle of **loving, giving and accepting.** This is perfectly balanced with the masculine principle of **power, authority and strength.**

Because GOD is the SOUL: - neither old nor young, nor male nor female, has the most perfect personality, there are so many different ways we can entertain ourselves in this highest and purest form of the relationships.

God as Teacher – Discovery of wisdom and truth
God as supreme guide – Directions for each step on the spiritual path.
God as friend – Conversation, support at any moment
God as Beloved – Sharing of intimacies, long-term support
God as Manager – Readiness to execute instructions
God as Child – Giving of all I have
God as Healer – Correct diagnosis and cure of weakness
God as Broker – Wise investment for my future.

"Lord wherever I am, You are with me" – It does not mean literally that the Supreme Being permeates everything; it's just a feeling, and not a fact.

God's power is purely spiritual. Birth and death, accidents and natural calamities are part of the interplay between human souls themselves and with matter directly. They are nothing to do with God

7.11 - SCIENCE AND THE SOUL: -
Mind is a tough thing to think about. Consciousness is the defining feature of the human species. Recent research suggests that our conscious minds play less of a role in making decisions than many people have long assumed. The **Dopamine neurons** are responsible for telling the rest of the brain what stimuli to pay attention to.

Older understandings implement in traditions as ancient as Judaism or Buddhism – in which subject and object, **mind and matter are more interfused than opposed**. Exploring the relationship between the physical brain and consciousness is not simply one of the last great intellectual frontiers, but it also sheds light on some of the most vexing life and death issues facing us today.

Consciousness is so tied up with what we think of as our inner selves, our spiritual being, that many of the greatest minds of history have assigned it to an order of reality entirely different from the rest of the natural, physical world. Plato, most influentially, separated the soul, or psyche, from the material body and argued that this reasoning part of our being was immortal. His idea was so powerful and attractive that it has kept philosophers intimately engaged with it to this day. Platonic ideas have left a lasting imprint on Christian beliefs. The body may die, many Christians hold, but the SOUL lives on, presumably extending in to eternity those qualities that we associate with our conscious minds and our sense of selfhood. The bodily organs sent perceptions and other information via the brain to the mind, located in the pineal gland in the middle of the head. Reflecting upon these data, mind then made decisions and directed the body's responses in words or deeds.

The astonishing hypothesis: - The scientific search for the soul.

According to this hypothesis "you", " your joys and sorrows, your memories and your ambitions, your sense of personal identity and free will, are in fact no more than the behavior of a vast assembly of nerve cells and their associated molecules. There are very specific neurons that sub serve consciousness. The real challenge is to develop generic techniques to selectively activate and deactivate specific groups of neurons to see how they are related to different conscious states. The neuromodulators are the underlying chemistry of mood, emotions and feelings. The emotions are the most basic form of consciousness. The consciousness produces orderly, grammatical representations of something out there in the world that is meaningful, but it does not create meaning. The consciousness may be the interface between the fundamental quantum world of information and the physical world that is more accessible to our senses.

Mind:
The mind is more than the sum of the parts that support it, and not just a machine that respond to external stimuli. Within religion itself there is also fresh

thought about the implications of the new science of mind for core religious principles and beliefs.

Consciousness:
The new science of consciousness by showing the inseparable links between mind and body, restore the original Christian conception of the unity of the person. As many Christian theologians now say like old Hindu and Buddhism philosophy that **Human beings do not have SOULS; they are the SOULS.** Here Christians and others might turn to the wisdom of Buddhism, in which the self is correctly understood not as an entity or substance but as a dynamic process.

Brain:
The brain, which does more than any organ, reveals least of all. The 3 lbs. lump of wrinkled tissue – with no moving parts, no joints or valves – not only serves as the motherboard for all the body's other systems, but also is the seat of your mind, your thoughts, and your sense that you exist at all. You have a liver, you have your limbs, and you are your brain.

Conclusion:
In recent years, the scientific study of consciousness has taken hold, if not always steady, steps in the direction of understanding the experience of wholeness and human spirituality in general. If religion can learn something valuable about the unity of body and mind from science, then science might be able to relearn something from religion about the deepest purpose of our minds.

THE MYSTRY OF CONSCIOSNESS: -
The major religions locate it in a soul that survives the body's death to receive its just deserts or blend in to a global mind. **For each of us consciousness is life itself.**

Scientists are trying to prove as to how 100 billion jabbering neurons create the knowledge-or illusion-that you are here. The hard problem is explaining how subjective experience arises from neutral computation. The problem is hard because no one knows what a solution will look like or even whether it is a genuine scientific problem in the first place. And not surprisingly, every one agrees that the hard problem (if it is a problem) remains a mystery. **Scientists have amassed evidence that every aspect of consciousness can be tied to the brain.** Using functional MRI, cognitive neuroscientists can almost read people's thoughts from the blood flow in their brain. They can tell for instance, whether a person is thinking about a face or a place or whether a picture a person is looking at is of a bottle or a shoe.

Death:

When the physiological activity of the brain ceases, as for as anyone can tell the person's consciousness goes out of existence. Attempts to contact the souls of the dead (a pursuit of serious scientists a century ago) turned up only cheap magic tricks, and near death experiences are not the eyewitness reports of soul parting the company from the body but symptoms of oxygen starvation in the eyes and the brain. A team of Swiss neuroscientists reported that they could turn out-of-body experiences on and off by stimulating the part of the brain in which the vision and bodily sensation converge.

Freedom:

Freedom is a state of mind. Understanding the self is the key to freedom. The more one understands the self, the easier it is to be liberated from the chains of waste and negativity. Freedom is to be uninfluenced and unaffected, to be at peace with the self. Real freedom is to experience the true essence of one's being.

Patience:

Patience is the willingness to work with the process of growth. The good, the positive and the true cannot be attained immediately or automatically, they require time and some form of process. Sometimes we have to act, but sometimes we have to wait. People often try to force things to happen. Occasionally force works, but then we are not left with the feeling of true accomplishment. If every inch of success is gained through a battle or a conflict, the victory is hollow.

The most important virtue needed for self-transformation is Patience. Without Patience you will lose hope in the transformation process.

As you travel the path you sometimes run into rough spots, where the foot slips and you find yourself suddenly not on the path, and there are wrong thoughts or words or behavior

Patience makes you cool and calm. It makes the journey possible.

The process of self-realization is not a ten-yard dash, it is the one hundred and fifty mile run, and you have to learn to pace yourself. Patience teaches you to pace yourself

You can't take help from God until there is patience of this kind

Where there is patience there is peace, where there is peace, there is love.

This is a whole new experience of what it means to be human

Balance:
The indication of balance in life is a sense of wellbeing, optimism and a clear conscience. The foundation for achieving this is to look after myself spiritually - making my mind peaceful, loving and thoughtful at all times. Then I will instinctively know how much to spend on my own well being and how much on fulfilling other responsibilities. I can only give my best to others when I am myself at my best.

Be Yourself:
Much of the tension in our lives arises when we consciously or subconsciously imitate others. If we listen to ourselves we will often here the voice of a parent, an older sibling, perhaps a charismatic teacher from school days. Imitation is the cheapest way to live. It is unnatural, and a sign that we are not thinking for ourselves. And deep down, our conscience knows it. We are under the thrall of another's personality, sometimes several. Awareness is the only way free. Reflect on what you say and do. Can you see or hear others in your thoughts, words and emotions? Don't struggle, don't resist, just be aware and choose to say and do the things YOU want to say and do...yourself. Gradually, the real authentic you will emerge from the shadows. And one day it will be your turn to turn to someone and gently say, "Be yourself!"

7.12 - DETACHMENT: -
Your need power to remain free from the influence of others. Detachment is this power. If you cannot remain detached from influences, you will not be able to keep your thoughts under control. From there it will be a down-

ward spiral until all trace of inner well-being is lost. The first step in detachment is to understand who you are as a spiritual entity. This allows you to detach yourself from your physical identity, and its world of limited thoughts and feelings and attach instead to your spiritual personality, the being of inner peace and power. A normal day will be filled with challenges to this detachment. On the one side will be your spiritual awareness, but on the other side will be the attraction towards human beings and material world. Detachment is not a question of becoming separate from the later, but of simply remaining conscience of yourself as a spiritual being whilst being in the world and playing your part. Detachment simply means to keep yourself centered in your spirituality.

How to Develop Detachment?
"We need to reach a state in which, while we are living in this world, we are detached from it. We need to realize that all the possessions of this world are transitory. They are an illusion."

"If we can get to a state where we can control our desires, then we will find that our life will move in harmony with its environment, our mind will be at peace, and we will be able to make tremendous strides towards the ultimate aim of our life, which is to know our real self and to be one with God."

"Being content does not mean inaction. We must still do our work in the world. We must still try to earn an honest livelihood. We must still do our best in whatever field we are placed. We must still do our best to provide for our families. The difference is that we do so with a spirit of detachment. We do our work but are not attached to the results."

"Let us not think that this is the real world. Let us recognize that this is the world of Maya, the world of illusion. But even though we are in this world of illusion, this is a grand opportunity that God has given for us to recognize ourselves. Let us know that each one of us has been created by the hand of God, has been created by God. That realization we will only have as we go within and experience the divine Light and Sound of God."

7.13 - WHAT IS THE SOUL? (Explanation in the story form)
Well worth reading. Enjoy!

The King & His Four Wives
Read This Carefully, very powerful thoughts.

Once upon a time there was a rich King who had four wives. He loved the 4th wife the most and adorned her with rich robes and treated her to the finest of delicacies. He gave her nothing but the best.

He also loved the 3rd wife very much and was always showing her off to neighboring kingdoms. However, he feared that one day she would leave him for another.

He also loved his 2nd wife. She was his confidant and was always kind, considerate and patient with him. Whenever the King faced a problem, he could confide in her, and she would help him get through the difficult times.

The King's 1st wife was a very loyal partner and had made great contributions in maintaining his wealth and kingdom. However, he did not love the first wife. Although she loved him deeply, he hardly took notice of her!

One day, the King fell ill and he knew his time was short. He thought of his luxurious life and wondered, "I now have four wives with me, but when I die, I'll be all alone".
Thus, he asked the 4th wife, "I have loved you the most, endowed you with the finest clothing and showered great care over you. Now that I'm dying, will you follow me and keep me company?"

"No way!" replied the 4th wife, and she walked away without another word.

Her answer cut like a sharp knife right into his heart. The sad King then asked the 3rd wife, "I have loved you all my life. Now that I'm dying, will you follow me and keep me company?"

"No!" replied the 3rd wife. "Life is too good! When you die, I'm going to remarry!" His heart sank and turned cold.

He then asked the 2nd wife, "I have always turned to you for help and you've always been there for me. When I die, will you follow me and keep me company?"

"I'm sorry, I can't help you out this time!" replied the 2nd wife. "At the very most, I can only send you to your grave." Her answer came like a bolt of lightning, and the King was Devastated.

Then a voice called out: "I'll leave with you and follow you no matter where you go." The King looked up, and there was his first wife. She was so skinny as she suffered from malnutrition and neglect.

Greatly grieved, the King said, "I should have taken much better care of you when I had the chance!"

In truth, we all have 4 wives in our lives: Our 4th wife is our body. No matter how much time and effort we lavish in making it look good, it will leave us when we die. Our 3rd wife is our possessions, status and wealth. When we die, it will all go to others. Our 2nd wife is our family and friends. No matter how much they have been there for us, the furthest they can stay by us is up to the grave. And our 1st wife is our SOUL. Often neglected in pursuit of wealth, power and pleasures of the world. However, our SOUL is the only thing that will follow us wherever we go.

Cultivate, strengthen and cherish it now, for it is the only part of us that will follow us to the throne of God and continue with us throughout Eternity.

When the world pushes you to your knees. You're in the perfect position to pray.

7.14 - SPIRITUALITY: -

"Spirituality is an awakening of the divine consciousness, which is within everyone. In order to take up the spiritual path we have to become more conscious. By taking alcohol or drugs, instead of expanding our consciousness, we dull it."

Spirituality is not only concerned with our own inner development. It is a way of living in which we also have love and concern for all other life in creation.

"Spirituality is recognizing that behind these outer names and outer labels we are all SOULs, a part of the one Creator. As such, we are all members of one family. When we develop this angle of vision, we no longer see through the eyes of prejudice and discrimination. We start breaking down the barriers that separate one human being from another. We start feeling like we are all connected at the level of soul."

Introversion

The ability to enjoy one's own company is one of the greatest gifts life has to offer. Learning to turn my thoughts away from all my responsibilities at the day's end and take my mind into a state of peace and benevolence enables me to carry greater and greater loads without feeling the burden. When my inner landscape is full of beautiful thoughts, everything I do is a pleasure. Gently, I calm down chaotic situations and offer comfort to troubled minds.

Introspection

Introspection is the attitude of going inside when it's necessary. It is especially applicable before a task or a busy day. The result of going inside is peace and calmness, which gives clarity to the intellect for making right decisions. Introspection does not mean avoiding the world, it means going inside and getting empowered to act along with others.

Positive Thoughts

A mother teaches her child with love and patience until the child learns. Be a mother and teach your mind to have positive thoughts and to let go of worries. Then when your mind needs peace, it will obey you.

The Wonder Of Silence

When the soul goes deep into silence, easiness emerges. The deeper I go into silence, the greater will be my power of tolerance. It is in very deep, extreme silence that the soul becomes elevated. It is in deep, deep silence that God can come in front of the soul.

Look Inwards

We all have three eyes. Two for looking out and one for looking in. Why would we want to look in when everything is happening 'out there'? Because the treasure we seek is inside, not outside. **What is treasure? Beauty, truth, peace, happiness.** You already have what you seek. You already are stunningly beautiful. You are already peaceful and loving. How come you don't know this? Simple, you never look inwards, beyond superficial memories or recent experiences, so you never see your own riches. Take a moment to stop, look in and see. Don't rush. Don't search. Just look. And be aware.

Miss Nothing

Being enlightened means being self-aware. Awareness of yourself means you don't miss anything inside. You are aware of things like the quality of your thoughts and feelings, of how you sometimes give your power to others, and how your self-esteem occasionally fluctuates. You don't miss anything because you know that knowing yourself is vital to being comfortable with yourself. Are you comfortable with yourself? No! Then be with your self, talk to your self, listen to your self today. Take a few moments out and have a meeting with yourself. Put yourself in your diary. Put your self at the top of your list. And write next to it, 'being with myself'. Miss nothing in your self.'

Seed Of Action

Acts of virtue emerge from deep within, from an inner sanctuary of silence from which inspiration flows. Every action has its seed in a thought and every thought is a creation of the thinker, the soul. I choose what thoughts I want to create and as is my thinking so are my actions and also my experience in life. Going within, I touch the stillness and pure love that lie at the core of my being and every thought that I create is of benefit to myself and of benefit to humanity.

MATURITY

As we mature spiritually there is less need to have our self-respect bolstered by praise and special attention. As our thought processes become more compassionate and less self-obsessed, we feel increasingly satisfied with our lives and ourselves. We relate to people more easily and feel no need to draw attention to our successes or complain about our problems.

Selfless service means that we help others without any desire for a reward. We serve because we have an innate desire in the core of our heart to help others."

Just as the highest tower needs a deep foundation, so too our higher thinking is based on going deep within.

Power On
Each day we all need to recharge our spiritual battery, otherwise the light of our consciousness becomes dim, thoughts become fuzzy, and decisions are impregnated with doubt. Power is available inside and outside. Inside us we have a spiritual center, at the core of our consciousness, pure radiant spiritual light. This is what we are. However it is now blocked by our attachments, the record of all our life experiences and many learned beliefs and perceptions. Outside us we have the sun of spirit, the source, invisible to our physical eyes but only one second away when we are able to be quiet and focus our mind. Meditation connects us to both sources of power - that's why meditation is the way to access the real vitamins and the minerals that spirit craves. The vitamin of pure love and the minerals of truth and wisdom. Take time to empower yourself today. Sit quietly and connect your mind to each source and allow yourself to recharge and renew.

Heal Yourself
The deepest wounds we all carry are locked in our subconscious (out of our awareness). Deep memories and subtle impressions, from unfinished experience, rooted in the past. The pain from those wounds comes to revisit, to block and paralyze us in the moment called now. We all know it comes without warning - "Why am I feeling this way, I didn't mean to do that, I don't know what made me say that." Healing does not mean finding and treating every single inner scar, which send it message to haunt us. It means going even deeper, past those wounds, beyond those distant memories and recording of unfinished business, to the core of our self, to the heart of our spirit, where we find the light and warmth of our own core qualities of love and peace. They are eternally present within us they are what we need to heal all our inner wounds. That's why this kind of deep healing is called spirituality and not therapy.

Remind Yourself
If you know a little of yourself, you will have realized that you are more than meets your eyes in the mirror in the morning. What you see is not what you

are. You see the form not the content, the body not the soul, and the matter not the mind. In quiet and profound moments, we innately know that is true. But we forget. The world tells us and wants us to believe that we are what we see - and we take the easy way out. We believe. That's why the awakening of spirit and the flowering of our spirituality (nothing to do with religion) means we have to keep reminding ourselves, a hundred times a day, I am a soul - not a body, I am an eternal spirit - not a perishable piece of meat. I am quality, not quantity. I am. Otherwise, freedom is not possible. And if we are not free, in the deepest space inside our own being, we cannot be truly happy.

Spiritual Language
To create the future we desire we need a spiritual language; we must speak from the heart and in the language of the soul - a language of trust, faith and higher values, of inner growth, love and listening.

Purity
A powerful, yet often misunderstood, aim of spiritual study is purity. Purity of the SOUL means to return to its original divine qualities. The SOUL has become so polluted with less than divine qualities; it can hardly enjoy being alive. Purifying the SOUL puts the higher self back in charge - useless and negative thoughts are removed and annoying habits finish. A pure SOUL cannot be touched by sorrow; indeed the power of purity is such, it serves to remove the sorrow of the whole world. Purity restores happiness - even bliss. All you need to do, in order to re-establish your purity, is want it. But you need to want it intensely, to the exclusion of everything else. The one thought, "I must become completely pure". Sparks a fire of love between you and God. This fire melts away all the pollution, and your purity becomes such a power that it frees you from all battles forever.

Divine Power
"What is that urge within man to persist in his quest for the Ideal? What is it that enables him to pursue his goal despite all obstacles, sacrifices and suffering? There is within each of us a divine impulse to reach beyond our seeming limitations to that, which is ideal and eternal."

PEACE
Peace consists of pure thoughts, pure feelings and pure wishes. When the energy of thought, word and action is balanced and stable, the individual is at

peace with the self, in relationships and the world. To exercise the power of peace look inward in order to look outward with courage, purpose and meaning.

Spiritual Progress

There is benefit for you in every situation. If, that is, you know how to look for it. The idea behind steady spiritual progress is to see every circumstance and situation (particularly those that challenge you) as a tailor-made lesson in your personal plan for self-development. For example, in a situation where hurtful or angry words were exchanged, why not see it as the chance either to perceive things about your own character which need changing or to rehearse some virtue or quality that you need to put into practice more often? Actually, we should be grateful for the opportunity to evaluate ourselves. In this way you can transform anything into a constructive lesson. Never think that you've learned enough and now can stop. You should love it when people try to correct you or give you advice. It keeps you alert and gives you plenty of opportunity to put your truth into practice. It's a sign of great danger to be unable to accept criticism and instead use your understanding to criticize others. Realize deeply the significance of every moment, and your spiritual progress will be assured.

Eye Of The Storm

A wise sea captain caught in a tropical storm knows that if he holds his vessel on the periphery it will get hurled from one side to the other. If he can reach the eye of the storm, he will enter a place of stillness. The storm will then subside and the ship can continue its journey. Similarly, when everything around me is changing in a very intense way, the best place for me to seek shelter and refuge is not on the outside, but deep within the self, where I can get in touch with my own inner being, find strength and stability, then come out and do whatever it is I need to.

Divine Help

Many times people report the feeling of divine help and strength when they come close to breaking point. Actually divine help is always there, but I am usually so busy doing things in my own little way that I only look for it when I face absolute defeat. The tranquil nature of enlightened souls comes from their ability to take God's help constantly. A state of true surrender will lead to the feeling of victory in everything I do.

Go Deep

Most of us think too much, especially about events and people, local and global, famous and not so famous. When we are always thinking about what is happening on the surface of life, the visible, then it is as if we are living a superficial life. Deep down inside there is a voice, a longing, and a calling to depth. It's our heart, reminding us to visit, explore and express the depths of us. Going deep and being deep requires time spent in solitude, some periods of introversion and a conversation with us. How on earth will we ever see what is in our heart unless we dive deep inside, switch on the light and look. Those who do will tell you it change everything. What do they see? Simple, only beauty and truth. They are always there, waiting for us to return. Waiting to welcome us and to introduce ourselves to our self.

Love

Love is a powerful force. It can take us to great heights and leave us feeling light and airy. Yet it has been the most abused and misused force. Many degraded things pass for love. True love is based on understanding, mutual trust and respect and not simply on transient emotions. Love is being in balance, that is, in harmony with the self, God and each other. Love dwells in the soul. We must allow this love to flow out and around us. Without love, all of life's treasures are locked away from our vision and experiences, for indeed **'love is the key.'**

CHAPTER 8

WHAT IS "HAPPINESS"?

8.01 – HAPPINESS: -

1. The quality or state of being happy.

2. Good fortune; pleasure; contentment; joy.

3. Pleasure, joy, exhilaration, bliss, contentedness, delight, enjoyment, satisfaction.

4. Happiness, bliss, contentment, felicity, imply an active or passive state of pleasure or pleasurable satisfaction.

5. Happiness - results from the possession or attainment of what one considers good: the happiness of visiting one's family.

6. Bliss - is pure or absolute happiness or supreme delight: the bliss of perfect companionship.

7. Contentment - is a peaceful kind of happiness in which one rests without desires, even though every wish may not have been gratified: contentment in one's surroundings.

8. Felicity - is a formal word for happiness of an especially fortunate or intense kind: to wish a young couple felicity (pleasure) in life.

9. It is a state of well being characterized by emotions ranging from contentment to intense joy.

10. It is emotions experienced when in a state of well-being.

11. It is a feeling the experiencing of effective and emotional state.

12. It is enjoying or showing or marked by joy or pleasure.

13. Whereas Unhappiness is experiencing or marked by or causing sadness or sorrow or discontentment.

Definition of Happiness

Happiness is a mental or emotional state of well-being characterized by positive or pleasant emotions ranging from contentment to intense joy. A variety of biological, psychological, religious, and philosophical approaches have striven to define happiness and identify its sources.

Various research groups, including Positive psychology, endeavor to apply the scientific method to answer questions about what "happiness" is, and how we might attain it.

Philosophers and religious thinkers often define happiness in terms of living a good life, or flourishing, rather than simply as an emotion. *Happiness* in this sense was used to translate the Greek Eudaimonia, and is still used in virtue ethics.

Happiness economics suggests that measures of public happiness should be used to supplement more traditional economic measures when evaluating the success of public policy.

Happiness is a fuzzy concept and can mean many things to many people. Part of the challenge of a science of happiness is to identify different concepts of happiness, and where applicable, split them into their components.

Money doesn't buy much happiness unless it's used in certain ways. "Beyond the point at which people have enough to comfortably feed, clothe, and house themselves, having more money - even a lot more money - makes them only a little bit happier." However we can sometimes get more happiness bang for our buck by spending it in prosocial ways. A Harvard Business School study found that **"spending money on others actually makes us happier than spending it on ourselves"**.

There are various factors that have been correlated with happiness, but no validated method has been found to substantially improve long-term happiness in a meaningful way for most people.

Psychologist Martin Seligman provides the acronym PERMA to summarize Positive Psychology's correlational findings: humans seem happiest when they have

1. *Pleasure* (tasty foods, warm baths, etc.),
2. *Engagement* (or flow, the absorption of an enjoyed yet challenging activity),
3. *Relationships* (social ties have turned out to be extremely reliable indicator of happiness),
4. *Meaning* (a perceived quest or belonging to something bigger), and
5. *Accomplishments* (having realized tangible goals).

Sociologists define happiness as the degree to which person evaluates the overall quality of his present life as a whole positively. In other words how much a person likes life he or she leads.

By happiness I mean here a deep sense of flourishing that arises from an exceptionally healthy mind. This is not a mere pleasurable feeling, a fleeting emotion, or a mood but an optimal state of being. Many people will talk about short-term happiness like a birth of a child, or an exam they have aced, or a sporting victory etc. The common factor of all these short-term experiences would seem to be the momentary disappearance of inner conflicts. The person feels in harmony with the world and the self.

Real happiness is the state of lasting well-being that manifests itself when we have freed ourselves of mental blindness and afflictive emotions. It is also the wisdom that allows us to see the world as it is, without veils or distortions. It is finally the joy of moving toward inner freedom and the loving kindness that radiates towards others. Ignorance is an inability to recognize the true nature of things and of the law of cause and effect that governs happiness and suffering.

8.02 - HAPPINESS IN LIFE: -

When wickedness prevails there is disorder in every field of life, but where goodness rules, order prevails and people are happy. They are happy not in the sense that their material needs are satisfied, but in the sense that they lead virtuous and contented lives. As for material possessions, some men have fortunes and yet have a distracted life. That is no sign of happiness.

The same law applies to the world of the living, which applies to the world of inert matter. As clay and gold are ultimately the same substance, so the saint and the sinner are ultimately one. They are both manifestations of the SOUL. The layer of uncleanliness has disappeared from over the saint's SOUL and is becoming ever thicker over the sinner's SOUL. We should have risen above this ordinary level only when we learn to have equal regard for either. He who rises above both happiness and misery has achieved Yoga. Yoga here means absence of suffering, never feeling miserable.

The speed of air can be measured by a meteorologist and that of electricity by a scientist; but no machine has yet been invented to measure the speed of the mind. It is unsteady and restless. We should withdraw it from every direction in which it flies and fix it in the right place, that is, in the SOUL.

He who acts towards others as if they were himself, will meet their needs as if they were his own, he would do to others what he will do to himself, will learn to look upon himself and the world as one. He is the true saint who is happy when others are happy and suffers when others suffer.

We should let no impurity enter our thoughts. Parents give us the human form, sometimes a form like their own. The subtle changes, which take place within us, become visible through our eyes. If we get a disease, we should believe that we ourselves are the cause of it. A person whose mind is so strong that he influences his surroundings instead of being influenced by them gets no disease. It is for our good therefore, to believe that our illness is the result of our own sins.

One should see oneself in the whole world and the whole world in oneself and act towards others accordingly. The ideal of non-violence had its origin in this realization – that when human life is full of suffering, we should cause suffering to no one.

Anger consumes many times more energy than does joy. It is because people spend more energy than they can afford that injustice and tyranny prevail in the world. Enjoyment of sense pleasure leads to death.

8.03 - RELIGION AND HAPPINESS: -

There is now extensive research suggesting that religious people are happier and less stressed. There are a number of mechanisms through which religion may make a person happier, including social contact and support that result from religious pursuits, the mental activity that comes with optimism and volunteering, learned coping strategies that enhance one's ability to deal with stress, and psychological factors such as "reason for being." It may also be that religious people engage in behaviors related to good health, such as less substance abuse, since the use of psychotropic substances is sometimes considered abuse.

The *Handbook of Religion and Health* describes a survey by Feigelman (1992) who examined happiness in Americans who have given up religion, in which it was found that there was little relationship between religious disaffiliation and unhappiness. A survey by Kosmin & Lachman (1993), also cited in this handbook, indicates that people with no religious affiliation appear to be at greater risk for depressive symptoms than those affiliated with a religion.

The Legatum Prosperity Index reflects the repeated finding of research on the science of happiness that there is a positive link between religious engagement and wellbeing: people who report that GOD is very important in their lives are on average more satisfied with their lives, after accounting for their income, age and other individual characteristics.

Surveys by Gallup, the National Opinion Research Center and the Pew Organization conclude that spiritually committed people are twice as likely to report being "very happy" than the least religiously committed people. An analysis of over 200 social studies contends that "high religiousness predicts a lower risk of depression and drug abuse and fewer suicide attempts, and more reports of satisfaction with sex life and a sense of well-being," and a review of 498 studies published in peer-reviewed journals concluded that a large majority of them showed a positive correlation between religious commitment and higher levels of perceived well-being and self-esteem and lower levels of hypertension, depression, and clinical delinquency. A meta-analysis of 34 recent studies published between 1990 and 2001 found that religiosity has a helpful relationship with psychological adjustment, being related to less psychological distress, more life satisfaction, and better self-actualization Finally, a recent systematic review of 850 research papers on the topic concluded that "the majority of well-conducted studies found that higher levels of religious involvement are positively associated with indicators of psychological well-being (life satisfaction, happiness, positive affect, and higher morale) and with less depression, suicidal thoughts and behavior, drug/alcohol use/abuse."

Happiness vs. Religion: -
Religious people are less stressed and happier than non-believers – WHY?

Some studies show that religion buffers its adherents from worry. Religious people are less depressed, less anxious and less suicidal than nonreligious people. And they are better able to cope with such crises as illness, divorce and bereavement.

Studies also show that the more a believer incorporates religion into daily living-attending services, reading scriptures, praying – the better off he or she appears to be on two measures of happiness: frequency of positive emotions and overall sense of satisfaction with life. Attending services has a particularly strong correlation to feeling happy, and religious certainty – the sense of unshakable faith in God and truth of one's beliefs – is more closely linked with life satisfaction.

We know that religion's benefits can be divided into following four areas:

1. **Social support** – Religion, after all, derives from the Latin Religion meaning "to bind together". – Linking individuals to families and ancestors, friends and community, clergy and congregation.
2. **Spiritual support** - If you believe there is GOD watching out, for you, which is profoundly comforting. It is the grand scale equivalent of thinking, if I can't pay my rent at the end of the month, my dad will help.
3. **A sense of purpose and meaning** – Doing good works through acts

of charity or prayer and meditation, provides another sense of connection to community for many believers. That is a key factor in Buddhism's capacity to foster happiness. A person might emulate the Buddha by imagining he's breathing in the suffering of others and breathing out energy to heal them.

4.   **The avoidance of risky and stressful behaviors.** – In a national study of thousands of adolescents, it was found that teens who attend services, read the bible and pray, feel less sad or depressed, less alone, less misunderstood and guilty and more cared for than their non religious peers. People can benefit from spirituality without subscribing to a particular doctrine.

Methodological considerations:

The studies cited above test only correlation, as opposed to causation; they do not distinguish between various possible explanations. These include the following:

- The religious *belief* itself in fact promotes satisfaction and that non-belief does not promote satisfaction and/or promotes dissatisfaction
- Satisfaction and dissatisfaction contribute to religious belief and disbelief, respectively (i.e. satisfied persons may be more inclined to endorse the existence of a traditionally defined deity than dissatisfied people)
- confounding variables may well promote satisfaction rather than religion itself.

Terror management:

Terror management theory maintains that people suffer cognitive dissonance (anxiety) when they are reminded of their inevitable death. Through terror management, individuals are motivated to seek consonant elements - symbols which make sense of mortality and death in satisfactory ways (i.e. boosting self-esteem). Research has found that strong belief in religious *or* secular meaning systems affords psychological security and hope. It is moderates (e.g. agnostics, slightly religious individuals) who likely suffer the most anxiety from their meaning systems. Religious meaning systems are especially adapted to manage death anxiety because they are unlikely to be disconfirmed (for various reasons), they are all encompassing, and they promise literal immortality. Citizens of the world's poorest countries are the most likely to be religious, and researchers suggest this is because of religion's powerful coping abilities.

Buddhism:

Happiness forms a central theme of Buddhist teachings. For ultimate freedom from suffering, the Noble Eightfold Path leads its practitioner to Nirvana, a state of everlasting peace. Ultimate happiness is only achieved by overcoming craving in all forms. More mundane forms of happiness, such as acquiring wealth and maintaining good friendships, are also recognized as worthy goals for lay people. Buddhism also encourages the generation of loving kindness and compassion, the desire for the happiness and welfare of all beings.

Catholicism:

In Catholicism, the ultimate end of human existence consists in felicity (contentment) (Latin equivalent to the Greek *eudaimonia*), or "blessed happiness", described by the 13th-century philosopher-theologian Thomas Aquinas as a Beatific Vision of God's essence in the next life.

In the *Nicomachean Ethics*, written in 350 BCE, Aristotle stated that happiness (also being well and doing well) is the only thing that humans desire for its own sake, unlike riches, honor, health or friendship. He observed that men sought riches, or honor, or health not only for their own sake but also in order to be happy. Note that *eudaimonia*, the term we translate as "happiness", is for Aristotle an activity rather than an emotion or a state. Happiness is characteristic of a good life, that is, a life in which a person fulfills human nature in an excellent way. People have a set of purposes which are typically human: these belong to our nature. The happy person is virtuous, meaning they have outstanding abilities and emotional tendencies which allow him or her to fulfill our common human ends. **For Aristotle, then, happiness is "the virtuous activity of the soul in accordance with reason": happiness is the practice of virtue.**

8.04 - LIFE IS PURSUIT OF HAPPINESS: - [17]

Happiness is what everyone is seeking for, but the majority seeks in things, which are evanescent and not real. No happiness was ever found in the senses or in enjoyment of senses. Happiness is found only in the spirit. We the immortal, the ever pure, the perfect spirit, think we are little minds and we are little bodies. It is the mother of all selfishness. As soon as I think I am a little body, I want to preserve it, to protect it, to keep it nice, at the expense of other bodies. If a small fraction part of the human beings living today can put aside the idea of selfishness, narrowness and littleness, this earth will become a paradise.

Common prudent human beings think that the purpose of our existence is to seek happiness, it seems like common sense. But isn't life based on seeking personal happiness by nature self centered, even self-indulgent?

Not necessarily, in fact survey after survey has shown that it is unhappy people who tend to be most self focused and are often socially withdrawn, brooding and even antagonistic (aggressive). Happy people on contrast are generally found to be more sociable, flexible, creative and are able to tolerate life's daily frustrations more easily than unhappy people.

The turning towards happiness as a valid goal and the conscious decision to seek happiness in a systematic manner can profoundly change the rest of our lives.

What is Heaven?
Heaven is the idea of happiness minus unhappiness. We want joys of this life minus sorrows. Naturally this is a good idea, but there is no such thing as absolutely good or as such thing as absolutely evil. For example there was a rich man in America who one day learnt from his accountant that he has only one million dollar left of his property. He thought, "What will he do tomorrow?" and therefore committed suicide. A million dollars were poverty to him.

What is joy and what is happiness?
These are relative terms. Joy for one may be sorrow for the other. Everyone's idea of pleasure and sorrow is different. Our pleasures and sorrows are always changing. It changes with the change of our necessities.

Modern medicine and Healthy Life: -
The skills of modern medicine are amazing. The miracles of healing performed by modern medicine are astounding. But the time has come when modern medicine must take a step forward. Doctors must find a way of treating the whole human being. Modern medicine takes care only of the body like a machine, which can be repaired when it goes out of order. **Man is a composite**

being built of body, mind and soul. Each one of us is essentially a soul. If the soul is sick, do whatever you do to the body, it will keep on moving from one sickness to another. We need to treat the whole human being.

Doctors should teach the psychology of mind. Always be positive in your outlook upon life and expect the best. Plant beautiful thoughts in your mind. Control your anger, and animal appetites. Many doctors are drawing a correlation between an individual personality and the nature of his disease. Give and forgive and live a healthy life.

1. The foundation of healthy body is a happy mind. Therefore let nothing agitate you or disturb your inner peace. Keep your upstairs (Brain) clean and your downstairs (Body) will be healthy.
2. Eat a balancEd diet.
3. Drink sufficient water.
4. Take plenty of fresh air and sunshine.
5. Laugh heartily. Laughter is at once a physical, mental and spiritual tonic.
6. You must have sufficient sleep.
7. You must have adequate exercise.
8. You must have proper elimination (via bowels, kidneys, lungs and skin)
9. Everyday you must spend some time in silence, Pray, Meditate, do your spiritual thinking.
10. You must adopt a cheerful and positive attitude.

How can we overcome stress?

To overcome stress you need to understand what stress stands for:

1. S – Smile - keep smiling
2. T – Tolerance - grow in tolerance
3. R – Relax – never be tensed
4. E – Easy – Take it easy but not be lazy
5. S – Service – keep serving
6. S – Silence – practice silence and thereby turn to God

Note: - Opposite of "STRESSED" is "DESSERTS"
              (unhappiness)   (happiness)

How can success be measured?

Success must not be measured in terms of money, power, prestige, influence, education, or standing in society. For a man may have all of these and yet his life may be full of misery, unhappiness, moral corruption, and ineffectiveness. Success should be measured by the yardstick of happiness, the ability to be happy and make others happy, the ability to be loved and to love, the ability to remain peaceful harmony with those around you, with your own self and with God's cosmic laws.

Success has three dimensions. – 1. The first is LENGTH, which is concerned with man's material needs, his hopes and aspirations, his desires and dreams. – 2. The second dimension is BREADTH, for the truly successful man should go beyond himself and reach outward to others. – 3. The third dimension is HEIGHT; he must go high and tap the hidden source of supply and wisdom, which we call GOD.

Western Happiness: -
The concept of achieving true happiness has, in the west, always seemed ill defined, elusive, an ungraspable. Even the word "happy" is derived from the Icelandic word happy, meaning luck or chance. Most of us, it seems, share this view of the mysterious nature of happiness. In those moments of joy that life brings, happiness feels like something that comes out of the blue. To the western mind, it didn't seem that sort of thing that one could develop, and sustain, simply by "training the mind".

Eastern Happiness: -
The concept of "training the mind for happiness" has a much broader meaning closer to 'psyche' or 'spirit'; it includes intellect and feeling, heart and mind. By bringing about a certain discipline, one can undergo a transformation of our attitude, our entire outlook and approach to living. When we speak of this inner discipline, it can of course involve many things, many methods. But generally speaking, one begins by identifying those factors, which lead to happiness, and those factors which lead to suffering. Having done that, one then sets about gradually eliminating those factors which lead to suffering and cultivating those which lead to happiness.

Perception of Happiness: -
Even if generic make up plays a role in happiness – and the verdict is still out on how large that role is – there is general agreement among psychologists that no matter what level of happiness we are endowed with by nature, there are steps we can take to work with the "mind factor' to enhance our feelings

of happiness. This is because our outlook largely determines our moment-to-moment happiness. In fact whether we are feeling happy or unhappy at any given moment often has very little to do with our absolute conditions but rather it is a function of how we perceive our situation, how satisfied we are with what we have.

What shapes our perception and level of satisfaction?
Our feelings of contentment are strongly influenced by our tendency to compare. When we compare our current situation to our past and find that we are better off, we feel happy. So we see how our feelings of life satisfaction often depends upon whom we compare ourselves to. Constant comparison with those who are smarter, more beautiful or successful than us also tends to breed envy, frustration and unhappiness. But we can use this same principle in a positive way, we can increase our feeling of life satisfaction by comparing ourselves to those who are less fortunate than us and by reflecting on all the things we have.

State of mind is key to happiness: -
There are many levels of happiness. In Buddhism, for instance, there is a reference to four factors of fulfillment, or happiness: **Wealth, Worldly Satisfaction, Spirituality, and Enlightenment.** Together they embrace the totality of an individual's quest for happiness. In a worldly sense, there are certain key elements that we conventionally acknowledge as contributing to joy and happiness. 1. Good Health is considered to be one of the necessary factors for as happy life. 2. Material facilities (Wealth) are another factor that we regard as a source of happiness. 3. An additional factor is to have friendship or companions. We all recognize that in order to enjoy a fulfilled life, we need a circle of friends with whom we can relate emotionally and trust. In order for individual to be able to fully utilize them towards a goal of enjoying a happy and fulfilled life, your state of mind is the key and it's crucial.

Without the right mental attitude, without attention to the mental factor, these things have very little impact on our long-term feelings of happiness. If one can maintain a calm, peaceful state of mind, then you can be a very happy person even if you have poor health.

So leaving a side the perspective of spiritual practice, even in worldly terms, in terms of our enjoying a happy day to day existence, the greatest the level of calmness of mind, the greater our peace of mind, the greater our ability to enjoy a happy and joyful life.

Secret of Happiness: -
As long as there is lack of inner discipline that brings calmness of mind, no matter what external facilities or conditions you have, they will never give you the feeling of joy and happiness that you are seeking. On the other hand, if you possess this inner quality, a calmness of mind, a degree of stability within, then even if you lack various external facilities that you would normally consider necessary for happiness, it is still possible to have a happy and joyful life.

Desire: -
There are two kinds of desires:

1. Positive Desire – like desire for happiness, desire for peace, the desire for more harmonious world, and friendlier world. Certain desires are very useful. The initial impulse desire shall be curbed but the other level of desire based on one's essential needs of food, clothing, and shelter, is something more reasonable.

2. Negative Desire – A desire is excessive or negative depends on the circumstances or society in which you live. This kind of excessive desire leads to greed – an exaggerated form of desire, based on over expectation. One interested thing about greed is that although the underlying motive is to seek satisfaction, the irony is that even after obtaining the object of your desire, you are still not satisfied. The true antidote of greed is contentment.

Inner Worth: -
We have seen how working on our mental outlook is a more effective means of achieving happiness than seeking it through external sources such as wealth, position or even physical health. Another internal source of happiness closely linked with an inner feeling of contentment is a sense of **self worth**. You can relate to people because you are still a human being, within the human community. You share that bond. And that human bond is enough to give rise to a sense of worth and dignity. That bond can become a source of consolation in the event that you loose everything else.

Happiness versus pleasure: -

Sometimes people confuse happiness with pleasure. True happiness relates more to the mind and heart. Happiness that depends mainly on pleasure is unstable. One day it's there, the next day it may not be. Everyday we are faced with numerous decisions and choices. Right choice is often difficult one – the one that involves some sacrifice of our pleasure. Pleasure is the beginning and end of the blessed life. Normally our underlying motive is to seek pleasure. Many researchers have chosen to side-step more philosophical speculations, and instead, a host of neuroanatomists have taken to poking around the brains hypothalamus and limbic regions with electrodes, searching for the spot that produces pleasure when electrically stimulated.

Real Happiness: -

A kind of happiness that is stable and persistent is real happiness. A state of happiness that remains, despite life's ups and downs and normal fluctuations of mood, as part of the very matrix of our being. With this perspective, it's easier to make right decision because we are acting to give ourselves something, not denying or withholding something from ourselves – an attitude of moving toward rather than moving away, an attitude of embracing life rather than rejecting it. This underlying sense of moving toward happiness can have a very profound effect. It makes us more receptive, more open, to the joy of living.

The path to Happiness: -

First our basic physical needs for Food, Clothing and Shelter must be met. But once these basic needs are met the message is clear; we don't need more money, we don't need greater success or fame, we don't need perfect body or even the perfect mate – right now, at this very moment, we have a mind or consciousness, which is all the basic equipment we need to achieve complete happiness.

So the first step in seeking happiness is learning. We first have to learn how negative emotions and behaviors are harmful to us and how positive emotions are helpful. For instance, hatred, jealousy, anger, and so on are harmful. We consider them negative states of mind because they destroy our mental happiness. On the other hand, mental states such as kindness and compassion are definitely very positive. They are very useful. If you maintain a feeling of compassion, loving kindness, then something automatically opens your inner door. Through that, you can communicate much more easily with other people. And that feeling of warmth creates a kind of openness. You will find that all human beings are just like you, so you will be able to relate to them very easily. Therefore cultivating positive mental state like kindness and compassion definitely leads to better psychological health and happiness.

Positive Mental State leads to Happiness: -
The systematic training of mind – the cultivation of happiness, the genuine inner transformation by deliberately selecting and focusing on positive mental states and challenging negative mental states – is possible because of the very structure and function of the brain. We are born with brains that are genetically hard wired with certain instinctual behavior patterns; we are predisposed mentally, emotionally, and physically to respond to our environment in ways that enable us to survive. These basic sets of instructions are encoded in countless innate nerve cell activation patterns, specific combination of brain cells that fire in response to any given event, experience, or thought. But the wiring in our brains is not static, not irrevocably fixed. Our brains are also adaptable. Neuroscientists have documented the fact that the brain can design new patterns, new combination of nerve cells and neurotransmitters (chemicals that transmit messages between nerve cells) in response to new input. In fact our brains are malleable, ever changing, reconfiguring their wiring according to new thoughts and experiences. And as a result of learning, the function of individual neurons themselves changes, allowing electrical signals to travel along them more readily. Scientists call the brain's inherent capacity to change "Plasticity".

By mobilizing our thoughts and practicing new ways of thinking, we can reshape our nerve cells and change the way our brains work. It is also the basis of the idea that inner transformation begins with learning (new input) and involves the discipline of gradually replacing our "negative conditioning" with "positive conditioning". Thus the idea of training the mind for happiness becomes a very real possibility.

Self Disciplined mind leads to Happiness : -
It is felt that self disciplined mind leads to happiness and an undisciplined mind leads to suffering. The definition of negative or unwholesome behaviors is those behaviors, which lead to suffering, and a wholesome behavior as one that leads to happiness. Traditionally, it has been considered the responsibility of religion to prescribe what behaviors are wholesome and what are not. However in today's society religion has lost its prestige and influence to some degree. And at the same

time, no alternative, such as secular ethics has come up to replace it. So there seems to be less attention paid to the need to lead a wholesome way of life. It is because of this that we need to make some special effort and consciously work towards gaining that kind of knowledge. We must also develop an appreciation and awareness of that fact. And changing how we perceive ourselves, through learning and understanding, can have very real impact on how we interact with others and how we conduct our daily lives. The proper utilization of our intelligence and knowledge is to effect changes from within to develop a good heart.

"Buddha Nature" leads to Happiness: -
"Buddha Nature" refers to an underlying, basic, and most subtle nature of mind. This state of mind present in all human beings is completely untainted by negative emotions or thoughts. Over the past two or three decades, there have been literally hundreds of scientific studies indicating that aggression is not essentially innate and that violent behavior is influenced by a variety of biological, social, situational and environmental factors. It is scientifically incorrect to say that we have an inherited tendency to make war or act violently. That behavior is not genetically programmed in human nature.

Reaching out to help others may be a fundamental to our nature as communication. One could draw an analogy with the development of language, which, like the capacity for compassion and altruism, is one of the magnificent features of the human race. Particular areas of the brain are specially devoted to the potential for language. If we are exposed to the correct environmental conditions, that is, a society that speaks, then those discreet areas of the brain begin to develop and mature and our capacity for language grows. In the same way all humans may be endowed with the 'seed of compassion'. When exposed to the right conditions – at home, in society at large, and later perhaps through our own pointed efforts – that "seed" will flourish. With this idea in mind researchers are now seeking to discover the optimal environmental conditions that will allow the seed of caring and compassion to ripen in children. They have identified several factors: having parents who are able to regulate their own emotions, who model caring behavior, who set appropriate limits on the children's behavior, who communicate that a child is responsible for her or his own behavior, or who use reasoning to help direct the child's attention to effective or emotional states and the consequences of her or his behavior on others.

We were not born with the purpose of causing trouble, harming others. For our life to be of value, we must develop basic good human qualities – Warmth, Kindness, and Compassion. Then our life becomes meaningful and more peaceful – Happier.

Establishing Empathy: -
One can attempt to increase compassion by trying to empathize with another's feeling or experience. That empathy is important not only as a means of enhancing compassion, but in dealing with others at any level, if you are having any difficulties, it's extremely helpful to be able to try to put yourself in the other person's place and see how you would react to the situation. Even if you have no common experience with the other person or have a very different life style, you can try to do this through imagination. You may need to be slightly creative. This technique involves the capacity to temporarily suspend insisting on your own viewpoint but rather to look from the other person's perspective, to imagine what would be the situation if you were in his shoes, how you would deal with this. This helps you develop an awareness and respect for another's feelings, which is an important factor in reducing conflicts and problems with other people.

There are some other factors that can help one deal with others more skillfully. First, it is helpful to understand and appreciate the background of the people you are dealing with. Second, be more open-minded and honest. These are useful qualities when dealing with others.

Basis of relationship: -
When we are dealing with trying to understand relationship problems, the first stage in this process involves deliberately reflecting on the underlying nature and basis of that relationship.

If one is seeking to build a truly satisfying relationship, the best way of bringing this about is to get to know the deeper nature of the person and relate to her or him on that level, instead of merely on the basis of superficial characteristics.

Compassion leads to Happiness:
Compassion can be roughly defined in terms of state of mind that is non-violent, non-harming and non-aggressive. It is a mental attitude best on the wish for others to be free of their suffering and is associated with a sense of commitment, responsibility, and respect towards others.

For instance, in marriage there is generally a component of emotional attachment. But if there is a component of genuine compassion as well, based on mutual respect as two human beings, the marriage tends to last a long time. In the case of emotional attachment without compassion, the marriage is unstable and tends to end more quickly.

In addition to the beneficial effects on one's physical health, there is evidence that compassion and caring behavior contribute to good emotional health. Studies have shown that reaching out to help others can induce the feeling of happiness, a calmer mind, and less depression.

8.05 -FACING SUFFERING AND OUR ATTITUDE TOWARDS SUFFERING: - [17]

If you look at your normal day to day life, however you often find that there are so many factors and conditions that cause pain, suffering and feelings of dissatisfaction, whereas conditions that give rise to joy and happiness are comparatively rare. In accepting that suffering is part of our daily existence, one could begin by examining the factors that normally give rise to feelings of discontent and mental unhappiness. Generally speaking for instance, one feels happy if you or people close to you receive praise, fame, fortune, and other pleasant things. And you feel unhappy and discontent if you don't achieve these things or if your rival is receiving them. And since this is the reality of our existence, our attitude towards suffering may need to be modified.

Our attitude towards suffering becomes very important because it can affect how we cope with suffering when it arises. Now our usual attitude consists of intense aversion and intolerance of our pain and suffering. However if we can transform our attitude towards suffering, adopt an attitude that allows us greater tolerance of it, then this can do much to help counteract feelings of mental unhappiness, dissatisfaction, and discontent.

So, how you perceive life as a whole plays a role in your attitude about suffering. For instance, if your basic outlook is that suffering is negative and must be avoided at all costs and in some sense is sign of failure, this will add a distinct psychological component of anxiety and intolerance when you encounter difficult circumstances, a feeling of being overwhelmed. On the other hand, if your basic outlook accepts that suffering is a natural part of your existence, this will undoubtedly make you more tolerant towards the adversities of life. And without a certain degree of tolerance towards your suffering, your life becomes miserable, and then it is like having a very bad night. That night seems eternal, it never seems to end.

The root causes of suffering are **desire, anger, greed, attachment and arrogance.** These are called **'five persons of mind'**. By generating insight in to the true nature of reality and eliminating afflictive states of mind such as desire, anger, greed, attachment, and arrogance, one can achieve a completely purified state of mind, free from suffering.

Suffering in West: -
As Western society gained the ability to limit the bodily or physical suffering caused by harsh living conditions by means of science, it seems to have lost the ability to cope with the suffering of the mind. Studies by social scientists have emphasized that most people in modern western society tend to go through life believing that world is basically a nice place in which to live, that life is mostly fair and they are good people who deserve to have good things happen to them. These beliefs could play an important role in leading a happier and healthier life. But the inevitable arising of the suffering undermines these beliefs and can make it difficult to go on living happily and effectively. In this context, a relatively minor trauma can have a massive psychological impact as one loses faith in one's basic beliefs about the world as fair and benevolent. As a result suffering is intensified. That is why the depression is more common in the west.

Suffering in East: -
Although pain and suffering are experienced by all human beings, but those brought up in Eastern cultures appear to have greater acceptance and tolerance for physical and mental suffering. Part of this may be due to their beliefs, but perhaps it is because suffering is more visible in poorer nations than it is in wealthier countries. In east when person becomes sick they are not marginalized, most cases they are not shipped off to nursing homes to be cared for by the health professionals, but they remain in community to be cared for by the family. Those living in daily contact with the realities of life cannot easily deny that life is characterized by suffering, that it is a natural part of existence.

Happiness means free of suffering: -
Of course, the wish to get free of physical and mental suffering is the legitimate goal of every human being. It is the corollary of our wish to be happy. Thus it is entirely appropriate that we seek out the causes of our unhappiness and do whatever we can to alleviate our problems, searching for solutions on all levels – Global, social, family, and individual. But as long as we view suffering as an unnatural state, an abnormal condition that we fear, avoid, and reject, we will never uproot the causes of suffering and begin to live happier life.

Self-mental Unrest: -
We often add to our mental pain and suffering by being overly sensitive, over reacting to minor things, and sometimes taking things too seriously. Therefore to a large extent, whether you suffer, depends on how you respond to a given situation.

We can see that there are many ways in which we actively contribute to our own experience of mental unrest and suffering. Although, in general mental and emotional afflictions themselves can come naturally, often it is our own reinforcement of those negative emotions that make them so much worse. For instance when we have anger or hatred towards a person, there is less likelihood of it's developing to a very intense degree if we leave it unattended. However if we think about the projected injustices done to us, the ways in which we have been unfairly treated and we keep on thinking about them over and over, then that feeds the hatred. It makes the hatred very powerful and intense. Of course it applies to when we have attachment towards a particular person, we can feed that by thinking about how beautiful he or she is, and as we keep thinking about the projected qualities that we see in the person, the attachment becomes more and more intense. But this shows how through constant familiarity and thinking, we ourselves can make our emotions more intense and powerful.

We also add to our pain and suffering by being overly sensitive, overreacting to minor things, and sometimes taking things too personally. We tend to take small things too seriously and blow them up out of proportion, while at the same time we often remain indifferent to really important things, those things which have profound effects on our lives and long term consequences and implications.

For example, say that you find out that someone is speaking badly of you behind your back. If you react to this knowledge that some one is speaking badly of you, this negativity with a feeling of hurt and anger, then you yourself destroy your peace of mind. Your pain is your personal creation. On the other hand if you refrain from reacting in a negative way, let the insult pass by you as if it were a silent wind passing behind your ears, you protect yourself from that feeling of hurt, that feeling of agony. So, although you may not always be able to avoid difficult situations, you can modify the extent to which you suffer by how you choose to the situation.

Suffering of change: -
It is extremely important to investigate the causes or origins of suffering, how it arises. One must begin that process by appreciating the impermanent, transient nature of our existence. All things, events and phenomena are dynamic, changing every moment, nothing remains static. Meditating on one's blood circulation could serve to reinforce this idea; the blood is constantly flowing, moving, it never stands still. This momentarily changing nature of phenomena is like a built in mechanism. And since it is the nature of all phenomena to change every moment, this indicates to us that all things lack the ability to endure, lack the ability to remain the same. And since all things are subject to change, nothing exists in the permanent condition; nothing is able to remain the same under its own independent power. Thus all things are under the power or influence of other factors. So at any given moment, no matter how pleasant or pleasurable your experience may be, it will not last.

Suffering in relationships: -
Relationship is a dynamic living system, composed of two organisms interacting in a living environment. And as a living system, it is equally natural and right that a relationship go through stages. Each of us repeatedly go through three stages **"Hold me tight", "Put me down", and "leave me alone".** In any relationship, there are different dimensions of closeness. – Physical, emotional, and intellectual. Body contact, sharing emotions, thoughts, and exchanging ideas are all legitimate ways of connecting with those we love.

The taste for suffering: -
The desire for happiness is essential to man. That desire inspires our every act, our every word, and our every thought so naturally that we are totally unaware of it, like the oxygen we breathe all our lives without thinking about it. Even if, ideally the satisfaction of all our desires were achievable, it would lead not to happiness but to the creation of new desires or, just as likely, to indif-

ference, disgust, or even depression. The fact is that without inner peace and wisdom, we have nothing we need to be happy. Happiness is the state of inner fulfillment, not the gratification of inexhaustible desires for outward things.

Easy life: -
Imagine what it would be like if we went through life never encountering an enemy or any other obstacle for that matter. If from the cradle to the grave everyone we met pampered us, help us, hand fed us (soft blend food, easy to digest), amused us with funny faces and the occasional "goo goo " noise. If from infancy we were carried around in a basket (later on, perhaps on a litter), never encountering any challenge, never tested – in short, if everyone continued to treat us like a baby. That might sound good at first. For the first few months of life it might be appropriate. But if it persisted it could only result in one becoming a sort of gelatinous mass, monstrosity realty – with the mental and emotional development of veal. It's the very struggle of life that makes us who we are. And it is our enemies that test us, provide us with the resistance necessary for growth.

Live and let live policy: -
The question is, how can we consistently and steadfastly maintain this set of underlying values and yet remain flexible?

First consider the few fundamental facts: 1) I am human being. 2) I want to be happy and I don't want to suffer. 3) Other human beings, like myself, also want to be happy and don't want to suffer.

Emphasizing the common ground one shares with others, rather than the differences, results in the feeling of connection with all human beings and leads to the basic belief in the value of compassion and altruism. It can be tremendously rewarding simply to take some time to reflect on our own value system and reduce it to its fundamental principles. It is the ability to reduce our value system to its most basic elements, and live from that vantage point, that allows us the greatest freedom and flexibility to deal with the vast array of problems that confront us on a daily basis.

To feel happy while suffering: -
There are three modes of suffering.

1. Visible suffering, which is self-evident.
2. Hidden suffering, this is concealed beneath the appearance of pleasure, for example food poisoning or bit by snake or house catches on fire.
3. Invisible suffering, this is hardest to distinguish because it seems from the blindness of our own minds, where it remains so long as we are in the grips of ignorance and selfishness. Ego clinging, selfishness or self-centeredness causes this.

Suffering will always exist as a universal phenomenon, but every individual has the potential for liberation from it. We all have the ability to study the causes of suffering and gradually to free ourselves from them. We all have the potential to sweep away the veils of ignorance, to free ourselves of the selfishness and misplaced desires that trigger unhappiness, to work for the good of others and extract the essence from our human condition. It's not the magnitude of the task that matters; it's the magnitude of our courage. The path is the process of using all available means to eliminate the fundamental causes of suffering by recognizing suffering, by eliminating its source, by ending the suffering and by practicing the path.

Managing suffering: -
If it is possible to relieve mental anguish by transforming one's mind, how can this process be applied to physical suffering? How do we endure crippling, virtually intolerable pain?

We should distinguish between two types of sufferings. Physical pain and the mental and emotional suffering. It is the mind that reacts to pain with fear, rejection, despondency, or feeling of powerlessness. Instead of being subjected to a single agony, we accumulate the host of them. There are various methods to overcome suffering.

1. One method uses mental imagery, when a powerful feeling of desire, anger, greed, attachment, pride, plagues one's mind, it is better to imagine yourself sitting in a serene place at the shores of ocean or on top of the mountain.
2. Another lets us transform pain by awakening ourselves to love and compassion. When we experience a powerful sense of empathy with the suffering of others, our impotent resignation gives way to courage,

depression to love, narrow mindedness to openness toward all those around us.

3. A third involves developing inner strength. This visualization is a powerful means to develop benevolence and compassion. It can be carried out anytime and during your day-to-day activities.

Realistic Expectations: -

It takes a long time to develop the behavior and habit of mind that contribute to our problems. It takes equally long time to establish the new habits that bring happiness. There is no getting around these essential ingredients, **Determination, Effort, and Time.** These are real secrets of Happiness.

When embarking on path to change, it is important to set reasonable expectations. If our expectations are too high, we are setting ourselves up for disappointment. If they are too low, it extinguishes our willingness to challenge our limitations and achieve our true potential. One should never loose sight of realistic attitude of being very sensitive and respectful to the concrete reality of your situation as you proceed on the path towards your ultimate goal. Recognize the difficulties inherent in your path and the fact that it may take time and a consistent effort. It is important to make clear distinction in your mind between your ideals and your standards. By which you judge your progress. Dealing with expectations is really a tricky issue. If you have excessive expectations without a proper foundation, then that usually leads to problems. On the other hand, without expectation and hope, without aspiration, there can be no progress. Some hope is essential. So finding the proper balance is not easy. One needs to judge each situation on the spot.

8.06 - MIND SCIENCE: -

Many in the West turn to religious beliefs as a source of happiness, but in the East it relies more heavily on reasoning and training the mind than on faith. The training of the mind involves the idea that positive states of mind can act as direct antidote to negative states of mind. And when this fact is combined with recent scientific evidence (Modern cognitive therapy for depressed people) that we can change the structure and function of the brain by cultivating new thoughts, then the idea that we can achieve happiness through training of mind seems a very real possibility.

Mind & Body Happiness:-
We humans have Body (Nature), and Mind & Intelligence (Nurture) and Mind is the seat of Soul. **Therefore God has two aspects Nature and Soul.**

Millions of us spend more time and energy pursuing the things money can buy than in engaging in activities that create real fulfillment in life, like cultivating friendships, helping others and developing a spiritual sense.

Good Deeds: will make you happy: -
- Dedicate your mind and soul to GOD
- Be jealous of none
- Be fount of mercy
- Be without egotism
- Be selfless
- Be ever forgiving
- Be always contented
- Be firm on your resolutions
- Cause no dread
- Do not be afraid of others
- Be free from exultation, sorrow and fear
- Be pure
- Be versed in action and yet remain unaffected by it
- Renounce all fruit, Good or Bad
- Treat friends and Foe alike
- Be untouched by respect or disrespect
- Do not get puffed up by praise
- Do not go under when people speak ill of you
- Love silence and solitude
- Have a disciplined reason
- Have complete harmony between Thought, Speech & Action

Happiness and Unhappiness
They both go together. If the question of how to be happy is dropped, then you begin to live i.e. Not bothering about happiness at all. That does not exist;

happiness does not exist at all. The more you want it, the more you search for it, unhappier you remain.

In the present world, full of electronics, if we practice following skills, we might find some happiness.

1   **Start the day with focused task: -** and don't allow your mind to wander while you do it. Research suggests that those who practice a little mindfulness (mental focus) in the morning have a better ability to stay focused throughout the day. A good task to choose might be the shower.

2   **Exercise with mindfulness (mental focus): -** Any sort of activity you do – walking, running, biking, swimming – can increase mental focus by boosting blood flow in the brain.

3   **Immerse yourself in a good book or movie:** - Reading a page-turner or watching a compelling movie or TV show can be a great way to practice mindfulness.

4   **Minimize multitasking:** - It's enemy of mindfulness – Stop texting while having lunch with friends. Don't check your email while you are helping the kids with your homework. And stop scanning the Internet when you get a call from a client. If you still sense your mind wandering, force your attention back to the task at hand.

5   **Practice 15 to 20 minutes of daily meditation:** - Those who practice regular meditation snap out of the brain's default wandering mode much faster than those who don't. If you meditate regularly, you prevent the cognitive decline in attention span that naturally occurs with aging.

6   **Give, Give and Give –** If you want to be happy, think of others and if you want to be unhappy think of yourself.

7   **Peace, Love and happiness –** Keep peace in the mind, love in the heart and happiness in the relationships.

8   **Open Mind –** The mind is like a parachute – it works best when it is open. How quickly we make assumptions, jump to conclusions and close our mind. How easily we form and hold fast to our opinions and then close our mind. How fast we make a judgment, slap on a label and then close our mind. A closed mind never knows the delight of playing with the possibilities, being enlightened by others point of view or enjoying the diversity of human life. An open and understanding mind never assumes, does not jump to conclusions and won't hold

fast to any opinion. Perhaps it is no wonder, a closed mind is not a very relaxed mind.

8.07 - THE NEW SCIENCE OF HAPPINESS: -
What makes the human heart sing?

For most of its history, psychology had concerned itself with all that ails the human mind; anxiety, depression, neurosis, obsessions, paranoia, delusions etc. The goal of practitioners was to bring patients from a negative ailing state to a neutral normal.

Over the decades, few psychological researchers had ventured out of the dark realm of mental illness in to the sunny land of the mentally hale and hearty. **They found that most people find happiness in family connections and friendships.** Survey showed 35% find happiness in children and grandchildren, 17% in family life, 11% in God/Faith/Religion and 9% in spouse. On the positive side, religious faith seems to genuinely lift the spirit, though it is tough to tell whether it's the GOD part or the community aspect that does the heavy lifting. It is important to work on social skills, close interpersonal ties and social support in order to be happy.

Measuring Happiness: -

Of course happiness is not a static state, even the happiest of people feel blue at times and even the bluest have their moments of joy. That has presented a challenge to social scientists trying to measure happiness. Also it is a simple fact that happiness is inherently subjective. As a result of research scientists find three components of happiness. **Pleasure** (the smiley face), **Engagement** (the depth of involvement with one's family, work, romance and hobbies), **Meaning** (using personal strengths to serve some larger end). About 50% of one's satisfaction with life comes from genetic programming. Genes influence such traits as having a sunny, easy going personality; dealing well with stress and feeling low levels of anxiety and depression. Humans were designed to be happy, creative and in harmony with the universe at all times.

Eight Steps Towards a More Satisfying Life: -

  1. Count your blessings.

2. Practice acts of kindness.
3. Savor life's joys.
4. Thank a mentor.
5. Learn to forgive.
6. Invest time and energy in friends and family.
7. Take care of your body.
8. Develop strategies for coping with stress and hardships.

The Natural High: -
Two key brain chemicals regulate how happy the body feels.

1. **Dopamine,** which is released in the nucleus accumbency and the frontal cortex, bathes neurons involve in memory and emotion, rewarding activities like eating and sex with pleasurable feelings.
1. **Endorphins,** which are chemically similar to morphine, promote pleasure by dampening pain and producing high.

The artificial High: -
Drug as can alter the brain's normal reward circuit, making it harder to feel pleasure without help.

8.08 - MONEY CANNOT BUY HAPPINESS: -
Millions of us spend more time and energy pursuing the things money can buy than engaging in activities that create real fulfillment in life, like cultivating friendships, helping others and developing spiritual sense. We say that we know that money can't buy happiness. Once your basic needs are met additional income does little to raise your sense of satisfaction with life.

Psychologists have found that the Forbes 400 richest Americans were only a tiny bit happier than the public as a whole, because those with wealth often continue to feel jealousy about the possessions or prestige of other wealthy people, even large sums of money may fail to confer well being.

Reference Anxiety: -

People tend not to ask themselves, does my house meet my needs? Instead they ask, is my house nicer than my neighbor's? If you own a two-bed room house and everyone around you owns a two-bed room house, your reference anxiety will be low, and your two-bed room house may seem fine. But if your two-bedroom house is surrounded by three and four bedroom house, your reference anxiety might rise. Our soaring reference anxiety is a product of the widening gap in income distribution. **It's all-relative.**

Earning capacity: -

As material expectations keep rising more money may engender only more desires. What people want in terms of material things and life experiences has increased almost exactly in lockstep with the post war earnings curve. That money never satisfies is suggested by telling this fact: polls show that Americans believe that, whatever their income level, they need more to live well. Even those making large sums said still large sums were required. We seem conditioned to think we do not have enough.

Future Perspective of Life: -

If we think our lot is improving, happiness follows. People's expectations about future may have more influence on their sense of well-being than their current state does. People living modestly but anticipating better days to come are likely to be happier than people living well but not looking forward to improvements in their living standards. Consider two people one earns $50,000 a year and foresees a 10% raise and the other makes $150,000 but does not expect any salary increase. The second person is much better off in financial terms but the first is more likely to feel good about life. People tend to focus on the negative part and ignore the positive. Fixated on always getting more, we fail to appreciate how much we have.

Final Note: -

Psychology and sociology aside, there is final reason money can't buy happiness: The things that really matter in life are not sold in stores. Love, Friendship, Family, Respect, a place in the community. The belief that your life has a purpose – those are the essentials of human fulfillment, and they cannot be purchased with cash. Everyone needs a certain amount of money, but chasing money is a formula for discontent. Too many Americans have made materialism and the cycle of work and spend their principal goals. Then they wonder why they don't feel happy.

8.09 - MARRIAGE AND HAPPINESS: -

Eternal love, the creation of new family, Approval of society – whatever, but everyone wants to know, **Will Marriage Make Me Happier?**

People have long believed that being unmarried makes people unhappy, but a long-term study shows that marriage does not necessarily make people one bit happier. The myth that marriage makes people happier and healthier probably stems from the fact that married people are indeed happier and healthier than single people, because married people are less likely to be in poor to fair health, smoke or drink heavily or suffer from such health problems as headaches and serious psychological distress.

Although past studies have stressed positive thinking as the key to a happy marriage, it turns out to be effective only in a short term. In the long run, you adapt back to the level of happiness you started with.

8.10 – MEDITATION AND HAPPINESS: -

With the help and encouragement of the Dalai Lama, neuroscientist Richard Davidson recruited Buddhist monks to go to Madison and meditate inside his functional magnetic resonance imaging (MRI) tube while he measured their brain activity during various mental states. For comparison, he used undergraduates who had no experience with meditation but got a crash course in the basic techniques, and experienced Meditators some of whom have spent 10,000 hours of their lives in meditation.

More interesting were the differences between the so-called adepts (highly skilled) and the novices. In the former there was significantly greater activation in a brain network linked to empathy and maternal love. Connections from the frontal regions, so active during compassion meditation, to the brain's emotional regions seemed to become stronger with more years of meditation practice, as if the brain had forged more robust connections between thinking and feeling.

But perhaps the most striking difference was in an area in the left prefrontal cortex- the site of activity that marks happiness. While the monks were generating feelings of compassion activity in the left prefrontal and swamped activity in the right prefrontal (associated with negative moods) to a degree never before seen from purely mental activity. By contrast, the undergraduate's controls showed no such differences between the left and right prefrontal cortex. **This suggests, says Davidson that the positive state is a skill that can be trained.**

8.11 – DON'T WANT EVERYTHING: -

We think of many aspects of life as a race – who gets the promotion, who gets the biggest salary, who has the nicest car. It's a race between us and everyone around us for these things.

Yet, we don't all need to have these things to succeed. What we need is what we need. Because some one else wants to be at the top or have the most or work the longest hours does not mean that you need those same things.

Success in life is not a matter of getting everything. That's impossible and wouldn't be much of joy even if it were possible. Success is a matter of getting what you need. Think of success as filling a box. You will be finished sooner not just by working harder to fill it but also by choosing a small box.

What success means is not universal. Studies of people who have attained nearly identical achievements in the workplace, for example, find great variation in their level of satisfaction, which some considering them tremendously successful and others considering themselves average or even failure.

8.12 - BIOLOGY OF HAPPINESS: -

In democratic societies, the well being of the masses – happiness for everybody – has become the focus of the "new science of happiness" and a main agenda of the state.

Happiness is more than the absence of unhappiness. Happiness is experienced both as fleeting sensations and emotions, and consciously appreciated as a permanent disposition of the mind. It encompasses two inseparable aspects: **Hedonic** (pleasure of the senses) and **eudemonic** (pleasure of reason; living well and doing well).

Darwin speculated that the emotions must be key to the survival of the fittest. With the emergence of self-awareness, emotions have become a new evolutionary force.

The emotional 'good' has become detached from the Darwinian 'Good', such that experiencing pleasure has become an end in itself.

Other people are also principal sources of social alarm and thus of psychological stress. It is here that the great advantage of the neo-cortex becomes apparent: it functions as an arbitrator to attribute quality and strength to social factors. The thoughts and actions of particular individual can render us excited or leave us indifferent. **Envy** is one of the most potent causes of unhappiness. It can be tempered or neutralized by mobilizing the neo-cortex. But the main source of stress for the human primate is probably fear and subjective sense of uncertainty, so the satisfaction of the need for security is a precondition for the unfolding of all other needs.

These capacities of mental self projection in to the past, the future, or the perspective of another individual, all enable a specifically human way of life: living within time. It seems that achieving zero pain and maximum pleasure has driven the evolution of the modern economy. We have been molded by evolution not to be happy, but to act on the phantasm of happiness. Occasionally the intense enjoyment of the present can escalate to reach a singularity of 'peak experiences', the 'single most joyous, happiest, most blissful moments of life.'

The west is especially rich in the things we call interesting, beautiful, delicious, cool, entertaining, and exiting. They make daily life more reinforcing, but they reinforce little more than the behavior that brings one in to contact with them. What is wrong with the life in the west is not that it has too many reinforces, but they are not contingent on the kinds of behavior that sustain the individual or promote the survival of the culture or species.

The emotional responses to the pleasant stimulus also weaken or completely cease, if stimulus remains constant. This phenomenon has been called the **Hedonic Treadmill.**

Artificial brain stimulation by electrical currents or by drugs replaces the meaningful natural activities of observing the environment and acting appropriately – in this way. Stimulation functions as an unusual reward, as a single response that suffices both to procure and consume it. It is in fact a short-circuiting of the natural mechanisms. Still there have been many utopians that envision that drugs will help us to achieve a perfect happiness.

Totally eliminating the suffering and blindly chasing pleasure are not paths to happiness. Posters on buses in London and other world capitals with the inscription "There is probably no God, now stop worrying and enjoy your life" give false advice. A program of mass happiness is actually a delusion. Happiness cannot be a set goal sold as consumer good. It can only spring up as a by-product of pursuing long term goals, intermittent with negative and positive emotions.

Sustainable happiness results from what we do, not from what we have. Chasing happiness as an aggregate of wealth and pleasure is a vicious spiral. A huge number of empirical studies show that vast amounts of material wealth do not make people happier once they have reached a certain level of financial security. Rather than crushing our spirits, the realization that we exist together for a narrow slice of time and space elevates us to higher plane of humanity and humility: a proud act in the drama of the cosmos.

Happiness isn't just a vague, overwhelming feeling; it is a physical state of the brain – one that you can induce deliberately. Scientists have discovered that happiness or related mental states like hopefulness, optimism and contentment appear to reduce the risk or limit the severity of cardiovascular disease, pulmonary disease, diabetes, hypertension, colds and upper-respiratory infections.

Doctors have known for years that clinical depression – the extreme opposite of happiness – can worsen heart disease, diabetes and host of other illnesses. But the neurochemistry of depression is much better known than that of happiness, mostly because the former has been studied more intensively and for much longer. A growing number of researchers exploring the physiology and neurology of happiness are starting to answer as to what happiness is in a clinical sense. At this point no one can say with precision. The word happiness is kind of placeholder for a constellation of positive emotional states. It is a state of well being where individuals are typically not motivated to change their state. They are motivated to preserve it. It's associated with an active embracing of the world, but the precise characteristics and boundaries have really yet to be seriously characterized in scientific research.

Two brain –imaging technologies - functional magnetic resonance imaging (MRI) which maps blood flow to active parts of the brain, and electroencephalograms which sense the electrical activity of neuronal circuits- consistently point to the prefrontal cortex as a prime focus of happiness. Scientists are confident that this part of the brain is a proximal cause of at least certain kinds of happiness. That suggests that some people are genetically predisposed to be happy by virtue of their busy prefrontal cortexes and research in infants confirms it. Neuroscientists have also learned over the past decade that the brain is highly plastic. It rewires it self in response to experience and that's especially true before the age of puberty. One might naively assume that negative experiences might destroy a happy personality.

Optimists may simply feel less stress than pessimists and thereby avoid the noxious biochemical cascades that stress is known to trigger. Another likely factor: optimistic, happy type seems to take better care of themselves than sad sacks do.

Does our happiness depend on that of others: -
(Joy shared is joy doubled; sorrow shared is sorrow halved)

When the selfish happiness is the only goal in life, life soon becomes goalless. We can never be truly happy if we dissociate ourselves from the happiness of others. This in no way requires us to neglect our own happiness. To love oneself is to love life. It is essential to understand that we make ourselves happy in making others happy. The goal of life is a deep state of well-being and wisdom at all moments, accompanied by love for every being. It is love that is always available, without showiness or self-interest.

Looking within, looking without: -
We willingly spend dozen years in school, then go on to college or professional training for several more; we work out at the gym to stay healthy; we spend a lot of time enhancing our comfort, our wealth and our social status. We put a great deal in to all this and yet we do so little to improve the inner condition that determines the very quality of our lives. What strange hesitancy, fear or apathy stops us from looking within ourselves, from trying to grab the true essence of joy and sadness, desire and hatred? Fear of the unknown prevails

and the courage to explore that inner world fails at the frontier of our mind. In pinning all our hopes on the external world, however, we can only end up being disappointed.

Can we cultivate happiness: -

If we try resolutely over the course of years to master our thoughts as they come to us, to apply appropriate antidotes to negative emotions and to nourish positive ones, our efforts will undoubtedly yield results that would have seemed unattainable at first. When it comes to physical performance we soon run in to limitations, but the mind is far more flexible. Why for instance there should be any limit to love or compassion. Why accept that but neglect our own transformation, which determines the quality of our lived experience? Is it better to just allow us to drift? Isn't that how we crash on the rock?

Pleasure vs. Happiness: -

Pleasure can be joined to cruelty, violence, pride, greed and other mental conditions that are incompatible with true happiness. Pleasure is the happiness of mad men, while happiness is the pleasure of the sages. Authentic happiness is not linked to an activity; it is a state of being, a profound emotional balance struck by a subtle understanding how the mind works. One who is at peace with one self will contribute spontaneously to establishing peace within one's family, one's neighborhood and circumstances permitting society at large.

Inner Freedom: -

Our inner freedom knows no limits other than those we impose on it or allow to be imposed on it. And that freedom also holds great power. It can transform an individual; allow him to nurture all his capacities and to live every moment of his life in utter fulfillment. When individuals change by bringing their consciousness to maturity, the world changes too, because the world is made up of individuals. No matter what your outer circumstances might be, there is always deep within you, a potential for flourishing. This is the potential for loving kindness, compassion and inner peace. This potential needs to be developed and matured in order to achieve a more stable sense of well-being. However this will not happen by itself. One has to develop it as a skill. For that begin by becoming more familiar with your own mind. This is the beginning of meditation.

EGO: -

Ego is a powerful attachment to the self and thus to the notion of "Mine" – my body, my name, my mind, my possession, my friends and so on – which leads either to desire to possess or to the feeling of repulsion for the "Other". This erroneous sense of a real and independent self is of course based on ego-centricity, which persuades us that our own fate is of greater value than that of others.

The western world holds the self to be the fundamental building block of the personality. Surely, if I eliminate my ego I will cease to exist as a person. But the genuine self-confidence is the natural quality of egolessness. Genuine confidence comes from an awareness of a basic quality of our mind and of our potential for transformation and flourishing, what Buddhism calls Buddha Nature, which is present in all of us.

The idea that a powerful ego is necessary to succeed in life undoubtedly stems from the confusion between attachment to our own image and the resolve to achieve our deepest aspirations. The fact is, the less influenced we are by the sense of our self's importance, the easier it is to acquire lasting inner strength. The reason for this is simple: self importance is a target open to all sorts of mental projectiles – jealousy, fear, greed, repulsion – that perpetually destabilize it.

We are obsessed with our success, our failure, our hopes and our anxieties and thereby give happiness every opportunity to elude us. When the self ceases to be the most important thing in the world, we find it easier to focus our concern on others. The sight of their suffering bolsters our courage and resolve to work on their behalf, instead of crippling us with our own emotional distress.

Depression or unhappy thoughts: -

In depression all that is happening in the present is the anticipation of pain in the future and present no longer exists at all. The inability to manage our thoughts proves to be the principal cause of suffering. Learning to tone down the ceaseless racket of disturbing thoughts is a decisive stage on the road to inner peace.

When a painful emotion strikes us, the most urgent thinking is to look at it head-on and to identify the immediate thoughts that triggered it and are fanning it. Then by fixing our inner gaze on the emotion itself, we can gradually dissolve it like snow in sunshine. Furthermore, once the string of emotions has been sapped, the causes that triggered it will seem less tragic and we will have won ourselves the chance to break free from the vicious circle of negative thoughts.

So we need to take a closer look at mind itself. The first things we notice are the currents of thought that are continuously flowing without our even being aware of them. The countless thoughts born of our sensations, our memories and our imagination are forever streaming through our mind. But also there is a quality of mind that is always present no matter what kind of thoughts we entertain. The quality is the primary consciousness underlying all thought. That faculty, that simple open presence, is what we may call **"Pure consciousness"**, because it exists even in the absence of mental constructs.

It is not easy to experience "Pure Consciousness", but it is possible. When a thought arises, try to see where it came from; when it disappears, ask yourself where it went. In that brief moment when your mind is not encumbered by discursive thoughts, contemplate its nature. In that instant when past thoughts have fallen silent and future ones have yet to emerge, you can perceive a pure and luminous consciousness unadulterated by your conceptual constructs.

Blame: -
It is tempting to systematically pass the blame on to the world and other people. When we feel anxious, depressed, cranky, envious, or emotionally exhausted, we are quick to pass the buck to the outside world; tensions with colleagues at work, arguments with our spouse etc. Systematically blaming others and holding them responsible for our suffering is the surest way to lead an unhappy life.

It is by transforming our minds that we can transform our world. We should not underestimate the consequences of our thoughts, words and actions. If we sow the seeds of poisonous plants along with those of flowers, we should not be surprised when the harvest is mixed. If we alternate between selfless and harmful behaviors, we ought to expect to get a sharply contrasting blend of joys and sufferings.

8.13 - EMOTIONS: -

**"One with compassion (positive emotions) is kind even when angry;
One without compassion (negative emotions) will kill even as he smiles."**

The goal in dealing with our emotions is not to rid us entirely of our emotions or to transcend it, but to manage our experience of it and the way in which it translates in to action.

Positive emotions broaden our thought-action catalog, widening the array of thoughts and actions that come to mind, including joy, interest, contentment, and love. Some scientists believe that developing such positive thoughts, therefore offers an indisputable evolutionary advantage, in as much as it helps us to broaden our intellectual and affective universe and to open ourselves to new ideas and experiences.

Negative emotions like hatred, jealousy or obsession, at the moment they form, they make us deeply uncomfortable. Moreover the actions and words they inspire are usually intended to hurt others. These disturbing emotions tend to distort our perception of reality and to prevent us from seeing it as it really is.

Short Meditation: –

People say they have no time for meditation. It's not true! You can meditate walking down the corridor, waiting for the traffic lights to change, at the computer, standing in a queue, in the bathroom, combing your hair, just be there in the present without the mental commentary. I do my meditation for 5 minutes as soon as I wake up in the morning, on the bed, to thank GOD that I have consciousness and ask for his blessings. Same way again I do my meditation for 5 minutes, in the night, on the bed, before lying down, to again Thank GOD for everything (good or bad) that happened that day.

Meditation is not about sitting quietly in the shade of the tree and relaxing in a moment of break from the daily grind; it is about familiarizing yourself with a new vision of things, a new way to manage your thoughts, of perceiving people and experiencing the world. The essential thing is to identify the types of mental activity that lead to well-being and those that lead to suffering, even when the latter afford us brief instances of pleasure. This investigation calls for a subtle assessment of the nature of the emotions.

The first phase of that analysis is to identify the way in which the emotions arise and then sit in a comfortable position. Your body remains in an erect but not tense posture with eyes gently closed. For 5 minutes, breathe calmly, noticing the in-and-outflow of your breath. Experience the gradual calming of chaotic thoughts. When thoughts arise, neither attempts to neither block them nor let them multiply. Simply continue to watch your breath.

Next instead of paying attention to outer sights, sounds and events, turn your gaze inward and look at the mind itself. Looking here means observing your awareness itself, not the content of your thoughts. Let the mind gently come to rest, as a tired traveler finds a pleasant meadow in which to sit for a while.

Then with the deep feeling of appreciation, think of value of human existence and of its extraordinary potential for flourishing. Be aware that this precious life will not last forever and that is essential to make the best possible use of it. Sincerely examine what counts more for you in life for you. What do you need to accomplish or discard in order to achieve authentic well-being and live a meaningful existence? When the factors that contribute to true happiness have become clear to you, imagine that they begin to bloom in your mind. Resolve to nurture them day after day.

End you meditation by letting thoughts of pure kindness embrace all living beings.

Finally we can meditate in a non-conceptual way on the very nature of the mind by looking directly at consciousness itself as an open presence, a pure awareness that always lies behind the screen of thoughts, or by contemplating the very nature of the thoughts that cross our mind. Meditation is followed up with action, that is, by being applied in every day life. Of what use is the great session of meditation if it does not translate in to improvement of our whole being, which can then place itself at the service of others? Once the seeds of the patience, inner strength, serenity, love, and compassion have come to maturity, it is to others that we must offer their fruit.

Inner Freedom: -
To be free is to be master of oneself. For many people such mastery involves freedom of action, movement, and opinion, the opportunity to achieve the goals they have set themselves. In the west that freedom means being able to

do whatever we want and to act on any of our impulses. But the inner freedom is a vast, clear and serene space that dispels pain and nourishes peace. Being free also means being able to follow the path of inner transformation. To achieve that, we have to overcome not only external adversity but also our innermost enemies: Laziness, lack of focus, and the habits that constantly distract us from or defer spiritual practice.

Renunciation: -

Renunciation is not about depriving ourselves of that which brings us joy and happiness – that would be absurd; it is about abandoning what causes us the inexhaustible and relentless distress. It is about having the courage to rid us of the dependency on the root causes of suffering. To do this we first have to identify and recognize these causes and then become mindful of them in our daily life. Renunciation involves simplifying our acts, our speech and our thoughts to rid ourselves of the superfluous.

Being free also means being able to follow the path of inner transformation. To achieve that, we have to overcome not only external adversity but also our inner most enemies. Like laziness, lack of focus, and the habits that constantly distract us from or differ spiritual practice.

Nature and Nurture: -

Are we born with varying genetic predisposition to happiness or unhappiness?

How do our upbringing and our life experiences favor or undermine our subjective well-being?

To what extent is it possible to modify our personality traits and generate a lasting sense of satisfaction?

What mental factors contribute to that transformation?

Many researches and studies have answered above questions in following three ways.

1. About 25 percent of our potential for happiness appears to be determined by Genes. Yet genes act more like a blue print that can be applied or ignored depending upon circumstances.

2. Outward conditions and other general factors, such as wealth, education, social status, hobbies, sex, age, ethnicity and so on have circumstantial influence, but account altogether for no more than 10 to 15 percent of the variable satisfaction quotient.

3. We can exert considerable influence on our experience of happiness and unhappiness through the way we live and think. How we perceive our life's events, and how we react to them.

8.14 - HOW TO ACHIEVE HAPPINESS: -

Happiness goes hand in hand with the capacity to assert one self with extroversion and empathy. Happy people are generally open to the world. They believe that an individual can exert control over oneself and one's life, while unhappy people tend to believe they are destiny's playthings. It would seem that the more an individual is capable of controlling one's environment happier the person is. It is interesting to note that in everyday life, extroverts experience more positive events than introverts, and neurotics have more negative experiences than stable people.

How do we explain that there is ultimately so little correlation – 10 to 15 % - between health, wealth, beauty, and happiness? Because it depends upon the way people perceive the world, which is more important to happiness than objective circumstances. It is also about the goals we set for our own lives. Having a lot of money necessarily plays a role in the happiness of someone who has set personal enrichment as his main objective, but it will have less impact on some one for whom wealth is a secondary importance.

Don't let your happiness be dependent on any object, person or situation: - It is the art of living, the purpose of our existence. Happiness is the true index of quality of life. Without happiness, life is dry and meaningless. With happiness, life immediately becomes fulfilling and wonderful. Happiness is an infectious feeling that immediately lifts the sagging spirits of people. Happy people keep themselves happy because they know the little ways to appreciate themselves and to see the humor and magic in each moment.

Happiness and Humanity: -

People are much more inclined to come to the assistance of a friend or of someone with whom they have something in common like ethnicity, nationality, religion and opinion, than to help a stranger to whom they feel no particular connection. The Buddhist approach is to gradually extend that sense of belonging to all beings. When our sense of belonging, extends to all living beings, we are intimately touched by their joys and sufferings. Those who believe themselves to be happiest are also the most humanitarians. When we are happy, the feeling of self-importance is diminished and we are more open to others. Acute depression is accompanied by difficulty in feeling and expressing love for others. Selfishness is the essential ingredient of true happiness.

True humility is freedom from all consciousness of self, which includes freedom from the consciousness of humility. The true humble man never knows that he is humble. The humble person has nothing to loose and nothing to gain. If one is praised, one feels that it is humility and not oneself that is being praised. If one is criticized, one feels that bringing one's faults to light is a great favor. Free of hope and fear alike, the humble person remains light hearted. People, who consider themselves superior, judge the faults of others more harshly and consider them to be less forgivable. Humble person makes decisions on the basis of what he believes to be right and sticks by them without concern for his own image or the opinion of others.

HOPE: -

Hope is defined by psychologists as the conviction that one can find the means to attain one's goal and develop the motivation necessary to do so. It is known that hope improves student's test results and athlete's performance, makes illness and agonizing debility more bearable, and makes pain itself (from burns, arthritis, spinal injuries, or blindness, for example) easier to tolerate. It has been demonstrated for instance, using a method to measure resistance to pain, that people who show a marked tendency to be hopeful are able to tolerate contact with a very cold surface twice as long as those who don't.

The optimist does not give up quickly. Strengthened by the hope of success, one perseveres and succeeds more often than the pessimist, especially in adverse conditions. The pessimist has a tendency to back away from difficulties, sink into resignation or turn to temporary distractions that will not solve one's problems. The pessimist will demonstrate little resolve, for one doubts everything and everyone, foresees the failure of every undertaking (instead of potential for growth, development and fruitfulness), and sees every person as a schemer and an egoist. One sees a threat in every new thing and anticipates catastrophe. In a word; when hearing a door creak, the optimist thinks it's opening and the pessimist thinks it's closing.

Time of Happiness: -
At the time of happiness, one gets completely involved in an activity for its own sake. There is a sense of transcending the Ego and Time. Every action, movement, thought follows inevitably from the previous one, like playing Jazz. Your whole being is involved, and you are using your skills to the utmost.

Consider walking just for the pleasure of walking, freely and firmly, without hurrying. We are present in every step. When we wish to speak, we stop walking and lend all our attention to the person, to speaking and to listening. Stop, look around, and see how wonderful life is: the trees, the white clouds, and the infinite sky. Listen to the birds, delight in the light breeze. Let us walk as free people and feel our steps growing lighter as we walk. Let us appreciate every step we take.

As satisfying as it may be to cultivate the experience of flow, it is still only a tool. If it is to make any long-term improvement in our quality of life it must be filled with human qualities, such as altruism and wisdom. The value of the flow depends on the motivation coloring the mind. It can be negative in case of the burglar, neutral of mundane activity- ironing clothes say - or positive when we are involved in a rescue operation or meditating on compassion. That experience is a source of inner peace and openness to the world and others.

Ethics of happiness: -
It is not possible to live happily if one does not live beautiful, righteous, and wise life; or to lead a beautiful, righteous and wise life if one is not happy. The goal of Buddhist ethics is to free all beings, including one-self, from momentary and long-term suffering and to develop the ability to help others to do so. In order to accomplish this we must equitably balance our own aspirations for well being that of others. It is not a question of defining good or evil absolutely, but of remaining alert to the happiness and suffering we cause by our deeds, our words, and our thoughts.

Thus the very core of ethics is our state of mind, not the form our actions take. If we relied solely on a deed's outward manifestation, it would be impossible to distinguish, for instance, between a white lie and a malicious one. If the killer asks you where the person he is chasing is hiding, that is obviously not the moment to tell the truth. The same holds true for an aggressive action. When a mother roughly shoves her child across the street to prevent the child from being hit by a car, the act is violent only in appearance; she has saved the child's life. Conversely if some one approaches you with a big smile and showers you with compliments only to rip you off, his conduct is non violent in appearance, but his intentions are actually malevolent.

Evil is not a demonic power external to ourselves, and good is not absolute principle independent of us. Everything occurs in our minds. Love and compassion are reflections of the true nature of all living beings – what we have called as basic goodness. Evil is a deviation from this basic goodness, which can be remedied.

Buddhism says that a person's goodness remains intact deep within even when it is horribly marred at the surface. This is not about naively ignoring the extent to which that good nature can be buried beneath hatred, greed and cruelty; rather it is about understanding that the mere fact of its existence always allows for its potential reemergence.

Thought to Destiny: -
Sow a thought and reap a deed,
Sow a deed and reap a habit,
Sow a habit and reap a character,
Sow a character and reap a destiny.

Radiate Happiness: -
Have you ever noticed that happiness is not a dependency, it is a decision? You don't actually need anything to be happy. It's not something that comes from outside, it comes from inside, and when you radiate a happy energy you'll be amazed what it attracts into your life. Don't worry, be happy...sound familiar? Decide now, be happy, and watch magic begin to enter your life.

Let Go: -

Just as the bird has to find the courage to let go of the branch in order to fly, so we also must let go of our branches if we are to know the exhilaration of soaring to the highest potential of our life. The branches we hold to areour inner attachments - our beliefs, ideas and memories. And then there are the outer attachments - people, possessions, positions and privileges are a few. But as long as we hold on to them we will live in fear (of letting go and loss) and we will never be free. And just watch those birds, by letting go of one branch they are able to spend the rest of their life alighting on a million other branches, and they enjoy the view from each. Are you flying and soaring in your life, or are you stuck on one branch, cursing others as they fly past. Go on, try it ...let go!

SPIRITUAL EDUCATION: -

A spiritual education teaches how to keep the mind free from tension and fluctuations. An unsteady mind is the result of letting you be strongly influenced by human Situations. Spiritual awareness keeps you centered and thus protected. You can claim increasing happiness and help others to do the same. This world is a supermarket of sorrow. Don't buy any! A good spiritual education teaches you how to be discerning in your shopping. Refuse to accept anything but happiness from others as well as the world.

Think Simply: -

With so many choices and decisions, so many demands from people and events, in our modern fast changing world, it's a real challenge to 'keep it simple'. Making it simple means making things easy and clear. The magic wand to wave over your life is 'planning and prioritizing'. Make plans, long and short term and then prioritize. Then practice taking one thing at a time, so you can have one thought at a time, with some space before you have to have your next thought. But don't get attached to your plans or priorities. Be flexible (easy) and yet focused (clear) and in this way you can teach yourself to think simply and act simply. One thought at a time. At your own pace. In your own space. A simple life is a contented life.

The Spiritual Aspect Of Healthcare: -

Silence, happiness, love and blessings are important aspects. Happiness leads to good health. It is only you who can give this medicine to yourself. Some bring illness to themselves through anger, greed, unfulfilled desires, expectations, suppression of feelings and relationships not based on true love. Look in your heart; you will know where your illness comes from. There are three ingredients for a long and healthy life: live with attention but without worry; use time in a worthwhile way; keep your thoughts pure, positive and filled with strength.

Peace, Love and Happiness: -
Keep peace in the mind, love in the heart and happiness in relationships.

Recipe For Happiness: -
Two heaped cups of patience,
one heart full of love,
two handfuls of generosity,
one headful of understanding and a dash of humor,
Sprinkle with kindness, add plenty of faith and mix well.
Spread over a period of a lifetime and serve to everyone you meet.

The Secret of Happiness: -
The secret of happiness is to be free of fear. Fear is like a toxin that runs through much of our thinking. It feeds on insecurity, feeling of loss, loneliness, inadequacy and attachment.

You are loveable and loving. Accept this as Truth. Appreciate and care for yourself - truly, deeply, intensely, in a way that reflects your real value. Then you will automatically have the same regards for all other living beings and things.

Truly and Permanently Happy: -
The secret to life's purpose is to be happy. In order to be truly and permanently happy, we have to fulfill our best intentions and act on them right away ... even if that means we start by just giving good thoughts to them.

Am I Happy?
If there is any sadness I make a strong effort to be free of it quickly, otherwise it grows like a vine in the rainy season: by midday I will be confused; by evening a whole jungle of weak, wasteful and negative attitudes will have taken deep roots in my mind. The result equals chaos. Sometimes I reach a stage where the attitude is: "So what if I feel the blues today? It is my life; no one else will be affected". Firstly, the more I allow myself to experience sorrow, the less time I have available to be happy and contented. It sounds

ridiculously obvious, but am I aware of the value of happiness? It is an extremely rare commodity, and the cost goes sky high. Secondly, is it my life? Yes, I am living it, but am I not a member of a family or a co-worker with others, and am I not part of society? If so, then every movement affects and is affected by those around me.

Daily Decisions: -
What I am experiencing at this moment is the result of choices and decisions made in the past; what I will experience in the future depends on choices and decisions I make now. Happiness is a daily decision.

8.15 - Finally Self-Transformation: -
Mere intellectual understanding is not enough. It is not by leaving the doctor's prescription by the bedside or learning it by heart that we are cured. We must integrate what we have learned so that our understanding becomes intimately bound up with our mind's flow. Then it ceases to be theory and becomes self-transformation.

I have been lucky enough so far to have had enough to eat and wear and a roof over my head. I consider my possessions to be tools, and there is not one I consider to be indispensable. Without a laptop I might stop writing, and without a camera I might stop sharing pictures, but it would in no way impair the quality of every moment of my life.

Inside Out:
There is essentially only one way in which you can bring about self-transformation - that's if you want to - but you will not think you need to if you are still taking your happiness from outside yourself, and still managing to tolerate the periods of unhappiness which result. As soon as your happiness is dependent on anything outside, you make yourself a slave to a condition, substance or perhaps a person. A slave is not free. And happiness is impossible if you are not free. Perhaps this goes some way to explaining why our happiness fluctuates. Real happiness does not go up and down. Real freedom means that your happiness comes from inside out. That will require detachment and renunciation, not least from the illusions and conditioning of society which would

have you believe happiness can be acquired from outside in. **Can you see it? Inside out, not outside in!**

Do Now:
Procrastination is not only the thief of time; it is the creator of subtle inner tension. You know you are cheating yourself. There are three secrets to overcoming procrastination.

1. Don't wait till you feel like doing it - the feeling will come only when you start doing it
2. List all the things you have to do and then prioritize the list.
3. Create a vision of the result and be motivated by the vision of the outcome, not the thought of the process.

And the options to those ideas?
1. Ask for help.
2. Completely forget about it, you don't have to do anything!
3. If there is anything you can learn from the process then see it is action learning.

GIVE:
Give happiness and you will receive happiness.
Give peace and you will feel peaceful.
Give sorrow and you will get sorrow in return.
Create thoughts and words that give only peace and happiness. The world is filled with worry and sorrow. Do something different.

CHAPTER 9

WHAT IS "ALL IS IN YOUR HEAD"?

9.01 – ALL IS IN YOUR HEAD: -

Being an engineer all my life, I have always been interested in matters of the science, and I've always had a somewhat conflicted relationship to religion. On the one hand, for anyone interested in humanity's further evolution, it's hard not to be excited by the latest findings of a discipline that, in a single 20th century, has managed to cure polio, crack the genetic code, send a probe to Saturn's largest moon, and invent the Internet. But on the other hand, there is something about science's tendency to reduce even life's greatest mysteries to the movements of matter alone that has always left me a little chilled. In the face of this unfolding world of meaning, purpose, and mystery, the notion that science held the keys to ultimate truth began to seem increasingly hard to accept. One result of this split personality is that whenever I'm confronted with the battle between science and religion, I always find it hard to take sides and end up in a sort of internal battle of my own.

The thriving field of neuroscience promises to fill that void and then some. Employing powerful new methods for studying the intimate workings of the brain, the pioneers of this increasingly self-assured discipline aspire to demonstrate once and for all that the mind, emotions, and even consciousness itself are entirely generated by the three-pound lump of gray matter in our skulls. For a generation of researchers in this field, the prime directive is to prove what Nobel laureate Francis Crick, who turned to neuroscience after co-discovering the DNA helix, called "the astonishing hypothesis":

That "you, your joys and sorrows, your memories and your ambitions, your sense of personal identity and freewill are in fact no more than the

behavior of a vast assembly of nerve cells and their associated molecules. You are nothing but a pack of neurons."

Despite the insistence of neuroscientists that our brains are the sole source of our experience and behavior, there are very strong reasons why most of us don't want to believe that this is the case. For most of us with religious or spiritual inclinations, accepting such a premise would eradicate, in one fell swoop, one of our most basic convictions—the belief in an immaterial SOUL or (if we're Buddhists) "mind essence" that transcends the physical body. Even for those of us who do not count themselves among the religious people, the notion that we are entirely reducible to brain stuff still seems to take away something essential—our humanity, our dignity, our sense of meaning.

There is something about the experience of consciousness itself, some kind of mystery inherent in the fact that we are conscious at all, that seems irreducible to the mere firing of our neurons. As convinced as the neuroscientists are of their case, I can't help feeling there must be more to the story.

I would have to dive into the unknown waters of brain science and find out for myself what the fuss is all about. What does it actually mean to say that our brains are the sole source of our experience? What evidence is there to prove it? And assuming it was true, would that mean that all of our spirituality is a trick?

Could the brain in fact be the soul?
Who had determined from an early age to disprove the existence of God and the Soul, made a passionate call for neuroscience to begin employing its growing scientific arsenal to demonstrate the material basis of consciousness?

Philosophers have been arguing about over the past few centuries. Ever since René Descartes gave birth to dualism by asserting the separation of Mind and Body, the big issue in the philosophy of mind has been figuring out how these two different substances—the mental and the physical—could interact with one another. On one hand, how could an objective, physical brain give rise to subjective, mental events? And on the other hand, how could those subjective, mental events—presumably not governed by physical laws—impact the objective, physical world?

Through the use of brain imaging techniques, it allows them to compare snapshots of the brain when a given perception is conscious and when it is not conscious. This, they hope, will ultimately give them some clues to understanding how neuronal activity correlates with consciousness. No matter how clear a snapshot we can get of what type of neuronal activity correlates with which sorts of conscious perceptions, we will still be no closer to understanding how the brain could possibly *produce* something like conscious experience itself.

Different Theories: -
The first thinker on record to suggest a link between mind and brain was the Pythagorean Alcmaeon of Croton, writing in the fifth century BC. Prior to that, across cultures, it was widely held that the Mind, or Soul, was located in the heart. The priests of ancient Egypt, for example, when preparing the body of the deceased for the afterlife, would pull out the brain, piece by piece through the nose, but would leave the heart intact, believing it to be the center of a person's Being and Intelligence. In most ancient cultures, the idea of dissecting a cadaver was taboo, so with no knowledge of the nervous system, it was only natural to conclude that the accelerated heartbeat that accompanied an excited mind was a clear indication of the bodily location of mental life. Even such great thinkers as Aristotle subscribed to this view. But, rigorous biologist that he was, Greece's greatest polymath was certain that the brain must serve some function. Noticing that it was cool to the touch, he concluded that it refrigerated the blood—a conclusion that also allowed him to account for the inordinately large brains of humans. Because of our unusual intelligence, he argued, our hearts produced more heat and, thus, required a larger cooling system.

Alcmaeon's brain-centered theory, however, did manage to persuade the likes of Hippocrates and Plato to abandon the prevailing "cardiovascular theory," and despite Aristotle's resistance to the idea, it was picked up by physicians during the early Roman period who broke the taboo against dissecting cadavers and discovered the nervous system branching out from the skull and spine. Although this view gradually took hold, and has remained dominant ever since, it was still being disputed as late as the seventeenth century, when philosopher Henry More wrote, "This lax pith or marrow in man's head shows no more capacity for thought than a cake of suet or a bowl of curds." It is also worth noting that the model of the brain that prevailed through most of the second millennium was very different from the model we subscribe to today.

Whereas we now see a vast, complex electrochemical network of some hundred billion neurons, these early anatomists were convinced that the Mind, or Soul, was a kind of etheric presence that lived in large "ventricles" or chambers in the brain, communicating its commands to the rest of the body through "vital spirits" that flowed through the nervous system's minute pathways.

Indeed, it has been this move away from a spirit-based view of the brain's workings toward a purely biological one that has led to the idea, so unpopular with the religiously inclined, that the mind, or soul, is ultimately reducible to brain activity.

Anatomy of Brain: -
It is hard for most of us to imagine what it would be like to have one of our most taken-for-granted faculties suddenly no longer available to us, like the ability to respond emotionally to our visual experience. Indeed, what is most intriguing about these stories is the way in which they challenge one of our most fundamental intuitions—our sense that the self is a single, unified whole. Repeated throughout the neurology literature are cases in which damage to a specific part of the brain leads to the loss of some specific aspect of our ability to perceive and respond to the world. Damage one part of my brain and I'll lose the ability to learn any new facts. Damage another part and I'll be unable to recognize faces. Damage another area and my experience of the world will remain intact, but I'll be unable to find the words I need to speak clearly about it. Damage still another part and I'll lose the ability to pay attention to half of my visual field, but I will be convinced that the half I'm seeing is the whole picture. As a result, in the morning, I'll only shave half of my face. Taken together, the data from neurology suggest that despite our brain's ability to organize our experience into a seamless unity, we are, in fact, made up of many parts, the loss of any of which can have dramatic effects on the whole.

However ignorant we may be of brain science, most of us are familiar by now with the idea that our brain has two hemispheres, a left one and a right one, each responsible for very different aspects of our behavior. Our dominant left brain, we are told, is more analytical; our right brain more emotional, creative, and intuitive. Although much of the popular psychology literature on the right brain–left brain distinction has been, in the eyes of neuroscience, exceedingly simplistic and inaccurate, the basic fact—known in the field as "hemispheric specialization"—is well established. In a normal brain, these two hemispheres communicate with one another through a large band of nervous tissue known as the corpus callosum (larger in women than in men, incidentally, accounting for their superior ability to multitask, among other things). But what would happen if the connection between these two halves of the brain was severed, leaving us, in effect, with two brains in our head? Would we end up with two different selves? Over the past few decades, a group of neuroscientists have had the chance to find out.

Epilepsy comes in many forms, some mild and some severe. In its worst manifestations, it brings with it nearly constant seizures that make life almost impossible for the patient. In an attempt to control these severe cases, in the 1960s neurosurgeons began cutting the corpus callosum to prevent the seizures from spreading from one side of the brain to the other. The procedure was remarkably successful, and to the relief of the doctors who pioneered the treatment, patients generally recovered well and were able to live relatively normal lives. But in these "split-brain" patients, psych biologist Roger Sperry soon recognized a rare opportunity to study the differences between the two hemispheres in a way that had never been possible before. Over the decades that followed, he pioneered a series of studies that ultimately earned him a Nobel Prize. Most of these split-brain studies focused on illuminating the functional differences between the two hemispheres, but along the way, Sperry and his colleagues began to realize that there were implications to what they were seeing that went far beyond the scope of their initial questions.

One of the most commonly known facts about hemispheric specialization is that the right brain controls the left side of the body and the left-brain controls the right side. Where visual input is concerned, the same rule applies. The left half of the visual field (of each eye) is routed to the right brain and vice versa. Knowing this, researchers realized that by presenting information quickly to only one side of the subject's visual field, they could ensure that the information only reached one side of the subject's brain. This technique provided the cornerstone of their research.

Employing this method, researchers had learned early on that the dominant left brain, with its ability to reason and use language, is the home of what we usually think of as the conscious mind. For instance, when asked to report on information that had been presented to their left-brain alone, subjects could speak about it quite normally. When information had been presented only to the right brain, by contrast, subjects seemed unaware of it. As the research progressed, however, the picture grew more complex. For instance, when the right brain was shown an image of a spoon, the subject's left hand (which is controlled by the right brain) could successfully identify an actual spoon from among an assortment of objects, even though the subject claimed to have no conscious knowledge of having seen it. Despite its inability to express itself, the right brain nonetheless seemed to have a will and mind of its own. Eager to test this, Scottish neuroscientist Donald MacKay devised a twenty-questions-type guessing game and successfully taught each of the two halves of a patient's brain to play it—first against him and then against the other half. But this image of the two halves of one brain competing with one another soon moved from the experimental to the macabre, as split-brain patients began to develop the bizarre malady known as "alien-hand syndrome."

The idea that splitting the brain amounts to nothing less than splitting the self is a challenging one with enormous implications for our understanding of the brain's role in creating consciousness and even individuality. Therefore, it is no surprise that it has remained a controversial finding, even among scientists. But for the man who was awarded the Nobel Prize for his pioneering work in this area, the experience of working with split-brain patients for many years all pointed in one direction. "Everything we have seen indicates that the surgery has left these people with two separate minds," Sperry wrote. "That is, two separate spheres of consciousness."

Cerebral Cortex (cerebrum): -
This is the most highly evolved part of our brain. The furrowed, quarter inch thick slab of gray matter that covers the surface of the brain is divided in two hemispheres and four lobes. Creativity generally resides in the right hemisphere, analytic ability in the left. **Frontal Lobe** – Area of brain just behind eyes, which controls intellectual functioning, including thought process, meaning and behavior. **Temporal Lobe** – Located on lower sides of the brain, the temporal lobes are responsible for smell, taste, hearing and visual associations. **Parietal Lobe** – Upper portion of the brain, just under top of skull. The parietal lobes are responsible for higher sensory and language functions. **Occipital Lobe** – located in the rear area of brain, the occipital lobes receive the visual information from the eyes.

9.02 - THE MIND IS I (oneself): -

Mapping the brain of course has not been an easy task. A dense tapestry threaded by archipelagoes (group of islands) of nerve cells, the brain consists of billions of neurons and trillions of synapses. It is the most complex object on the planet. The heart pumps blood, the lungs ingest oxygen, the stomach absorbs nutrients, but the functions of the brain are manifold. It monitors the body's basic processes, coordinates physical movement, perceives, thinks, acts and feels. It is an executive branch of government that ceaselessly plans, reacts and interacts with the organic world around it.

But if you define consciousness as mental content – the information contained in the thoughts that is reportable by the person, and which they can reflect on and talk about it, in that sense the consciousness is a valid subject of scientific study.

Consciousness: -

There are many levels, from basic perception of the environment to the higher consciousness, which is the capacity for self-awareness. Sense of identity is probably a mixture – a nested hierarchy – of coordinated functions arising out of several areas of the brain. But the right hemisphere is the dominant source of the self. Some scientists believe that the right hemisphere is not simply dominant in the formation of the self-awareness, but it is essential. There are definite neural correlates of higher order consciousness that, if you mark them out, the person is no longer conscious, no longer capable of self-awareness. Just tenth of an inch beneath the furrowed ridges of gray matter that covers the right front side of the brain, is a layer of tangled cell tissue that makes us uniquely human. There may be other similarly minuscule areas of the brain that contribute to consciousness, but the right prefrontal cortex – located just above the right eye – is the primary source of self awareness.

Nature vs. Nurture: -

Is this a religiosity, a function of environment of how we are brought up, or as many neuroscientists now believe that it is a function or reflection of brain activity. **In other words we are hard wired for GOD.**

The relationship between brain chemistry and consciousness is one that, in the neuroscience age, is hard to get away from. As neurobiologists have deepened our understanding of the powerful neurochemicals that underlie our moods and motivations, words like adrenaline, endorphins, dopamine, and serotonin have become part of our vernacular. And for those who have spent any time studying the field, it has become increasingly difficult not to think of human behavior in chemical terms.

If the study of brain damage and neurochemistry provides the beginnings of an outline of the profound link between brain and mind, powerful new brain scanning techniques promise to fill out the details in living color. By providing a picture of the brain's blood-flow patterns when engaged in particular activities, PET, SPECT, and MRI scans are enabling researchers to map the regions of the brain like cartographers once charted the contours of the globe.

Discovering the biological basis of speech and perception is, however, just the beginning. With experimental methodologies improving by the month, even the more complex aspects of our experience, such as emotion, reason, motivation, and will, are beginning to give up their secrets. **In *Mapping the Mind*,** science journalist Rita Carter writes: "It is now possible to locate and observe the mechanics of rage, violence, and misperception, and even to detect the physical signs of complex qualities of mind like kindness, humor, heartlessness, gregariousness, altruism, mother-love, and self-awareness."

The profound implications of these findings are not lost on the neuroscience community. Indeed, one of the more interesting new areas of discussion is what has become known as neuron-ethics. According to psychologist Martha Farah, brain imaging in particular has opened up an ethical can of worms with its unprecedented ability to peer into the previously private reaches of the individual mind. For instance, with neuroimaging, it has now become possible to tell when someone is being deceitful, or even when he or she is deceiving him or her. Enter lie-detection 3.0. Scientists can also discern whether someone was involved in a crime by showing them objects from the crime scene and seeing how their brain responds. Welcome to the new forensics, as marketed by Brain Fingerprinting Laboratories, Inc. It is even possible to tell whether someone is an illegal drug user by showing them photos of drug paraphernalia and seeing whether the brain enters a "craving state." Meet the new war on drugs.

Then there is what Farah refers to as "brain typing." Using these same methodologies, neuroscientists can now look behind the scenes of your persona and find out what sort of human being you really are. Do you secretly harbor racial prejudices? By watching your brain while you look at pictures of racially diverse faces, brain scanners can provide an answer. How about sexual preferences? By showing you a variety of erotic imagery, we can see who or what turns you (or your brain) on. (And don't bother trying to suppress your response. Your brain looks different when you do that too.) Are you a risk-taker? A pessimist? An introvert? Neurotic? Persistent? Empathic? Even such core personality traits as these are now laid bare before the new neuron-interrogation.

9.03 - ETHICAL ISSUES INDEED

Within the discussion around neuron ethics, however, there is a larger issue coming to the front that some feel may rattle the very foundations of the way we think about ethics itself. In civilized culture, our ethical norms and even our legal system are built on the notion of individual responsibility. When judging the actions of another, we hold him or her accountable for having freely chosen those actions for good or ill. But if we look at the picture of the human being emerging from neuroscience, many feel that there is little in it to support the idea that we freely choose our actions. If our actions are entirely caused by the brain, and the brain is in turn shaped entirely by the interaction between genes and environment, where does free will enter the equation? This may seem like philosophical nonsense, given that one of our most basic human intuitions is our sense of our own freedom to choose. But prominent neuroscientists claim that this deterministic picture of human behavior has, in fact, been reinforced by a number of experiments that seem to show that our brain makes choices before we are conscious of having made them, that in fact, conscious will is an illusion.

This bizarre notion, which is widely held within the neuroscience community, is clearly not one that will go over easily with the public at large. In fact, on the controversy scale, it may run a close second to what is no doubt going to be the most hotly disputed neuroscience claim of all—**the notion that, as Farah puts it, even our "sense of spirituality" is itself a "physical function of the brain."**

9.04 - MEDITATION AND BRAIN: -

During meditation or prayer, there is an increase in activity in the prefrontal lobes, a region responsible for such higher faculties as intention, will, and the ability to focus our attention. But it was another one of the science findings, in particular, that seemed to create the entire stir.

If you look at the back of the brain, Newberg said, "you can see that it is much less pronounced during the meditation session than before. This is the posterior parietal lobe, what I call the orientation-association area. It's the part of the brain that allows us to orient ourselves in space that gives us a sense of boundary between ourselves and the rest of the world. What we hypothesized was that the sense of unity, or oneness, that people experience during meditative practice would be correlated with a reduction of activity in this area. And this is exactly what the neuro-imaging shows."

People asked Newberg, "Do you think your research shows that religious experience is completely reducible to brain activity?

Is God all in our head?"

Newberg responded, "Let's say we were to take the materialist position that the only way we experience anything is through the brain. This means that the only way we can tell whether something is real is through our brain. The brain is the organ that discerns what is real. Okay, now this presents a slight problem for the materialist position because when people have mystical experiences, they universally report that they have experienced something that is *more real* than our everyday material reality. Which means that the brain perceives God, or pure consciousness, to be more real than anything else. So if the brain is what determines what is real and what isn't, and this is a universal experience of human brains across cultures, where does that leave us?"

But it can give no clear answer as to where consciousness comes from. On the other hand, if we take a religious perspective and say that consciousness is primary, it's not so easy to explain the existence of matter. Newberg feels that perhaps consciousness and matter are two ways of looking at the same thing. But he thinks the bottom line is that we really don't know yet.

Newberg further states that for all the evidence neuroscience seems to present for the case that the brain creates the mind, the reality is that nobody has yet been able to explain, let alone demonstrate, how it could actually do such a thing. **The mind/body problem is as mysterious as ever.** And although this doesn't seem to be persuading the neuron-scientific community at large to question its materialistic assumptions.

9.05 - THE ART OF MEDITATION: -

As meditation is demystified and mainstreamed, the methods have become more streamlined. There is less incense burning today, but there remains a nugget of Buddhist philosophy: the belief that by sitting in silence for 10 minutes to 40 minutes a day and actively concentrating on breath or a word or an image, you can train yourself to focus on the present over the past and the future, transcending reality by fully accepting it. In its most modern form, it has dropped the creepy mantras that have you memorize a secret phrase or syllable; instead you focus on a sound or on your breathing. The brain like the body also undergoes subtle changes during deep meditation. The first scientific studies in '60s and '70s basically proved that meditators are really, really focused.

How to Meditate: -
1. Find a quiet place, turn off the lights. The fewer distractions you have, the easier it will be to concentrate.
2. Close your eyes. The idea is to shut out the outside world, so your brain can stop actively processing information coming from the senses.
3. Pick a word any word. Find a word or phrase that means something to you, whose sound or rhythm is soothing when repeated.
4. Say it again and again. Try saying your word or phrase to yourself with every out breath. The monotony will help you focus.

Which Form of God should we meditate?
Fix your attention on that form which appeals to you most: but know for certain that all forms are the forms of ONE GOD alone. He is blessed indeed who has known all as one.

Scientific Discovery: -
What scientists are discovering through these studies is that with enough practice, the neurons in the brain will adapt themselves to direct activity in that frontal. Concentration- oriented area of the brain.

Frontal Lobe: This is the most highly evolved part of the brain, responsible for reasoning, planning, emotions and self-conscious awareness. During meditation, the frontal cortex tends to go offline.

Parietal Lobe: This part of the brain processes the sensory in formation about the surrounding world, orienting you in time and space. During meditation, activity in the parietal lobe slows down.

Thalamus: The gatekeeper for the senses, this organ focuses your attention by funneling some sensory data deeper in to the brain and stopping other signals in their tracks. Meditation reduces the flow of incoming information to a trickle.

Reticular Formation: As the brain's sentry, this structure receives incoming stimuli and puts the brain on alert, ready to respond. Meditating dials back the arousal signal.

Meditation Flavors: -
The meditation practice itself comes in many flavors, from the purely spiritual to mostly physical.

Concentrative: Meditative technique that directs the mind to a single focus, such as on breath or mantra.

Mindfulness: Teaches an evenhanded, accepting awareness of whatever arises in the senses.

Movement: heightens the awareness of sensations of movement, such as in walking or Tai Chi.

Visualization: Generates a mental image, from simple crosses or a single square of color to complex symbols such as the elaborate mandalas of Tibetan Buddhism.

Loving-kindness: Cultivates a positive mood or beneficent outlook through the contemplation of such feeling as compassion for all people.

Transformation: Seeks Solace or the solution to specific problems by turning negative emotions in to positive energies.

9.06 - NDE (NEAR DEATH EXPERIENCES): -

The simple fact that people have these experiences does not in itself prove anything one way or the other regarding the existence of consciousness outside the brain." Simply put, how do we know the NDE is not just a brain-generated illusion? According to the "dying brain hypothesis" as put forward by psychologist Susan Blackmore, all of the specific phenomena associated with the classic NDE can be accounted for by established brain responses to the "severe stress, extreme fear, and cerebral anoxia" that would naturally accompany a brush with death.

Yet riddled throughout the NDE literature are accounts that seem to suggest that there is more going on in these experiences than can as yet fit into the materialist picture. For instance, several physicians and nurses have reported patients being able to describe in detail events that happened when they were clearly unconscious, comatose, or even clinically brain dead. So far, the research into NDEs has been largely anecdotal, and as yet, no one has provided the kind of independent verification of data that would stand as scientific proof. For the scientific researcher, the interesting question is this: **When does the NDE occur?** If it could be shown scientifically that the near-death experience occurs during unconsciousness, as suggested by those who have survived a cardiac arrest, when all brain function has ceased and there is apparently no mechanism to mediate it, this would be highly significant, because it would suggest that consciousness can indeed exist independently of a functioning brain.

If the mind is not contained in the brain, then just where exactly is it? The traditional dualist answer, around since Descartes' time, is that it is a separate immaterial substance that interacts with the brain and body in some mysterious way. Trying to figure out how this interaction occurs is what launched the debate over the mind/body problem in the first place. But today, thanks to advances in scientific theory over the past century and a half, some new ways of thinking about the matter are starting to emerge.

If brains behave as quantum objects, then it opens the possibility that our brains are connected, or entangled, with everything. In which case we can think of psychic phenomena not as a mysterious process of information being sent from one place to another and somehow getting into your head, but more as a change of attention within the brain. If the whole universe is already inside your head because you're bio-entangled with it, then if you wish to see what is in somebody else's head or what's in a hidden envelope somewhere else, or what's on the other side of the world right now or last year, you simply need to attend to the portion of your brain that is entangled with that state.

9.07 - MIND AND BRAIN: - [33]

In recent years, philosophers, theologians, cosmologists, and even mainstream cognitive scientists have joined the fray, developing powerful critiques and alternative theories that attempt to expand the frame of our thinking about the mind and brain.

Since the human nervous system is the most complex piece of hardware on the planet, it's no surprise that the most complex form of consciousness accompanies it. Though still eschewed by most mainstream philosophers and scientists, this view is gaining ground, particularly among the alternative intelligentsia, in large part because it provides a potentially non-reductionist framework for understanding the relationship between the mind and the brain (even if some of its proponents, like Chalmers, use it as an argument for the possibility of conscious machines—if all matter is conscious, after all, why couldn't a super-complex computer be as conscious as you or me?).

Is it possible that it will be science's failure to solve the mind/body problem that will ultimately lead to materialism's undoing? Could neuroscience's bold attempt to penetrate the mysteries of the human psyche be that one step too far that brings the entire edifice crashing to the ground? It is of course far too early to say, but if such an eventuality were to unfold, given the mythic implications, it would no doubt give the gods—and perhaps even Icarus—a good chuckle.

GOD versis NEURONS:
Still, in the face of such multilayered complexity, one can't help but feel compelled to reach for synthesis, whether it's God or the Neurons that are doing the compelling.

I find the materialist notion that the mind is an irrelevant byproduct of brain function about as plausible as the dualistic idea that consciousness is some ghostly ethereal substance that exists entirely independent of the brain. The truth, it seems, must lie somewhere in between. But where exactly?

Just how the brain's neural network could function as a "tuning system" for consciousness, however, is still something I'm struggling to visualize.

I'm also tempted to go with some version of the emergence idea, as it seems the closest to hard science to say that consciousness in some way comes out of the brain. But as one philosopher pointed out to me, **"Until someone explains *how* emergence occurs, we might just as well say GOD did it."**

Perhaps the most promising and ultimately satisfying theories are the integral ones that acknowledge the essential reality of different levels and dimensions of existence, allowing interiors and exteriors, consciousness and matter, to be seen as different sides of the same event, neither reducible to the other. Where mind and brain are concerned, however, even the most integral theories have thus far been unable to explain *how* the two interconnect, leaving the mind/body problem a mystery for another day.

CONSCIOUSNESS:
One thought experiment is imagining that our brain really is generating our consciousness. Think about it—this whole three-dimensional experience of sound, color, thought, feeling, and movement all somehow arising out of the organic functions of this wrinkled slab of tofu-like substance in your head. It seems hard to imagine, but if it were true, what would that say about the nature of matter itself? In fact, if I think about it in this way long enough, I start to wonder which would really be mind-boggling—to find out that the brain doesn't create the mind, or to find out that it does.

There are levels of who we are that simply cannot be understood by looking at our neurons alone. Although we may not lose our humanity to neuroscience, however, it does seem likely that as research progresses, we will have to let go of a few ideas—possibly even some big ones—about what our humanity is made of. The great specter of brain science is that it will demonstrate that we are merely conscious organic machines, that all of our experience and behavior originates in the brain. Based on the evidence from frontier science alone, it doesn't seem likely at this point that it will quite be able to do that. But let's say that it were able to show that *most* of our behavior and experience is rooted in the brain. What would that mean? Well, for starters, we'd have to come to terms with the fact that we're a lot more organic machine than we'd like to think—that, as much as we savor the nuances of our personal wishes, aspirations, and personalities, most of our responses are driven by genetic and social conditioning wired into our brains on a level we cannot see.

However, even if we take the materialist position that the brain is the sole mediator of experience and the final arbiter of truth, we are left with the fact that human brains across the ages have universally concluded that the spiritual reality glimpsed in mystical experience is in fact of a higher order than the ordinary reality we experience every day.

And this leads us to what may be the most interesting point of all. For as Newberg's research demonstrates, there is little doubt that the brain is at least a big part of what is enabling us to perceive that higher order. This means that, in what may be the greatest miracle we know, life somehow managed to evolve an organ capable not only of reflecting on itself but of perceiving something higher than itself—perceiving, even, that which many believe to be the very source and creative driver of the cosmos. Looked at in this way, the brain suddenly starts to seem a lot less like some frightening organic computer that we'd do well to distance ourselves from and a lot more like a rather mysterious and even spiritual event in its own right. After all, if it can do all that, who knows what kind of genius and untapped potential live within its folds? Given that human evolution is still in its early days, it in fact seems likely that the awesome powers of the human brain have only begun to reveal themselves. If we can use our gray matter to avoid destroying ourselves, we may find that the story of humanity's higher potentials is just getting started.

9.08 - THOUGHT POWER: -

All that we are is the result of what we have thought, it is founded on our thoughts and made up of our thoughts.

Thoughts are ink in the pen with which we are writing our destiny.

As you think so you become. By changing one's thought pattern, one can change one's life.

Thoughts are things, thoughts are forces, and thoughts are the building blocks of life.

Destiny is not matter of chance; it is a matter of choice.

A thought if it is constantly held in mind, will drive us to action, if it is a thought of service, it will lead us to an act of service, if it is a thought of impurity, it will lead us to an act of impurity.

Thoughts take more time and space in our lives than actions.

Thought creates an action: –

An action, which is repeated, creates a habit and a habit is a terrible thing. The sum total of our habits makes our character. It is character that determines our destiny. If we wish to change our destiny, we must begin to change our thoughts. We must change our pattern of thinking. Our minds need to be cleansed of thoughts of lust, hatred and greed, passion and pride, selfishness and miserliness, greed and arrogance, envy and jealousy, resentment and ill will. There are those who nurture thoughts of hatred, envy and jealousy in their hearts how can they ever be happy?

Hatred and happiness can never dwell together, even as darkness and light can never live together.

Thought Control: –

So many of our ills would be cured, if only we could change the pattern of our mind. Change the mind and you change the world. The modern world has gone astray, because it lays undue emphasis on the "work" side of life. Work has its place in life, but more important than "work" is "Thought". Take care of your thoughts, because every thought is a force, which we generate for our good, or evil.

No it is not our fault if evil thoughts come to us and tear in to bits the fabric of good life, which we may have gradually built. But it is our fault if we welcome evil thoughts and let them germinate in the soil of our minds. Out of them will grow trees of bitter fruits, which we shall be compelled to swallow. If we have good thoughts – thoughts of love and compassion, beauty and joy, faith and freedom, of peace and wisdom – we invite to ourselves good forces, forces of light and in that measure, we create heaven around ourselves.

Positive and Negative Thinking: –
It is not that the man with a positive attitude refuses to recognize the negative side of life. Life has a negative side, a dark side also. The pathways of life are strewn with difficulties. But the man with the positive attitude refuses to dwell on the negative side of life. He looks for the best results from the worst conditions. Surrounded by the trials and tribulations, he looks for some place to stand on. Conditions may be adverse, yet he continues to expect good things. It is an inviolable law of life, that when you expect good, good will comes to you. There are people who always think negative. Speak to them of something and they will tell you "It can not be done! It is impossible! There are people who always think of diseases and death. Those are the ones who, through the magnet power of their own thoughts, draw disease to themselves. They are their own enemies.

Vibrations: –
Each one of us is vibrating to a particular frequency like a tuning fork. Tuning fork vibrates to 118, 186, 212 frequency and so on. Each one us vibrate to a particular frequency. The frequency at which one is vibrating is different from the other. When both people's frequencies are in harmony with each other, they like each other. But if they are in disharmony, then for no apparent reason they do not like each other. **The spirit is vibratory.** In the measure in which I invite spirit in to my life, in that measure I will be more and more vibratory. Every vibration contains certain power. There are vibrations that are very powerful, while others are less powerful. Each one of us is the generator of vibrations. There are people of such powerful vibrations that they can move out and heal other people or help other people. A blessing is a vibration that moves out of the holy ones to us.

Will Power: –

Willpower should be understood to be the strength of mind, which makes it capable of meeting success or failure with equanimity. Strong will power must be developed and this comes through practice and through control over one's thoughts. Our minds must be filled with the thought of GOD if we are to grow in will power; otherwise it is very easy to slip. Prayers can increase will power by resolving to give up something which one relishes, and you can strengthen your will power through studies of biographies and sayings of men, women of will power.

9.09 - PAIN AND SUFFERING IN LIFE: -

There is a difference between physical pains, which is a physiological process, and suffering, which is our mental and emotional response to the pain. So the question arises – can finding, an underlying purpose and meaning behind our pain modify our attitude about it? And can a change in attitude lessen the degree to which we suffer when we are physically injured?

To view pain not as universal enemy as seen in the west but as a remarkable, elegant, and sophisticated biological system that warns us of damage to our body and thus protects us.

There is no doubt that our attitude and mental outlook can strongly affect the degree to which we suffer when we are in physical pain. Let's say, for instance, that two individuals, a construction worker and a concert pianist suffer the same finger injury, while the amount of physical pain might be the same for both individuals, the construction worker might suffer very little and in fact rejoice if the injury resulted in a month of paid vacation which he or she was in need of, whereas the same injury could result in intense suffering to the pianist who viewed playing as his or her primary source of joy in life.

The idea that our mental attitude influences our ability to perceive and endure pain is not limited to theoretical situations such as above; it has been demonstrated by many scientific studies and experiments. Researchers looking in to this issue began by tracing the pathways of how pain is perceived and experienced. Pain begins with a sensory signal – an alarm that goes off when nerve endings are stimulated by something that is sensed as dangerous. Millions of signals are sent through the spinal cord on the base of the brain. These signals are then sorted out and a message is sent to higher areas of the brain telling of pain. The brain then sorts through the prescreened message and decides on the response. It is at this stage that the mind can assign value and meaning to the pain and intensify or modify our perception of pain.

We convert pain in to suffering in the mind.
To loosen the suffering of pain, we need to make a crucial distinction between the pain of pain and the pain we create by our thoughts about the pain. Fear, anger, guilt, loneliness, and helplessness are all mental and emotional responses that can intensify pain. So, in developing an approach to dealing with pain, we can of course work at the lower levels of pain perception, using the tools of modern medicine such as medications and other procedures, but we can also work at the higher levels by modifying our outlook and attitude.

Other experiments with human beings, involving hypnosis and placebos, have also demonstrated that in many cases the higher brain functions can overrule the pain signals from the lower stages on the pain pathway. They not only warn us and protects us, but it unifies us. Without pain sensation in our hands or feet, those parts no longer seem to belong to our body. **It is our suffering that is the most basic element that we share with others, the factor that unifies us with all living creatures.**

Suffering according to Buddhism: -
According to Buddhism all suffering is due to desires and that liberation involves their suppression, by following the "Noble eight fold path"

1. Right Action
2. Right Belief
3. Right Aspiration
4. Right Speech
5. Right Livelihood
6. Right Endeavor
7. Right Thought
8. Right Meditation

9.10 - DEALING WITH ANGER AND HATRED: -

Even though under rare circumstances some kind of anger can be positive, generally speaking anger leads to ill feeling and hatred. And as far as hatred is concerned, it is never positive. It has no benefit at all, It is always totally negative. We cannot overcome anger and hatred by suppressing them, but we need to actively cultivate the antidotes to hatred – like patience and tolerance. In order to be able to successfully cultivate patience and tolerance you need to generate **Enthusiasm, a strong desire to seek it.**

Feelings of anger and hatred arise from a mind that is troubled by dissatisfaction and discontent. So one can prepare ahead of time by constantly working towards building inner contentment and cultivating kindness and compassion. This brings about some calmness of mind. In seeking to eliminate anger and hatred, the intentional cultivation of patience and tolerance is indispensable. The only factor that can give you refuge or protection from the destructive effects of anger and hatred is your practice of tolerance and patience. When anger does occur, research has shown that actively challenging, logically analyze, and reappraising the thoughts that trigger the anger can help dissipate it.

Patience and Tolerance: -

In our day-to-day life experiences, tolerance and patience have great benefits. For instance developing them will allow us to sustain and maintain our presence of mind. So if an individual possesses this capacity of tolerance and patience, then even in spite of living in a very tense environment, which is very frantic and stressful, so long as the person has tolerance and patience, the person's calmness and peace of mind will not be disturbed. True tolerance or patience has a component or element of self-discipline and restraint, or humility in it. The realization that you could have acted otherwise, you could have adopted a more aggressive approach, but decided not to do so. The end result, or a product of patience and tolerance is **forgiveness**. When you are truly patient and tolerant, then forgiveness comes naturally. It's possible to let go of the negative feelings associated with the events.

Meditation on anger: -

For the few minutes of meditation everyday, simply let your mind remain on the resolution not to fall under the influence of anger and hatred. Because if one does become angry, one loses the peace of mind, lose composure and assume ugly physical appearance.

Let us visualize that someone whom you dislike, someone who annoys you, causes lot of problems for you or gets on your nerves. Then see how you feel, see whether that causes the rate of your heartbeat to go up and so on. Examine whether you are comfortable or uncomfortable, see if you immediately become more peaceful or if you develop a mental uncomfortable feeling, judge for yourself. So far few minutes, three or four minutes perhaps, judge and experiment. Then in the end of your experiment, if you discover that "Yes, it is of no use to allow that irritation to develop, then say to yourself" In future, I will never do that " develop that determination. Finally for last few minutes of meditation, place your mind upon that conclusion or determination.

Anger Patiently: -
To never get angry is a tall order for almost any human being. So when we see anger as failure, and we try not to be angry and fail, it is so easy to turn the gun on ourselves when our anger comes. We blame ourselves and put ourselves down for not being able to control us. Don't turn the gun in yourself. Don't give yourself a guilt trip. We spend our lives learning anger, so we are not going to unlearn all the beliefs and habits, which create our irritations, frustrations and angers in a few days, or even a few weeks. So be easy on yourself. Healing the inner scars, forgiving us, transforming those habits, are all aspects of this inner work, and they take a little time. Be patient; be gentle and merciful with yourself. And if you do decide you want to forgive and heal yourself, if you do decide you don't want to be a slave to others words and actions, if you do decide you want to be free of your negative feelings, one of the secrets is not to fight or struggle with those old habits. Accept them when they come, for whatever reason, and you'll be amazed how quickly the habit of those feelings is dissolved. All healing begins with acceptance, including the healing of our feeling.

9.11 - DEALING WITH FEAR, ANXIETY AND WORRY: -
In the course of lifetime many people will suffer from devastating degree of anxiety and worry severe enough to meet the criteria for the medical diagnosis of an anxiety disorder, that serve no useful purpose and do nothing but undermine their happiness, and interfere with their ability to accomplish their goals.

Mental Effect: -

The human brain is equipped with an elaborate system designed to register the emotions of fear, anxiety and worry. This system mobilizes us to respond to danger by setting in motion a complex sequence of biochemical and physiological events. The adoptive side of worry is that it allows us to anticipate danger and take preventive action. But excessive anxiety and worry can have devastating effects on the mind and body, becoming the source of much emotional suffering and even physical illness. On mental level, chronic anxiety can impair judgment, increase irritability, and hinder one's overall effectiveness.

Physical effects: -

Excessive fear, Anxiety and worry can cause depressed immune function, heart disease, gastrointestinal disorders, fatigue, and muscle tension and pain. Scientists have recently discovered a gene that is linked to people who are prone to anxiety and negative thinking.

How to overcome Anxiety: -

1) In most severe cases of anxiety, medication can be useful part of the treatment regimen. 2) Working on improving our physical health through proper diet and exercise can also be helpful. 3) Cultivating compassion and deepening our connection with others can promote good mental hygiene and help combat anxiety states. 4) Cognitive intervention – This technique involves actively challenging the anxiety generating thoughts and replacing with well-reasoned positive thoughts and attitudes.

How to overcome Fear: -

There are many types of fear, 1) These kinds of fear are very genuine, based on valid reasons, fear of violence or fear of bloodshed fro example. 2) Fear about the long-term negative consequences of our negative actions, fear of suffering, fear of our negative emotions such as hatred. 3) There are fears of our own mental creations like childish fears to scare away the child. 4) There are fears based on mental projection. This kind of fear is related to hatred. In dealing with fear, one need to first use one's faculty of reasoning and try to discover whether there is a valid basis of your fear or not.

How to overcome worry about a variety of Day-to-Day problems: -

To reduce that kind of worry is to cultivate a thought – If the situation or problem is such that it can be remedied then there is no need to worry about it. – If there is no way out, no solution, no possibility of resolution, then also there is no pointing being worried about it, because you can not do anything about it anyway. Some type of anxiety may have biological roots like some people tend to get sweaty palms, and for this medical treatment may be useful. In any case the sincere motivation acts as an antidote to reduce fear and anxiety.

Motivation: -

If you develop a pure and sincere motivation, if you are motivated by a wish to help on the basis of kindness, compassion, and respect, then you can carry on any kind of work, in any field, and function more effectively with less fear or worry, not being afraid of what others think or whether you ultimately will be successful in reaching your goal. The closer one gets to being motivated by altruism, the more fearless one becomes on the face of even extremely anxiety-provoking circumstances.

Generally being honest with oneself and others about what you are or are not capable of doing can counteract that feeling of lack of self-confidence.

What is energy healing?

Our entire body is one big energy field. Hidden beneath the physical surface are levels of emotions, thought patterns and learned beliefs. Imbalances and energy blockages on these levels manifest as emotional discomforts and even physical illness. The most effective way to treat an illness is to uncover its root cause and begin the healing process from the deepest emotional level. Conventional medicine takes a different approach to healing and can encounter difficulties in determining the actual cause of a disease. Energy healing compliments traditional treatments offering a holistic healing solution encompassing body, mind and soul.

9.12 - BRAIN WAVES: -

Scientists have known for years that brain activity can be measured in wave patterns. Broadly speaking, the brain generates four kinds of patterns:

1. Delta waves – Seen most often in sleep.

2. Theta waves – When you are daydreaming or catnapping.
3. Alpha waves – often observed when you are aware but relaxed, like during a massage or a long run.
4. Beta waves – These are the key one for cognitive processing.

By measuring these waves, the body wave device can determine when your concentration has peaked and therefore when you are primed to make an important decision.

So how exactly does the Body Wave device works?

The Technology is based on electro-encephalography (EEG), the study of how brain activity – from automatic impulses like breathing to active thoughts like what to have for dinner – excites neurons to emit brain waves. This electrical activity originates in the brain but is transported along the central nervous system. You can wear the body wave device on your arm or actually anywhere on the skin, which is highly sensitive to changes in the central nervous system. The sensors register the electrical charges that occur in your brain when you concentrate hard. The act of concentration necessitates the firing of neurons in careful synchrony. That synchrony produces a unique electrical signature that can be measured. When you stop concentrating the synchrony breaks and the signature changes. The Body Wave device then transmits this change through a simple receiver plugged in to a USB port. A computer can tell you, in real time, whether you have been focused or were pondering what to do this weekend.

9.13 - WILL POWER AND SELF CONTROL: -

Self-control is a matter of balance. The mid-brain region governs desire. The prefrontal cortex governs control. We work that will power muscle everyday – and like any muscle, it often goes weak. Also like a muscle, however will power can be strengthened and growing number of researchers, using brain scans, virtual reality and more are learning what kind of psychic exercises it takes to get us in shape. Much of that research hasn't made it into popular consciousness yet, but the more scientists publish, the more we all learn.

Our brain operates at three levels: **I will, I won't and I want**. For many of us, the I want part wins. It is easy to call lot of this as addiction, particularly when drugs, alcohol or behaviors like gambling are involved. But that can be superficial. Addiction is not always easy to define, but it might best be described as knowing that substance or behavior is wrecking your life and yet being unable to stop. Failure of will is more about behaviors that are compromising your life – making it less healthy or prosperous than it could be – yet can not quite be controlled even though you try.

But if will power is illusive, it's also trainable and cultivatable. The simple truth is that the brain evolved from the back to the front. The back is the wanting part. The front is the restraint part, and they are both with us all the time. The goal of the rising band of willpower researchers is to make peace between back and front.

Good Feelings: -
Good feelings for others are like ointments that can heal wounds and re-establish friendship and relationships.

Good feelings are generated in the mind, are transmitted through your attitude and are reflected in your eyes and smile.

Smiling opens the heart and a glance can make miracles happen.

Easiness: -
As we grow in strength in our spiritual life, we give up the habit of worrying. It serves no purpose other than to make us feel tense and miserable. When I stop fretting about things that are beyond my control and focus instead on generating optimistic and kind thoughts, my life can begin to flow in ever more positive directions. Such a light and easy approach to life enables me to take everything in stride.

Personal change: -
When you do not upset yourself thinking about how others must change and instead you concentrate on your own change, good things start to happen. First, you will feel better about yourself. Second, you will start to have positive feelings towards others and start to understand them. Third, others start having a more positive attitude towards you.

There are many hidden benefits in personal change.

Staying Peaceful (Free from Desires): -

Desires cause peace to disappear. You think that acquiring things will make you feel secure, but the reality is that the more you have the more fear there usually is of losing it, and the further you are from peace. Desires are the cause of all conflicts.

When you want something and cannot get it you become frustrated. Learning to be free from desires is learning how to stay peaceful.

9.14 - DETACHMENT: -

Detachment is best learnt from God, who sees everything but never stops loving. It is best demonstrated by the Lotus flower, which touches mud, touches rock bottom but never loses its beauty. Beauty means to keep growing - always.

How to Develop Detachment?

"We need to reach a state in which, while we are living in this world, we are detached from it. We need to realize that all the possessions of this world are transitory. They are an illusion."

"If we can get to a state where we can control our desires, then we will find that our life will move in harmony with its environment, our mind will be at peace, and we will be able to make tremendous strides towards the ultimate aim of our life, which is to know our real self and to be one with God."

"Being content does not mean inaction. We must still do our work in the world. We must still try to earn an honest livelihood. We must still do our best in whatever field we are placed. We must still do our best to provide for our families. The difference is that we do so with a spirit of detachment. We do our work but are not attached to the results."

"Let us not think that this is the real world. Let us recognize that this is the world of Maya, the world of illusion. But even though we are in this world of illusion, this is a grand opportunity that God has given for us to recognize ourselves. Let us know that each one of us has been created by the hand of God, has been created by God. That realization we will only have as we go within and experience the divine Light and Sound of God."

CHAPTER 10

WHAT IS "ONE GOD"?

10.01 – ONE GOD

Monotheism: - is the belief in the existence of ONE GOD or in the oneness of GOD. Monotheism is characteristic of Abrahamic religions (Judaism, Christianity, Islam) and also recognizable in numerous other religions such as Zoroastrianism, Bahá'í Faith, the Sikh tradition and even Hinduism.

Monotheism is the belief in a singular God, in contrast to polytheism, the belief in several deities. Polytheism is, however, reconcilable with inclusive monotheism or other forms of monism and the distinction between monotheism and polytheism isn't clear-cut or objective.

GOD, the Cause of all, is ONE. This does not mean one as in one of a pair, nor one like a species (which encompasses many individuals), nor one as in an object that is made up of many elements, nor as a single simple object that is infinitely divisible. Rather, GOD is a unity unlike any other possible unity.

Zoroastrianism: - is a monotheistic religion (although early Zoroastrianism is often regarded as dualist) which was once one of the largest religions on Earth. Zoroastrianism is generally believed to have been founded around the 1st millennium BC. By some scholars, the Zoroastrians ("Parsis" or "Zartoshtis") are credited with being the first monotheists and having had significant influence in the formation of currently larger world religions.

Abrahamic religions: - The major source of monotheism in the modern Western World is the narrative of the Hebrew Bible, the scripture of Judaism. The text of the Bible states that Judaism began with divine revelations from "God most high" to Abraham and to the people of Israel through Moses. The understanding of the transmitters of the biblical text was that the Bible uniformly presents ONE GOD as creator of the world and the only power controlling history. In their understanding, references to other "GODs" are to non-existent entities or angelic servants of GOD, to whom humans mistakenly ascribe reality and power.

Judaism: - It provides a clear textual source for the rise and development of what is named Judaism's ethical monotheism which means that:

(1) There is ONE GOD from whom emanates one morality for all humanity.
(2) GOD's primary demand of people is that they act decently toward one another.

The GOD of ethical monotheism is the GOD first revealed to the world in the Hebrew Bible. Through it, we can establish GOD's four primary characteristics:

1. God is supernatural.
2. God is personal.
3. God is good.
4. God is holy.

Christianity: - Historically, most Christian churches have taught that the nature of GOD is a *mystery*, in the original, technical meaning; something that must be revealed by special revelation rather than deduced through general revelation. Among early Christians there was considerable debate over the nature of Godhead, with some factions arguing for the deity of Jesus and others calling for an Arian conception of God.

TRINITY: - The doctrine of the Trinity — that GOD the Father, GOD the Son, and GOD the Holy Spirit are each equally and eternally the ONE TRUE GOD — is admittedly difficult to comprehend, and yet is the very foundation of Christian truth.

TRI-UNITY — The teaching of the Bible concerning the Trinity might be summarized thus. GOD is a Tri-unity, with each Person of the Godhead equally and fully and eternally GOD. Each is necessary, and each is distinct, and yet all are ONE. The three Persons appear in a logical, causal order. The Father is the unseen, Omnipresent Source of all being, revealed in and by the Son, experienced in and by the Holy Spirit. The Son proceeds from the Father, and the Spirit from the Son. **With reference to God's creation, the Father is the Thought behind it, the Son is the Word calling it forth, and the Spirit is the Deed making it a reality.**

Islam: - The holy book of Islam, the Qur'an, asserts the existence of a single and absolute truth that transcends the world; a unique and indivisible being who is independent of the creation. The indivisibility of Allah (GOD) implies the indivisibility of GOD's sovereignty which in turn leads to the conception of the universe as just, coherent and moral rather than as an existential and moral chaos (as in polytheism). Similarly the Qur'an rejects the binary modes of thinking such as the idea of a duality of GOD by arguing that both Good and Evil generate from God's creative act and that evil forces have no power to create anything. GOD in Islam is a universal GOD rather than a local, tribal or parochial one; an absolute who integrates all affirmative values and brooks no evil.

Hinduism: - cannot be said to be polytheistic, as all great Hindu religious leaders have repeatedly stressed that **GOD IS ONE** and his forms are many, the ways to communicate with him are many and focusing or concentrating on the icon is one of those ways. The number of auspicious qualities of GOD are countless, with the following six qualities being the most important:

- *Jñ na* (Omniscience), defined as the power to know about all beings simultaneously
- *Aishvarya* (Omnipotent/Sovereignty) which consists in unchallenged rule over all
- *Shakti* (Omnipresent/Energy), or power, which is the capacity to make the impossible possible
- *Bala* (Omnibenevolent/Strength), which is the capacity to support everything by will and without any fatigue
- *V rya* (Omnibenevolent/Vigor), which indicates the power to retain immateriality as the supreme being in spite of being the material cause of mutable creations
- *Tejas* (Omnitruth/Splendor), which expresses His self-sufficiency and the capacity to overpower everything by His spiritual effulgence

Sikhism: - is a monotheistic faith that arose in northern India during the 16th and 17th centuries. Sikhs believe in ONE GOD who is timeless, omnipresent, and supreme creator.

The Bahá'í: - view of GOD is monotheistic. GOD is the imperishable, uncreated being who is the source of all existence. He is described as "a personal GOD, unknowable, inaccessible, the source of all Revelation, Eternal, Omniscient, Omnipotent, Omnipresent, Omnibenevolent and Omnitruth. Although transcendent and inaccessible directly, his image is reflected in his creation. The purpose of creation is for the created to have the capacity to know and love its creator. GOD communicates his will and purpose to humanity through intermediaries, known as Manifestations of GOD, who are the prophets and messengers that have founded religions from prehistoric times up to the present day. The ONENESS of GOD is one of the core teachings of the Bahá'í Faith. Bahá'ís believe that there is one supernatural being, GOD, who has created all existence. GOD is described as "a personal GOD, unknowable, inaccessible, the source of all Revelation, eternal, omniscient, omnipresent and almighty."

Chinese view: - This faith system pre-dated the development of Confucianism and Taoism and the introduction of Buddhism and Christianity. It has features of monotheism in that Heaven is seen as an Omnipotent entity, endowed with personality but no corporeal form. From the writings of Confucius in the *Analects*, we find that Confucius himself believed that Heaven cannot be deceived, Heaven guides people's lives and maintains a personal relationship with them, and that Heaven gives tasks for people to fulfill in order to teach them of virtues and morality. However, this faith system was not truly monotheistic since other lesser gods and spirits, which varied with locality, were also worshiped along with *Shangdi*. Still, variants such as Mohism approached high monotheism, teaching that the function of lesser gods and ancestral spirits is merely to carry out the will of *Shangdi*, akin to angels in Western civilization.

10.02 - ONE GOD WHO IS FATHER OF ALL: -

GOD, who made the world and everything in it, is Lord of heaven and earth and does not live in man-made churches, temples or mosques. Nor does he need anything that we can supply by working for him, since it is he himself who gives life and breath and everything else to everyone. From one man he created all races of mankind and made them live throughout the whole earth. He himself fixed beforehand the exact times and the limits of the places where they would live. He did this so they would look for him, and perhaps find him as they felt around for him. Yet God is actually not far from anyone of us; as someone has said, *'In him we live and move and exist.'*

There is but ONE GOD. He is all that is. He is the Creator of all things and He is all-pervasive. He is without fear and without enmity. He is timeless, unborn and self-existent. He is the Enlightener and He can be realized by grace of Himself alone. He was in the beginning; He was in all ages. The True One is, was, and shall forever be. He is one, He is the first. He is all that is. **Eternal Truth is His Name**. He is the creator of all. Fearing naught, striking fear in naught; timeless is His image. Not begotten, He is self-existent. He was in the beginning; He is through all ages; He shall be the One who lives forever. Beyond thought, no thinking can conceive Him. How true it is that God has no favorites, but that in every nation those who are God fearing and do what is right are acceptable for him."

The One God is the Father of all, we are all his Children.

The One God is the cause of all causes; knowledge and wisdom are His Gifts to us. He is not far, He is not near, and He is with us all. Praise the Lord with abiding love. If I can unite in myself, in my own spiritual life, the thought of the East and the West, of the Greek and Latin Fathers, I will create in myself a reunion of the divided Churches, temples & mosques and from that unity in myself can come the exterior and visible unity of these places of worship. For, if we want to bring together East and West, we cannot do it by imposing one upon the other.

Our religious traditions at their most authentic should free us to find traces of GOD in all things. GOD loves all manner of our being in the world and has made all things in harmony. As in our inner work, so our communal work for justice and peace is futile if we insist on the primacy of one form of being human over another, of one religion over others, or by choosing a mono-cultural path toward Joy for all beings that share this planet. God loves our infinite diversity and has choreographed an ordered dance of different stars.

10.03 - ONE GOD – ONE FAITH: -

There is only one God, one faith. Let the people believe firmly and do not fear anything.

Every prayer, which comes from the heart, is agreeable to God.

I maintain that every major religion of the world - Buddhism, Christianity, Confucianism, Hinduism, Islam, Jainism, Judaism, Sikhism, Taoism, Zoroastrianism - has similar ideas of love, the same goal of benefiting humanity through spiritual practice, and the same effects of making their followers into better human beings... Differences of dogma may be ascribed to differences of time and circumstance as well as cultural influences.

No one faith is perfect. All faiths are equally dear to their respective devotees. What is wanted, therefore, is a living friendly contact among the followers of the great religions of the world and not a clash among them in the fruitless attempt on the part of each community to show superiority of its faith over the rest

NAMASTE: - is the form of greetings by Hindus, which means - I honor in you that place in you where the LORD resides, and when you are in that place in you, and I am in that place in me, then there is only ONE of us."

GOD OF LOVE: -

I go for refuge to God who is ONE in the silence of Eternity, pure radiance of beauty and perfection, in which we find our peace. He is the bridge supreme, which leads to immortality, and the Spirit of fire, which burns the dross of lower life. **He is the God, the God of love.**

The entire world is being driven insane by this single phrase: "My religion alone is true." O Mother, you have shown me that no clock is entirely accurate. Only the transcendent sun of knowledge remains on time. Who can make a system from Divine Mystery? But if any sincere practitioner, within whatever culture or religion, prays and meditates with great devotion and commitment to Truth alone, Your Grace will flood his mind and heart, O Mother. His particular sacred tradition will be opened and illuminated. He will reach the one goal of spiritual evolution. How I long to pray with sincere Christians in their churches and to bow and prostrate with devoted Muslims in their mosques!

All religions are glorious!

The Christian is not to become a Muslim, a Hindu or a Buddhist, nor is a Muslim, a Hindu or a Buddhist to become a Christian. But each must assimilate the spirit of the others and yet persevere his individuality and grow according to his own law of growth. If the Parliament of Religions has shown anything to the world, it is this: It has proved to the world that holiness, purity, and charity are not the exclusive possessions of any church in the world, and that every system has produced men and women of the most exalted character. In the face of this evidence, if anybody dreams of the exclusive survival of his own religion and the destruction of the others, I pity him from the bottom of my heart.

One God explained in the form of a joke: -
There were three friends, a Christian, a Muslim and a Hindu. They were to cross a river one day, but the river was flooded with water. Christian goes first, prays for Jesus Christ and started walking towards the river, slowly the water recedes and he crosses the river. The Muslim goes second, prays for Allah and started walking towards the river, slowly the water recedes and he crosses the river. Hindu thought in his mind that Christian prayed for only Jesus Christ and crossed the river, Muslim prayed for Allah only and crossed the river, so I am going to pray for all my Gods and they will surely come and save me. So he started chanting "Hare Rama, Hare Krishna, Hare Radhe Shyam, Hare Vishnu Bhagwan etc. and slowly started walking towards the river, but the river water did not recede and he drowned. In heaven he was produced in front of God and he started complaining to God that he prayed for so many Gods and no one came to save him. God said " Oh Stupid Hindu, **I am only One God with many names and forms**, when Christian called me, I wore the clothes of Jesus Christ and went to save him, when Muslim called me, I wore the clothes of Mohamed and went to save him, but when you called me with so many names, I just kept on changing the clothes to suit that name and I could not come to rescue you.

10.04 - ONENESS OF WHOLE UNIVERSE: -
The other great idea that the world wants today is that eternal, grand idea of the spiritual oneness of the whole universe, the only **Infinite Reality**, that exists

in you and in me and in all, in the self, in the soul. **The infinite oneness of the Soul** - that you and I are not only brothers, but are really one - is the eternal sanction of all morality.

One should lead mankind to the place where there is neither the Vedas nor the Bible nor the Koran; yet this has to be done by harmonizing the Vedas, the Bible, and the Koran. Mankind ought to be taught that religions are but the varied expressions of the Religion, which is **Oneness,** so that each may choose the path that suits him best.

In whom is the Universe, Who is the Universe; in whom is the Soul, Who is in the Soul, Who is the Soul of man; to know Him, and therefore the Universe, as our Self, alone extinguishes all fear, brings an end to misery, and leads to infinite freedom. Wherever there has been expansion of love or progress in well-being of individuals or numbers, it has been through the perception, realization, and the practicalization of the Eternal Truth - **the Oneness of All Beings.**

Without the foundation of the non-dualistic Absolute, dualism breeds fanaticism, exclusiveness, and dangerous emotionalism.

FORMS OF GOD: -
Suppose we all go with vessels in our hands to fetch water from a lake. One has a cup, another a jar, another a bucket, and so forth, and we all fill our vessels. The water in each case naturally takes the form of the vessel carried by each of us. So it is with religion. Our minds are like those vessels. God is like the water filling the different vessels. And in each vessel the vision of God comes in the form of the vessel. **Yet He is ONE**; He is God in every case.

The Entire Universe is One Narrow Bridge, which we are all learning to cross without fear.

Life is the light of GOD, the expression of Divinity. It is divine. It is the stream of eternal Being, a flow of existence, of intelligence, of creativity, of purity, and of bliss. Life is unity. Life is unity in GOD consciousness.

Ecumenism: -
This is an outreach of love to all fellow Christians, as affirming all that we have so mercifully received from the Lord and share in common, and as trying to

be ONE as much as we can in response to Christ's prayer, and above all as trying to stand together before the Lord in complete openness so he can lead us all into oneness in the possession of the ONE FAITH. In fact very devoted Christians, oftentimes very kind, and, are very pleasing to the Lord. Yet they certainly have a perception of things that is very different from others. For them it is impossible to please the Lord outside of the True Faith. Therefore most who are called "Christians" are not in fact Christians; their Sacraments are not true Sacraments, they have no grace, they cannot be saved or in any way please God.

Before ecumenism can make any real progress, there has to grow a widespread good will and desire for unity at the cost of the sacrifice of separate identity.

The ecumenical path is surely, by human vision, a long, difficult one, stretching far into the future. But with GOD, all things are possible. And the most important thing is prayer, with fasting and humbling ourselves before GOD. GOD will only hear prayer from a sincere heart, one that really shares the concern of Christ's heart for all his flock. Without this concern our prayer for union is only words.

Yes, we all have our different perspectives, even those of us who have faith in Christ, the Son of God, love him, and are dedicated to being his followers and disciples. He sure leads a mottled flock. I wonder if we do not put awful human limitations on our loving and all-powerful God's universal and soothing will. **Christ did die for all!**

10.05 - PRAYER FOR ONE GOD: -

There is only one GOD. He is the supreme truth.
He the Creator is without fear and without hate.
He the Omni-present pervades the universe.
He is not born, nor does he die to be born again.
By his grace shall though worship him.

Before time itself, there was truth.
When time began to run its course, he was the truth.

Even now he is the truth And Even more shall truth prevail.

Not by thought alone can he be known, though one think a hundred thousand times.
Not in solemn silence, nor in deep meditation.
Though fasting yields an abundance virtue, it cannot appease the hunger for truth.
No, none of these, or by a hundred thousand other devices can GOD be reached.
How then shall the truth be known?
How the veil of false illusion be torn?
Thus runneth the writ divine,
The Righteous path – let it be thine.

10.06 - COSMIC INTELLIGENCE AS ONE GOD OF ALL HUMANITY:

Applying the Life Cycle principle to the whole of universe, we see that Intelligence must be the lord of creation, the Cause. The beginning therefore is the Intelligence. At the beginning that intelligence becomes involved like a seed, the cause, and in the end that intelligence becomes evolved like a tree, the effect. The sum total of this intelligence displayed in the universe must therefore be involved as Universal Intelligence. Call it by any other name; it is absolutely certain that in the beginning there is that **Infinite Cosmic Intelligence.** This cosmic intelligence gets involved, and it manifests, evolves itself until it becomes the perfect man, called the Christman, the Buddha-man, the Brahman, the Allah, the Lord etc. and then it goes back to its own source. **This Cosmic Intelligence is called GOD.** That is why all the scriptures preach that we come from God and go back to God. All the hopes, aspirations, and happiness of humanity have been centered in that word. Therefore all the various forms of cosmic energy, such as matter, thought, force, intelligence, and so forth, are simply the manifestation of that cosmic intelligence, or, as we shall call it the **One Supreme Lord.**

10.07 - SELF REALIZATION FOR ONE GOD: -

Though evil and good are both conditioned manifestations of the Soul, yet evil is more external coating and good is the inner coating of the **Real Man, the SELF**. Unless the man cuts through the layer of evil, he cannot reach the layer of good, and unless he has passed through both layers, of good and of evil, he cannot reach the self. So the man of realization says, "All this talk in the world about its little religions is a chatter; Self Realization is the soul, the very essence of religions."

Suppose we have realized this oneness of the universe, suppose we know that we are that one Infinite Being: and suppose we have realized that this Self is the only Existence, and that it is the same self which is manifested in all these various phenomenal forms – what becomes of us after that? The religious realization does the greatest good to the world. People are afraid that when they attain to it, when they realize that there is but ONE, the foundation of love will dry up, everything in life will go away, and all that they love will vanish for them, as it were in this life and in the life to come. People never stop to think that the greatest workers in the world have been those who bestowed the least thought on their own individualities. Such a man becomes a world mover. For him the little self is dead and GOD stands in its place; for him the whole world becomes transfigured. That which is painful and miserable will all vanish; struggles will all depart, instead of being a prison house, where everyday we struggle and fight and compete for a piece of bread, this universe will then be to us a playground.

This will be a great good to the world resulting from such realization. If all mankind today realizes only a bit of that great truth, the aspect of the whole world will be changed; in place of fighting and quarrelling there will be a reign of peace. With it will vanish all jealousy; all evil will vanish away for ever; Gods will then live upon this earth. This very earth will become heaven – and what evil there can be when Gods are playing with Gods, when gods are working with Gods and Gods are loving Gods. That is the great utility of **Divine Realization**.

No one can make a spiritual man of you. You have to teach yourself, your growth must come from inside. Therefore give up all ideas that you can make men spiritual. It is impossible. There is no other teacher for you than your own SOUL. Recognize this. This is called **SELF REALIZATION**.

Useful energy: -

We have been told from childhood that we cannot work if we do not have the passion for work. But that is not true. The less passion there is, the better we work. The calmer we are, the better it is for us and greater is the amount of work we can do. When we let loose our feelings, we waste so much energy, shatter our nerves, disturb our minds, and accomplish very little work. The energy, which ought to have gone in to work, is spent as mere feeling, which counts for nothing. It is only when the mind is very calm and collected that the whole of energy is spent in doing good work. That is why the man who becomes angry never does a great amount of work, and the man whom nothing can make angry accomplishes so much. A person who gives way to anger or hatred or any other passion cannot work; he only breaks himself to pieces and does nothing practical. It is the Calm, forgiving, equable, well-balanced mind that does the greatest amount of work. There are two tendencies in human nature; one to reconcile the ideal with life and other to elevate life to the ideal. All the powers in the universe are already ours. It is we who have put our hands before our eyes and cry that it is dark; know that there is no darkness around you.

10.08 - ONENESS: -

There is but one Life, one World, one Existence, everything is that ONE. The differences are of degree and not of kind. All of us are going towards the same goal. The difference between weakness and strength is one of degree. The difference between virtue and vice is one of a degree. The difference between heaven and hell is one of a degree. The difference between life and death is one of a degree. All differences in this world are of degree, and not of kind, because ONENESS is the secret of everything. All is the one, and the one manifest itself either as thought or life or soul or body. This being so, we have no right to look down with contempt upon those who are not developed exactly in the same degree as we are. Condemn none.

There is only one life, one world, and this one life and one world, appears to us to be manifold. This manifoldness is like a dream. When you dream, one dream passes away and another comes. None of your dreams are real. Dream comes one after another, scene after scene unfolds before you. So it is in this world of ninety percent misery and ten percent happiness. Perhaps after a while it will appear ninety percent happiness, and we shall call it heaven. But time comes to the humans, when the whole thing vanishes and this world appears as GOD himself, and his own sole as that God. Everything that makes for ONENESS is truth. Love is truth and hatred is falsehood, because hatred makes for multiplicity. It is hatred that separates man from man; therefore it is wrong and false. Love unites and love makes for ONENESS. For love is Existence, God Himself, and all this is the manifestation of that one love.

Scriptures is not the proof of your conduct, but you are the proof of scriptures. How do you know that book teaches the truth? Because you are truth and you feel it. What is the proof of the Christ and Buddha of the world? That you and I feel like them. That is how you and I understand that they were true. Our prophet soul is the proof of their prophet soul. Your Godhead is the proof of God Himself. If you are not a prophet there has never been anything true of God. If you are not God there never was any God and never will be.

The living God is within you, and yet you are building churches and temples and believing all sorts of imaginary non-sense. The only God to worship is the human soul in the human body. Of course, all animals are temples too, but the man is the highest, the greatest of all temples. If one cannot worship in that, no other temple will be of other advantage. The moment one has realized that God is sitting in the temple of every human body, the moment one stand in reverence before every human being and see God in him, that moment one is free from bondage, everything that binds vanishes and he/she is free. He whom you are worshiping as unknown and are seeking throughout the universe has been with you all the time. You are living through him and He is the eternal witness of the universe. When one really begin to love the world, then one understands what is meant by the brotherhood of mankind and not before.

If you cannot worship your brother man, the manifested God, how can you worship a God who is un-manifested? Even Bible says, "If you can not love your brother whom you have seen, how can you love God whom you have not seen?" If you cannot see God in the human face, how can you see him in the clouds or in images made of dull, dead matter or in the mere fictions of your brain?

Let us therefore, find God not only in Jesus of Nazareth, but also in all great ones who preceded him, in all who have come after him, and in all who are yet to come. Our worship is unbound and free. They are all the manifestations of the same Infinite GOD. They are all pure and un-selfish; they suffer and give up their lives for us poor human beings.

10.09 - THE IDEAL OF UNIVERSAL RELIGION: -

Wherever our senses reach or whatever our minds imagine, we find there in the action and reaction of two forces, the one counteracting the other and thus causing the constant playoff the mixed phenomena which we see around us or which we feel in our minds. Religion is the highest plane of human thought and life, and herein we find that the working of these two forces has been most marked. The intense love that humanity has ever known has come from religion, and the most diabolical hatred that humanity has known has also come from religion. No other human motive has deluged the world with so much blood as religion; at the same time, nothing has brought in to existence so many hospitals and asylums for the poor' no other human influence has taken such care of humanity than religion. **Nothing makes us so cruel as religion, and nothing makes us so tender as religion.**

Yet out of the midst of this noise and turmoil, this strife and struggle, this hatred and jealousy of religions and sects, there have arisen, from time to time, potent voices drowning all this noise – making themselves heard from pole to pole, as it were – proclaiming peace and harmony. If it is difficult to bring harmony and peace on the physical plane of life - the external and gross side of it – then it must be a thousand times more difficult to bring harmony and peace to rule over this internal nature of human beings.

We all have been hearing from the childhood of such things as love, peace, charity, equality and universal brotherhood; but these have become to us mere words without meaning, words that we repeat like parrots. Some ignorant people took those words to play with them and they made religion a mere play with words and not a thing to be carried in practice. It has become part of patriotism to profess a certain religion; and patriotism is always partial. To bring harmony to religion is always very difficult.

We see that every religion there is in three parts. **First there is philosophy** – which presents the whole scope of that religion, setting forth its basic principles, its goals, and the means of reaching that goal. **The second part is the mythology** - which is philosophy made concrete. It consists of legends relating to the lives of people or of supernatural beings. Basically these are stories of supernatural beings made around the philosophy. **The third part is Ritual** – This is still more concrete and is made up of forms and ceremonies, various physical attitudes, flowers and incense and many other things that appeal to the senses.

We will find that all recognized religions have these three elements. Some lay more stress on one and some on another. Each religion brings out its own doctrine and insists upon them as being the only true ones. Fanatics will even draw sword to compel others to believe as they do. Nobody in the world is able to make out the fine distinction between history and mythology, as it exists in the brain of some people. We are all human beings, but we are not equal in our brains, in our powers and in our bodies. Therefore the universal mythology is impossible. Neither can there be one universal ritual. Variety is the first principle of life. Just as we have recognized unity as our very nature, so must also recognize variation.

Through the high philosophy or low, through the most exalted mythology or the grossest, through the most refined ritualism or complete fetishism, every seed, every soul, every nation, every religion, consciously or unconsciously is struggling upward towards GOD. Each one of us is trying to arrive at the realization of GOD. He is GOD in every case. This is the only recognition of universality that we can get. That plan alone is practical which does not destroy the individuality of any main religion and at the same time shows him a point of union with all others. But so far all the plans of religious harmony that have been tried, while proposing to take in all the various views of religion, have in practice tried to bind them all down to few doctrines, and so have produced more new sects, fighting, struggling and pushing against each other. **We all human beings should join together in our minds for the Realization of ONE GOD and call it UNIVERSAL RELIGION.**

In this world there are thousands and thousands of varieties of minds and inclinations. A thorough generalization of them is impossible, but for our practical purposes let us divide **human mind in four classes**.

1. **Philosophical Mind (Jnana Yogi)**–who wants to weigh everything and use his intellect even beyond the possibilities of human thinking.
2. **Mystic Mind (Raj yogi)** – Whose mind wants to analyze its own self, to understand the workings of human mind.
3. **Emotional Mind (Bhakti Yogi)** – who loves the sublime and the beautiful to an excessive degree. He loves great souls of all times, the prophets of religion.
4. **Active Mind (Karma Yogi)** - the worker, there is tremendous energy in his muscles and in his nerves.

Now a religion to satisfy the largest portion of mankind must be able to supply food for all these various types of minds. I want to propagate a religion that will be equally acceptable to all minds. It must be equally philosophic, equally emotional, equally mystical and equally conducive to action. Religion must be able to show the philosopher, how to realize that knowledge that teaches that this **WORLD BE ONE**, that there is but one existence in the universe. Religion must be able to teach mystic, the science of mental analysis. If the emotional person comes, we must sit with them and laugh and weep in the name of the Lord. To the active man we must work with him with all the energy. To become harmoniously balanced in all these four directions is my ideal religion. And this deal is attained by Yoga (Union of body and mind) and those 4 minds of four kinds of yogis.

We find in all living beings there are **three instruments of knowledge.**

1. **Instinct** – This lowest instrument of knowledge, mostly in animals.

2. **Reasoning** – Most highly developed in humans. Yet even reason is insufficient. Reason can go only a little way and then stops, it cannot go any further, and if you push it further, the result is helpless confusion. This world, this universe, which our sense feel or our mind thinks about, is but one atom, of the infinite, projected on to the plane of consciousness. Within the narrow limit defined by the network of consciousness works our reason, and not beyond. Therefore there must be other instrument to take us beyond; and that instrument is called Inspiration.

3. **Inspiration** – which belongs to God-Men. Now let us take the Jnana-Yogi, the philosopher, and the thinker, he who wants to go beyond

the visible. He is the man who is not satisfied with little things of this world. His idea is to go beyond the daily routine of eating, drinking and so on. Not even the teachings of books, not all sciences will satisfy him. His soul wants to go beyond all that in to the very heart of Being, by becoming one with the Universal Being. To him God is the Life of his Life, the Soul of his Soul, God is his own self, nothing else exists which is other than God. To such humans Religion will not remain the bundle of ideas or theories, or an intellectual assent; it will enter in to his very self. By means of our intellectual assent we may subscribe today to many foolish things, and change our minds altogether tomorrow. But true religion never changes.

Religion is realization – not talk or doctrines or theories, however beautiful they may be. It is Being and becoming – not hearing or acknowledging. It is the whole Soul's becomes changed in to what it believes. This Self Realization is the Universal Religion.

10.10 - ALL RELIGIONS BELIEVE IN ONE GOD: -

We find that all GODS are understood as different aspects, personalities, or facets of ONE GOD, which pervades the entire universe.

> "God hath made of one blood all nations that dwell upon the face of the earth".
> > The Bible, Acts 17:26

> "All creatures are members of one family of God".
> > Mohammed (Islam)

> "Human Beings, all, are as head, arms, trunk, and legs like one another."
> > The Vedas (Hinduism)

> "One thing we know, all men are brothers."
> > Chief Seattle (Native American)

"All people are your children, whatever their belief, whatever their shade of skin."

Jewish prayer book

Reading the Bible gives the impression that **GOD is much more of a spiritual force or energy that exists everywhere**, than a man sitting on a throne above the clouds.

The word GOD refers to something that we cannot describe with words, and trying to assign a gender to GOD is putting a limit on something that has no limits. If all the religions are in fact describing, and praying to, the same GOD, then it changes our perspective on the role religion plays in our lives. It makes us easier to believe that this GOD does indeed exist. In fact it challenges us to consider that the chances are quite low that the religions, in all their variety, would describe GOD so similarly just by coincidence, and this forces even the skeptic to ponder the existence of GOD.

10.11 - ONE SOUL: -

All the religions tell us we have an immortal SOUL that survives death. We find that all religion, from Christianity to native religions in Africa, tells us of mysterious aspect of our being, we call the SOUL. Not surprisingly, they don't just agree on the mere existence of the SOUL but they also agree on how to describe it.

Some Asian scripture quotations tell us clearly and directly that we are one with GOD. This teaching has been somewhat overlooked or forgotten in western religion. Priests and Rabbis don't seem to focus today on our connection to GOD. But it is difficult to read the scriptures and not to get the message that there is something inside us, mostly unknown to us that are divine. This is none other than our SOUL, and it is not just "something" inside us – it is us, it is what we truly are – ONE WITH GOD. But we should not forget that we have a body, and responsibilities in the world. Remembering that we have a SOUL also will help us to do the things that are important in life in honest and truthful way. Realizing that we are a SOUL is quite comforting. Knowing that there is a part of us that does not die, is eternal and un-harmful, can cause a beautiful peace and contentment to overcome difficulties of our lives.

Seeking Truth through Meditation and/or Prayers: -

There are some questions that most, if not all, of us have on our minds. *Who am I? Where do I come from? When is there a God? Why did I come here? What is God and so on?*

The real answer to these questions cannot be spoken of in words. We are talking about spiritual knowledge or wisdom called Enlightenment. **One cannot absorb the spiritual knowledge until he or she has adopted the basic rules of love and respect for others.** Knowledge of one's true self is knowledge of the Soul and this is what enlightenment is centered on. It involves a full life of inner searching as well as learning from relationships with others. All the religions give us some specific guidance in seeking the truth about the universe and ourselves.

Along with good old fashion reading and studying, Meditation and Prayer are two Keys.

Meditation: - While prayer can be called talking to God, meditation can be called listening to God. Meditation is quieting or controlling of the mind (Thought process). As a simple exercise, close your eyes for one minute and try to think of only one thing – it does not matter what it is. You will notice that other thoughts come and go constantly, sometimes they seem random or unrelated. It is almost impossible to stop it. The mind is sometimes called the endless chatterbox. Meditation is the practice of picking a focus – something to look at, a thought to think about, a mental image, a sound in our mind or anything – and trying to think only about that one thing for a period of time. Meditation is not necessarily the stopping of thought, but the process of letting go and distancing from the outside world. Through persistence, the other thoughts that bombard the mind eventually become less frequent. What happens next is beyond description. The positive effects of meditating have been shown over and over again in scientific studies.

Blood pressure decreases and an enhanced state of relaxation occur. Many people report a renewed feeling of positive energy and/or creativity after meditating. When we practice concentrating in meditation, it carries over to our regular life, making it easier to stay focused on our work and daily tasks. Some doctors now even prescribe daily meditation to relieve stress and prevent heart disease. It has been confirmed that deep meditation is a unique state of consciousness and the brain emits unique brain waves during meditation. – One of the great things about meditation is that while it is essentially a spiritual practice, it requires no faith, no belief in God, and anyone from any religion can practice it without feeling that they are sinning. – Whether the goal is to seek spiritual knowledge, or just to learn how to relax, meditation is a valuable tool for everyone.

Prayer: - Prayer is counterpart to meditation. While meditation is passive, a way of observing, listening, or focusing, prayer is more active. It is literally talking to God. Prayers can take many forms. It can be communal activity as on holy days or private type of prayer, which can be done anywhere at any time. Prayer can involve much more than asking. You can talk to God about anything. Talk about your feelings, what is important to you, or why you are sad or happy. But remember that it is not the old man up in the sky that we are praying to, but we are praying to our SOUL for others SOULS. For maximum effectiveness, direct your focus inwards, to the center of you're Being; knowing that this is where you have a direct connection to God. Prayer is one aspect of religion, which is universal. The important thing is what prayer means to you. If you start with what it means to you, the emotion will naturally follow.

10.12 – ONE SET OF CODES: - [7]
Most religions have similar set of codes.

Ten Commandments	Buddha's Precepts	Hinduism
Thou shall not kill	Abstain from killing	The following quote from the Bhagavad-Gita in many ways resembles the 10 commandments and the Buddha's Precepts
Thou shall not steal	Abstain from stealing	Fearlessness, Purification of One's existence, Cultivation
Thou shall not commit adultery	Abstain from adultery	Of spiritual knowledge, Charity, Self Control,
Thou shall not bear false witness	Abstain from lying	Performance of sacrifice, study of scriptures, Austerity and
Thou shall not take the name of the Lord in vain	Abstain from slander (in-sult)	Simplicity, non-violence, Truthfulness, Freedom from
Thou shall not covet thy neighbor's house	Do not covet (desire or want) other's property	Anger, Renunciation, Tran-quility, Aversion to fault
Thou shall have no other Gods before me	Do not speak harshly	Finding, Compassion and Freedom from covetous-ness,
Thou shall not make unto thee any Graven image	Do not engage in idle talks	Gentleness, Modesty and steady determination,
Honor thy father and mother	Do not show hatred	Vigor, Forgiveness, Forti-tude, Cleanliness, Freedom from
Remember the Sabbath day and keep it Holy	Think righteously	Envy, and the passion for honor.

10.13 - DIVINE LOVE: -

One must fall in love with GOD. Therefore it is necessary to establish some relationship with GOD. Make GOD your father or mother or brother or friend or master or the hearts beloved. Let everything you do to strengthen this relationship with G.OD

Live with GOD all the time. Therefore talk to him, again and again. Engage yourself in a loving, humble, intimate conversation with GOD.

Speak softly. Treat everyone with love and kindness. Do not see the faults of others. For every blow you receive, give back a blessing.

He who loves GOD, fears to do anything, which may displease GOD. He services to live a life of purity.

Whatever you do, do it for the pure love of GOD.

The law of love is the law of service. Go out of your way to help others and rejoice in the will of GOD.

God upsets our plans to set up his own, and His plans are always perfect. Man proposes and GOD disposes.

You pray in your distress and in your need; with that you might pray also in the fullness of your joy and in your days of abundance.

The greatest undeveloped resource of the world is **Faith** and the greatest unused power is **Prayer**.

10.14 - GOD AS CAUSE AND EFFECT: -

All the following qualities – intellect, knowledge, the absence of ignorant attachment, forgiveness, truthfulness, control of the senses, serenity, happiness and suffering, birth and death, fear and absence of fear, non-violence, inward poise and contentment, austerity, making gifts, good name or evil reputation among men, these conditions exist in all creatures and GOD is the cause of each one of them. The creator of all beings is also the cause of all the good and evil, which we see in these beings. There is no doubt at all that he who believes in GOD from the depth of his heart and obeys the Lord who dwells in him attains to a state of serenity which is never perturbed.

Neither Christians nor Muslims nor Jews nor Hindus have risen above the worship of the personal GOD. Even a person who aspires to cultivate devotion exclusively for the Un-manifest worships some visible symbol. We can of course understand with our intellect the idea that the body is unconnected with the SOUL, but has anyone ever been able to say what his state after death will be. The spiritualists and the theosophists are not correct, in my view, about what they say concerning spirits, in the sense that no one has been able to know and tell the whole truth.

GOD is described as having two aspects. Under one aspect we should know him as **NATURE** and under the other as **SOUL** as the **cause of the experience of happiness and misery.**

Anyone who has become free from the egotistic idea of being the author of anything, and who recognizes every moment of his life the authority of the GOD will never commit sin. It is in egotism that sin has its source. There is no sin where there is no consciousness of the "I".

10.15 - THEORIES OF ONE GOD: -
BIG BANG THEORY: -

The scientific theory of creation is that there was a Big Bang, which created the material elements (earth, water, gases, chemicals etc.). These material elements then somehow combined together and created the various planets and one species of living beings. These living beings then somehow changed their bodies and became another species, and so on. In this way the 8.4 millions species of living beings we know were created. This is termed as evolution, thus one body changes in to another and so on.

The Big Bang theory is the dominant scientific theory about the origin of the universe. According to the big bang, the universe was created sometime between

10 billion and 20 billion years ago from a cosmic explosion that hurled matter in all directions.

In 1927, the Belgian priest Georges Lemaitre was the first to propose that the universe began with the explosion of a primeval atom. His proposal came after observing the red shift in the distant nebulas by astronomers to a model of the universe based on relativity. Years later, Edwin Hubble found experimental evidence to help justify Lemaitre's theory. He found that distant galaxies in every direction are going away from us with speeds proportional to their distance.

The Big Bang was initially suggested because it explains why distant galaxies are travelling away from us at great speeds. The theory also predicts the existence of cosmic background radiation (the glow left over from the explosion itself). The Big Bang theory received its strongest confirmation when Arno Penzias and Robert Wilson, who later won the Noble Prize for this discovery, discovered this radiation in 1964.

Although the Big Bang theory is widely accepted, it probably will never be proved; consequently, leaving a number of tough, unanswered questions like

1. What or who caused the Big Bang?

2. If a Big Bang created all the universes and millions of planets, then according to scientific logic, it should be possible to create a small planet or something with a small bang. Can any scientist create anything with a bang?

3. Some chemicals mixed together created the first living being. The scientist has all the chemicals in the world; can they mix them and create a living being?

4. All the millions of planets are shaped like a sphere, is this by chance?

5. The sun has been giving exact amount of sunlight to the various planets including earth for millions of years. Is this by chance? Too much sun or too little can destroy all life on earth.

The final answer to all these unknown questions is **ONE GOD** who himself cannot be known.

Intelligent designer (GOD) theory vs. Darwin's theory of evolution: -
Because Darwin's theory is a theory, it is still being tested as new evidence is discovered. The theory is not a fact. Gaps in the theory exist for which there is no evidence.

Intelligent design is an explanation of the origin of life that differs from Darwin's view. The intellectual underpinnings of the latest assault on Darwin's theory come not from Bible-wielding fundamentalists but from well-funded think tanks promoting a theory they call intelligent design (ID). Their basic argument is that the origin of life, the diversity of species and even the structure of organs like the eye are so bewilderingly complex that they can only be handiwork of higher intelligence called GOD.

But many scientists and science teachers do not think that there is any valid criticism. Many tens of thousands of scientists reject I.D's core argument, that evolution can produce complex structures. Take the eye, I.D theorists say it could not have evolved bit by bit because a bit of an eye has no survival value; it would never have been passed on. Biologists see it differently. They say for example, a primitive light-sensing patch of skin- a forerunner of the retina- could help animals detect the shadows of predators.

Finally it is accepted that evolution as the best scientific explanation for life as we know it, but ONE GOD is ultimately responsible for the process.

10.16 - TRUE PRAYER: -
"When prayers end in a silent devotional yearning for union, without words, without thoughts, we have reached the highest form of prayer, which is **Meditation.**"

"Unless the cry comes from the heart, it is not effective.

So a prayer to be heard by the Lord, no matter what we are praying for, must come from the bottom of the heart. Only when the soul itself is weeping, crying out, is the prayer effective."

"There should be unison between the heart, the tongue and the brain. The prayer which comes from the heart and is expressed through the mouth and in which we have full confidence intellectually, will be heard."

"Praying to God is a positive step. When one prays to God it is recognition that there is a power greater than us. It is the awareness that we are not as great and powerful as we think we are, but that some higher force is there to come to our aid."

"The process of inversion, of going within, has been called differently in different ages by different saints and mystics. Some of them called it Concentration, some called it Inversion, and others called it Meditation, while others called it Prayer. These are all different names for trying to find ourselves, find God, and be one with God."

"Whenever we pray, not for our personal benefit but out of compassion for somebody else who is suffering, the Master may grant relief because we do not gain anything personally from it, neither are we making the prayer just for show. It is a spontaneous cry of the heart out of our compassion for a suffering man or for suffering humanity. The Master does listen to those prayers and grants them."

"When we meditate, we are praying to God to please enlighten us. So it is the highest treasure that we can find. Any thing that we pray for-let's say that we pray for a new house, a new car, or a promotion at work-these are all things of this world which are temporary, which we're going to leave behind the moment we physically die. But if we can gain enlightenment, if we can know who we truly are, then that gain will be with us forever. So meditation is the highest form of prayer-meditation is when we listen to God."

10.17 - GRATITUDE AND THANKFULNESS: -

"Prayer and gratitude grant inner peace and harmony to withstand the hazards of physical life, which is a passing phase of the soul in its long journey back to the True Home of the Father."

Gratefulness is a state in which we need to be. It is a state of recognizing that whatever happens to us is happening for our highest good. It is a state in which we really believe and act in these words: **'Sweet is Thy Will.'** We need to get into that state to be able to fulfill the purpose of our lives, which is to be one with GOD."

GOD'S BOXES: -

I have in my hands two boxes, which God gave me to hold.

He said, "Put all your sorrows in the black box, and all your joys in the gold box."

I heeded His words, and in the two boxes, both my sorrows and joys I stored. But though the gold became heavier each day, the black was as light as before.

With curiosity, I opened the black, I wanted to find out why, and I saw, in the base of the box, a hole, from which my sorrows had fallen out by.

I showed the hole to GOD, and thought, "I wonder where my sorrows could be."

He smiled a gentle smile and said, "My child, they're all here with me."

I asked God, why He gave me the boxes, why the gold, and the black with the hole?

"My child, the gold is for you to count your Blessings, the black is for you to let go."

10.18 - GOD IS ONE (proved by mathematics)

Dear friends, do you agree that we have 26 alphabets in English, as given below

A B C D E F G H I J K L M N O P Q R
1 2 3 4 5 6 7 8 9 10 11 12 13 14 15 16 17 18

S T U V W X Y Z
19 20 21 22 23 24 25 26

With each alphabet getting a number, in chronological order, as above, study the following, and bring down the total to a single digit and see the result yourself

Hindu
S h r e e   K r i s h n a
19+8+18+5+5+11+18+9+19+8+14+1=135=9

Muslim
M o h a m m e d
13+15+8+1+13+13+5+4=72=9

Jain
M a h a v i r
13+1+8+1+22+9+18=72=9

Sikh
G u r u   N a n a k
7+21+18+21+14+1+14+1+11=108=9

Parsi
Z a r a t h u s t r a
26+1+18+1+20+8+21+19+20+18+1=153=9

Buddhist

G a u t a m

7+1+21+20+1+13=63=9

Christian

E s a M e s s i a h

5+19+1+13+5+19+19+9+1+8=99=18=9

Each one ends with number 9

THAT IS NATURE'S CREATION TO SHOW THAT GOD IS ONE.

CHAPTER 11

WHAT IS "FINAL FAITH"?

11.01 - WHAT IS FAITH?

Faith is confidence or trust in a person or entity. Depending on the religion, faith is belief in a single GOD or multiple Forms of GOD or in the doctrines or teachings of the religion. Informal usage of faith can be quite broad, including trust or belief without proof, and "Faith" is often used as a substitute for **"hope", "trust" or "belief".**

Some critics of faith have argued that faith is opposed to reason. In contrast, some advocates of faith argue that the proper domain of faith concerns questions which cannot be settled by evidence.

Fideism is not a synonym for religious belief, but describes a particular philosophical proposition in regard to the relationship between faith's appropriate jurisdiction at arriving at truths, contrasted against reason. It states that faith is needed to determine some philosophical and religious truths, and it questions the ability of reason to arrive at all truth.

I have faith that GOD exists, but you do not show it in your daily life. If you had faith that GOD exists, you would not be a liar and thief and murderer, or criminal. We are all liars. No body has faith in GOD. We know that he does not exist. Therefore, with impunity we are cheating, murdering, robbing, making money from others, evading taxes etc. Our way of life proves that we are sure that there is no GOD. Today's human population is a cancer on nature. We are destructive; we are destroyers of everything including our SOUL and ourselves. Therefore take a big leap inside you and find your SOUL (conscious) and make use of your fullest time in the present, for the present, knowing that what I am not in the present and I don't have in the present, I will never have in the future. So live in the present and do well to yourself and others.

- Faith is loyalty or allegiance to a cause or a person.
- It is the act of binding yourself (intellectually or emotionally) to a course of action that means it is a commitment or dedication.
- It is strong belief in a SUPER NATURAL POWER.
- It is an institution to express belief in a DIVINE POWER.
- It is complete confidence in a person or a plan.

Faith makes things possible; it does not make them easy.

When I am continuously being battered by the storms of life, and my very spirit is ebbing away, then all I need to do is hang onto that gift called **'Faith'**, that one support which will weather the storms. FAITH does not depend on a clever head, only belief: belief in the self and the strength that lies within. **FAITH** is the seed of victory and the foundation of making the impossible possible.

This is living Faith: - Faith can transform your life, enabling you to enjoy a close, personal relationship with GOD. Faith can offer freedom from the shackles of worry, doubt and fear. It can bring strength, hope and wisdom in the face of problems and challenges.

11.02 - MEANING OF FAITH IN DIFFERENT RELIGIONS: -

Bahá'í Faith:

In the Bahá'í Faith, faith is ultimately the acceptance of the divine authority of the Manifestations of God. In the religion's view, faith and knowledge are both required for spiritual growth. Faith involves more than outward obedience to this authority, but also must be based on a deep personal understanding of religious teachings. By faith is meant, first, conscious knowledge, and second, the practice of good deeds.

Buddhism:

While faith in Buddhism does not imply "blind faith", Buddhist faith nevertheless requires a degree of faith and belief, primarily in the spiritual attainment of Gautama Buddha. Faith in Buddhism centers on the understanding that the Buddha is an Awakened being, on his superior role as teacher, in the truth of his Dharma (spiritual teachings), and in his Sangha (community of spiritually developed followers). Faith in Buddhism can be summarised as faith in the Three Jewels: the Buddha, Dharma and Sangha. It is intended to lead to the goal of enlightenment, or bodhi, and Nirvana. Volitionally (power of decision making), faith implies a resolute and courageous act of will. It combines the steadfast resolution that one will do a thing with the self-confidence that one can do it.

Christianity:

Faith in Christianity is based in and on the work and teachings of Jesus Christ. In this way Christianity declares not to be distinguished by its faith, but by the object of its faith. Faith is an act of trust or reliance. Rather than being passive, faith leads to an active life aligned with the ideals and the example of the one being trusted. It sees the mystery of God and his grace and seeks to know and become obedient to GOD. To a Christian; faith is not static but causes one to learn more of GOD and grow; it has its origin in GOD.

In Christianity faith causes change as it seeks a greater understanding of GOD. Faith is not fideism or simple obedience to a set of rules or statements. Before the Christian has faith, they must understand in whom and in what they have faith. Without understanding, there cannot be true faith and that understanding is built on the foundation of the community of believers, the scriptures and traditions and on the personal experiences of the believer.

Mainstream psychology and related disciplines have traditionally treated **belief** as if it were the simplest form of mental representation and therefore one of the building blocks of conscious thought.

Hinduism:

The Hindu faith is based on the premise that logic and reason are not conclusive methods of knowing a dramatic or literary work. Spiritual practice (*sadhana*) is performed with the faith that knowledge beyond the mind and sense perception will be revealed to the practitioner. The schools of Hindu philosophy differ in their recommended methods to cultivate faith, including selfless action (*karma-yoga*), renunciation (*jnana-yoga*) and devotion (*bhakti-yoga*).

Islam:

In Islam, faith (*iman*) is complete submission to the will of God, which includes belief, profession and the body's performance of deeds, consistent with the commission as vicegerency (an administrative deputy of a king) on Earth, all according to God's will.

Iman has two aspects:

- Recognizing and affirming that there is one Creator of the universe and only to this Creator is worship due. According to Islamic thought, this comes naturally because faith is an instinct of the human soul. This instinct is then trained via parents or guardians into specific religious or spiritual paths. Likewise, the instinct may not be guided at all.
- Willingness and commitment to submitting that God exists, and to His prescriptions for living in accordance with vicegerency (an administrative deputy of king). The Qur'an is the dictation of God's prescriptions through Prophet Muhammad and is believed to have updated and completed the previous revelations that God sent through earlier prophets.

Judaism:

Faith itself is not a religious concept in Judaism. Although Judaism does recognize the positive value of *Emunah* (generally translated as faith, trust in God) and the negative status of the *Apikorus* (heretic), faith is not as stressed or as central as it is in other religions, especially as it is in the faith possessed Christendom. It could be a necessary means for being a practicing religious Jew, but the emphasis is placed on practice rather than on faith itself. Very rarely does it relate to any teaching that must be believed. Classical Judaism does not require one to explicitly identify God (a key tenet of faith in Christianity), but rather to honor the idea of God.

Sikhism:

Sikhism, the fifth-largest organized religion in the world, was founded in 15th-century Punjab, India on the teachings of Guru Nanak Dev and ten successive Sikh gurus, the last one being the sacred text Guru Granth Sahib. The core philosophy of the Sikh religion is described in the beginning hymn of the Guru

Granth Sahib. There is one supreme eternal reality; the truth; imminent in all things; creator of all things; inherent in creation. Without fear and without hatred; not subject to time; beyond birth and death; self-revealing.

11.03 - FAITH IN GOD: -

"One of the most important qualifications for the aspirant is faith. There are three kinds of faith: (i) faith in ONESELF, (ii) faith in the GOD and (iii) faith in LIFE. Faith is so indispensable to life that unless it is present in some degree, life itself would be impossible. It is because of faith that cooperative and social life becomes possible. It is faith in each other that facilitates a free give and take of love, a free sharing of work and its results. When life is burdened with unjustified fear of one another it becomes cramped and restricted....Faith in GOD becomes all-important because it nourishes and sustains faith in oneself and faith in life in the very teeth of set-backs and failures, handicaps and difficulties, limitations and failings. Life, as man knows it in himself, or in most of his fellow-men, may be narrow, twisted and perverse, but life as he sees it in GOD is unlimited, pure and untainted. In GOD, man sees his own ideal realized; GOD is what his own deeper self would rather be. He sees in the GOD the reflection of the best in himself which is yet to be, but which he will surely one day attain. Faith in GOD therefore becomes the chief motive-power for realizing the divinity which is latent in man.

11.04 - CRITICISM OF FAITH:-

Some critics argue that religious faith is irrational and see faith as ignorance of reality: a strong belief in something with no evidence and sometimes a strong belief in something even with evidence against it. Bertrand Russell noted, "Where there is evidence, no one speaks of 'faith'. We do not speak of faith that two and two are four or that the earth is round. We only speak of faith when we wish to substitute emotion for evidence." In the rationalist view, belief should be restricted to direct observation in the past and present.

Evolutionary biologist Richard Dawkins criticizes all faith by generalizing from specific faith in propositions that conflict directly with scientific evidence. He describes faith as mere belief without evidence; a process of active non-thinking. He states that it is a practice which only degrades our understanding of the natural world by allowing anyone to make a claim about nature that is based solely on their personal thoughts, and possibly distorted perceptions, that does not require testing against nature, has no ability to make reliable and consistent predictions, and is not subject to peer review.

11.05 - DEFINITION OF FAITH: -

1. Confidence or trust in a person or thing: faith in another's ability.
2. Belief that is not based on proof: He had faith that the hypothesis would be substantiated by fact.
3. Belief in GOD or in the doctrines or teachings of religion: the firm faith of the Pilgrims.
4. Belief in anything, as a code of ethics, standards of merit, etc.: to be of the same faith with someone concerning honesty.
5. A system of religious belief: the Christian faith; the Jewish faith.
6. The obligation of loyalty or fidelity to a person, promise, engagement, etc.: Failure to appear would be breaking faith.
7. The observance of this obligation; fidelity to one's promise, oath, allegiance, etc.: He was the only one who proved his faith during our recent troubles.
8. Christian Theology. The trust in GOD and in His promises as made through Christ and the Scriptures by which humans are justified or saved.

11.06 – MAYA (ILLUSION): - [2]

MAYA in its final form is neither idealism nor realism, nor is it a theory. It is simple statement of facts, as they exist – what we are and what we see around us. Maya is the statement of the facts of this universe. And this is MAYA.

Death is the end of life, of beauty, of wealth, of power, of virtue too. Saints die and sinners die, kings die and beggars die. They are all going to death. And yet this tremendous clinging to life exists. Some how, we do not know why, we cling to life; we cannot give it up. And this is MAYA.

A mother nursing her child with great care: all her soul, her life, is in that child. However she may try, she cannot shake off the bondage she is in. And this is MAYA.

Reformers arise and preach that learning, wealth, and culture should not be in the hands of a select few; and they do their best to make them accessible to all. These may bring happiness to some, but perhaps as culture grows, physical happiness lessens. The knowledge of happiness brings the knowledge of un-happiness. The least amount of material prosperity that we enjoy is elsewhere causing the same amount of misery. This is the Law. The young perhaps, do not see it clearly, but those who have lived long enough and those who have struggled enough will understand it. And this is MAYA.

Animals are living upon plants, men upon animals, and worst of all, upon one another – the strong upon the weak. This is going on everywhere as a life cycle. And this is MAYA.

The animal man lives in his senses. If he does not get enough to eat, he is miserable, or if something happens to his body, he is miserable. In the sense both his misery and happiness begin and end. As soon as man progresses, as soon as his horizon of happiness increases, his horizon of unhappiness in-creases proportionately. We who are progressing know that the more we progress, the more avenues are opened to pain as well as to pleasure. And this is MAYA.

Desire is never satisfied by the enjoyment of desires; it only increases the more, like fire when butter is poured upon it. This is true of all sense enjoyments; and all the enjoyments of which the human mind is capable. They are nothing. They are all within MAYA, within this network, which we cannot get out of. And this is MAYA.

All religions are more or less attempts to get beyond nature – the crudest or the most developed, expressed through mythological stories of Gods or angels or demons, or through stories of saints or seers, great men or prophets, or through the abstraction of philosophy – all have that one object; all are trying to get beyond these limitations. In one word, they are all struggling towards freedom. This nature, this universe, is what is called MAYA? And this is MAYA.

To humans the universe appears real, yet at the same time not real, and we appear awake, yet at the same time asleep. This is a statement of fact, and this is what is called MAYA. We are born in this MAYA, we live in it, we think in it, we dream in it. We are spiritual men in it, we are devils in it and we are Gods in it. Stretch your ideas as for as you can, take them higher and higher, call them infinite or by any other name – even these ideas are within MAYA. The whole of human knowledge is a generalization of this MAYA. Everything that has form, everything that calls up an idea in your mind, is within MAYA, for everything that is bound by the laws of time, space, and causation is within MAYA. And this is MAYA.

With every breath, with every pulsation of the heart, with everyone of our movements, we think we are free; and the very same moment we are shown that we are not: we are born slaves, nature's bond slaves, in body, in mind, in all our thoughts, in all our feelings. And this is MAYA.

Whatever may be the position of the philosophy, whatever may be the position of metaphysics, so long as there is such a thing as death in the world, so long as there is such as a weakness in the human heart, so long as there is a cry going out of the heart of man in his very weakness, there will be faith in GOD. And this is MAYA.

11.07 - INTELLECTUAL FAITH: -
A man must have not only Faith, but also intellectual Faith.

Materialists call it Matter, whereas spiritualists call it GOD.

Materialist would say "Eat, drink and be merry, there is no GOD, SOUL or HEAVEN".

The salvation depends on the Rationalistic Religion – Non duality, Oneness, the idea of Impersonal God – is the only religion that can have any hold on Intellectual people.

We want today that bright sun of intellectuality joined with the heart of Buddha, the wonderful, infinite heart of love and mercy. This union will give us the highest philosophy. Science and religion will meet and shake hands. Poetry and philosophy become friends. This will be the religion of the future, and if we can work it out, we may be sure that it will be for all times and people.

When a scientist makes the assertion that all objects are the manifestation of one force, does it not remind you of the GOD?

Why should human beings be Moral? Because through morality is the path towards freedom and immorality leads to bondage.

11.08 – GOAL OF THE UNIVERSAL RELIGION: -

Universal religion can apply to everyone, and that religion must not be composed of only specific parts, but it must always be the sum total and include all degrees of religious development.

We should have a combination of the greatest heart with the highest intellectuality of infinite love with infinite knowledge.

The final attributes to God should be Infinite Existence, Infinite knowledge and Infinite Bliss.

Our Goal should be Harmony of Existence, Knowledge, and Bliss Infinite.

If we take the world as it is then nothing will be left to us but Evil. But there is something beyond this world. The life in five senses, life in the material world is not all, it is only superficial. Behind and beyond is the Infinite, in which there is no more evil. Some people call it GOD, some Brahaman, some Allah, some Jehovah, Jove and so on.

What we really want is head and heart combined.

The goal of every religion is the same, that each is trying to teach the same thing (Self Realization), the difference being largely in the methods and stills more in language. At the core of all sects and of all religions have the same aim; they only quarrel for their own selfish purposes.

11.09 - SELF REALIZATION FOR FAITH: -

The closer we are to the center of circle, the closer we are to the common ground in which all the radii meet; and the farther we are from the center, the more divergent is our radial line from others.

The **external world** is only one part of the whole of phenomena. There are other parts: **the mental, the moral and the intellectual** – the various planes of existence – and to take only one part and find a solution of the whole is simply impossible. Therefore we have to find a center where all the planes of existence start. Now where is that center? **It is within us.** The ancient sages penetrated deeper and deeper until they found that in the inner most core of the **Human Soul is the center of the whole universe.**

Matter is only an infinitesimal part of the phenomenal universe. Actually in every moment of our day-to-day life, great part is played by Thought and Feeling than the Material phenomena outside. Materialistic people think that the whole phenomena are only in touch, taste, sight, hearing and smell, but in fact it is deep inside you in your thoughts and feelings.

Those who are evildoers, whose minds are not peaceful, can never see the light. It is to those who are true in heart, pure in deed, whose senses are controlled, that self manifests itself. **This is self-realization.** If the power to satisfy our desires increases in arithmetical progression, our desires increase in geometrical progression.

This world is nothing but a shadow of reality. We must go to reality. **Renunciation** will take us there. Renunciation is the very basis of our true life. Every moment of goodness and real life that we enjoy is when we do not think of ourselves. This little separate must die. Then we shall find that we are in the Real, and that Reality is GOD, and he is our own true nature, and he is always in us and with us. Let us live in him and stand in him; it is the only joyful state of existence. **Life on the plane of the spirit is the only life. Let us all try to attain to this realization.**

Wherever there are business and business principles in religion, spirituality dies. Religion does not consist in erecting temples or building churches or attending public worship. It is not to be found in books or in words or in lectures or in organizations, **Religion consists in realization.** We all know as a fact that nothing will satisfy us until we realize the truth by ourselves. However we may argue, however much we may hear, but one thing will satisfy us, and that is our own realization, and such experience is possible for everyone of us, if we will only try. The first idea in this attempt to realize religion is that of renunciation. As far as we can, we should give up. Darkness and Light, enjoyment of the world and enjoyment of GOD, will never go together.

GOD exists or not: -
We have to analyze our own souls and find what is there. **We have to understand it and realize what is understood. That is Religion.** So the question of whether there is GOD or not can never be proved by argument; for the arguments are as much on one side as on the other. But if there is GOD, he is in our own hearts.

The turmoil and fight and difference in religions will cease only when we understand that religion is not in books and temples, it is in actual perception. Only the man who has actually perceived GOD and the SOUL is religious. We are all atheists, and yet we try to fight the man who admits being one. We are all in the dark; religion is to us mere intellectual assent, mere talk, and mere nothing. Religion begins only when actual realization begins in our souls.

Faith in Oneself: -
The new religion says that he is the atheist who does not believe in himself. But it is not selfish faith; it is the doctrine of Oneness. It means faith in all because you are all. Love for you means love for all. – Love for animals, love for everything; for you are all. This is the great faith, which will make the world better. You know little of that which is within you, for behind you is the ocean of infinite power and blessedness.

Hear day and night that you are that Soul. Repeat it to yourself day and night till it enters in to your veins, till it tingles every drop of blood, till it is in your flesh and bone. Let the whole body be full of that one idea: "I am the birth-less, the death-less, the blissful, the omniscient, the omnipotent, ever glorious SOUL. Then all your actions will be glorified, transformed, deified, by the very power of this thought. If matter is powerful, thought is omnipotent.

11.10 - ANALYTICAL THINKING WEAKENS RELIGIOUS BELIEF: -
Most of the world's population believes in GOD, or Forms of GOD, but alongside them there are also hundreds of millions of nonbelievers. What makes one a believer or not?

Religious faith is likely a complex phenomenon, shaped by multiple aspects of psychology and culture. The researchers, Ara Norenzayan and Will Gervais of the University of British Columbia in Canada, showed in a series of clever studies that at least one factor consistently appears to decrease the strength of people's religious belief: **analytic thinking.**

In one study, the researchers correlated participants' performance on a test of analytic thinking with measures of their religious belief. The thinking task included three problems requiring participants to analytically override their initial intuition. For example, one question asked: "A bat and a ball cost $1.10 in total. The bat costs $1 more than the ball. How much does the ball cost?" The immediate, intuitive response is 10 cents. Those who take the time to figure out the right answer (5 cents) are judged to be more analytical, and these people tended to score lower on the measures of religious belief.

There are surely many factors at play here, but the researchers say their results suggest that one's style of thought may be a crucial contributor to religious belief. Intuitive thinkers are more likely to be religious; analytical types, less so. "One explanation for belief is that it is based on a number of intuitions we have about the world around us. People don't necessarily come to belief because they reason into it. Intuition helps us," says Norenzayan.

That's not to say that one way of thinking is more valuable than the other, only that the friction between intuitive and analytical thinking may help explain the origins of religious belief — or disbelief. "We know that in human psychology there are two systems of thinking. System one is intuitive; it is rapid and effortless. System two is analytical, and is more reasoned and thoughtful. Our study supports the idea that analytic thinking can push people away from intuitive thinking," says Norenzayan.

The authors stress that their findings only scratch the surface of how religious belief develops. Faith is a complicated thing, influenced by culture and experience, Norenzayan says, such as those who find religion during situations of fear or morality. "We are not saying that analytical thinking turns people against religion. ... There are lots of things going on," says Norenzayan. "Our findings do not suggest one form of thinking is better than the other either. We don't believe that. Both are important and both have costs and benefits."

11.11 - NARCISSISM (EGOTISM) AND RELIGION AS UNETHICAL MIX: -

Can't get enough of yourself? Narcissism can certainly be a social turn-off, and a new study from Baylor University shows that its least appealing features may have the strongest effect on those least likely to be so self-focused: the religiously devout.

Researchers at Baylor University surveyed a group of 385 undergraduate students who answered questions about how acceptable they found certain ethically sketchy behaviors, such as an underpaid company executive padding his expense account by $3000 a year, to assess their moral judgment. The students also answered questions about how religious they were, how often they went to church and how important religion was in their lives. Overall, those who were classified as nominal or devout Christians were more likely to show better ethical judgment than skeptics (those who were not very religious).

But when the scientists added an additional information on the students' narcissistic tendencies, the more devout participants tended to make the least ethical judgments. "Both the nominal and devout groups show degrees of poor ethical judgment equal to that of the skeptics when accompanied by higher degrees of narcissism (egotism), a finding that suggests a dramatic transformation for both nominals and the devouts when ethical judgment is clouded by narcissistic tendencies," study author Chris Pullig, chair of the department of marketing at Baylor said in the statement. "For both of these groups as narcissism increases so does the tendency to demonstrate worse ethical judgment." Narcissism is sufficiently intrusive and powerful that it entices people into behaving in ways hostile to their most deeply-held beliefs.

The effect of narcissism appeared to be strongest among those identifying themselves as religious; there was little effect on the skeptics as they showed no changes in ethical judgment regardless of where they stood on the narcissism scale.

Therefore, it is reasonable to hypothesize that even though an individual's religious commitment would logically preclude unethical behavior, a person might be seduced by his or her own narcissism into engaging in acts that are unethical and possibly illegal.

It seems that for narcissists, even those whose religion teaches them otherwise, it's all about them.

11.12 - RELIGIONS' SECRET TO HAPPINESS: ITS' FRIENDS, NOT FAITH:-

Religion can be good for your health, and especially your mental health, according to the latest studies, which show that church-goers are happier and more satisfied with their lives than those who don't attend services. But what exactly is it about religion that is so beneficial to health?

Some might argue that it is the power of faith in a being or power beyond ourselves. But according to a study led by Chaeyoon Lim, a sociology professor at University of Wisconsin-Madison, the reason religion makes us happy may have more to do with friends than with faith.

Using data from the Faith Matters Study, a survey of U.S. adults conducted in 2006 and 2007, Lim and his colleagues found that 33% of those who attended religious services every week and reported having close friends at church said they were extremely satisfied with their lives, while only 19% of those who went to church but had no close connections to the congregation reported the same satisfaction.

The evidence substantiates it is not really going to church and listening to sermons or praying that makes people happier, but making church-based friends and building intimate social networks there.

The results support the idea that friends and acquaintances can have a powerful, even contagious effect on our health. It's clear that our social network, regardless of how close or distant we are to the people in them, can influence our health. Scientists have shown that even people separated from you by up to three degrees can influence your weight, your happiness, or even whether you quit smoking or are prone to loneliness.

The sense of community that religion promotes is an important part of helping people to feel involved and worthwhile, and therefore may contribute to an overall sense of happiness.

11.13 - HOW FEELING OF GRATITUDE BREED HAPPINESS AND WELL-BEING: -

If you need another reason to give thanks at the dinner table, how's this: people who maintain an "attitude of gratitude" tend to be happier and healthier than those who don't. Adults who feel grateful have more, than who do not, according to studies conducted over the past decade. They're also less likely to be depressed, envious, greedy or alcoholics.

One research has found that grateful students reported higher grades, more life satisfaction, better social integration and less envy and depression than their peers who were less thankful and more materialistic. Additionally, feelings of gratitude had a more powerful impact on the students' lives overall than materialism. Gratitude should be chronic in order to reap all of its benefits.

Feeling gratitude must be ingrained into your personality, and you must frequently acknowledge and be thankful for the role other people play in your happiness.

For older children and adults, one simple way to cultivate gratitude is to literally count your blessings. Keep a journal and regularly record whatever you are grateful for that day. Be specific. The real benefit comes in changing how you experience the world. Look for things to be grateful for, and you'll start seeing them.

Studies show that using negative, derogatory words — even as you talk to yourself — can darken your mood, as well. Fill your head with positive thoughts, express thanks and encouragement aloud and look for something to be grateful for, not criticize, in those around you, especially loved ones.

11.14 - REAL GOD: -

I had learned that one's GOD is what a person obeys. The word *Lord means Master* – one you obey. Most people I had discovered are obeying false GODs, rebelling against the one true *CREATOR*, who is the supreme ruler of the universe.

Then who and what is Real GOD?

GOD is the creator, who designed, formed, shaped and created MAN.

GOD is the creator of all – of everything in this vast universe – the stars, the galaxies in endless space, this earth, man and everything in the earth. That is what GOD is. He is the GENERATOR, OPERATOR and DESTROYER of every SOUL and NATURE.

What GOD does?

He Creates! He designs, forms and shapes. He gives Life! He is the great giver. And his law – his way of life – is the way of giving, not getting, which is the way of this world. He is the OPERATOR of every SOUL and NATURE.

But what is God like? Who is GOD?

There have been many conceptions. Some believe GOD is merely the GOD of good intentions, within each human – merely some part of each human individual. Some have imagined GOD was some kind of idol composed of gold and silver, or carved out of wood, stone or other material. The Israelites thought, while Moses was communing with GOD on mount Sinai, that GOD was, or looked like, a Golden Calf. Many think GOD is a single individual Supreme Personage. Some thought he was a spirit.

But the generally accepted teaching of traditional Christianity is that GOD is a Trinity – GOD in three persons. Father, Son, and Holy Spirit, which they call a "GHOST". The word Trinity is not found in the bible, nor does the bible teach this doctrine.

What is GOD's form and shape?

God said, let us make man in our image, after our likeness. We know the form and shape of man. That is the image, likeness, form and shape of GOD.

GOD's Nature and Character: -

The character of both GOD the father and Christ the son is that of Holiness, Righteousness and Absolute perfection. That character might be summed up in the one word Love, defined as out flowing, loving concern. It is the way of giving, serving, helping, sharing. It is the way devoid of desire, lust and greed, vanity and selfishness, competition, strife, violence and destruction, envy and jealousy, resentment and bitterness. GOD's inherent nature is the way of Peace, Justice, Mercy, Happiness and Joy radiating outward toward those he has created.

11.15 - MYSTERY OF CIVILIZATION: -

Let us stop to think about it, but when you do, could anything be wrapped in more mystery than this world's civilization?

How to explain the astonishing paradox. A world of human minds that can send astronauts to the moon and back, produce the marvels of science and technology, transplant human hearts – yet cannot solve simple human problem of family life and group relationships, or peace between nations?

The developed nations have made awesome progress. They have produced a highly mechanized world providing every luxury, modern convenience and means of pleasure. Yet they are cursed with crime, violence, injustice, sickness and disease, broken homes and families. At the same time more than half the world is living in illiteracy, hopeless poverty, filth and unpleasantness. Violence and destruction are rapidly multiplying. Many ask, why? If GOD exists, does he allow so much violence and human suffering?

Humanity was created on earth for a glorious and wonderful purpose. GOD was reproducing himself. Stated another way, GOD's purpose was to create humanity to become supremely happy and joyful in peace and perfect comfort, to become productive, creative, and joyfully successful with eternal life. But to accomplish it, humanity must make its own decisions.

11.16 - THE ROLE OF FAITH IN CROSS-CULTURAL CONFLICT RESOLUTION - [34]

One of the most important findings of cross-cultural conflict resolution research is that religion is a perpetual and perhaps inevitable factor in both conflict and conflict resolution. Religion, after all, is a powerful constituent of cultural norms and values, and because it addresses the most profound existential issues of human life (e.g., freedom and inevitability, fear and faith, security and insecurity, right and wrong, sacred and irreligious), religion is deeply implicated in individual and social conceptions of peace. **To transform the conflicts harassing the world today, we need to uncover the conceptions of peace within our diverse religious and cultural traditions, while seeking the common ground among them.**

When we speak of the role of faith in cross-cultural conflict resolution, our challenge is to honor the diversity of the world's humanistic and spiritual traditions while seeking common ground among them, **that common ground is that we are all same GOD's creation, he is our GENERATOR, OPERATOR and DESTROYER.** What we need is an agenda for research, dialogue and activism that is global in conception and responsive to common challenges of peacemaking and coexistence within and among the world's many traditions. It is no longer sufficient for transnational peace agendas to be defined primarily by the cultural experiences and perceived security threats of a particular nation or culture. **We need new frameworks for organizing knowledge about religion, culture and spirituality** – frameworks that recognize the powerful role that faith and belief play in conflict and conflict resolution, and that do not privilege one culture as 'normal' and label another as 'exceptional'. **Education of the masses about different religions is the key in resolving conflicts.**

Many Religions, One Community: -
Our contemporary situation raises many serious questions:

How can different cultures and faith groups find ways to live together in peace and prosperity in a shared society? To what extent are tensions between different faith groups and cultures inevitable? How should these tensions be understood and handled? History provides us with a number of resources for thinking about these questions and about how we might answer them today.

The Rise and Fall of Islamic countries highlight a period in history when Christians, Muslims and Jews lived together and flourished. At the height of this era, people of these different faiths and cultures learned each other's languages, translated each other's great works of literature, philosophy and science, and benefited from a time of peace and prosperity. **But this period of peace and prosperity was brought to an end by interfaith conflict, misunderstanding and intolerance.** What implications do this historical period and its decline have for interfaith and cross-cultural relations in our community, our nation and in the world today?

Defining the Role of Religion in Conflict and Peacemaking: -
Peace and conflict resolution are both universal and particular; similar as well as divergent approaches derive form and vitality from the cultural resources of the people. When we examine peacemaking and conflict resolution across cultures, we discover both common themes and significant differences, both of which enhance our general theories of conflict resolution and help to create constructive channels for the perennial religious impulse.

Primarily, this occurs through pre-suppositions regarding the nature of reality and society, the purpose and ultimate meaning of life, and the means by which to live an 'authentic' ideal life – the life of inner and outer peace. Religious concepts of peace, then, embody and elaborate upon the highest moral and ethical principles of a given society and define the terms and conditions for individual and social harmony.

Religion in Conflict Situations: -

In promulgating the ideals and values held in highest esteem by groups and individuals, religion profoundly influences goal-seeking behavior in conflict situations, by establishing the criteria or frames of reference for determining the rightness and wrongness of events. Viewed from a religious perspective, conflicts are interpreted not only as ruptures in horizontal relationships between human beings, but also as ruptures in one's vertical relationship with the divine.

Religion and Conflict Resolution: -

The religious cosmology of a group, in privileging some values and ideals over others, specifies how restoration, wholeness and healing can be achieved through distinctive paths of resolution adopted by different cultures. The ruptures experienced in conflict situations often require symbolic or other social exchange found within collective cosmologies. In this way, conflict resolution strategies manifest distinctive conceptions of peace, which illuminate the terms and conditions necessary for social harmony to be both understood and experienced.

Islam and the West: A Search for Common Ground: -

One distinction that many observers of Islam fail to make concerns the difference between revivalism and fundamentalism. Islamic revivalism is a broad-based social and political movement directed toward internal renewal. First and foremost, it is a response to a widely felt disorder that has left Muslim societies weak and unable to meet the modern world on their own terms. Although its manifestations are remarkably widespread, Islamic revivalism is not a monolithic movement, nor is it equivalent to the militant fundamentalism – a reaction to foreign incursions and perceived threats to identity and security – that captures the attention of the media. Among the world's major historical powers, only the Muslims, as a people, have not reversed the decline in their global status. The Japanese, the Chinese, the Indians, and the Europeans have all regained their world influence. The Islamic revival is a way that Muslims are defining who they are. Under conditions of cultural, economic and political marginalization, large numbers of people are returning to deeply embedded religious discourses as they search for authentic values and alternative means of responding to their problems.

Today's challenge for the West is to live up to its liberal tradition, which requires continual openness to new revelations of truth. Today's challenge for Muslims is no more than the expansion of the original ideas of Islam.

The Changing Context of Human Spirituality: -
We stand at the conjunction of two perspectives. One is the emotional perspective felt by many Westerners – the view that, if not for the revival and increasing political activism of non-Western cultural traditions such as Islam, all would have been well. This perspective points to the calamitous events of September 11, 2001 and states that its peace has been shattered. The other perspective – a perspective of hopelessness that is common among Muslims as well as members of many other non-Western cultural traditions – is born of experiences of exclusion, suffering and resentment that have accumulated over a considerable period of time. From their perspective, peace and justice have long been absent from the world. A precarious and even humiliating state of existence has been the norm, not peace.

Where do we go from here? What contribution can faith make to this state of affairs? We need to experience ourselves in relationship, not out of relationship. In a world of collapsing boundaries, cultures need to experience their commonality. This is necessary if the suffering that Americans and Westerners are undergoing in the face of scourges like terrorism is to find its counterpoint in the suffering of those who turn to militant belief systems or who are unable to prevent their companions from doing so.

In other words, divergent worlds of perception – **Islam and the West, the South and the North – must move from isolation toward unity.** To do so, we need to stimulate reflection, find meaning in mutual tragedies and share our most sacred values, including our conceptions of peace. Such activities permit a search for meaning and commonality. The discovery of commonality, in turn, makes reconciliation possible, through the re-identification and reaffirmation of the core spiritual precepts upon which our religious narratives, images and values have been built. In the process, we may also derive common responses to shared human suffering.

11.17 - RECITATION BY BUDDHISTS: -

The meaning of Nam-myoho-renge-kyo – This is Lotus Sutra
This is the mystic law

Many people associate Buddhist religious practice with silent, interior meditation. But the practice of vocalizing, reciting and chanting various teachings has played a vitally important role in the history of Buddhism. Using our voices to express and convey the state of our inner life – whether that is one of joy, gratitude, despair or determination – is central to our identity as humans. Likewise it is through song, the voice, that human beings have given primary expression to their innermost feelings of-and desires for-harmony with all life. The voice serves as a vital link between us, our fellow humans and a universe that is itself vibrant with the rhythms of life and death.

What then does "Nam-myoho-renge-kyo" mean.?
The phrase can be literally translated as " I devote myself to the lotus sutra of the wonderful law."

Nam: - derives from Sanskrit and means to venerate (worship or idolize) or dedicate oneself.

Myoho: - corresponds to Sadharna and may be translated as "wonderful or mystic law". It is simply the mysterious nature of our life from moment to moment, which the mind can not comprehend or words express. " The great power of the mystic law...embraces everything, brings out the positive possibilities of all situations, transforming everything toward the good, reviving and giving new life to all experiences."

Renge: - The lotus Flower – The fact that the lotus flower already contains seeds when it opens, symbolizes the principle of the simultaneity of cause and effect. The idea that cause we make are engraved in the deepest, the most essential realms of life, and on this plane we immediately experience the effects of our thoughts, words and deeds. **The fact that lotus flower sends forth white blossoms from roots sunk deep in muddy water, express the idea that our higher nature is brought forth through committed engagement with the often difficult or disagreeable realities of life and society.**

Kyo: - signifies the Sutra, the voiced and transmitted teaching of the Budha. The chinese character for Kyo indicates the threads that run continually through a woven fabric. It represents the words and voices of all living beings. Kyo may also be defined as that which is constant and unchanging in the three existences of past, present and future.

When with our mouths we chant the mystic law, our Buddha nature, being summoned, will invariably emerge.

11.18 - RECITATION BY HINDUS: -

What is Gayatri?

Gayatri is a Sanskrit word – Ga means to sing – Yatri means protection. Gayatri is not new or independent goddess. Gayatri means those who worship her, get protected.

What is the gayatri Mantra?

OM BHOOR BHUVAHA SWAHA TAT SAVITUR VARENIYAM BHARGO DEVASYA DHEEMAHI DHIYO YO NAHA PRACH-DAYAT

Meaning of Gayatri Mantra: -

Translated it means: - " Oh God, though art the giver of life, the remover of pain and sorrow, the bestower of happiness; O creator of the universe, may we receive thy supreme, sin-destroying light, may though guide our intellect in the right direction".'

Gayatri is a Mantra (Hymn), which inspires righteous wisdom. It's meaning is that the Almighty God may illuminate our intellect, which may lead us to righteous path. This is the most important teaching. All the problems of the person are solved if he is endowed with the gift of righteous wisdom. Having endowed with farsighted wisdom, a man is neither entangled in calamity nor does he tread wrong path. Righteous wisdom starts emerging as soon as me-thodical recitation of this mantra is performed.

OM	Almighty God
BHOOR	Embodiment of vital or spiritual energy
BHUVAHA	Destroyer of suffering
SWAHA	Embodiment of happiness
TAT	That (indicating God)
SAVITUR	Bright, luminous like sun
VARENIYAM	Supreme, best
BHARGO	Destroyer of sins
DEVASYA	Divine
DHEEMAHI	May receive
DHIYO	Intellect
YO	Who
NAHA	Our
PRACHODAYAT	May inspire

One should contemplate these feelings daily for some time. By such contemplation, the meaning of Gayatri Mantra is fully assimilated in the heart of the person. The result in few days, his mind gets diverted from evil deeds and he starts taking enthusiasm in righteous thinking and good actions.

11.19 - FINAL PRAYER FOR EVERY FAITH: -
Have mercy upon me O Lord, hear me as I pray.
Cleans me from my sin, create faith within my heart.
Grant me patience in my trail, and peace to my troubled heart.

FINAL THANKS TO GOD: -
Thank you God for nice world to see,
Thank you God for birds to sing,
Thank you God for food to eat,
Thank you God for everything you give us.

A PRAYER FOR THE WORLD: -
Let the rain come and wash away the ancient grudges,
The bitter hatreds held and nurtured over generations.

Let the rain wash away the memory of the hurt, the neglect,
Then let the sun come out and fill the sky with rainbows.
Let the warmth of sun heal us, wherever we are broken,
Let it burn away the fog, so that we can see each other clearly,
So that we can see beyond labels, beyond accents, gender or skin color.
Let the warmth and brightness of the sun, melt our selfishness,
So that we can share the joys and feel the sorrows of our neighbors.
And let the light of sun be so strong that we see all people as our neighbors.
Let the earth, nourished by rain, bring forth flowers to surround us with beauty, and let the mountains teach our hearts to reach upward to heaven.

DAILY MORNING PRAYER: -

Dear GOD,
Today I woke up
I'm Healthy
I'm Alive
I'm Blessed
I apologize for all my complaining
I'm truly grateful for all you have done in my life.

11.20 - FAITH'S PLACE: -

Belief in Spiritual power is a universal trait. We were custom-made for religious experience. The human brain even at its ancient, primitive core is less an organ of impulse than a machine of reason. We are built to make sense of things. Our brains restlessly scan the world for patterns in chaos and causes in coincidence. We crave explanation and when faced with the ineffable, sometimes we create the answer. **For many people, the answer to the most indescribable question of all – "Why do we exist?" – is GOD.**

Neuroscientists have spent years studying history, myth and biology in their quest to understand the universality of spiritual experience and its evolutionary function. In his studies of the brains of Tibetan monks and Franciscan nuns, radiologist Andrew Newberg seeks out the relationship between neural activity and mystical experience. Many scientists believe the connection between the brain and spirituality, which suggests that **there is a physiological basis for religion – that human beings, in essence, are hard-wired for GOD.**

Some neuroscientists theorize that Homo sapience have evolved the capacity to experience GOD primarily through the amygdale, a small almond shaped structure buried deep in the brain. The amygdale along with the hippocampus and hypothalamus, make up the limbic system, the first formed and most primitive part of the brain, where emotions, sexual pleasure and deeply felt memories arise. Spiritual experience is not based on superstition but instead is real, biological and part of our primitive biological derives.

May be the ability to experience GOD and the spirituality sublime is an inherited limbic trait. May be we evolved these neurons to better cope with the unknown, to perceive and respond to spiritual messages because they would increase the likelihood of our survival. **Consciousness create so much anxiety** that our species had to come up with the cognitive adaptation to deal with the pain of our intelligence – being able to think about our own mortality for instance. So it came up with the brain modification that allows us to believe in an alternative reality, that when we die there is a spiritual part of us that will live forever.

Am I religious? No, I am Spiritual? Yes, I certainly do not believe in anthropomorphic (something not human) GOD. I would say that the kingdom of GOD is inside us all. The brain is the chamber of GOD. It allows us to realize GOD and contemplate GOD, whatever GOD is.

11.21 - THE BIOLOGY OF BELIEF: -
Science and religion argue all the time, but they increasingly agree on one thing: a little **spirituality may be very good for your health**. – Spirituality predicts for better disease control. A large body of science shows a positive impact of religion on health. The way the brain works is so compatible with religion and spirituality that we are going to be enmeshed in both for a long time.

When people engage in prayer, it is the frontal lobes that take the lead, since they govern focus and concentration. During very deep prayer, the parietal lobe powers down, which is what allows us to experience that sense of having loosed our earthly moorings.

Fasting: -
Faith and health overlap other ways too. One of the staples of both traditional wellness protocols and traditional religious rituals is the cleansing fast, which is said to purge toxins in the first case and purge sins or serve other pious ends in the second. Jews fast on Yom Kippur, Catholics have lent, Muslims observe Ramadan, and Hindus give up food on 18 major holidays. Done right, these fasts may lead to a state of clarity and even euphoria. This in turn can give practitioners the blissful sense that whether the goal of food restriction is health or spiritual insight, it's being achieved. When the body is deprived of calories, first the liver and then fat compensate for the deficit, providing energy for needy cells. This altered body chemistry can affect the brain, leading some to feel an otherworldly connection.

Faith and Health: -
Religious belief is not just a mind question but involves the commitment of one's body as well. People who maintain a sense of gratitude for what is going right in their lives have reduced incidence of depression, which is itself a predictor of health. People who believe their lives have meaning live longer than people who don't. Given the generally higher incidence of obesity, hypertension and other lifestyle ills among African Americans, the church is in a powerful position to do a lot of good. The body is a temple, and the connection can be made between the physical body and religious and spiritual well-being.

Common Faith: -
A Hindu believes there are many paths to God. Jesus is one way, the Qur'an is another, and yoga practice is a third and so on. None is better than any other, all are equal. The most conservative Christians have not been taught to think like this. They learn in Sunday school that their religion is true, and others are false. Jesus said, " I am the way, the truth and the life. No one comes to the father except through me." Americans are no longer buying it. At present 65 percent Americans believe that "Many religions can lead to eternal life" Also the number of people who seek spiritual truth outside church is growing. 30% of Americans call themselves "Spiritual, not Religious". You are not picking and choosing from different religions, because they are all the same. It's about whatever works. If going to Yoga works, great - and going to Catholic

mass works, great. And if going to Catholic mass plus the Yoga plus the Buddhist retreat works, that's great too. **That means whatever gives the peace in mind called spirituality is good.**

HINDUISM: -

The object of the Hindu religion is the sublime one: to achieve the union with the eternal spirit, which the Hindus call Brahman, rather than God, and represented by the sacred syllable "OM". The grand purpose of its theology is to define Brahman – as far as it may be possible. Hindus believe that Ultimate Reality is so profound, ineffable and illimitable that it can neither be described nor debated. Yet the Hindus have made fantastic efforts to describe the divine and its relationship to the world. They hope to reach their goal of union with Brahman not only through ritual but also through **the common ideals of Hindu ethics: Purity, Self-Control, Detachment, Truth, Nonviolence, Charity, and Compassion toward all living creatures.**

Hindu deities are like a museum of religion, presenting almost every stage in the evolution of man's thinking about God. The early Gods, as in all primitive religion, personified the forces of nature: a Sun God, a Wind God, and a God of Fire. As morality advanced in to metaphysics, the seers became dissatisfied with the notion of many Gods and resolved all the diversities of nature in to one common source, **"Reality is ONE"**.

In Hindu mythology Brahman appears in the form of the **God Brahma (GENERATOR)** to create each universe, the form of **God Vishnu (OPERATOR)** to sustain it, and the form of **God Shiva or Mahesh (DESTROYER)** to be its eventual destroyer. Brahma is somewhat like a Christian GOD except that Brahma creates each universe out of eternally existing material, not out of nothing as GOD does according to Judaea-Christian tradition.

The Hindu also has different concept of reality. The realistic westerner, from the Hindu point of view, is usually preoccupied with MAYA, the world of appearance as, and in the end his realism will lead to disillusionment. In Maya though there is progress of the individual back to Brahman, there is no final purpose towards which the whole world seems to be moving. There is no social progress, as westerner would like to think, only endless repetitions. Unlike westerners, Hindus do not see time as an arrow or a flowing river but as a pool of water. At intervals there are waves or ripples in the pool, but the pool itself remains unchanged.

Hindus think that their religion is not only the most ancient in the world but also the most modern and the best suited to resolve the problem of the world's many conflicting faiths.

Hindu philosophy that all religions are equally valid may well sweep the world in the next twenty-five years. This thesis is congenial to the contemporary European and American mind.

Hindus consider themselves to be the representative of 21st century understanding, and the Christians along with the Moslems, to be the epitome of the religious exclusiveness and bigotry, which must disappear in the modern world.

O PILGRIM OF ETERNITY (Human beings)

DO THY DAILY WORK,
BUT ENTANGLE NOT THYSELF
IN ANY FORM, IN ANY FINITE THING

AND KNOW THAT THIS WORLD IS BUT A BRIDGE

LINGER NOT ON THE BRIDGE

BUT MOVE ON TO THE SHRINE
O PILGRIM OF ETERNITY

11.22 - FINAL FAITH OR BELIEF: -
Psychologists often carve thinking into two broad categories: **intuitive thinking**, which is fast and effortless (instantly knowing whether someone is angry or sad from the look on her face, for example); and **analytic thinking**, which is slower and more deliberate (and used for solving math problems and other

tricky tasks). Both kinds of thinking have their strengths and weaknesses, and they often seem to interfere with one another. Recently there's been an emerging consensus among researchers that a lot of religious beliefs are grounded in intuitive processes.

To Gervais and Norenzayan, the findings suggest that intuitive thinking, likely along with other cognitive and cultural factors, is a key ingredient in religious belief. Through some combination of culture and biology, our minds are intuitively receptive to religion. If you're going to be unreligious, it's likely going to be due to reflecting on it and finding some things that are hard to believe. **"In some ways this confirms what many people, both religious and non-religious, have said about religious belief for a long time, that it's more of a feeling than a thought,"** says Nicholas Epley, a psychologist at the University of Chicago. But he predicts the findings won't change anyone's mind about whether God exists or whether religious belief is rational. "If you think that reasoning analytically is the way to go about understanding the world accurately, you might see this as evidence that being religious doesn't make much sense," he says. "If you're a religious person, I think you take this evidence as showing that God has given you a system for belief that just reveals itself to you as common sense."

Make a Difference: -
"We can all make a difference…. What is required is that we have faith in GOD that everything that is happening in our life is for our highest good. As we live in that positive mode, we are able to bring happiness and joy into any atmosphere."

There is part of you that is perfect and pure. It is untouched by the less than perfect characteristics you've acquired by living in a less than perfect world. It is filled with divine qualities, so is a constant state of resourcefulness and well-being. Its total absence of conflict and negativity of any sort makes this part of you a Still-Point; a deep, enriching experience of Silence.

Make time to practice reaching this inner place of Silence. It will bring you untold benefit.

Belief Power: -
So why do you have so many beliefs? And why is the world not becoming a

better place with so many believers? To answer this question, we need to go back to the moment of 'truth' which was lost to our awareness...some time ago. Beliefs are only present because we have lost our connection with the eternal truths, and our awareness of those truths. For example, while you believe you are what you see in the bathroom mirror in the morning, it is not the truth of who you really are. You are not your physical form - you are simply spirit, or that which animates the form. The experience (not the belief) of this truth liberates you from the fear of ageing and decay. Spirit (self) does not grow old and does not die. But then, you must not believe me (or disbelieve me). **When you experience, there is no longer a need to believe, because now you know...THE TRUTH.** This is why belief is not the truth and why truth is more powerful than belief, and why belief and truth are never found in bed together. So what is the truth? Are you a physical being having the occasional spiritual experience, or are you a spiritual being had a physical experience. If you say both that's called avoidance!

The Final Analysis: -
People are often unreasonable, self-centered: Forgive them anyway.

If you are Honest, People may cheat you, but be Honest anyway.

What you spend years to build, someone could destroy overnight. Build anyway.

The good you do today, People will often forget tomorrow. Do Good anyway.

You see, in the final analysis it is between you and GOD; it never was between you and them anyway.

Why worry, have faith: -
I can make a hobby out of worrying. I worry about the noise and then complain when it is too quiet. I worry about having too many sunny dry spells and then complain when it rains. I may even be worried about worrying too much. It is essential to take an honest interest in what goes on around me, and of course it is always wise to analyze a situation and take the necessary precautions to avoid being influenced by anything negative. However, when all is said and done, my tense and burdened mind will not be able to function clearly enough to arrive at a suitable solution to a problem. Maybe I should just do the best

that I can and beyond that leave it in the hands of GOD. To have faith in the self, faith in GOD and faith in GOD's plan is a sure way to remain clear and free of burdens.

Eye of Faith: -
When I am continuously being battered by the storms of life, and my very spirit is ebbing away, then all I need to do is hang onto that gift called '**Faith**', that one support which will weather the storms. Faith does not depend on a clever head, only belief: belief in the self and the strength that lies within. Faith is the seed of victory and the foundation of making the impossible possible.

"Faith is not blind. Faith is seeing with the eyes of the mind. Even as we have two physical eyes with which we are able to see wonderful things that are around us- trees, flowers, stars, streams, hills and dales, forests and mountains, even so with the eyes of faith we can perceive goodness, peace and calm around us."

CHAPTER 12

WHAT IS "LIVE AND LET LIVE"?

12.01 - LIVE AND LET LIVE CONCEPTS: -
Cliché not to interfere with other people's business or preferences. I don't care what they do! Live and let live, I always say. Your parents are strict. Mine just live and let live.

Believing that other people should be allowed to live their lives in the way that they want to, They seem as a society to have a very live and let live attitude towards issues like gay rights.

To accept other people as they are, although they may have a different way of life, I firmly believe in live and let live, and if people don't rob, cheat or beat their wives, I have no complaints.

An idiom expressing the modern concept that one should let others live their lives as they see fit.

Live and let live is the spontaneous rise of non-aggressive co-operative behaviour that developed during the First World War particularly during prolonged periods of Trench Warfare on the Western Front. Perhaps one of the most famous examples of this is the Christmas Truce of 1914. In the early months of immobile trench warfare, the truces were not unique to the Christmas period, and reflected a growing mood of "live and let live", where infantry units in close proximity to each other would stop overtly aggressive behavior, and often engage in small-scale fraternization, engaging in conversation or bartering for cigarettes.

It is a process that can be characterised as the deliberate abstaining from the use of violence during war. Sometimes it can take the form of overt truces or pacts negotiated locally by soldiers. At other times it can be a tacit behaviour—sometimes characterised as "letting sleeping dogs lie"—whereby both sides refrain from firing or using their weapons, or deliberately discharge them in a ritualistic or routine way that signals their non-lethal intent.

Live and Let Live: - A form of the Golden Rule

When we *live and let live*, we don't need to criticize, judge, or condemn others. We have no need to control them or try and make them conform to our way of thinking. We let others live their own lives and we live ours.

This simple slogan helps center us on our own recovery and on living our own life in the best way we know how. *Live and let live* is one of the keys to peace in our lives. When we practice tolerance in our lives we are liberated to work on our own issues. When we use this slogan we end many of the conflicts in our lives and gain the ability to stop new ones before they build into big ones.

Benefits with friends: -

Having good friends and a close family may prolong life, according to an analysis of 148 studies that focused on relationships. The studies assessed the strength of a person's social ties by looking at factors including marital status, household size, participation in group activities, number of social contacts, and self-reported levels of support or isolation. Overall participants (average age 64) with strong social ties increased their odds of survival by 50%, over an average age 7 ½ year period, compared with those who were more isolated. The authors found that healthy social relations are as good for you as quitting smoking and better for you than exercising or loosing weight. Of course doing all those health-promoting things while friends and families support you would be better still.

12.02 - BRIDGES OF INSPIRATION: -

Bridges of Service and Charity.
Bridges on the path of Duty and Devotion.

Bridges between Poor and Wealthy.
Bridges between different minds.

We understand now we are but one.
If we look for differences there are but none.
Such disparity exist only in the mind,
For in every heart and soul breathes the Lord Divine.

Bridge Builders: -
We give but little when we give of our possessions, it is when we give ourselves that we truly give. I found that in giving of myself, I feel myself growing more and more. Towards which direction and to which destination, I know not, but it sure does, make me a happier person and makes me have a smile on my face when I go to bed at night.

Meditation: –
It is a method of raising self-awareness leading to self-realization. Meditation stills the mind and empowers the intellect to achieve insight and understanding of the spiritual laws and principles, which sustain harmony and can bring natural renewal at all levels of life on earth. Meditation will enhance your inner virtues & inner peace.

Self Realization: –
Self-awareness and self-realization are cultivated in order to realize one's true spiritual identity and nature. In the meditative state, the self is experienced as conscious energy taking the form of a point of light. This spiritual energy, the Soul, is experienced as both different and separate from the energy of the Material body.

Consciousness: –
The role of the mind and the interplay between, the intellect and the personality is understood through a process of self-observation. The meditator learns to be quiet and control the mind, allowing the conscience to be clearly heard. Conscious awareness of the soul is then developed, allowing full understanding of the self.

Relationship with God: –
As meditation helps consciousness move beyond self-limiting beliefs, the presence of GOD is experienced in the state of YOGA (a system of body and mind control) – a mental link with the source of spiritual power.

12.03 - WHY PRAYER COULD BE GOOD MEDICINE

Neuroscientists are documenting changes in brain scans of meditating Tibetan Buddhists and praying nuns. They are trying to see whether meditation/prayer has meaning to people that translates into biology and affects a disease process.

Prayer and faith speeded recovery in illnesses ranging from depression to stroke to heart attack. Medical acceptance has grown along with solid scientific data on prayer's impact on health. About 75% of studies of spirituality have confirmed health benefits. If prayers were available in pill form, no pharmacy could stock enough of it.

Scientists and spiritualists in general believe that GOD heals people in supernatural ways, but Science cannot shape a study to prove it. But we now know enough, based on solid research to say that meditation and prayer, much like exercise and diet, has a connection with better health.

Is prayer good medicine?

Dozens of studies have shown that individuals, who pray regularly and attend religious services, stay healthier and livelonger than those who rarely or never do – even when age, health, habits, demographics and other factors are considered. Prayer – Whether for oneself (petitionary prayer) or others (intercessory prayer) – affects the quality, if not quantity of life. It boosts morale, lower agitation, and loneliness and life dissatisfaction and enhances the ability to cope in men, women, the elderly, the young, the healthy and the sick. Another study has found that those who prayed regularly had significantly lower blood pressure than the less religious. A third study showed that those who attended religious services had healthier immune systems than those who did not. In studies at several medical centers, meditation/prayer and faith have been shown to speed recovery from depression, alcoholism, hip surgery, and drug addiction, stroke, rheumatoid arthritis, heart attacks and bypass surgery. Those who pray stay healthier and live longer than those who don't.

How does prayer do these things?

Some scientists speculate that meditation/prayer may foster a state of peace and calm that could lead to beneficial changes in the cardiovascular and immune systems. Using sophisticated brain-imaging techniques, Dr. Andy Newberg of the university of Pennsylvania, author of "Why God won't go away" has documented changes in blood flow in particular regions of the brain during prayer and meditation. This could be the link between religion and health benefits such as lower blood pressure, slower heart rates, decreased anxiety and an enhanced sense of well-being.

Can prayer heal others?

At nine medical centers around the country, 750 patients with potentially life-threatening heart problems participated in the MANTRA (Chant) project, a recently concluded randomized trial of intercessory prayer or distant healing. The names of half the patients were given to groups – including Carmelite nuns, Buddhist monks, Sufi Muslims and Evangelical Congregations- who prayed for their recovery. In the next few months they found that in a pilot study, prayer recipients had 50% to 100% fewer complications.

Skeptics remain dubious, "The premise behind distant healing is not scientific." Even writers on spirituality, concede that science may never prove that prayer can heal others. That does not mean that people should not take advantage of this wonderful tool that is right at their fingertips.

12.04 - GOOD THOUGHTS AND ACTIONS
(With concept of Live And Let Live)

When you build a home, every brick counts. When you build character, every thought counts.

Good relationships: -
In order to create good relationships...
- with your mind, think about what you have to learn from others,
- with your eyes, look into good qualities of others,
- with your words, recognize, value and appreciate their accomplishments,
- with your actions, cooperate and do something for others.

Good Feelings: -
Good feelings for others are like ointments that can heal wounds and re-establish friendship and relationships. Good feelings are generated in the mind,

are transmitted through your attitude and are reflected in your eyes and smile. Smiling opens the heart and a glance can make miracles happen.

Be a humming bird: -

No matter how bad people may seem, they possess at least one virtue. Be like the humming bird and pick out the sweetness of everyone's character.

Love All: -

Love can never be exclusive. The sun does not choose to shine on some flowers in the garden and not others. Love is inclusive and has many faces - caring, listening, sharing from the heart, just accepting someone for what they are right now, is all acts of love, as long as you seek nothing in return. It all starts with acceptance of yourself - you're just fine as you are right now, warts and all. It's not that you will stay that way forever - but you might, if you don't accept. The secret key to the greatest door called love is acceptance. First yourself, then others (especially the ones you currently resist) and eventually all.

Kindness: -

Kindness in words creates confidence.
Kindness in thinking creates perceptiveness.
Kindness in giving creates love.

Resolve Conflict: -

There has probably never been a time where there has been so much fear and conflict across the world, not just across oceans and borders but also across the breakfast table. In fact many now prefer conflict to peace, as they become addicted to the actions of anger and aggression, and the adrenaline rush, which results. They don't really want conflict to end, in fact, they will say that some conflict is good to get things done and stimulate change. They are not aware that they are killing themselves. All conflict is simply a symptom of attachment to a position. And as we know, this generates fear, and fear, if allowed to stay, eventually kills it's host. All solutions are based on detachment or letting go. But that will be difficult until we can see that all possession is an illusion, that we have nothing to lose and that there are no victories in winning.

World like hand: -

The world is like a hand and its continents like our five fingers. Each finger is different and unique. Yet it is only when they all work together that whatever we put in our hand to succeeds.

Live Purposefully: -

If you do not live life on purpose you live life by accident.

Why do some days feel like a motorway pile up?

It is because you have not sorted out your purpose yet.

The highest purpose is always giving or serving others, without wanting anything in return.

This is why relaxation is always impossible if we are always on the take.

There is an overall purpose of your life, and each of the many scenes, which fill your day, are opportunities to serve your purpose.

Take time to think deeply, listen to your intuition, and with patience, the reason why you are here, and what you uniquely have to give, will occur to you. Then you can live your life on purpose.

Charity: -

It is very good to give financial aid to the suffering, orphans and widowed, provided these three points are kept in view:

a) We should not pride ourselves on being charitable, because we are doing no more than our duty. Everything we hold is on the account of our Master.

b) In giving, we should not expect any reward either in this world or in the next; otherwise we are only lending money on interest.

c) We should not expect any kind of praise or service from those to whom we give. Such charity is very helpful for the purification of the mind."

Respect: -

It is always easy to expect and demand respect from others. It is simple to criticize others for not being respectful or for being rude or for not showing the proper appreciation. It is difficult to ask respect from myself.

Without respect I can never gain respect from others. Without self-respect I will always be performing self-defeating actions. Without self-respect I will always be looking outside myself and will constantly be at the whims and fancies of other people's dispositions. I cannot get respect by asking for it. I only receive it when I give it to myself and to others.

Manage Emotions: -
When the energy of our consciousness is out of our control - the mind is agitated. We are being emotional. The solution is to detach from the inner storms, stand back and observe the hurricane pass. Detached observation withdraws the energy, which your emotions require to sustain them. When you watch your own anger, it dies. If you don't detach from it, and observe it, it will be your master. Today is the day to practice positive, detached observation, and each emotion-filled moment is the opportunity. This is 'real' work. The work of one who is a master of his or her own consciousness. Are you a master or a slave?

Never Battle: -
Never fight. Nothing is worth fighting for. Wisdom never fights, it waits patiently, speaks positively, releases easily, sees benefit in everything and envisions a future of abundance...knowing that all needs will be met at the right moment, in the right way. If you think life is a struggle you will always be struggling, if you think life is a breeze, your attitudes and actions will convey lightness and easiness. And that's what attracts everything you need, and much more. Make today a breeze not a battle.

Sin Bin: -
It's a great idea in sport. Too many fouls and you're out of the game for a short period. The same happens in real life, but we are not aware of it. Sin essentially means forgetfulness, or more specifically, to forget yourself, to forget who you truly are, a pure, peaceful and loving spiritual being who occupies and animates a physical form. It is this forgetfulness that makes us commit what we call sinful action. If another person insults you, and you become angry in response, the sin is the anger, which you create not the insult. You are asleep to the truth that you just hurt yourself, and that you are the creator of your anger not the other person. And now you have a recording in your consciousness that contains an image of the other surrounded by the energy of anger. You put it there, not them. Next time you see them, up comes the anger again, and in that moment you are at your least effective, paralyzed by self created anger, you are effectively out of the game until you cool down. Interesting isn't it. Never get angry, at anything, or anyone, anytime. It's a sin!

Do your best: -

"As human beings our job is to do the best and leave the results in God's hands. When we leave the results in God's hands, then nothing of this world bothers us anymore. It is only then that we start to live according to the principle of **"sweet is Thy will."**

Love thy neighbor: -

"People in our modern world have become so isolated and so self-centered that they do not take the time to learn who their next-door neighbors are. We should take the time and say hello to those who live next door to us. We should inquire how they are. A few kind words or a small conversation with them goes a long way. It does not cost anything to offer them a helping hand."

Pursue Wisdom: -

Each day is filled with a hundred choices and decisions, and wisdom is our best guide. Wisdom comes from three places - **experience, learning and our deepest intuition**. Each day is an opportunity to gather and use all three. Experience comes from engaging with life, learning comes from observing, and intuition comes from listening to yourself. At the end of the day sit down and write down what was the main experience, what did I learn and what did I hear...from myself? You did listen to yourself...didn't you?

Interfere Love-fully: -

One of the deepest habits we learn is interfering in others' lives. Even if we are not actively interfering there is a good chance it's happening in our heads. Then, when people don't do what we want them to do, which is usually all the time, our ability to relax is non-existent. If you want to interfere successfully in someone else's life, try this lovely approach. **It begins with acceptance, continues with acknowledgement, is empowered by appreciation and ends in actualization.** Only in this way can we help others be all that they can possibly be, and what else is life for, but to help others to be all that they can be. Only by making love practical in this way, can we heal our own habits of criticism, envy and blame. **Accept, Acknowledge and Appreciate.** It doesn't mean you have to agree, comply or condone. The paradox is that we ourselves will receive the same in the process, not only from ourselves, as we become what we give, but from others along the way. Why? It's the law!

Nonviolence: -

"We need to teach people how to meditate, how to live in a nonviolent, peaceful way, and how to help end the suffering of others. Let us teach people to reject the infliction of pain and instead inject affection and love."

"If we stop reacting in anger to all those in our families, at our jobs, and in our communities, how much longer will others continue to bother us?"

"Even with different thoughts, different words, and different deeds, we have an utmost duty to make this atmosphere peaceful. If we are bringing disharmony into the atmosphere, if we are bringing pain into the atmosphere, if we are bringing strife and tension into the atmosphere, then we are wasting the time of many, many other people."

"If we walk on the path of nonviolence, the whole world comes close to us and we draw close to the whole world. Our life is then lived for every human being who shares the planet."

"On the path of love we have to walk with great sensitivity, with great caution, so we do not trample on the delicate hearts of other living beings. This care that we take not to injure others is called nonviolence."

"You have to meet certain basic requirements if you wish to raise the edifice of spirituality. First is the practice of nonviolence. **Do not hurt anyone's feelings**. This is the first essential for knowing God."

MATURITY: -

As we mature spiritually there is less need to have our self-respect bolstered by praise and special attention. As our thought processes become more compassionate and less self-obsessed, we feel increasingly satisfied with our lives and ourselves. We relate to people more easily and feel no need to draw attention to our successes or complain about our problems.

Selfless service means that we help others without any desire for a reward. We serve because we have an innate desire in the core of our heart to help others."

Just as the highest tower needs a deep foundation, so too our higher thinking is based on going deep within.

Real Love: -
The problem nowadays is that love is interpreted on a gross level. Just as many people are attracted to the size and glitter of a fake diamond, so are they swayed by false, superficial love? There is no value in either. A real diamond is often quite small, but it is flawless. That is where it's value lies. Real love is like a tiny diamond: it is not flashy and it is without a single flaw. Real love is one hundred percent pure. There is nothing artificial mixed into it. It is clean. There are no ulterior motives in real love.

We may do well in the world and make the world a better place, but we are still prisoners. We are still caught in the cycle of life and death. Along with helping others in the world, we must also look to finding a way out of suffering."

Embrace Change: -
When you are aware and accept that everything around you is constantly changing, and that you have no control over 99.99% of it, you are able to embrace change like a close friend! Change is like a river, constantly flowing and moving things around. The river of life is constantly bringing you ideas, people, situations – each one is an opportunity to be enriched or to enrich others, and to learn. Change is the play of the universe as it entertains us in the biggest light and sound show of all time. Why not sit back and enjoy the show!

Faith in Others: -
If there is a need to take responsibility for something, then of course, you should. However, if a situation is not your business, or someone else is in charge, then don't get caught up in it. If you want to help, you can still involve yourself in a more subtle way through faith. Faith in others does a lot of work. **It doesn't mean blind faith** - observing helplessly while keeping your fingers crossed - it means to remain alert to what's going on, and then to fill another with the strength of your faith to such an extent that they feel able to do what-ever needs to be done. This means having faith, but also donating the power of your faith. If the other person is honest and truthful, your faith will work for them. In this way, we can learn to truly help each other.

Resist Not: -

Have you ever noticed that resistance leads to persistence? And behind all resistance is self-created fear. The only way to relax and stay relaxed is acceptance. You don't have to agree, or follow, or condone, but acceptance means you begin any interaction with a serenity, which invites others to engage with you. And out of engagement comes the satisfaction of creative expression and an enriching relationship. That's relaxation in action!

Simplicity: -

Peace is simplicity. Simplicity is beauty. Choose a day as your day of simplicity. Speak little, and listen with attention. Do something incognito and nice for a person you are close to. Eat simple and natural food. Create time periods for not doing anything - just walk, look around, live the moment. Have your mind open to a more profound and silent sensitivity. Appreciate each scene and each person as they are. In the evening, write down your discoveries. Observe the state of your mind

Compassion: -

A compassionate person develops an eye for spotting the qualities that make each person special. Even when others are at their lowest ebb, it is possible to help them restore their self-belief by keeping a firm, clear vision of their goodness and specialties. Taking a gently encouraging approach, I must never give up on anyone.

Generosity: -

Generosity means more than just giving. It also means to cooperate with others. The greatest act of generosity is to see beyond the weaknesses and mistakes of others, helping them to recognize their innate value.

Depth of Humility: -

Humility means to understand the self and through that to understand others as well. Humility is the attitude where a person is not attached to his or her opinion and feelings. Humility is the most natural expression of truth. It helps in better understanding of truth. Humility is the basis for maintaining self-respect. Humility does not mean bowing down and being subservient to others. Humility allows you to see benefit in everything. Developing humility brings a lot of comfort and ease into your life.

Never tell lies: -
Never tell lies. Why do we tell lies? Only to meet our own ends. We want to deceive others, we want to seize the rights of others, and for that we tell lies. Be truthful. Don't even think of telling a lie or of acting or posing. Say what you are. We like to appear to be good, but we are something else. At heart of hearts we are not what we appear to be. We must be true to our own selves. Even though you know you are doing wrong you purposely do it; you do it intentionally. **What is truthfulness? When your heart, brain and tongue agree. That is truthfulness."**
"If we can begin to realize and accept the fact that we are not perfect, and if we do not hide from others the fact that we have faults, then we can eliminate many of our failures in deceit, falsehood and hypocrisy. We can always succeed in fooling a few people, but in the final analysis, when we are untruthful we are only fooling ourselves."

The Truth: -
One of the nicest things about telling the truth is that you don't have to remember what you said.

Banish Ego: -
Ego is not just having a big head. Ego is present every time you feel any kind of fear, or hear yourself saying, "That's mine!" The truth tells us that nothing is 'mine' or 'yours', we are all trustees, and fear is only present where there is the voice of attachment. So where there is ego, there is attachment, and where there is attachment there is fear, and where there is fear there cannot be love and where there is no love there is misery. **This is why there is so much unhappiness in the world.** Detach from everything, and you will banish ego, fear will be no more, only then can true love return, and our oldest friend happiness will feel it is then safe to make reappearance in your life.

Radiate Light: -
Each one of us is a walking radiator. Mostly we radiate thoughts and attitudes. From deep within we radiate our state of being, and the essential, original and eternal state of every being is peaceful and loving. But we block and distort this energy with our attachments. Attachments turn love into fear, peace into anger and then distort our attitudes and actions towards others. This is neither relaxing for ourselves, or for those around us. Which is why detachment is the secret to living lightly and lovingly. To be a radiator that people come to for real warmth, what do you need to detach from today? If you don't detach then you

will stay attached, and then you will see others and life itself as a threat, and your tension will keep them away. But they cannot threaten you. Only your dependency on a thing, or an idea, or an opinion can be threatened. What needs to be released today? What needs to be released so the light can come through?

Go Giver: -

It's been said that you cannot give away what you do not have. One of the most spiritual important insights or secrets in life is that you already have, and always have had, what you need to give away! If you impart the message that 'I am not worthy' the universe will send it straight back in many shapes, forms and circumstances. When we say 'give me' we are imparting this message. We are saying we think we need to get something to complete ourselves or prove our worth. Most of us are taught to live a life of give me, give me, and give me, always striving, desiring, wanting, and struggling. We do so only because we think that when we get what we want we will be fulfilled and esteemed by others. But it's an illusion. We are all already complete and worthy but we cannot know it and experience it, until we give it away! Only giving allows us to know what we are and what we have within. Ask the question – how can I serve? The intention to serve will point you towards what you need to give. If the intention is real it also generates the will. The most successful people in life are not go-getters, but go-givers!

Resource Full: -

We each have the three energies we need to learn to manage – **Body, Mind, and Soul/Spirit.** All three need a good diet - Body needs pure food (vegetarian), your Mind needs positive ideas and images, and the Spirit that you are needs time in silence and stillness to refresh and renew. These are our resources, and each one needs topping up, otherwise we run on empty and disease comes to visit.

Kindness: -

Great souls take advantage of every moment and every opportunity to give happiness to others through kindness in their thoughts; such souls are willing to overlook weaknesses and mistakes and have the desire to help everyone reach their potential.

Manners: -

A person of wisdom and spirituality has very beautiful manners that have grown from genuine respect and love for the whole of humanity. Manners in this sense have nothing to do with culture or education: it is simply a question of humility.

When we are at the receiving end of such manners, we feel that some deeper part of us has been honored. In fact, none of us deserves anything less.

A Benevolent Attitude: -
-When you extend pure love to everyone with selfless motivation that is an attitude of kindness. -When you send good wishes and pure feelings to those who are in deep sorrow, that is an attitude of mercy. -When you see the virtues rather than the weaknesses in people that is an attitude of compassion. -When you bless and uplift someone even as they defame you, that is an attitude of forgiveness. -When you tolerate a situation and take responsibility as well as give cooperation even when not appreciated that is an attitude of humility and self-respect. -Every second, every moment and every breath of your life is nurtured by attitude. -Instead of speaking too much and wasting your energy, become experienced in the sweetness of introversion.

Peace (non-violence): -
Not to cause anyone sorrow even in your thoughts is complete non-violence.

Speak Sweetly: -
Nature did not like hardness in speech, so there is no bone in the tongue.

Spiritual Love: -
It is when we silence the chattering of our mind that we can truly hear what is in our heart and find the still, clear purity that lies within the Soul. Spiritual love carries us into the silence of our original state of being. This silence contains the power to create harmony in all relationships and the sweetness to sustain them.

Honesty: -
Honesty is to speak that which is thought and to do that which is spoken. There are no contradictions or discrepancies in thoughts, words or actions.

Sweetness: -
Sweetness is a virtue that searches with patience for the good in every person and situation.

Unconditional Acceptance: -
Accepting the self and others unconditionally allows everyone to remove their masks and feel at ease with who they are.

Lasting Fragrance: -
Tread lightly upon this earth, seeing, understanding but never imposing. Thoughtful, Independent, be Gracious in victory and defeat. Free of possessiveness, so ease of mind sweetens relationships. Like the scent of a rose the untroubled spirit imparts a lasting fragrance.

Tolerance: -
If you realize that everyone is an individual with his or her own unique part to play, then the power of tolerance is easy to develop.

Keep Faith: -
To limit your faith to one set of beliefs or an institutional belief system is to commit intellectual suicide. We shut down the possibility of being enlightened and enriched by others' experiences, which may be derived from their beliefs. We build a barrier between our fellow travellers and ourselves and then feel threatened, even in small and subtle ways, by someone of a different faith. The deepest faith is the intuitive conviction that all is as it should be, despite appearances, and that every human being is intrinsically good, despite appearances. This reminds us to keep our minds open, not take the law into our own hands, and look out for the best in others, regardless of what they say or do. This is faith in life, not faith in a set of learned or inherited beliefs. Have you ever noticed how people don't go to war over their faith in life?

Love, Purity, Peace, Wisdom: -
When you build a house, every brick counts. When you build a character, every thought counts. You are what you think. Love, purity, peace, wisdom - the more you think of these qualities, the more you will become them.

Choice: -
As we can see, we have a choice. One, we can go to work and sail through the day without becoming bogged down with thoughts involving desire, anger, greed, attachment, and ego so we can return home each night with a clear mind; or two, we can choose to become involved in everyone else's business and entangle ourselves with thoughts, words, and deeds of desire, anger, greed, attachment, and ego that will stick to our mind like glue as we leave our job and will trouble us at home when we try to meditate. The choice is ours to make.

The Virtue of Sweetness: -

Just as eating and serving something sweet makes your taste buds feel sweetness, and for a while after you remain happy, become sweet-natured yourself so that words filled with sweetness are constantly spoken. Such sweet words make both you and others happy. Use this method to always sweeten everyone's mouth; constantly maintain sweet attitude, sweet words and sweet actions.

Greatest Powers: -

Gentleness, love, humility, forgiveness are the greatest powers in the world.

Faults: -

Very often, we become blind to our faults. We magnify the faults of others. A little reflection, a period of calm introspection, can set the balance right.

Renunciation: -

Renunciation is a much-misunderstood concept. It is not about giving up what is good and beautiful and much needed materialistic things. But it is about disengaging oneself from the unsatisfactory and moving with determination towards what matters most. It is about freedom from mental confusion and self-centered afflictions, meaning through inside and loving kindness.

12.05 – FINALLY HOW TO LIVE AND LET LIVE: -

Following are some of the lessons I have learnt for last fifteen years, after reading good scriptures, holy books and magazines.

Meditation: -

In these troubled times, if we can learn to meditate and find a place of calm and peace within ourselves every day, we will be able to face the challenges of life. Not only do we ourselves live more happy and balanced lives, receiving the joy of God's love, but also we begin to radiate the peace and joy that we experience to those around us. We begin to see all others, indeed all life forms, as part of GOD.

Inner and Outer Peace: -

If each of us learned the art of meditation, this world would be filled with people who are peaceful and kind. There would be an end to wars and conflicts.

We would each attain inner peace and happiness and help radiate it to all those around us. We would not only have peace within, but we would also have peace without.

If followers of every religion truly observed the teachings of their great saints, the whole world would be an abode of love. People would be having direct experiences of GOD. People would have love for all humanity and all creation. There would be no wars, no crime, and no discord. There would be joy and peace on our planet.

Enjoy Moments of Silence: -
When you open your eyes in the morning, sit for a moment and appreciate the gift of a new day, create a peaceful thought and enjoy some moments of silence throughout the whole day. Thank GOD that you have consciousness.

Transformation: -
By transforming ourselves, we can transform others, including our family, community, society, and eventually the whole world. Opportunities come by creation, not by chance. It is my prayer that the spirit of unity enlivens each of you and that we rest not until the whole world is an abode of peace and love. If you speak badly of others, the negative energy that you put out into the universe will return to you. The same is true of positive energy

Cultivate Silence: -
Behind all creation is silence. Silence is the essential condition, the vital ingredient for all creation and all that is created. It is a power in its own right. The artist starts with a blank canvas - silence. The composer places it between and behind the notes. The very ground of your being, out of which comes all your thoughts, is silence. The way to silence is through meditation. When you arrive in your own silence you will know true freedom and real power. Stop, take a minute, and listen to the silence within you today. Then be aware of what disturbs your inner silence. It could be negative thoughts, memories, and sensations. And when you are aware, you will know what is draining your creative power, and you will know what needs to change...on the inside!

Brotherhood And Unity: -
Understanding the worth and dignity of every human being is the key to brotherhood and unity.

Comparison with Others: -

Comparing yourself with others will leave you vulnerable on three counts: **you'll either feel inferior, superior or impressed.** All three of these states are dangerous because they all disregard the underlying principle of our true connection with each other - mutual love and regard, based on independently generated self-esteem. To protect yourself from this vulnerability, make sure that your attention remains turned within, towards the spiritual experience of pure pride. Staying centered in your elevated self-respect will help you remain undisturbed by others around you. Keep asking yourself, "Who am I?" "How would my spiritual personality respond to this event or person?" this will help to center you further, and allow you to enjoy the successful efforts of others. We start to recognize that Light within others. Then the outer differences that separate us start to dissolve. We no longer see a person's hair color, eye color, or skin color. We no longer see the way people dress or speak. Instead we see one Light expressed by many different outer coverings, each beautiful in its own way."

Inner Light and sound: -

If all seven billion people on our planet spent time daily connecting with the inner Light and Sound, each would realize his or her unity and would live a life of love. So let each of us begin with ourselves.

Life: -

Your thoughts guide you to your destiny. If you always think the same you will always get to the same place. Think in a new way and you will be a new person. Give happiness to all and you will live in peace. Create peace in your mind and you will create a world of peace around you. It is time to end this insanity and violence. It is time to lay down our swords and guns and instead offer each other flowers of love. It is time to live up to the message of love and peace brought to us by our religious founders and spiritual teachers."

Pure Peace: -

Why do we find it hard to be at peace with each other, the world and ourselves? Imagine a lake that is flat and calm and pure - it is so clear you can see the bottom. Even when the wind blows it only ruffles the surface. All is still and peaceful in its depth. Then the first polluting chemicals of the new factory and farm come rolling down the hill and into the water. Immediately it starts to cloud over and bubble a little. Chemical reactions are taking place and the purity is lost. **When purity is lost peace is lost.** It is the same with human consciousness. We are innately peaceful beings. Peace is our deepest inner state of being, our true nature. To be at peace is to be in our natural state, but only when our consciousness is pure and clean and true. As soon as the pollutants of any negative images are allowed in, or we allow old memories and experiences to disturb us into negative thinking, our purity and therefore our inner peace are gone. It's not the external event or person that takes our peace away - it's because we give them permission to enter and give them life in our minds. Keep your mind and heart free of all pollution, and peace will always be with you.

The Power of Thoughts: -

Thoughts are more powerful than actions because they are the creators of actions. You have to keep in mind that the thought-waves of your good wishes and pure feelings, your vibrations of peace and love, can once again bring harmony in nature and happiness in the world.

If you are depressed, you are living in the past. If you are anxious, you are living in the future. If you are at peace, you are living in the present.

Godly Love: -

Let us carry in our heart the prayer that the whole world be intoxicated with godly love and those we each find spiritual union with the Lord. Where the world's philosophies end, there the true religion starts.

Diamond Consciousness: -

When you look at the world through your physical eyes, you will see all the facets of our diversity: culture, race, personality, religion and so on. Seeing only through your physical eyes, it is easy to become stubborn and to try to prove yourself right. However where there is stubbornness there is no love. And trying to prove the self-right is equally offensive. A diamond will sparkle even in the dust; you do not ever need to prove that you are right. In the face of the dangers that come from seeing only with the physical eyes, always think: now is the time to go beyond all divisions, beyond all that limits, and our sense of self. Whatever the race, the religion, and the class - our consciousness now has to go beyond all of that.

Resolve Conflict: -

There has probably never been a time where there has been so much fear and conflict across the world, not just across oceans and borders but also across the breakfast table. In fact many now prefer conflict to peace, as they become addicted to the actions of anger and aggression, and the adrenaline rush, which results. They don't really want conflict to end, in fact, they will say that some conflict is good to get things done and stimulate change. They are not aware that they are killing themselves. All conflict is simply a symptom of attachment to a position. And as we know, this generates fear, and fear if allowed to stay, eventually kills it's host. All solutions are based on detachment or letting go. But that will be difficult until we can see that all possession is an illusion, that we have nothing to lose and that there are no victories in winning.

Lost: -
If wealth is lost, nothing is lost; if health is lost, something is lost; if character is lost, all is lost.

Real Love: -
The problem nowadays is that love is interpreted on a gross level. Just as many people are attracted to the size and glitter of a fake diamond, so are they swayed by false, superficial love? There is no value in either. A real diamond is often quite small, but it is flawless. That is where it's value lies. Real love is like a tiny diamond: it is not flashy and it is without a single flaw. Real love is one hundred percent pure. There is nothing artificial mixed into it. It is clean. There are no ulterior motives in real love.

Seed Of Action (Creativity): -
Acts of virtue emerge from deep within, from an inner sanctuary of silence from which inspiration flows. Every action has its seed in a thought and every thought is a creation of the thinker, the SOUL. I choose what thoughts I want to create and as is my thinking so are my actions and also my experience in life. Going within, I touch the stillness and pure love that lie at the core of my being and every thought that I create is of benefit to myself and of benefit to humanity.

Do not try to be great, try to be good, for being good is great.

Pursue Wisdom: -
Each day is filled with a hundred choices and decisions, and wisdom is our best guide. Wisdom comes from three places - **experience, learning and our deepest intuition**. Each day is an opportunity to gather and use all three. Experience comes from engaging with life, learning comes from observing, and

intuition comes from listening to our self. At the end of the day sit down and write down what was the main experience, what did I learn and what did I hear...from myself? You did listen to yourself...didn't you?

The Spiritual Aspect Of Healthcare: -
Silence, happiness, love and blessings are important aspects. Happiness leads to good health. It is only you who can give this medicine to yourself. Some bring illness to themselves through anger, greed, unfulfilled desires, expectations, suppression of feelings and relationships not based on true love. Look in your heart; you will know where your illness comes from. There are three ingredients for a long and healthy life: live with attention but without worry; use time in a worthwhile way; keep your thoughts pure, positive and filled with strength.

Attitudes: -
When you extend pure love to everyone with selfless motivation that is an attitude of kindness. When you send good wishes and pure feelings to those who are in deep sorrow, that is an attitude of mercy. When you see the virtues rather than the weaknesses in people that is an attitude of compassion. When you bless and uplift someone even as they defame you, that is an attitude of forgiveness. When you tolerate a situation and take responsibility as well as give cooperation even when not appreciated that is an attitude of humility and self-respect. Every second, every moment and every breath of your life is nurtured by attitude.

Be Awe – full: -
Look out on life with amazement, not shock. The variety, the diversity, the manner of every person, the beauty amidst the drudgery, the contrasts, the opportunities, the heroism in the lives of ordinary people, your gifts, your talents, your friends - even just one friend - is all awesome. Live in awe, and entertain wonder, and you will be knocking on the door of true love. Don't kill it with cynicism or criticism; don't sabotage your life with moaning and complaining. Open the eyes in your head and the eye in your intellect and choose to see the stunning, awesome, diverse beauty of life happening around you right now. Meet it with your heart and you will enrich and be enriched in one single moment.

Contentment: -
The more positive the thoughts flowing through my mind, the more contented I will feel. It is easy to feel contented when we are praised and appreciated but

to remain contented when we are being criticized and rejected is the mark of real spiritual strength. The way to develop this level of strength is to learn about GOD's way of loving. Only when I am in deep contemplation can I see GOD showing me the kind of love I need to express so that I myself never reject or criticize and always generate good wishes for others. Then I will feel satisfied no matter what life throws at me.

ACKNOWLEDGMENTS

1. The Story of My Experiments with Truth
    Mohandas K. Gandhi – Autobiography

2. VIVKANANDA – The Yogas and other works
    by Swami Nikhilanada

3. Mystery of the Ages by Herbert W. Armstrong

4. The Reason for GOD – Belief in an age of Skepticism
    by Timothy Keller

5. THIS, I BELIEVE by Donald D. Day

6. A Manual of Self Unfoldment by Swami Chinmayananda

7. The Message that comes from Everywhere by Gary L. Beckwith

8. Kindle the Light by T.L.Vaswani

9. The Bhagavad Gita according to Gandhi

10. The World's Religions by Ninian Smart

11. Pathways to Higher Consciousness by Ken O'Donnell

12. The Spiritual Powers of the Soul by Brahma Kumaris

13. The Demon-Haunted World by Carl Sagan

14. Spiritual Solutions by Deepak Chopra

15. Dada Answers – Questions you have always wished to ask
    By J. P. Vaswani

16. After We Die, What Then by George W. Meek

17. The Art of Happiness – A Handbook for Living
    by His Holiness The Dalai Lama and Howard C. Cutler

18. The Divine Life – Astrology and Reincarnation
    by A. T. Mann

19. You Can Live Forever in Paradise on Earth
    by watch Tower Bible and Tract Society of Pennsylvania

20. Sometimes God Has A Kid's Face – The story of America's Exploited
    Street Kids
    by Bruce Ritter

21. He Can Who Thinks He Can by Orison Swett Marden

22. Translation of THE QURAAN by Abdullah Yusuf Ali

23. Sense and Nonsense in Psychology by H. J. Eysenck

24. Reinventing Your Life by Jeffrey E. Young and Janet S. Klosko

25. HAPPINESS by Matthieu Ricard

26. Living The Simple Life by Elaine ST. James

27. MOTHER TERESA – Come Be My Light
    by Brian Kolodiejchuk

28. Extracts from Ninian Smart, University of California Cambridge University Press.

29. Time magazine article on Abraham.

30. Memoirs of 1 Million Daimoku by Torrie Pattillo.

31. Healing Power of Faith by Harold G. Koenig

32. The Power of the Mind by Swami Vivekananda

33. Is God all in your head ? by David Chalmers

34. The role of Faith in Cross-Cultural Conflict Resolution by Abdul Aziz Said and Nathan C. Funk

AUTHOR'S AUTOBIOGRAPHY
(SIMPLE LIVING, HIGH THINKING)

STAGE 1 OF MY LIFE – (Brahmacharya - The Celibate Student)

I was born on November 19th, 1939 in village Thut Bojraj, district Nawabshah, state Sindh, country India. I passed my childhood in Karachi and Sukkur, two big cities of Sindh. After more than three hundred years of British rule, India finally won back its freedom on August 15, 1947. All the patriotic hearts rejoiced at seeing India becoming a sovereign nation and the triumph of hundreds and thousands of martyred souls. It was a birth of a new nation and a new beginning. **The only fact that marred the happiness of the fruits by the blood of martyrs was the fact that the country was divided into India and Pakistan, based on religion alone, and the violent communal riots between Muslims and Hindus took away a number of lives.** Whole state of Sindh became part of Pakistan and Extreme Muslims were chasing/killing Hindus. In the movie Gandhi, produced and directed by Richard Attenborough, where actor Ben Kingsley played the role of Mahatma Gandhi, you can spot me as eight-year-old boy sitting on top of the train, running from Sukkur to Karachi and then by ship to Kandla port and then by train to Ajmer city of Rajasthan state in India. We had to leave all our property (Land and Buildings) and come to India by ship and become refugees. We eight of us (I, my father, my mother, my two older sisters and two younger sisters and my younger brother) came to the city of Ajmer in state of Rajasthan, India, in January 1948 and stayed with couple of other refugee families. Almost all the Hindus from Sindh state came to India, but Mahatma Gandhi told Hindus in India, to let the Muslims stay back in India and adopt the non-violence policy. That is why Mahatma Gandhi was assassinated by a Hindu Nathuram Godse on January 30,1948. I with my two elder sisters was admitted in school. I joined 4th grade instead of 3rd grade and my father wrote my date of birth as January 19, 1941 by mistake, because there was no paper work, it was all by memory. This gave me advantage of 2 years over other kids. In May 1948 my father had to leave us in the hands of our uncle and go to New Delhi, where he was offered a clerical job by the central government of India. We joined him in May 1950, when he was allotted a house in a newly built refugee colony called Rajinder Nagar, with no electricity, no city water and no city sewer system. A Sindhi school was set up in tents for refugees from Sindh.

Somehow in June 1954, I graduated from Sindhi high school (10th grade) in New Delhi, India, at the official age of 14 and in 1959 I graduated from Engineering College affiliated with the Gujarat university, at the official age of 19 and earned BE Civil (bachelor of civil engineering) degree. Thus became one of the youngest engineers in India. I had received good scholarship during all my college life. By this time two more sisters and one more brother were born in New Delhi, making total of nine children. My eldest sister (Meena) helped my mom at home and with children, till she got married in 1957, whereas my second oldest sister (Vimla) started working as the telephone operator after high school to financially support the family. She started evening classes for BA in private college, where she fell in love with a Bengali (from west Bengal state) boy S K Dutta, which my father did not like because he was not Sindhi (from Sindh state) and forbid her to go to college. When I came home from engineering college, my sister cried and told me all about her love affair and she said she was ready to elope with her boy friend and get married. I somehow convinced my father that now we are in New Delhi, where there are people from all states of India, we have lost our whole Sindh state 10 years ago and now we have to mix and match with people of all states, so please forgive my sister Vimla. He somehow agreed and in October 1958 we had first Interstate Wedding in New Delhi.

In November 1959 I joined engineering design office of CPWD (Central Public Works Department) in New Delhi with good pay and that helped to raise the standard of living of our family. My father asked me to stay home and study for the UPSC (Union Public Service Commission) test for Class 1 engineering job with Government of India. He will not let me do any work around the house and will wake me up early morning at 5:00 AM to study. Finally in 1962, I was selected to be Assistant Executive Engineer in North Eastern Railway whose head quarters were in Gorakhpur UP (Utter Pradesh state of India). By this time my father taught me **"Work like Labor and live like Lord"** because money you get after hard work was important at that time, specially for family of 11 members. My mother was pious Hindu mother, every Thursday she used to collect all the ladies of the neighborhood and read a chapter from Ramayana, Mahabharata or Guru Granth Sahib. **From her I learnt to have faith in GOD.**

In August 1963, (at an official age of 22) I joined North Eastern Railway with head quarters at Gorakhpur, UP, India. After 18 weeks training in Lucknow (big city of UP), I was posted as assistant engineer in Samastipur (a small town in Bihar state of India and was divisional head quarter of North Eastern railway). This was executive job and had about 250 people under me. During next two years I learnt a lot about designing & maintaining the railway track, bridges and buildings, controlling floods, dealing with subordinates and bosses, dealing with contractors (honest and dishonest), court cases and vigilance cases etc. **In fact I grew up to be a man to understand right from wrong.** After a false vigilance case and inquiries from the Railway Board Authorities, my Chief Engineer realized that it was not the job of simple and honest person, so he transferred me to the design office at Gorakhpur as Assistant Executive Engineer (AEN) of design.

STAGE 2 OF MY LIFE – (Grihastha - Family Life)

Before I could resume my duty as design engineer in Gorakhpur, I had to go to Roorkee engineering college for two months training (Nov. & Dec. 1965) and then four months training in Railway staff college in Baroda (Jan to April 1966). During this time my parents were able to find a suitable girl for me, and I was engaged on Dec. 12, 1965, with Ratna Khushalani (a daughter of business man of Calcutta, India). We got married in New Delhi on **May 21st, 1966**, after I finished all my trainings. After our honeymoon in Kashmir, we came back to Delhi, purchased some furniture and came to Gorakhpur, where a nice bungalow was allotted to me. We lived happily thereafter, I was busy in design office and Ratna kept herself busy by joining railway officer's wives club and do some social work for railway employees. We had few railway employees as our servants (though illegal but customary from British days) to do our domestic work in garden and kitchen. Since Ratna and I were now settled in Gorakhpur, I decided to help my family. I invited my middle brother Ramesh to come to Gorakhpur and stay with us. In May 1967, I helped him in getting admission in Government Polytechnic in a diploma course of civil engineering at Gorakhpur.

On morning of 21st January 1968, at 9:30AM Ratna gave birth to a baby boy in railway hospital at Gorakhpur. My Mom had come from New Delhi to help us with the baby and my father consulted the pundit/astrologer in New Delhi to pick the letter for baby's name, based on his birth time, position of stars and planets etc. He called us and told me that letter has come out as "S". According to Hindu religion on 6th day my Mom performed some rituals and ceremonies called "Naamkaran" to protect the baby from evil spirits, and we named the baby as Shailender Kumar (Shelly). In March I took my mom back and she told Ratna to come to New Delhi as soon as possible so that everybody could see the baby. After celebrating our 2nd anniversary on 21st May 1968, I sent Ratna to New Delhi with the baby to my parents, so that my brothers and sisters also can play with the baby because it was vacation time for them.

After about 2 weeks I left for New Delhi and came to know that Ratna and Shelly had gone to stay with her cousin for few days because it was very hot and they had window air conditioner and her father had also come there from Calcutta. Ratna's first cousin Uttam Khushalani was squadron leader in air Force and had nice government flat. Next day on 2nd June 1968 I went there and was shocked to find out that Shelly was sick and was crying in peculiar way and his stomach was swollen. She said that child specialist doctor of "All India Institute of medical sciences (AIIMS)" is being consulted and he has diagnosed him for colic infection. I put Shelly in my arms and let his head rest on my shoulder and requested Uttam to take us by car to the doctor's residence, which is in AIIMS campus, and there was doctor's residence near hospital. Whole time Shelly was in my arms but he was crying in peculiar way and was shaking his head. Doctor after examining him, gave him some water to drink and asked us to take him to children ward of hospital and get him admitted there because his condition was getting serious. I took Shelly back in my arms and told every one, let us rush to the hospital. While we were all walking fast to the hospital I heard Shelly take a deep sigh and stopped crying. His head was on my shoulders and I was holding him in my arms. Ratna's father thought that he is tired and must have fallen a sleep. In few minutes we reached children ward on 5th floor and went to emergency room. I kept Shelly on the stretcher and was shocked to see his mouth wide open. Doctor immediately told us to go out. Ratna and I could not control and cried out loud. Ratna sat on bench in corridor and I tried to look inside through glass pane of door. I saw doctor on duty was trying mouth-to-mouth resuscitation. One lady doctor and other apprentice doctors also tried to give external oxygen but all in vain. Our Shelly had slept forever. I forced open the door, took Shelly in my arms and we all came by car to Rajinder Nagar. When we reached home, everyone was surprised to see us in this condition. My mother cried out loudly and almost fainted. My sisters and brothers also started crying. On hearing loud cries neighbors also gathered. I laid Shelly on the floor and then everybody sat on the floor and started praying for his soul to rest in peace. Next day morning at 9:00AM Pundit (Priest) was called to perform the funeral rites, and then we took his body to the cremation ground. After 12th day ceremony (as per Hindu scriptures, soul is still around for 12 days) Ratna and I went to Calcutta for a week before going to Gorakhpur. On 1st July 1968, I resumed my duty as AEN Designs in Chief Engineer's office of North Eastern Railway.

From 16th August to 24th October 1968 I was assigned for two months training to Indian Railway school of Advanced Permanent Way Engineering, Poona. After my training I was posted as Assistant Executive Engineer (AEN) in Lucknow, UP (Utter Pradesh) state of India. Here I was in charge of maintenance of all officers Bungalows, new construction and open line maintenance of all railways Buildings, Bridges and Rail-track of 250 miles. I had total staff of about 1000 working for me including 5 trolley men to push or start the engine and operate it and 2 gardeners and 1 cook. For Ratna also happy days were back again. She lived like a queen. She joined Railway officers wives club and used to play cards 3 times a day. During 1969 there was one passenger train accident in my jurisdiction, luckily no one died but about 100 passengers were injured who were immediately transported to nearby hospitals. Sometimes in September 1969 I had the scooter accident in which I had dislocated my right elbow bones. After 6 weeks when my cast was removed doctor suggested some exercises for the arm, to straighten it, but due to my laziness and busy life I did not do proper exercise and my right arm remained in bow shape forever.

Immigration to USA: -

In January 1968 I learnt from newspapers and from other railway officers that US and Canada have relaxed the immigration rules for qualified Engineers, Doctors, and Accountants. I immediately wrote to both embassies in New Delhi and got the complete information and application forms. It was a very good opportunity for me to fulfill my long desire to go abroad, so I immediately filed the immigration papers for USA and Canada during my visit to New Delhi in March 1968, when I went to leave my mother, who was with us in Gorakhpur during the birth of our son Shelly. Everyone was thrilled with this idea because no one from my family had gone to foreign countries. Ratna's two cousins had gone to USA for further studies and were still there. So the time passed by, my son Shelly had expired in June 68, I was sent for training to Poona and then transferred to Lucknow in October 68, but still no response to my applications.

Finally in January 1969, USA embassy responded and wanted me to collect following six documents. 1. Affidavit of support from someone in USA, so that I will not be burden on US Govt. in case of financial need. 2. Passport. 3. Marriage certificate. 4. Police certificate. 5. Birth certificate. 6. 3 passport size photographs. Since Ratna and I decided to go to USA together, we had to get the affidavit of support for both of us from her cousin brothers. She wrote nice letters to both of them. After about 4 months one of them replied in negative because he was sending affidavit for his brother and he suggested that since I was in good position in Railways, I should not try to come to USA because the job situation for engineers was not good and life was tough in USA. This letter disappointed me a little bit but I did not give up and tried to get other documents. Passport was no problem, my office clerk knew some one in passport office and he got us a joint passport. Marriage certificate was also no problem, Ratna and I went to court with an influential person and magistrate gave the marriage certificate right at that moment based on the affidavit given by both of our parents. Police certificate came from passport office by itself. Birth certificate we both had, because in our high school certificates our birth dates were mentioned. We got our passport size photographs taken by a professional photographer.

This way whole year of 1969 passed, I had collected all my required documents except the affidavit of support from someone in USA. We were enjoying our life in nice Bungalow in nice city called Lucknow with lots of servants, officers club and we were respected and mostly invited in local functions of Sindhi Association to which we were introduced by Ratna's aunt, who had been living in Lucknow for last 10 years. One day we were invited to attend the wedding of a Sindhi boy (Vachani) who had come from USA (He was student and on work visa in US) with an American girl for Hindu style wedding. Ratna's aunt knew that family very well. This was in January 1970 that I thought of trying to get an affidavit of support from him in Lucknow court. So I inquired about his arrival and requested him if he could spare few hours, before his wedding, with us to the local court and he agreed. So next day we went to the court with him and I took the influential clerk with me. Affidavit was prepared by the magistrate's clerk on court stamped paper, he signed, magistrate signed and in 2 hours I had the affidavit, but still Mr. Vachani had to send me the verification of his pay and verification of his bank account, which he did in Feb. 1970 when he went back to USA after his wedding. In March 1970 Ratna and I went to New Delhi and straight to the USA embassy with all the required documents. They arranged for our medical the next day and on third day on 20th March 1970 they gave us our visas for USA in a closed brown envelope. This visa was valid for four months only i.e. up to 20th July 1970. At home everyone was happy specially my father who wanted me to go to foreign country. We came back to Lucknow and news spread fast among officers and staff that we were going to USA. My Chief Engineer was also glad to know about it and he was ready to give me 6 months leave immediately.

Now I started to get the tickets for New York and went to different travel agents in Lucknow and Delhi. All agents wanted me to collect following 3 documents, which were required by law for the immigration visa holders. 1. Clearance from reserve bank of India that I do not have any land or immovable property here in India. 2. Tax clearance certificate from tax collector's office. 3. Resignation letter from railway authorities. The first certificate from reserve bank was no problem since I did not own any immovable property in India. Second certificate gave me little problem because railway books were not maintained properly, but somehow by paying about Rs. 500 as my tax dues, I managed to get that certificate. The third certificate was difficult because I did not want to resign from my current job but I wanted to go on leave from Railways to try life in USA. Ratna's cousins in USA had mentioned tough job situation for engineers at that time because both of them were engineers, and my father was also adamant that I should not resign from this class 1 service of Indian Railways. Considering these problems I dumped visa papers in one corner and convinced Ratna to forget the whole thing.

In first week of July 1970 I had to go to Calcutta on railway office business and I took Ratna with me. There in Calcutta I explained the whole situation to my Father-in-law (Mr. Awatsing Khushalani). First he asked me **"Dev, are you spiritualistic or materialistic?"** I answered "materialistic of course ". He said in that case he would try to help me. Next day he took me to one of his friends who had the travel agency. That agent was smart, he suggested that if I buy a return ticket to USA, he will arrange for my boarding the plane as a tourist without showing the immigration papers which I could keep in my hand bag and open only at New York Airport, and this way I was entitled for $108 of foreign exchange instead of only $8 (Rs. 64) which emigrants will get as per government of India rules, because government of India considers the emigration of qualified people as Brain Drain. I told Ratna to pack immediately to leave Calcutta next day because in 10 days we had to come back to Calcutta to catch plane on July18th, so that I can reach New York before expiry date of my visa, which was July 20th. I immediately sent a telegram to my father in Delhi about this sudden program. So on 10th morning we reached back to Lucknow. I explained the whole situation to my Divisional Engineer, who was considerate to understand as to why I could not do the job for which he had sent me to Calcutta. That night I left Ratna at Lucknow and told her to pack my clothes, while I was gone for a day to Gorakhpur. My Chief Engineer Mr. Mehta immediately sanctioned my 6 months leave and then I met my colleagues and friends, who gave me a farewell party at one of my old boss's house. On 12th morning I reached back to Lucknow and on 13th gave the charge of my office to my colleague in Lucknow till new AEN is posted. I was given a warm send- off party in office where all my inspectors and staff were present. On 13th night we left Lucknow for Delhi, leaving everything behind in the bungalow, which I could retain for 2 months. In Delhi we stayed for 2 days with whole family, met all neighbors, relatives, my school friends and almost everyone was thrilled that I was going to America. I requested my father that after a month when Ratna comes back he should accompany her to Lucknow, try to sell the furniture etc. or pack everything and bring home. So with all these happy moods, Ratna and I left Delhi for Calcutta on 15th night by train and reached Calcutta on 16th July 1970 in the evening. In Calcutta also everyone was happy. Ratna's brothers gave me a real treat in different restaurants and cinemas etc. Finally on 18th July 1970 we all came to Dum-Dum airport by car. This was first time that I was boarding an airplane, so I was little bit nervous and was also afraid of being caught with the immigrant visa. But by the grace of God, the travel agent arranged everything nicely, my suitcase was booked and I had one briefcase in hand. I bid good-bye to everyone; they put garlands and took pictures. I bid good-bye to my dearest wife Ratna and boarded the Air India jet 707 for USA.

First 6 months in USA: – (July 1970 to December 1970)

In the afternoon at 4pm of July19, 1970 Boeing jet 707 landed at John F Kennedy airport in New York. Throughout the journey I stayed in plane, which stopped at Bombay, Beirut, Zurich and London. In the plane food was no problem, it was Air India plane so they served Indian style vegetarian as well as non-vegetarian good food. At Kennedy airport I passed through immigration office where I showed my visa envelope and got the green card (it was sort of my ID card that I was legal alien and permanent resident of USA). Then through the customs was no problem. Finally I came out of the International arrivals building with my suitcase in one hand and a brief case in the other hand, in this new world where I was complete stranger and knew no one. There were lot of mixed feelings and strange thoughts, which passed my mind. Did I do the right thing by coming over here? Is it going to be good for my family's future and mine? Will I be happier or not? Why did I leave my wife, my parents, my whole family, my friends and my relatives? Will I meet and make good friends here? I said to myself, since I am here let me find some shelter before it gets dark. American counselor in Lucknow had made me member of YMCA and had given me the map of Manhattan New York and had marked the location of YMCA in Sloan House NY. I was guided by the information center to catch airport terminal bus and YMCA is couple of miles from there. So I did get bus and arrived east side terminal at 1st avenue and 34th street, whereas YMCA was between 8th & 9th avenue on the 34th street, which was 2 miles away. I was told to stand outside for cross-town bus. I was waiting there for bus for about ½ hour without any signs of bus, so I stopped a taxicab and asked him to take me to YMCA. He quoted $5 as the fare but since I was good in math. I worked out the fare for 2 miles as per his posted rate on the door, $0.50 for first 1/5th mile and $0.10 for each additional 1/5th mile, so it came to $1.40. I told him that according to the rate posted on the door of your cab fare comes to $1.40 but still I will give you $2 and not $5. On that he argued a little bit and finally said, "you foreigners do not know anything about New York taxi, we do not run on meter here" and he went away. Somehow after some time bus came and charged me only $0.30 and I reached YMCA. Here in YMCA charge for a room was $5.25 instead of $2.00 per night as American counselor had told me. I showed him my YMCA membership card and on that he gave me a discount of 25cents and charged me only $5.00 per night. I had no choice but to take it. Next day morning I got up early to get ready in search of a job. I went to bathroom for morning ablutions and I saw that there were 4 toilet seats with no partition in between and similarly there were showers with no partition. This was new to me and I was pretty shy person, so I skipped the bath but toilet I had to use. I ate quick breakfast in cafeteria of YMCA where I met one guy from Pakistan who was also new to the town and was a civil engineer. So we both purchased one newspaper and looked for civil engineering jobs. We went to few agencies, filled their forms but no luck. Next day we went to few companies but they were asking for our resume. It was hard for us to understand as to what they meant by resume, we showed them our certificates but they did not want to see those. Somehow we looked in the telephone book yellow pages and found a place where they prepare the resume. We gave them our job history and they put them in proper resume format and asked us to come back after 2 days and get 100 copies of resume, for which they charged $10 from each of us. This way 4 days passed with no luck. I was paying $5 for a room and about $5 per day for food plus transportation and phone calls. So in 4 days I had already spent about $50 out of my $208, which I brought from India. $108 was foreign exchange from the airline with return ticket and $100 my father in law had arranged from black market by paying Rs.13 for each dollar, whereas official rate was Rs.8. So I suggested to my friend as to why don't we look for a cheaper place to live till we get our resume. On 5th day we met one South Indian guy on the road and we asked him if he knew a good place to live. Luckily he knew one Mr. Donald Buck who rents rooms to single immigrants in Flushing Queens where he lives with his uncle. Next day we went to flushing and met Mrs. Buck who had only one room left which was big enough for 2 beds and rent was $30 per week. That was great $15 each per week as compared to $35 per week in YMCA. We immediately rented the room and on 7th day moved out of YMCA. Though from Flushing to Manhattan it was about 45 minutes ride, it was costing us only 30 cents each way by subway.

This building was 2 stories and there were 4 rooms with common kitchen and bathroom at each level. We were total 9 of us in the same building because we were 2 in the same room. Each one of us had a bed, bed sheets and some blankets. 5 were Indians, 2 from Pakistan and 2 from Iran. We all became good friends and were helping each other. One of the Indians in our adjacent room was a Sindhi. Next week when we got our resume, we started mailing them and we were going personally also to the engineering companies. I was looking for design engineers job whereas my roommate was looking for job in soil laboratory. Somehow after about 3 weeks he got job in Clifton New Jersey and he moved there, so I went to YMCA to find the roommate to replace him. Luckily I met with one Gujarati (From Gujarat state of India) boy who was chartered accountant in India and had come to USA only 2 days ago. I suggested him for sharing a room with me, which will fall much cheaper and had the cooking facility. He immediately agreed and moved with me. He was good cook so we purchased some pots, dishes and started our own breakfast and dinner, and lunch we used to eat out. This way almost one month passed. I had good living and eating facility but no job. I had mailed and given away all my 100 copies of resume but somehow there were no engineering jobs or many would say come after Labor day, which is first Monday of September, which was still 3 weeks away. In the mean time I learnt from newspaper that city of New York needs engineers of all types in its different agencies and they were conducting open examination for junior engineers and assistant engineers category every Thursday. All the legal permanent residents were eligible to apply.

I immediately rushed to that office and got the forms and syllabus. Borrowed books from some people whom I had met by now and purchased few guidebooks. I stopped going out and studied hard. In 2 weeks I was ready to take the junior engineers exam. And 3rd week took senior engineers exam. I think I did pretty well in both exams. While I was desperately trying to get some engineering job in USA, my money was finishing fast. By end of August 1970 I had only $50 left. So I wrote letters to Calcutta for help and called Ratna's cousins for lending me some money. Both her cousins felt empathy for me and each of them sent me a check of $100. Ratna's daddy also wrote to his friend in Bombay, who had his adopted son Vishnu kumar in Jamaica plains New York close to Flushing. He also came to see me and was ready to lend me some money and I told him to wait for some time. This all-monetary help gave me some encouragement and I started looking for job again. I used to go to Manhattan by subway and then walk through Avenues and Streets to go to different consulting engineering firms. By now I had maps and fairly good idea of Manhattan, so I used to plan my way so that I have to do minimum walking. Everyday I used to walk miles and miles, with my full suit and tie and a fountain pen clipped on my left pocket, in search of engineering job. One day I was passing by 46th street between 7th and 8th avenue, a girl who was sitting in front of a door on stool got up and asked me if she could borrow my pen. I immediately gave her my fountain pen, which she took and went inside. After about 10 minutes I knocked on the door, she opened the door and asked me to come in. I peeped inside and did not like the place, I realized that it was brothel and she was the prostitute. She started patting my cheeks and said "Don't you like girls." I said, "No, I want my pen back". She shouted at some one "Mary, give him his pen, he does not want us to use his pen." Reluctantly she gave me my pen and I ran away from that place.

After Labor Day I went for interview to a small consulting engineering firm called "Harwood & Gould consulting engineers". During interview Frank Harwood asked me about pile foundations design, which I had done in CPWD design office in Delhi. He was happy with my answer, so he hired me at $160/week i.e. $4/hr. i.e. $8000/year. Though it was not much pay for qualified engineer like me, but something was better than nothing. So on September 14, 1970 I started working as an engineer with minimum pay. During this time Ratna wrote that my father had met with a scooter accident and fractured his knee and she was having difficulty in getting the passport and she needed an affidavit of support from me. In October I sent her affidavit with a certificate from Frank Harwood, and my savings bank statement in which I had about $400. She tried to get all her papers including marriage certificate again (the original was lost in mail) by getting the affidavit from my mother and her mother. Finally she got the passport and visa and sent me telegram in November 1970 that she is going back to Calcutta with all the papers and plans to fly to USA from there in early December 1970 before Christmas which is her birthday. I was in two minds, whether to write her to delay her arrival here or to start the search for an apartment. Winter was fast approaching, evenings were pretty cold and I had taken up an evening job as cashier in Macy's departmental store for Christmas rush. Macy's World's Largest Departmental store was across the street from Harwood & Gould on the 34th street, so it was quite convenient. It was during the weekends only that I could look for an apartment in Flushing. It was difficult to get an apartment immediately because everywhere there was a big waiting list. Finally I decided to give $180, which was equal to one month rent, to an apartment superintendent as a bribe, plus $360 as two months rent in advance, I was able to get an apartment in Flushing from December 1st, 1970. I gave this happy news to Ratna and in return she sent a telegram that she is arriving New York on 15th Dec. 1970. I rushed to purchase a used 2nd hand King size mattress for $50 and received Ratna in an empty apartment with only this mattress tucked in one corner.

Settled in USA: - (Jan 1971-Dec 1974)

After few days stay in the apartment all alone, while I was gone to office and then to Macy's, Ratna felt lonely and bored and she had no one to talk to, because in the apartment complex all the men and women had gone for their jobs. So starting with New Year, she thought of going out in search of job. We got her resume made and every night I used to make her program to go to different employment agencies and make a walking route map for her. In the morning we both used to go to Manhattan by subway #7 to Time Square and then she was on her own, sometimes she used to get lost and used to call me to guide her the right way. Luckily in 15 days she landed up with a good job as an accountant with a financial corporation 'Walter E. Heller' in the Pan Am Building and my holidays job at Macy's had ended. So we started our regular routine, to get up early, make breakfast, take sandwich for lunch, go to Manhattan by subway, she used to get off at Grand Central and I used to go to time square and then walk to my job. In the evening we used to meet at Grand Central and come back home together. Gradually we started our savings, bought essential furniture, carpet, TV, vacuum cleaner, utensils, crockery, blender, toaster etc. etc.

New York city (NYC) personnel office informed me that I have passed Junior Engineer's exam and have failed in Assistant engineer's exam. So on Feb 22, 1971, I joined the New City Department of Transportation (DOT) with the idea that I will be doing Bridge Design. Frank Harwood wanted me to finish the pile design of his project and offered me to work on Tuesdays and Thursdays from 5:30 to 8:30 in the evening as overtime at $5 per hour. But unfortunately when I joined DOT of NYC, I was assigned to do paving design, which was basically drafting work on the drawing board. I did not like the job at all. After May 1971, when I finished overtime with Harwood & Gould, I started applying for job again. This year during summer we took vacation to Canada by greyhound bus. We visited Montreal. Ottawa, Thousand islands, Niagara Falls, Buffalo, and Rochester. This was our first nice sight seeing vacation after our honeymoon in Kashmir. In fall I joined New York City College for MS (masters in civil engineering) and I was asked to take two under graduate courses, GRE (graduate record examination) and TOEFL (Test of English as foreign language) before I could be admitted to the graduate class. By spring of 1972, I successfully finished both under graduate courses, GRE and TOEFL and I was admitted in MS starting from the fall semester of 1972. I sent the copy of my admission letter to my chief engineer in Indian Railways and he granted me 5 years education leave till July 1975. So I thought my life was set with regular routine of home, office, and college in New York City for next 5 years.

Since in our minds we both were settled with good jobs and nice apartment, Ratna showed a desire to have a child and stop our family planning, which we were continuing since the death of our son Shelly. Ratna stopped taking the birth control pills and within a month she became pregnant. In fall 1971 I received an interview call from a small design company in New Jersey. Since I did not have the car, it was difficult to reach this place; first I had to take subway from Flushing to Manhattan, then Penn-Central Railroad from Penn station to a small town Metuchen in NJ and then by taxi to the Raritan center. It took me 2 hrs. from home to office. At the interview I did very well, so I was offered the job of 'structural engineer' to design the structures of Power Plants Precipitators and Flue ducts and its supporting structures for a salary of $14000/year. They agreed to pay me all the transportation expenses for 3 months till we move to NJ and had good medical insurance and life insurance policies. I came home and gave good news to Ratna. She was unhappy at first that what will happen to her job but then we decided that she has to quit the job in any case, because she was pregnant. For few nights I could not sleep well because with great difficulty we had settled and now we had to make a move so soon. Friends and relatives thought that I was being foolish in leaving such a secured job, but I was unhappy at that job which was not very challenging, so I finally decided to quit NYC-DOT and move to NJ. On October 18, 1971, I joined 'Middlesex engineers' company in NJ. I commuted to work for 3 months, I used to leave home at 6am, and it used to take me 2 hrs. each way and it was during severe winter months. One night a week I used to go to NYC College which was on the other side of Manhattan and that day I used to reach home at 11pm. During weekends we used to come to NJ in search of an apartment. We found the apartment in Elizabeth NJ close to railroad for my commuting and also close to bus stop for Ratna to commute to work till June 72 as per doctor's advice. Elizabeth town was half way between Metuchen and Manhattan. Finally with the help of friends we moved to NJ in Jan. 72 and settled down once again for regular routine.

In NJ we found that it was necessary to have car to go about, because local transportation was not good. I took driving lessons, passed the written test and driving test at first instant. In Feb. 72, we purchased our first car Blue Dodge Dart four-door sedan from the show room for $3000 and had to take $2500 loan from bank. By May 31,72 Ratna had to quit her job because we were expecting the baby, and unfortunately by mid May I was also laid off from 'Middlesex Engineers' because they lost a big design job which they were hoping to get from Research Cottrell Corp. On top of it I had just sent $5000 to my father in India at the black-market rate of Rs.12 per dollar where as govt. rate was Rs.8 per dollar, because he was building a new house in nice diplomatic enclave called Vasant Vihar in New Delhi India, for us, since we were planning to go back in 1975. I became very nervous once again. Hastily I mailed lot of resumes to engineering companies all over United States. One day I saw advertisement in papers by 'Jacobs Engineering co.' for Structural Engineers, I immediately rushed to the place by car, it was not far from Elizabeth, and so I was first person to be interviewed. Chief Structural Engineer Mr. John Scott was impressed by my resume and interview and told me to wait till next week, so that he can interview other candidates and then select suitable person. But I could not wait for a week, so after 3 days I visited him again and requested him that I need the job and I will perform it to his satisfaction. He finally was convinced and hired me as Structural Engineer at the rate of $15000/year. So from June 1st 1972, I started working as structural engineer for Jacobs Engineering Company. My boss Mr. John Scott was so pleased with my work that in 6 months time he had promoted me as group leader and made me in charge of a small project from January 1973. I even did not claim a single penny from unemployment office since I was able to get job in 10 days time.

First American Baby was born on July 4, 1972: -
Now we were ready to receive newcomer in this world. On night of July 3, 1972 Ratna started labor pains, we immediately contacted the doctor who advised us to stay home till the frequency of contractions was 5 minutes. So whole night we remained awake till 8 in the morning, when I took her to 'Elizabeth General Hospital', which was about 2 miles from our apartment. We reached there by car in 5 mts. and Ratna was immediately booked and taken to the labor room. Since July 4th is America's Independence Day and National holiday, so I stayed in hospital and was peeping through the door in the labor room till Dr. Poch came and nurses started preparing her for delivery. Finally at 12:10pm on July 4, 1972, a baby girl was born. Both the baby and Ratna were OK. I immediately rushed to post office nearby and sent telegrams to New Delhi and Calcutta that 'A princess was born'. I took one-week vacation from office because I had to take care of Ratna and new baby whom we named Priya (means Lovely in Hindi). After 3 days when Ratna came home, neighbors started visiting us from the apartment complex. One Jewish family felt pity on us that there was no one of our family here to help us, so the lady (who was on disability leave) volunteered herself to look after Ratna and baby when I start going back to work in 2 days. She was really good and even she did some grocery shopping for us. After sometime we started calling her as Priya's Godmother.

C F Braun & co. (June 4, 1973 to Dec 15, 1982): -
For last one year I have been working for Jacobs Engineering as structural group leader and learnt to design Petro-Chemical Industrial Plants. I learnt that its main competitor was C F Braun & co., which was much bigger consulting engineering company than Jacobs. So I applied there for the post of

senior structural engineer. I was immediately selected after a short interview and its office was in Murray Hill NJ, only five miles from Elizabeth. This company was called the Cadillac of design companies and was #10 in the list of design and construction companies listed in 'Engineering News Record' magazine. It had beautiful office with wood paneled individual offices with glass door in front. Each person including VP, chief engineer, all engineers & draftsmen including secretary had individual office. There was dress code, white shirt and conservative suit with tie for men and ladies could wear only skirts and dresses but not pant suits. For men suit means matching pants & jacket and short hair. We were supposed to wear our suit all the time except when we were sitting in our office that we could take the jacket off. Outside building surroundings were also neat and clean, with nice grass, flowers, shrubberies and trees. Canteen was subsidized and was like posh restaurant. Tables were set with napkins and silverware and we had to buy our food from the counter and bring it to the table. Cards and chessboards were supplied to play at lunchtime. Company head quarters were in Alhambra California and it was owned by three brothers (sons of Carl F Braun the founder). I liked this company very much. In short time I was promoted as Project Civil Engineer (in charge of structural, civil and HVAC engineers, and architects working on my projects). In this petrochemical industry chemical engineer was normally the project manager who used to select project civil engineer, mechanical engineer, and electrical engineer from different departments. I handled the projects of Mobil oil refinery, PVC plants, Hess refinery, and a fertilizer plant, which was built in Anchorage Alaska. In Anchorage there is only 3 months construction time, therefore whole plant was built in modules on barges in Seattle. Foundation was built during 3 months of summer and modules were put on the foundation by cranes and bolted. This was first of its kind of Petrochemical plant built in modules. Each module contained all the equipment, piping, conduits etc., these modules were built on barges in Seattle, and then moved to anchorage, where these were just bolted, piping and all conduits were connected at site. I liked this job as Project Civil Engineer for petrochemical plants very much, so I decided to stay with this company (C.F.Braun & co.) forever.

Cont. on page 392

Masters in Civil/Structural Engineering (MS) - June 1974: -
When we moved to NJ, I transferred all my credits to Newark college of Engineering and in fall of 1972, I started attending evening classes twice a week. June 1974, I graduated with A grades in most of the subjects.

Visit to India in October 1974: -

Since my job was secured with good company (C.F.Braun & co.) and I graduated with MS from Newark College of Engineering and we decided to permanently settle here in the United States, so we decided to go to India in October 74 during Diwali time for a visit for four weeks. We flew to Delhi after one-day break at Paris where we saw the Eiffel Tower. At Delhi we stayed with my parents (Mom, Dad, 2 sisters & 2 brothers) in Old Rajinder Nagar, New Delhi, India. Priya was only two years old baby and was adored by everyone. When I told them about my decision to go back to US and settle down there permanently and therefore I had to tender my resignation to Indian Railways, my father was little upset, and he asked me if I will be able to help my younger brothers and sisters. I told him that after 5 years as permanent resident I will be able to apply for American citizenship and then I can sponsor my blood related brothers and sisters. Finally he agreed and accompanied me to the Railway Board, where I tendered my resignation. After 2 weeks we went to Bombay for a visit and stayed with Ratna's uncle. Ratna's elder brother Sunder was also there, with whom we did some sight seeing. After 3 days stay in Bombay we flew to Calcutta, where I told the whole story to my father-in-law, who also became happy to hear my final decision. Ratna's mom wanted her and baby Priya to stay back and spend some time with her. I agreed to that request and left for Delhi, where I took flight for New York. Ratna and Priya came back to USA after about a month.

First House in USA-July 1975: -

After we came back from India with the decision that we are going to settle here in USA, we decided to look for a house, get US citizenship and try for 2nd baby. In Berkley Heights NJ near C F Braun, we could not afford to buy a house there, so we shifted our search North and West of the company. One of my colleagues in office was also looking for a house and he found one in Succasunna NJ (a small town in North West Morris County). He suggested a house in back of his house, where they were getting divorce and had to sale the house. This was about 25 miles away from office but we could car pool. The gas price at that time was 30 cents per gallon and was going up due to Saudi Arabia embargo. We immediately went to see the house, negotiated the price with the owners because they did not have to pay the realtor fee, and finally agreed on the price of $40,000. So on July 15, 1975 we moved in our first home at 5 highland avenue, Succasunna, NJ 07876. Succasunna was a small town of Roxbury Township in Morris County NJ. Our house was 3-bed room split house and was about 24 years old. Priya was 3 years old, so we admitted her in a nursery school in a Lutheran church nearby.

One Sunday we were invited by Priya's nursery school for a social function. After the morning Lutheran faith sermons there were snacks before children's program. During that time Pastor of the church approached us and said "It seems you are new in town so why don't you sign our register and come to church every Sunday". In the register there were questions about our previous old church and new church. I answered both questions and wrote **"My Own Mind"**. Next day Pastor called and said "Your answer regarding church was quite interesting, why don't you come to the church and we will have a talk". I replied, "I do not go to church, mosque or temple regularly, except on some social functions, because I believe that my God is my **'Soul & Nature'** for which I always thank GOD in my mind. I pray GOD in my own mind in one corner, where I have pictures of most of the Gods including Jesus Christ. These pictures remind me of the good philosophies of all religions to follow".

Dev's US Citizenship-September 1975:
I was sworn in as US Citizen. I then applied for my younger sister Rajkumari and younger brother Rajkumar for immigration to USA. I told my father that they should get married in India and then come to US. Finally both came to US with their spouses in 1978. After that my father wanted me to apply for my brother Ramesh Kumar also, which I did and he also came with his spouse in1980. After my youngest sister Aruna's wedding and immigration to USA in 1980, my Mom and Dad were left alone and my Mom had lot of health issues, so I decided to apply for their immigration too. They also arrived USA in March 1982.

2nd American baby was born-November 1, 1975: -
In July 1975 when we moved in our first house, Priya was 3 years old and Ratna was 6 months pregnant. On Oct. 31, 75 evening we were sitting in family room, waiting for kids to come for Halloween candy, Ratna thought her baby bag in her belly had burst. So we left candies with our neighbors and put note on front door and immediately left for the Dover General Hospital, NJ. At 12:15am of Nov 1, 1975 Brinda (a holy place called Brindaban in India) Tahiliani was born.

Professional Engineer's license in NJ (PE/NJ)-April 1976: -
This was a three-part exam for total 16 hrs and I wanted to take all three parts at the same time. I prepared hard for this exam and also took some evening classes in Rutgers University after my MS. So one Saturday I took part 1 for 4 hrs in the morning and part 2 for 4 hrs in the afternoon. Next Saturday I took part 3 for 8 hrs with ½ hr break. Luckily I passed all three parts at the first attempt and got full Professional Engineers license in NJ (PE/NJ). My Chief engineer at C F Braun was happy and made me Project Civil Engineer.

Professional Engineer's license in NY (PE/NY)-October 1977: -
After getting PE/NJ, I applied to New York State for getting PE/NY on reciprocity basis, so that I do not have to take exam again. After a year in October 1977, I was granted PE/NY.

Ratna's US Citizenship-Feb. 1978: -
Ratna's dad was asking us to help Ratna's elder brother Sunder and get him some job there in US. He did not get along with his father in business of manufacturing crusher jaws and assembling the crushers. So Ratna applied for citizenship and became US citizen in Feb. 1978 and applied for her brother Sunder, who came with his family (wife & 2 daughters) on immigration to USA in1980.

2nd visit to India-August 1978: -
Since we were fully settled in our house, and I was happy with my job with C F Braun and Ratna was busy with both girls and housework, Priya was in 1st grade and Brinda had started going to nursery school, so we decided to visit India again to introduce to children the life in India. I took 4 weeks vacation and flew to Delhi via London, where we stayed for 3 days with my high school friend, who had migrated to London. We stayed for 2 weeks at New Delhi with my parents and then flew to Calcutta to spend 2 weeks with Ratna's parents. It was nice and short stay and we mostly did sight seeing at both places and came back home to US.

Fall from ladder-Oct. 1978: -
On a sunny bright and crisp day of fall season, I took a day off from C F Braun, because I had to go for general physical check up for the first time. I went to Dr. Kostelnick, whose office was in Roxbury shopping center in NJ. He examined me and gave me clear bill of health. I came home and decided to fix

the living room bow window, whose one pane was cracked. I had not done any work around the house with my own hands so far, neither in India nor here in US. At home in childhood my father did not want me to do anything in house except study and play, because I was the eldest son born after my two sisters and thus became the favorite son of the family. When I joined railways I had lot of labor at my disposal to take care of all domestic work and I did not have to do anything with my own hands. So I went to Rickles hardware store and bought glass to the measurements, nails and putty. I went outside on a 5ft. ladder outside the living room window and fixed the glass of windowpane. I was so excited that I hurriedly came down the ladder, missed the last rung and fell between the bushes in such a way that my left leg was bent under my body and I could not straighten it. I shouted for Ratna, but all the doors and windows were closed. This highland avenue was a dead end street, so no cars passed by for almost an hour. Finally Ratna opened the front door and said, "What are you doing in the bushes". I asked her to call ambulance because I had fallen from ladder and cannot get up. After a while ambulance came and took me to Dover General hospital. I called for Dr. Kostelnick, first thing he said "you told me in the morning that you have never been to hospital in US and now you are in hospital". He pulled my leg with a rope over a pulley and attached the weights to it to straighten my leg. Next day orthopedic surgeon came, took some X-rays and found that my left leg Tibia bone was cracked. He put the cast from knee to ankle and said that bone should heal itself in 6 weeks time. I had no choice but to go to office on crutches with my car pool colleagues. After 6 weeks he cut open the cast and slowly everything became normal.

Started playing Golf-June 1979: -
In C F Braun, it was company rule that in summer months from June to September, we used to work for 9 hrs daily Mon thru Thursday and for 4 hrs on Friday, so that employees can play golf for the rest of Friday. My draftsman George Timer was the Golf League organizer. George approached me in May 79 and said "Dave you have right elbow broken (by motor cycle accident in India) and now the left leg Tibia Bone (fall from ladder while fixing window pane) has made your left leg week, so now you have perfect combination for playing Golf in which you need the left arm and the right leg". One day during lunchtime, he took me to a sports shop and made me buy good set of clubs made by Wilson, a bag and dozen golf balls. He made me join the Golf classes in Roxbury high school. So from June 79, I started playing in C F Braun golf League.

Moved to new House-October 1979: -

For last 6 years I had good job with C F Braun and good pay, so we had saved about $10K and we had two beautiful girls aged 7 and 4, so we started looking for a dream house. We came to know that new houses are being built in Succasunna about 2 miles west of our current house. We immediately went to see the model. We liked the 4-bed room colonial house for a price of $100K. We selected the flat lot with 1-acre land with woods in the back where a family of deer lived. Sales person told us that it will take 6 months to build and we can get mortgage with 10% down. I used to come every weekend to see the progress. Finally in October 79 we moved in this new house and sold the old house with 25K profit.

During the sale of this old house, many prospect buyers came to see the house. One buyer looked at the pictures of all kinds of Gods including Jesus Christ placed on a table in our master bedroom. He did not like the idea that picture of Jesus Christ was placed with all other pictures, so he pulled me aside and told me that I should remove the picture of Jesus Christ. I asked why? He said that Jesus Christ is the only SON OF GOD. I said no; all of them are Forms of ONE GOD of good philosophies including Jesus Christ and moreover this is my house still, so I can do what I feel like doing, when you buy this house I will take away all those pictures and you can do what you feel like doing.

This new house had at 2nd level, a master bedroom with attached bath, Priya's room, Brinda's room & a guest room and a full bathroom with double sink. At 1st level we had Living room, Dinning room, Family room with fireplace, Kitchen, Laundry room and a half bath. There was full basement under the house. In 1982 I got the basement finished. In 1986, I got the in-ground swimming pool built in after cutting 40 trees because Priya and Brinda developed warps in the YMCA pool. So we were very happy family and decided to live in this house forever.

Cont. from page 387

C F Braun & co.-(June 4, 1973 to December 15, 1982): -

I was very happy working for C F Braun as project civil engineer and was getting good pay with nice benefits; good working atmosphere, good bosses and I liked the work of design and construction of industrial structures. C F Braun usually gets projects from its regular clients but in 1979 we realized that petrochemical industry was slowing down and not many new projects were being awarded to our company, so when we finished Mobil refinery project in Dec.

1979, I was asked if I will be willing to go to Alhambra California in head office on a temporary assignment as senior structural engineer for Nuclear Power Plants. I was shocked because just in October 79 we had moved in a big new house with woods in the back yard of 1 acre lot, girls were small 7 & 4 years old, so I did not want to leave Ratna alone, because it gets scary in the night. I came home and told Ratna about it. She is very brave and bold lady and immediately gave me permission to go. Next day in office my chief engineer told me that I could fly home every 3 weeks for week-end at company expenses and in addition to increase in pay I will get $50 per day for living expenses and a company rented car. Therefore on January 5, 1980, I left NJ with one mechanical engineer, for California. Within a week we found an apartment in Pasadena and rented a car. C F Braun office was in Alhambra, which was about 10 miles from our apartment. My boss here and colleagues were all nice people and I was given the job of analyzing structures for a nuclear plant, by means of a computer program. We had to punch the cards and hand over to the computer operator for processing. My friend and I had joined the bowling league and the camera club as our pass time. In March 1980 Ratna came alone for a week to visit me in CA, and left Priya & Brinda with her sister in NJ. Again in July 1980 all three came to visit CA during summer vacation. I took two weeks vacation and started by car from LA to San Francisco. On the way we saw Sequoia and Yosemite parks where we stayed for 2 nights in the cabin. Then we stayed for 2 nights in San Jose with Ratna's cousins and then went to lake Tahoe before we came back. Next week we went to Hoover Dam and Los Vegas. One day I took whole family to Disney land, Hollywood, Universal studio and enjoyed 1 ½ month in California with my family. On August 15, 1980, they left for NJ. In Oct. 1980, my boss in NJ called me to come back because he had small project for me. I was happy to come back to my family in new house and started working as project manager for revamp project of Hess Refinery on NJ Turnpike.

January 1981, we got the news that C F Braun has been sold to Santa Fe International because all the three sons of Carl Braun wanted to retire. This was an oil rigging company and had lot of rigs in Kuwait for drilling oil. President of Santa Fe International was friendly with king of Kuwait. After Labor Day in 1981, when we went to work, we saw a big banner on front gate. "We are Kuwait Petroleum Corporation". During office hours our VP called all employees and explained that Santa Fe president was having dinner with Kuwait king, when the king mentioned that he is planning to form a Kuwait Petroleum Corporation to build a Petro Chemical Complex in Kuwait and he was looking for a design company, so our president sold him this C F Braun & co. After that some employees were sent to Kuwait, which offer I refused. C F Braun in NJ and CA started losing projects. All our previous clients withdrew their projects and will not give us new projects because we had become the foreign company now. In 1982 we were very slow. Finally management decided to close NJ branch. I was given a choice to move permanently to CA office and work on Nuclear power plant for which I was already familiar. This time I refused the offer because all my family including my parents and Ratna's family, whom we had sponsored to come to USA, were now all settled in NJ. All my plans to stay with C F Braun forever were shattered. I started applying for a job of senior structural engineer or senior project manager, but there was recession of engineering jobs, because petro-chemical industry and nuclear industry were not getting the permits to be built here in US due to some political reasons. Finally C F Braun and company closed their office in NJ on 31st, December 1982.

Parents to USA (March 1982 – Sep. 1984): -
After my both brothers and two sisters came to US on immigration and permanently settled here, there was no body left at home to take care of my Mom & Dad. My mom was very sick and she had lot of complications. So in 1981, I processed their immigration papers, which were immediately approved and both of them arrived USA on immigration in March 1982. They stayed with we three brothers turn by turn every month, till July 82 when my Mom was admitted in hospital for treatment. She did not improve much and day-by-day she became very week, till March 83 when she passed away. My father became very lonely after that, because he had no friends. He tried to keep himself busy, by working on cash register in a supermarket, but still he was bored here. So finally in Sept. 84 he decided to go back to India and be with his friends and stayed in our old house in Old Rajinder Nagar New Delhi India, where he has been living since 1950. In addition to that he started taking care of our newly built house in Vasant Vihar New Delhi and resolve the complaints of the tenants.

General Public Utilities (GPU) Nuclear (Dec. 82 to Dec. 89): -
Before C F Braun closed NJ office, I had made my resume and started sending out. Luckily in the beginning of Dec. 82 I was called for interview by Mr. Rochino (Manager of Engineering Mechanics Dept.) of General Public Utilities Nuclear division in Parsippany NJ. He was impressed by my resume and interview and my 10 months experience of designing Nuclear power plant

structures. He took me out for lunch to a nice restaurant and after that when we came back to office, he offered me a job of Senior Structural Engineer with salary of $60k/year and very good health insurance and other benefits. So on Dec. 15, 82, I left C F Braun, before they closed NJ office and joined GPU Nuclear in Engineering Mechanics Dept. GPU owned, operated and maintained two Nuclear plants, one is Oyster Creek Nuclear Power Plant in Oyster Bay NJ (This is the oldest Nuclear Power Plant in USA) and second is Three Mile Island (TMI) Nuclear Power Plant in Pennsylvania near Harrisburg. At TMI there were 2 reactors and in March 1979 unit 2 had an accident, which had the partial meltdown, which resulted in the release of small amounts of radioactive gases and radioactive iodine in the environment. At the time of accident in unit 2, unit 1 was on outage for refueling. Nuclear Regulatory Commission (NRC) did not allow this unit to be started back, till all the new regulations were complied with. So GPU had decided to develop lot of projects to comply with NRC regulations and had decided to close unit II, after cleaning it thoroughly and then filling the reactor with concrete. All the utility companies in US were asked to comply with new code standards of seismic qualification of plant equipment of Nuclear Plants built before 1975. Seismic Qualification Utility Group (SQUG) was formed by all Nuclear Plant Owners in US in early 1983 to investigate and develop the use of actual earthquake data, as means of assessing the seismic adequacy of electrical and mechanical equipment in operating plants. I was selected to be GPU representative in SQUG.

In SQUG, we used to collect Earthquake experience data from various sources including: analysis or tests conducted for previous qualification programs, documentation on equipment and facilities that have experienced earthquake and data from operating dynamic loading or other dynamic environments, meaning machinery that vibrates under normal operation. The SQUG procedure called General Implementation Procedure (GIP) was developed and I was proud to be part of it from 1983 to 1986. I was very happy and my boss Mr. Rochino, who had PHD in mechanical engineering was also very happy and he suggested that we (I, him & my mid manager Leon Garibian) form a company and give lectures to employees of other utility companies, to educate them on '**Seismic Qualification of Nuclear Power Plant Equipment**' for a fee to cover our expenses. So we formed a company called 'East-West Engineers' and started giving lectures in our own time, in the evening & weekends, to utility companies and engineering colleges. This we did for 2 years (86 to 88), when all of sudden, VP of GPU fired Mr. Rochino and hired another PHD professor as manager of Engineering Mechanics dept. I became very unhappy and did not come to know the reason for it. I was not getting along with my new boss and was confident that he did not know much about the SQUG program or seismic qualification of nuclear plant equipment. So one day he was guiding me technically in the wrong direction and I instantly said 'Don't be ridiculous'. He immediately took the letter opener (a sharp and pointed object) and pointed towards me and said, "you have not seen an angry Italian". After that day he made my life difficult, started finding faults on all my designs and reports. But I liked my work, my family was set in new house and it was only half an hour drive from Succasunna to my GPU office in Parsippany, it was close to our video store which Ratna was managing, Priya was in 11th grade, Brinda was in 7th grade, so I did not want to quit the job, but I had no choice. After I gave my resignation I decided to file a court case against my boss for harassing and threatening me. I hired a lawyer, who issued a notice to him personally and to GPU as a company. GPU management did not want to go to court, because of company's reputation, so their company lawyers started negotiating with my lawyer and finally we agreed on $ 10,000 as compensation and I left GPU by December 1989.

Wedding in India and on way back tour of Europe - August 1984: -

Ratna's youngest brother (20 years younger than Ratna) Sunil Khushalani was getting married in India. At this time I was happy with my good job with GPU Nuclear, children were in school, Priya was 12 and Brinda was 8, and Ratna was housewife, so we decided to attend this wedding, which will give the children an idea of Indian wedding. We flew to Calcutta direct with our Jewish friend's son Jason Matzner and attended the three days of wedding festivities. After that Ratna stayed back with her parents and I took both girls and Jason to New Delhi by air-conditioned train called 'Rajdhani Express'. I introduced Priya & Brinda to all relatives. We made one day round trip to Agra by 'Taj Express', to see the Taj Mahal and back to New Delhi. After about a week stay in New Delhi, we flew back to Calcutta. After few days stay there we all flew to London and then to Rome. After sight seeing in Rome for couple of days, we started the tour of Europe by Euro-rail. We visited Rome, Tower of Pisa, Zurich and Frankfurt. From Frankfurt we flew back to New York via London.

Priya's sweet sixteen-birthday party – July 4, 1988: -

Adjacent to video store, there was a Theater Restaurant, where we decided to celebrate Priya's sweet sixteen birthday. We invited all our friends and relatives to come and have nice dinner and watch a live play at the same time. At the end of the play we cut the cake and wished Priya happy birthday. After that our good Jewish friends (Matzner family) suggested that we all should go to New York and watch Macy's fire works. This became a tradition every year for about 5 years.

Disney Cruise - August 1989: -

We went to Bahamas on a Disney cruise and visited Disney world in Florida for the second time.

Video Store called 'Video Zone' - (Aug 84 to June 92): -

In May 1984 my friend Gobind Hirani was laid off from his accounting job with 'Two Guys' departmental store, which went out of business. At that time new video player came in the market with movies in VHS tapes. People started renting the VCR from video stores to watch movies at home. At that time there were very few video stores here & there and people were travelling far to rent the videos. Gobind approached me to invest 50% cost to open the video store in Morris County, so that we can make profit by renting the VCRs and the VHS tapes of the movies. So we had the verbal agreement that each of us will put down $20K to buy about 4 VCRs and about 200 VHS tapes of latest movies, He went for training to Connecticut and started looking for a shop in Morris county. Finally in August 1984 we opened a video store called 'Video Zone' in Mountain lakes NJ. This was next town to Parsippany near my GPU office. We registered a corporation called 'GURU Inc.' and had an agreement that he will manage the store Monday thru Saturday from 10am to 6pm and since I continued working for GPU in my engineering job, I agreed to manage the store during evening hours 6pm to 9pm, Mon thru Friday and Sunday 11am to 6pm. Each of us will draw a salary of $10/hour. Due to our hard work and long hours, our Video Zone became a success in one year, so we employed part time high school girls to help us during our busy time from 5pm to 9pm. We hired an accountant to pay quarterly taxes. We started making good profit, but one day I found some paperwork for sale of some movies, which were not accounted for in the business accounts. I confronted my partner Gobind, who denied and said that he did not get time to account for it, so I kept quiet. But I lost trust in him, so I kept watch on the accounts and caught him same way two other times. I discussed with my wife Ratna & my younger brother Rajkumar, who had lost his job in early 1986 and both agreed to manage the store if I buy it. So I told Gobind that I do not want to be his partner anymore. We got the store assessed by an accountant and he assessed the value of store inventory and future profit prospects, as $120k. So I told him to give me 60k to call it quit, but he did not agree to it. So we hired a lawyer, who told us to sit down and start bidding on the price of store, starting with 40k as our original combined investment. So we basically auctioned the store and finally when I bid 120k, he jumped at it and said, let Dev buy it for 120k and give him 60k (all my savings at that time). I was shocked because he did not have the job, so I agreed to pay him 60k and asked my brother Rajkumar to manage the store and we will pay him $12/hour and he will get 25% of profit share. He agreed to replace Gobind.

After about 6 months, Rajkumar saw good profit in this video store, he learnt the business, and decided to open his own store in his town of Lake Hopatcong. Ratna at that time was working as part-time & temporary accounting job with Hertz Corporation for renting cars and trucks. So I asked her to quit the job and manage the store during daytime and evening time her brother Sunder had agreed to manage and help her on hourly basis, because I was busy with newly formed company 'East-West Engineering' and my regular engineering job with GPU. So from 1987, Ratna and I became the sole owners and we made good profit and in 2 years time period we got more than 60k in profit. By 1990 lot of video store chains (like Palmer Videos & Block Buster) opened up, so the Mom & Pop video stores like ours had tough time competing with them. Business became slow, so in 1992 we decided to sell the store. In June 1992 we got the offer of about 120k and we sold it. But after six months the new owner realized that there was no profit at all, and he was losing money. May be he could not manage it, so he filed a civil suit against us that we had fudged the books and showed him bogus profit. We engaged the lawyer and argued in court, but he won the case by verdict of 6 jurors. I had to pay him 20k back. Thus the court case ended in 1996.

Difficult decade of life – Jan. 1990 to March 1998: -
After I left GPU in Dec. 89, I updated my resume and started applying for job again and I applied for unemployment also. Within a week I found out that Petro chemical and Nuclear Power Plant industries have slowed down and there were no regular jobs in design offices, so I accepted temporary assign-

ments within two weeks, before the unemployment could kick in. I worked as temporary structural engineer for three years for design of maintenance projects with Foster Wheeler corp. Jacobs Engineering co. and Research Cottrell corp. I got tired of these temporary assignments and moving from company to company; therefore in 1993 I decided to start my own consulting company (R & D Engineers), which stands for Ratna & Dev or Research & Design. I started this engineering company to do Bridge design and Inspections, because after few highway accidents, Federal Govt. required all states to do Biennial Inspections of all bridges and they developed the standards for structural inspections. I was the only employee of my company and had 30 years experience as structural engineer. After sometime large consulting companies who had projects from states of NY & NJ, hired me as Consulting Engineer and Team Leader for Bridge inspections? It was real physical work, going up and down the bridges, going up in cherry picker to inspect the underside and the bearings of the bridges. As team leader I inspected 200 bridges of Queens Borough NY working for Volmer Associates NY as sole employee of R & D Engineers and had to commute by inspection van for 1½ hour each way. Then in August 1994 my company R & D Engineers was offered a similar job by Maguire group NJ to inspect bridges of whole Garden State Parkway (GSPky) from North to South. VP of Maguire group was so impressed by my credentials of education & experience and my practical work, that in couple of months he offered me a permanent job of Chief Structural Engineer (CE) in his company, because their lady CE was pregnant and wanted to quit. I immediately accepted the job, because to look for consulting work every year was becoming difficult, because both girls were in college and Ratna had picked up full-time job as teller in the bank and I needed steady income. I was given staff of 20 people (engineers, draftsmen and bridge inspectors) to manage two main projects 1. Finish inspection of all bridges (about 250) of GSPky from Mahwa town in North NJ to Atlantic City in South NJ. We completed this project in March 1996. 2.Widening of Route 287 from Bridge water to Morristown in NJ to make High Occupancy Vehicle (HOV) lane, including widening of 12 bridges. We completed the design part of this project in Sept. 1996 and awarded the contract for construction.

As Chief Engineer of Maguire Group I was responsible to submit proposals to towns of NY & NJ for their advertised projects of design, construction and inspection of bridges. VP of Maguire Group started coming to NJ every week to help me in proposals, because head office was in New Britain Connecticut.

In six months of sending proposals, we did not win any project. I became nervous and I did not want to move to Connecticut, so I started applying to NJ consulting companies and NJ department of transportation (NJDOT). In June 1997 I accepted the job of Deputy Chief Engineer with Frederic R Harris (a big consulting engineering company with head office in NYC) with little less pay. My job was to research different materials and methods to rehabilitate the elevated highway in front of Holland Tunnel. This was a turnkey project from NJDOT, to design and build this high way. By Dec.97 I finished the research and submitted to NJDOT. At that time NJ economy was getting slow and state Government was cutting its future projects, with the result that this project was put on hold (postponed for sometime). I became nervous again and started applying outside for engineering job of any kind. By this time I had about 5 years of experience in design, construction and inspection of Bridges. In April 1998 I was called for interview with the Port Authority of NY & NJ in their NJ office. Paul Crist (Engineer of Projects) interviewed me. He was impressed by my resume and interview and he asked me as to why I wanted to leave Frederick R Harris, a big consulting company for this temporary job through an agency. I explained to him the fear of losing my job and I had two daughters in college. Next day Paul called me and offered me a job of Project Manager as temporary job for one year to manage the maintenance projects of 4 bridges connecting NJ with NY (George Washington Bridge, Goethals Bridge, Bayonne Bridge and Outerbridge Crossing). So on April 28 1998, I joined The Port Authority of NY&NJ as Temporary Engineering Project Manager.

During my above difficult time, we had following family activities: -

Brinda's Sweet Sixteen party – Nov. 9, 1991 – We celebrated Brinda's sweet sixteen party in firehouse of Blair's town because Brinda was doing her high school at Boarding school called Blair Academy.

2nd Cruise to Bahamas – December 1991 – During Christmas vacation, we flew to Fort Lauderdale and boarded on to cruise ship for Freeport and took boat to other small islands.

20 Days vacation to Spain (started 12/7/1992) – Priya had gone to Madrid through Boston University (BU) for fall semester of her Junior Year. When Brinda got Christmas vacation we decided to fly to Madrid and visit Spain. Priya had finished her semester, so we rented the car (Stick shift) and went around whole Spain. We visited Madrid, Toledo, Cardoba, Seville, Granada, Elconti and Barcellona, where they had 1992 summer Olympics that year.

Trip to India – March 1995 – Ratna & I made quick trip to India. We landed in New Delhi and stayed with my lonely father. He was living all alone in old house where I grew up. He had got this house rebuilt as three-storied house and was living in ground floor. We realized that he was in the initial stages of Alzheimer's disease. I noticed that he had written a check of Rs.10 Lakhs (1,000,000) to a developer, whom he had sold the Vasant Vihar building for One Crore rupees (10,000,000), and he did not remember it at all. Developer had become good friend of my father and they both used to sit and drink scotch almost everyday. I contacted the developer, who denied having received a check from my father and we had no time to fight with him in court. After 2 weeks we flew to Calcutta and stayed with Ratna's lonely mother in their old house where Ratna grew up. We realized that her health was also deteriorating fast. For few days we went to Visakhaptnam by train to visit my sister and then back to Calcutta. Next day we flew to New Delhi and from there we flew back to New Jersey.

15 day vacation to Chile in Dec. 1996: - Brinda had gone to Chile for fall semester of junior year through her Bates college. So when Priya came for Christmas vacation from Buffalo medical college, we flew to Santiago Chille. We rented the car (stick shift) and travelled to North Chile and visited places and then to South and visited a burning volcano and other cities.

Education of our children (1990 to 1998): –
In 1990 Priya graduated from high school and joined Boston University (BU) for liberal arts. Same year Brinda graduated from 8th grade and joined Blair Academy (private boarding school) for high school. This time I was struggling for job as mentioned above, so I took lot of parent loans and other educational loans to pay their fees. Brinda did not want to go to Roxbury high school because there were few bomb threats during Priya's 4 years of high school. She chose this private school because her friends were going there. Again in 1994 Priya graduated from BU, and joined Albany medical college for MS in biology and Brinda graduated from high school in Blair academy and joined Bates College in Maine. By this time I could afford their college expenses because I was working as consultant for bridge inspections through my own company R & D Engineers and was making good money. In 1996 Priya got her MS degree,

passed MCAT and joined university of Buffalo medical college with scholarship and some student loans she took in her own name. I had to give her money only for lodging and boarding. She became pediatrician and graduated from medical college in 2000, started her residency and became independent. Brinda got her BA in political science from Bates College in 1998 and decided to work for non-profit organization in Boston for couple of years and in 2000 she joined Brandies University for Business Management. She had saved enough money for her fees but I paid her for lodging and boarding till she graduated in 2002 and started working for non-profit organization again. In 2004 she got scholarship to do Masters in teaching and by 2005 she started working as History teacher in Boston school system and became independent.

Our Parents (1990 to 1998): -
My Mother and Father had come to US on immigration visa in 1982 and due to sickness my mom had passed away in 1983 and after that my father had gone back to India because he felt lonely here. Ratna's Mother and Father visited us in 1989. Her father was sick at that time. I took him to our primary physician, who checked him and found nothing wrong, so he asked him if he was afraid of death, and he replied 'NO'. When he went back to India, in a year's time in 1990 he passed away due to natural causes. During our last visit to India in 1995 we found that Ratna's mom was sick and in Dec. 1997 she passed away. My father who was all alone in old house where I grew up, but he had got that house gutted down and rebuilt as 3 storied building. He had tenants in 2nd & 3rd storey flats and he was living in ground floor area. He also owned one other building in Vasant Vihar, New Delhi India, which he got built in 70s and I had sent him some money from US. There tenants were giving him lot of trouble and he could not manage, so he sold that building in 1994 for one crore (Ten million) rupees. In 1995 during our visit, I realized that he was loosing his memory and was in initial stages of Alzheimer's disease. The developer whom he sold the building became his regular visitor, friend and scotch drinking buddy. He had issued a check of 10 lakhs (one million) rupees to him and he did not remember it at all. I tried to get it back from the contractor but he denied it. I did not have enough time to drag him to court. So when we came back to US, I consulted my brothers and decided to bring our dad here in NJ for treatment. In 1996 my younger brother Rajkumar went to India, found his old immigration card (green card) and brought my father back to US because his Alzheimer disease was advancing fast. We three brothers were living within 30 to 45 minutes drive, so we took turns and kept him for a month each time.

But slowly as his dementia increased, we tried to get his Indian Rupees converted in to US dollars and transfer to our accounts here. One day in the evening when Ratna came home, she found that he had left the stove burning since lunchtime. The other day he went for walk in the evening and got lost and landed at our neighbors house and claimed that it was his house, Ratna had to go and bring him home. I realized that his Alzheimer's was advancing fast, so in 1998 we decided to put him in sub-acute home in Andover NJ, which was about one hour drive from my home. I used to visit him every Sunday and slowly he started forgetting my name and did not recognize me also. Finally in 2003 he passed away. I consoled my family that for last 5 years he was the happiest man, because he had no worries, no desires, no anger, no greed, no attachments and no vanity.

Priya's Engagement (July 1997) and Wedding (June 1998): -
Priya Tahiliani (Priya) met Andrew Wagner (Drew) in senior year at BU in 1994. Drew got through MCAT and was admitted in University of Buffalo (UB) Medical College, whereas Priya decided to do MS in biology at Albany Medical College. But both kept the friendship active and in 1996 when Priya finished MS and got through MCAT, she succeeded in getting admission in UB Medical College, where Drew became two years senior to her. Both continued to be friends in Buffallo and visited us in NJ for couple of times and we liked Drew. Surprisingly in July 1997 Drew proposed her after getting our approval and she agreed to be his wife. When Priya told us about this engagement, we decided to throw a big engagement party for our friends and relatives. This party was held in Moghul Indian Restaurant in Morristown NJ. Drew's parents and relatives also came from Buffallo. Wedding day was fixed as 20th June 1998 (Father's Day), immediately after Drew graduated from UB Medical College as urologist.

A day before the wedding on 19th June 1998, we celebrated the **Mehndi Day** at our home, outside on lawn and invited all our friends and relatives. Mehndi or Hanna is a paste that is bought in a cone shaped tube and is made into designs for women and men. The use of mehndi and turmeric is described in the earliest Hindu Vedic ritual books. It was originally used for only women's palms and never for men, but as time progressed, it became common for men also to wear it for fun. Haldi (staining oneself with turmeric paste) as well as mehndi are Vedic customs, intended to be a symbolic representation of the outer and the inner sun. Vedic customs are centered on the idea of "awakening the inner light". Traditional Indian designs are of representations of the sun on the palm, which, in this context, is intended to represent the hands and feet. On this day according to Hindu customs the bride gets her hands and feet decorated by the paste of an herb called Mendi (Hanna). This ceremony was followed by lunch to all the guests.

On June 20, 1998 we had posh wedding in Brook-lake country club in NJ. We rented the hall for whole day. Since this was interfaith wedding between Catholic Christian groom and Hindu bride as Ecumenical couple, for the first time in NJ, so Star Ledger news paper showed interest in the story and were invited. First we had the Christian wedding inside the hall at 12 noon followed by a cocktail hour. During this hour both bride and the groom and families of both changed their clothes to Hindu style. Outside mandap (stage) was set up in front of lake. It was sunny, bright and hot summer day. Grooms party started in a procession from right side of the lake and everyone from both sides started dancing while moving towards mandap, which was decorated with real fresh flowers. In the mean time Priya was getting ready with Indian sari and jewelry. After making Drew stand in front of the mandap I went to escort Priya and brought her in front of Drew. Both exchanged Jai mala (garland of real rose flowers) and then sat in front of fire and Pundit started Hindu ceremony rituals. After this Hindu wedding ceremony we had 2nd cocktail hour followed by reception (Dinner and Dance). This was really a Gala wedding. I have framed the article written by Star Ledger and have preserved VHS tapes and a DVD of the wedding along with the album. I told everyone that I got a Son (Drew) as my father's day gift.

The End of the 20th Century (Jan. 99 to Dec. 2000): -
First the good news came from my boss Paul Crist that he was happy with my work as temporary engineering project manager with The Port Authority of New York and New Jersey (PANYNJ), so my temporary assignment will continue indefinitely. So from March 99, I became comfortable in my job and by talking to colleagues I came to know that this is the way PANYNJ hires the employees till the permanent position is available. PANYNJ is big semi-government organization to maintain and operate 35 facilities in NYC and NJ.

Second good news was that in May 2000, Priya graduated from University of Buffalo Medical College and we gave a big party in her honor to all our friends and relatives.

Third good news was that 1999 stock market was doing well. Lot of technology companies had sprung up due to Internet, search engines, personal computers, cell phones etc. In 1998 when I joined The Port Authority, one of my colleague and neighbor suggested to sell the mutual funds and buy stocks in these High Tech. companies called .com companies. So I did that and by Sept. 1998 I had $600,000 invested in stock market, which grew in 1999 and by March 2000, my portfolio grew to $1 million.

Fourth news was bad news that by end of March 2000, stock market crashed, but all the financial advisors on TV & Radio kept on saying that people should not panic, it is only temporary, so I became greedy and did not touch my money in IRA and Brokerage accounts with Charles Schwab. I neither put more money in to it, nor took it out till the end of December 2000. By that time stocks had lost more than 60% of its value and my portfolio came down to about $350,000. In Dec. 2000 I sold all the individual companies stocks and bought some mutual funds as per the recommendations of the Morning Star magazine.

Fifth news was also bad news that in 2001 there was mutual funds fiasco, due to insider trading and I being individual investor with full time job for 8 hrs with PANYNJ and 2 hrs commute each way by car, train, & bus or walk, I could not pay much attention to my finances, till my portfolio reduced to $250,000, when I withdrew all my money from Charles Schwab brokerage firm in 2004.

STAGE 3 OF MY LIFE – (Vanaprastha - The Hermit in Retreat)

Start of new Millennium- Year 2001: -

Permanent job with Port Authority of NY&NJ

Since May 1998 I have been working as Temporary Engineering Project Manager for The Port Authority of New York and New Jersey (PANYNJ) in Jersey City near Holland Tunnel. It used to take me 2 hrs. each way to commute to work. I used to leave home at 6AM and come back home at 6PM, but it was worth it, because I liked my job and pay was good. One day in March 2001, I read in Engineering News Record that PANYNJ is looking for project managers. I asked my boss Paul Crist about it and he said yes I can apply for the job like anybody else and will have better chance of being selected. So I did that and was called for interview. Luckily Paul Crist was one of the three members of the selection committee who interviewed me. All the 3-committee members were younger (in 40s) than me, whereas I was 60 years old at that time and much more experienced than them. Therefore after few technical questions, they asked me as to how long was I planning to work. I said 'at least 10 years'. **So I was selected and on May 28, 2001, I became regular employee of PANYNJ as Senior Project Manager with all the government benefits with good medical insurance coverage for whole family, free of any premium.** Next day I told Ratna to cancel her medical plan from her bank where she was full time teller. Priya and Brinda were both over 26 and were no longer our dependents.

First Grand Child (Grand Daughter) was born (July 11, 2001): -

On July10th Andrew Wagner, our son-in-law called that Priya has been admitted in hospital in Connecticut and baby can come out any moment but we should not rush because his parents were home (They had bought this house in Sturbridge MA, because it was 45 mts drive for Priya to go to Children hospital in Hartford Connecticut where she was doing her residency and was about 30 mts drive for Drew to drive to Worcester hospital where he was doing his residency). Ratna and I decided to leave NJ in the morning and before we could leave our home, Drew called that Priya has given birth to a baby girl. So we decided to postpone our journey to next day. We did our thankful prayers to God and called our offices. Ratna took one-month vacation from First Union Bank and I took 3 days off from PANYNJ. The second day we started from our home at 10AM and reached hospital in Hartford in 3 hrs. Baby girl (Genevieve Sonia Wagner) was very cute. Priya and baby Genna were doing fine. In the evening we all left hospital for Sturbridge. We all had fun for three days, Drew's parents and we became good friends and everyday after lunch we used to go to hospital. On 3rd day Priya came home, Drew's mom and dad left for Boston to their daughter's place. Ratna stayed back for a month and I used to come every weekend.

Attack on America (WTC attack on September 11, 2001): -
Around 8:55 AM while I was busy in office writing a report for one of my bridge projects, I heard my boss shouting in the hallway that the tower one is on fire. I along with rest of my colleagues of The Port Authority of NY & NJ (PA) followed him to the parking lot and watched the smoke coming out of the tower one. I had just joined PA in May 2001 as project manager in the Engineering Department of PA, located in Jersey City near Holland Tunnel across the river from The World Trade Center (WTC). While we were watching the fire on tower one, around 9:04 AM we saw a plane flew over us and headed towards tower two for the direct hit. We were all stunt as to what happened and we saw a smoke coming out of this tower too. We were shocked and we turned the car radios on to find out that this was a terrorist attack on America. We just stood there in the parking lot with our eyes and ears open. As the world watched Tower Two collapsed to the ground at about 10:00 AM, unfortunately, this horrible scene was duplicated at 10:30 AM when Tower One also crashed to the ground. We started praying for our colleagues in tower one because PA corporate office was in that tower. PA owned and operated WTC at that time and about 43 PA police and about 43 civil employees of PA lost their lives. This terrorist attack brought about the death of approximately 3,000 men, women and children from nations around the world. My mind was very much disturbed by this incident and could not sleep in the night for quite some time and had lot of nightmares.

Heart attack & Quintuple Bypass Surgery (January 5, 2002): -
On January 5, 2002 around 5AM, I shoveled the snow from my driveway, came up in to my master bathroom to shave and shower and get ready for office. While applying the shaving cream on my face, I passed out and fell on the bathroom floor. My dear wife Ratna heard the big thud, shouted my name but I did not respond. She got up from the bed and came in to bathroom and saw me lying unconscious on the floor. She was shocked and ran back to the bedroom and called for ambulance. Then she came back in to bathroom and saw me sitting on the floor. She asked, "Do you know what happened to you"? I

responded "Nothing happened, I am just going to shave and shower and go to office". She said NO, you are not going to office today, so come and lay down on bed, ambulance is coming and we have to go to hospital in Dover NJ. There an emergency doctor found some enzymes in my blood and said that I had heart attack and they have to do Cardiac Catheterization (CC). By this time I was in good spirits and kept on denying that I had heart attack. So they transported me immediately to the St. Clairs hospital in Denville NJ, where Dr. Robert Wang a renowned Cardiologist performed the CC and told us that I had 3 arteries 90% blocked and 2 arteries were 50% blocked. That means they have to do Open Heart Triple bye pass surgery. Whole family was scared of this risky procedure. After 3 days they transferred me to Morristown Memorial Hospital in NJ, where heart surgeons performed the successful open-heart surgery. Next day Surgeon came and told me that they performed Quintuple Bye Pass Surgery and cleaned up all my five arteries, because he said that my pump (Heart) was good and healthy but all my pipes (arteries) were clogged. We all had a big laugh. After six weeks I went back to work.

Ratna's Left Knee surgery (July 2003): -
Ratna had pain in her left knee for very long time. Sometimes in 1973, doctor had taken out water from her knee to relieve her from pain. Again in 1986 she tore her ligament of this knee, for which an orthopedic surgeon performed an orthoscopic surgery. After that she developed the rheumatoid arthritis in her whole body and she started getting pain in her knees, hands, legs and arms. Since she is short and over weight and she had to stand most of the time in bank where she worked as bank teller, she started getting pain in the knees, specially in this left knee. An orthopedic surgeon Dr. Rosenzwieg saw that cartilage had dried out, so he suggested the total knee replacement. We had no choice but to go through this surgery. She stayed in hospital for 3 days and for 7 days in Kessler Rehabilitation center in NJ. After that for 4 months, she had to go for physical therapy to Kessler, where I used to take her in the evening because it was only 10 minutes drive from our home. After 4 months of disability leave, she went back to work.

Second Grand Child (Grand Son) was born on May 3, 2004 –
Drew decided to spend one year of his residency in children hospital in London, so whole family left for London and spent a year (July 2002 to June 2003) there and came back to US. Priya and Drew were still living in Sturbridge Massachusetts when Zachary Sunil Wagner was born on May 3, 2004. He was

first boy born in our family after Shelly. Ratna and I left NJ in the morning and reached Sturbridge in the afternoon. We stayed in Days- Inn because Drew's parents and some of his relatives were staying in their house. After two days we moved in Priya's house, because Drew's parents and relatives left for Buffalo and Priya came home from hospital. Ratna stayed back for 2 to 3 weeks till Priya went to work and both kids were put in daycare center. By the end of June 2004 both Priya and Drew finished their residency. Priya finished 4 years residency as Pediatrician and Drew finished his 6 years residency as urologist. In July 2004 they moved to Baltimore because Drew got Fellowship in Johns Hopkins to learn Minimum Evasive Surgery in urology (Robotic surgery of kidneys), while Priya worked as regular Pediatrician for a pediatric group. Genna started nursery school and Nanny took care of Zachary.

Ratna's Right knee surgery (July 2004): -

During rehabilitation of left knee last year, Ratna put too much pressure on right knee and due to rheumatoid arthritis; her right knee started having lot of pain. Dr. Rosenzwieg said that it happens and X-Ray showed that there was no cartilage left in this knee also. So complete knee replacement is the only solution. Since her left knee was completely healed, she agreed for this operation exactly after one year. Surgery went well, she stayed in hospital for 3 days and then 7 days in Kessler rehab. Center and then 4 months at home with outdoor Physical Therapy. In November 2004, it was her niece Shilpa's wedding, so Ratna wanted to buy some clothes. In Oct. 2004 by jeep we went to Indian clothing store in Parsippany. After some shopping we came back to the parking lot, Ratna approached jeep from passenger side and I went from driver's side. As I was getting in to my seat, I heard Ratna shouting Help Help. I immediately ran out to her side and saw her lying on the ground with her right knee bleeding. I asked her as to what happened, she responded that while climbing up in to jeep, she picked her left leg up but she could not stand on right leg, so she fell down. I immediately called ambulance and then tried to stop her bleeding. One passerby ran to a restaurant and brought some ice and other passerby tore his shirt and tied it around her bloody knee. After about 10 mts. Ambulance came and took her to the same St. Claires Hospital in Denville where she had this knee surgery done. I had followed the ambulance by jeep. In emergency room physician's assistant just tore her pants and cleaned the wound and left it open and said that we have to wait for Dr. Rosenzwieg, who was luckily in hospital but was busy in surgery room. After one hour he came to emergency room and saw that Ratna's right knee-cap was broken. He did not waste any time; he said his surgery room is ready because we have to do surgery. He himself rolled her bed through the hallway and took elevator to the fourth floor and straight to the surgery room. After 2 hrs he came out from the surgery room and said that he has removed the broken small piece of kneecap and extended the ligaments and tied to the remaining portion. She can go home and after 2 weeks start physical therapy of her right knee all over again. Finally Ratna had to go to her niece's wedding on crutches.

Alaska Tour (July 8 to 22, 2006): -
Since Ratna was physically fine except minor arthritic pains and was retired, we decided to take Alaska tour by Holland America as advertised by the America Automobile Association (AAA). This was a fully guided tour. We flew to anchorage and then next day we boarded on McKinley Explorer train to Denali National Park. It was a whole day ride in a beautiful train on a scenic route with guide explaining everything. We stayed here for two days. First day we visited Husky Homestead, restaurant where all waiters and waitresses played drama. Second day we took 8 hrs tour of Tundra Wilderness by bus. Third day we took McKinley Explorer train to Fairbank, where we spend a day visiting town. This was the North most city in Alaska. Then by bus to Alaska pipe line, a Gold Mine, and reached TOK town. After shortstop there, we came to Eagle town, which was an old Air-force base. There we boarded in a Yukon Queen Boat, which travelled along Yukon River and took us across the Yukon River to the town called Dawson in Canada. Dawson was old town, which had flourished during Klondike Gold Rush between 1896 and 1899. Dawson city's main industries are tourism and Gold Mining. From Dawson city we came to White horse city by bus. This is capital of Yukon. From here we boarded on to White Pass & Yukon Route Railways (built in 1898 during Klondike Gold Rush). This narrow gauge railroad is International Historic Civil Engineering Landmark called the Railway built of gold. We reached town of Skagway by this train. Skagway means the windy place with white caps on water. Here we boarded on Zudar Dam Ship of Holland America. Here we were surprised that our cabin was upgraded because we had filled the form stating that we were celebrating our 40th anniversary. They gave us the full suite at the back of the ship with balcony. It had bar, elegant bath and we got Captain's key of the ship by which we can go to any facility available on the ship. Ship took us to Glacier Bay with the marvelous view of Glaciers. We saw snow melting which made the big roaring sound like earthquake. Then ship came to town of Katchikan, where we took a bus-boat tour and saw the

salmons in river and bald eagles on the trees. Finally the ship reached Vancouver, from where we flew back to NJ.

Brinda's Engagement (July 23, 2006): -
In 2005 after Brinda joined Boston school system as teacher and bought a condo in Boston near her school, she told us that she is set in her life now and she is ready for marriage. So we started looking for Indian boys. We got few proposals, but all were in different towns. Neither boy nor Brinda were ready to move. So Brinda decided to go on Internet site (match.com). Finally in October 2005 she found a professor in Boston Curry College. His name was John Neiswender and he was PHD in Criminal justice. I checked his credentials on Internet, which were good. Brinda started dating him. After couple of month's courtship, Brinda liked him and was happy that she met him. We told her to bring him home in NJ during Christmas time of 2015, so we can meet him. Since December 25th is Ratna's (my wife's) birthday, we normally have family gathering at our place in NJ. Brinda and John came a day earlier because John had to leave on 25th morning to his home in Pennsylvania, where his Mom, Sister & Niece live, and 25th Dec. is his niece's 7th birthday also. So on 24th we invited Maya (Ratna's sister) and her husband Jim. Priya (our elder daughter) and her husband Andrew also came on 24th. We all six of us met John, talked to him and liked him. After John left for PA we gave OK to Brinda, and guided her that no sex before marriage. So in March 2006, aftergetting our approval, he proposed her and she said yes. The engagement date was fixed for July 23, 06, when Brinda and John both will be on vacation. John had changed his religious faith from Christianity to Buddhism, so he wanted the engagement and wedding according to Hindu customs only. For engagement we suggested Sindhi Temple in NJ and he agreed to that. We had Prayers in Sadhu Vaswani Temple in Closter NJ and big Langar (lunch for all and paid by us). Everybody including John, his mother and sister wore Indian dresses. Brinda's friend who came from California, took all pictures during this engagement ceremony.

Brinda's Mehndi ceremony (July 14, 2007) and Wedding (July 15, 2007):
After their engagement last July, John decided to move in Brinda's condo and Brinda agreed to it in spite of Ratna's objection. Somehow the year passed by nicely and they started making preparations for the wedding in Boston. They hired a wedding planner, reserved the hall, arranged for its decorations inside for reception and Mandap (Stage) outside for Hindu wedding. Since John has adopted the Buddhist religion, they both decided to have Hindu Wedding only.

Surprise came to us while John and Brinda were visiting us in NJ in March 07, that John asked us if he could adopt our last name "Tahiliani". We were shocked because this is not done in any religion. Normally the girl adopts the boy's last name. Ratna & I discussed about it, consulted some relatives. Since we are Sindhis, that means we come from Sindh State (now in Pakistan), where Ratna & I were born, we are not very orthodox Hindus, so we agreed. John became happy and he arranged to change his last name, along with his marriage certificate in court. All the wedding arrangements including the invitation cards etc. were being arranged by Brinda and John, except the financial arrangements. Brinda had given us the estimate and we agreed to spend about 100k including her new car as gift.

A day before the wedding we celebrated the **Mehndi Day** at Priya's house, outside on the lawn and invited all our friends and relatives. Mehndi or Hanna is a paste that is bought in a cone shaped tube and is made into designs for men and women. The use of mehndi and turmeric is described in the earliest Hindu Vedic ritual books. It was originally used for only women's palms and never for men, but as time progressed, it has become a custom for men also to wear it for fun. Haldi (staining oneself with turmeric paste) as well as mehndi are Vedic customs, intended to be a symbolic representation of the outer and the inner sun. Vedic customs are centered on the idea of "awakening the inner light". Traditional Indian designs are of representations of the sun on the palm, which, in this context, is intended to represent the hands and feet. On this day according to Hindu customs the bride gets her hands and feet decorated by the paste of an herb called Mehndi (Hanna). This ceremony was followed by lunch to all the guests.

Finally the day arrived, we came from NJ and stayed in Hyatt hotel in Boston where wedding was arranged. Program started with Mango Lassie (Butter milk) in the hallway where all guests had gathered. Then I guided all guests to come out to receive the groom (John) who was dressed like Maharaja on white horse. Outside in a parking lot everyone danced on nice Indian music by DJ (magic Mike). Then whole procession came to the gate (made of real flowers) in front of an open-air wedding ground. Ratna greeted the groom with some pooja (prayers) at the entrance. John then entered in to Buddhist temple (it was hotel Gazebo decorated with status of Budha, Ganesha & Hindu Gods). After short prayers Ratna & I escorted John thru the aisle between guest chairs to the Mandap (an stage for Hindu ceremony). After making him stand there with Ratna, I left to bring Brinda from her room where she was waiting for me. Wedding planner made us stand at the end of line. First was Zachary Wagner (our first grandson) as ring bearer to go and give ring to John and then Genna Wagner (our first grand daughter) and Katie Nieswender (John's niece) went as flower girls and then there were 7 bride's maids all dressed in same color sari, who went out dancing. At last we went out towards Mandap and I handed over Brinda's hand to John. They both exchanged Jai Mala (garland of real rose flowers) and took their seats in front of fire. Pundit started the Hindu ceremony, which lasted for one hour. After that we had the cocktail hour and finally reception. At the start of reception Brinda & John surprised everybody by dancing on an Indian film song. After that dinner and dance continued till 12 mid-night.

Ratna had Shingles (May 2008): -

After our 42nd anniversary on May 21, 2008, Ratna got the rash on her left arm. We thought it might be allergic reaction of some food she ate at the restaurant last night. So I applied a cream on her arm and waited for the whole day. Next day her rash had increased, so we called our primary doctor, who immediately asked Ratna, if she had chicken pox in childhood, she said yes. Doctor suggested that we should immediately go to the hospital and she will meet us there. At hospital (St. Claires in Denville NJ) in emergency room as soon as we explained that she has shingles, they registered her and put her in Isolation-ward because this is a contagious disease. She was then visited by many different kinds of doctors, who prescribed different medicines for her cure. She remained in that isolation ward for 7 days. Priya and Brinda with their families visited her from Boston. Finally after 7 days she was cured and released from hospital. Next day our primary doctor gave me the vaccine injection as a precaution.

Sunder Khushalani (Ratna's elder brother) passed away (August 08): -

One night around 10pm we got the call from Laju (Ratna's sister-in-law) that Sunder was admitted in hospital yesterday and now his condition is getting worst. Ratna & I immediately got ready and rushed to the hospital in New Brunswick. After one-hour drive when we reached hospital, it was too late, he had already passed away. Everyone was crying including Ratna. Since I was the eldest in the family at that moment, I tried to remain calm and consoled everybody and asked them to say good-bye to Sunder and performed short prayers in his room. After that everybody left for home and I asked Laju to make funeral arrangements near there tomorrow. Sunder was Ratna's eldest brother whom she had sponsored to come to US in 1980. He was nice guy, has two beautiful daughters. Next day funeral parlor in Edison NJ took the body from hospital and third day was set for funeral rituals (Wake), Pooja (Prayers) and cremation at the same place.

Cruise to Caribbean islands (April 17 to 26, 2009): -

This was arranged by a group of ladies in Senior Center of Succasunna NJ. We all boarded the bus from the center to the Sea Port on the Hudson right across from the Liberty Science Center. We all got our cabins at different areas and different levels of the ship as per the booking, so we decided to have dinner at the same table, which we reserved for 7pm everyday. This ship called the Explorer of the Seas of Royal Caribbean Cruise Lines was very big, there were 2000 passengers and about 1000 crewmembers. Ship started from NJ shore in the afternoon, passed under the Verrazano Bridge and its mast was only a foot below the lowest girder of the bridge. 2nd day we were on the ship and entertained ourselves with different activities like miniature golf, chess, play, art etc. 3rd day early in the morning we reached San Juan in Port Rico. We took the tourist bus for sight seeing the whole city and then came back to the ship in the evening. Ship sailed out at 4pm and 4th day morning we reached St. Thomas Island. Here also we took the tourist bus for sight seeing the whole island. Again the ship sailed out at 4 pm and 5th day morning we reached Samana city of Dominican Republic. Here also we took tourist bus for sight seeing of this beautiful city. As usual the ship sailed again at 4pm and 6th day we reached Labadi Island in Haiti. Here the ship was docked far from the island and all the passengers were taken to the island by motorboats. This island had lot of fun things to do like nice beach, snorkeling, shopping area etc. Again the ship sailed out at 4 pm and we started journey back home. 7th day we were on the ship whole day and 8th day we reached back to NJ port and took bus with all Succasunna seniors and reached home.

Vasudev Demla (my youngest sister Aruna's husband) passed away (August 2009): -

One night we got call from some one (he was nephew of Vasu) that Vasu all of sudden passed away tonight. Ratna and I were shocked to hear. We knew that he had Lupus and Epilepsy. Due to these diseases he had heart attack couple of times and one artery was blocked with hardened calcium. But last couple of years he was doing fine with proper medicines. My middle brother Ramesh who was also in NJ, called and said that we should go to Texas immediately.

My younger brother Rajkumar, who is in Waco Texas, also called and said that we should fly to his place and then he will take us all from his town to Aruna's place in College Station. We agreed to that and flew to Dallas from Newark and then by small plane to Waco. Rajkumar met us at the airport and drove us to College Station in about 2 hrs. He took us to a motel owned by Aruna and after quick wash we went to Aruna's house. There was chaos in the house because Vasu's 5 brothers & 2 sisters with their families, and Aruna's daughter Anjali and son Vishal had all come. Vasu's body was already taken away by the funeral home. Everyone was crying because he was young only 56 years old. I immediately picked up a book of Sukhmani Sahib (a religious book of Sikhs, in which we Sindhis believe in), which was lying there near Vasu's picture and started reading it loud. Slowly everyone gathered around me and took turns in reading it. After consoling Aruna and requesting everyone to calm down, we came back to the hotel. Next day we all got together at the funeral home which had the church attached to it. We had some prayers and speeches by Vasu's nephews and nieces, while his body lay there in front of us. I also spoke few words and recited few paragraphs from the Jap Ji Saheb (also a book of Sikhs). Then whole caravan of cars went to a cremation place, which was little far. After some prayers by Pundit (Indian priest), his body was cremated. Third day morning after doing some prayers with Aruna, we all left for Waco to Rajkumar's house. On the 4th day we took flight back to Dallas and then to New Jersey.

New Lexus Hybrid car (August 2009): -
In 2009 Federal Govt. started the 'cash for Clunkers' program, in order to boost the car sales, because in 2008 all the car companies were at the verge of bankruptcy along with big banks. We decided to take advantage of this deal because our 1994 Jeep Cherokee was like a clinker car. We always had one good family car for Ratna and other one as commuter's car for me. This time we wanted a luxury car for Ratna because I was planning to retire in few years, so we started looking for Mercedes Benz or Lexus car. Once we went to Warnock Lexus dealer on Route 10 in NJ and the sales person told us that we just missed to see a demo car of new 2010 first hybrid model of Lexus, which gives 35 mph and price is only $45,000. He showed us the brochure of that car and its factory installed options. It was luxury hybrid car with all modern options including navigation system. Ratna also liked it so we decided to buy it. We placed the order with all the options and we were supposed to get delivery in September. But in August the manager of dealership called that they were getting a car of same model HS250h and same color and all options (except

minor 3 options) as we had ordered and $1000 less. Ratna and I discussed and agreed to buy it as soon as it arrives. When we took the delivery on August 10th, 2009, the manager said that we would be the first people on the road with this Luxury Hybrid Lexus car, because no other dealer has got the delivery as yet.

Third grand child (2nd Grand son) – October 23, 2009: -

One day Priya called from Boston and said on speakerphone "Guess who is pregnant?" We both said Brinda. She said No, she is pregnant. She said that since she and Drew are settled with their jobs, (Drew as Urologist in Harvard university hospital and she as part time pediatrician in a pediatric group) and they were settled in big old house in Newton (10 miles from Boston), they decided to have a third baby after 5 years gap. So Noah Wagner was born on October 23rd, 2009. We came to her place after a week because first week Drew's parents stayed with them. Ratna stayed back for two weeks and I went back to NJ. After 2 weeks I came to pick up Ratna. Priya, baby & whole family were doing well.

Fran Wagner (Drew's Father) passed away: -

One day in early mid January 2010 on snowy day Priya called that her father-in-law (Fran Wagner) passed away due to severe heart attack. We were all shocked, though we knew that he had heart problem. We immediately called Drew and his mother Amalia (in key west Florida) and gave them our condolences. They mentioned that his body would be flown to Buffalo and that is where funeral ceremonies will be done. He was a nice person and took good care of our daughter Priya. On December 25, 2009, we had met him @ Priya's house for Christmas celebrations and now he was gone. Ratna and I packed our new Lexus on January 29, 2010 and headed for Buffalo to pay our respect and last homage to him. On 30th morning was his wake and burial and in the afternoon Ratna wanted to see Niagara falls in winter, so we went there and saw the frozen falls and frozen river, though the water was flowing underneath. On 31st there was a function in his honor in a bar and restaurant, where he was the frequent visitor. On February 1st, 2010 we checked out of hotel and came back home.

Maya Khemani (Ratna's only younger sister) passed away – May 28, 2010:

Laju Khushalani (Ratna's sister-in-law) called in the evening to inform us that Maya passed away. As soon as I came from office, Ratna & I immediately rushed to Valley hospital in Bergen county NJ. Jim's (Maya's husband) friends had collected outside the hospital. When we entered the room, where Maya's body was lying, we saw Jim (my brother-in-law) and his two sons Sharad and Sumeet were all crying. Ratna and I approached near her bed and recited some prayers in our minds that her soul rests in peace and then consoled everybody to remain calm. After a little while I went and asked the nurse as to what we have to do next. She said that body would remain in that room till we make arrangements with funeral parlor people, who will come and take away the body. So I told everybody that let us go home and make arrangements. We all came to Jim's house, where we tried to keep everybody calm and quiet. Sharad and Sumeet said that in the morning they would call the funeral parlor and Indian temple pundit and make all the arrangements. So Ratna & I came back home late in the night. Wake and cremation was set for the third day. All the friends and families (including Priya & Brinda from Boston) came for the wake and Pooja (Hindu prayers). After that we all went in a procession to the cremation place. There also Pundit (Indian priest) performed Pooja before the cremation was done in oven. Again on 12th day as per our Hindu customs, prayers were arranged in a temple. That time also all friends and relatives got together and prayed that her soul rests in peace, because she had suffered a lot due to her breast cancer.

Yellow Stone Park, Mt. Rushmore, & Great Teton tour (August 29 to Sept. 5, 2010):

We took this two weeks guided tour with Caravan tours. We flew to Rapid City and stayed in hotel arranged by Caravan. This was a nice city with statues of different US presidents at each corner. Next day morning we boarded the Caravan tour bus with lady guide and visited Crazy Horse and Mount Rushmore and reached the Sheridon town of Wyoming. Next day we boarded the bus again and visited Buffalo Bill (The plains Indian museum) and CODY museum, till we reached the town of Billing in Montana, where we saw Yellow Stone Rocks. From Billing we went to Yellow Stone Park and reached Old Faithful Lodge. This was very old lodge, built of wooden logs and located near the Old Faithful Geyser, which erupts at regular intervals every day. This was really a wonderful site, where all gathered to watch it erupt at the announced time as if some body turned the switch on. Next day we took the tour of whole Yellow Stone Park by bus, along the Yellow Stone River and saw lot of Hot Geysers and Hot spots where Lava was flowing in different colors. Next day we went to Grand Teton Mountains and took rowboat ride on the Snake River. From there we went to Jackson Hole Wyoming, where we had dinner in

Chuck Wagon Diner. From there we went to Salt Lake City in Utah and visited Sabarnical temple. This is the Mormon temple and was gorgeous. It had the assembly hall where you can hear the sound of pin dropping from one corner to the other. From there we flew back home.

Ratna's Fall & Right Elbow Surgery (March 2011): -

We were invited for dinner at Ramesh Tahiliani's (my brother's) house. After dinner we came out in front. Ratna while coming down the steps, she was still talking to Seema (my sister-in-law). After 2 steps she thought that she had reached the ground, so she left handrail and started walking. So she missed the third step and fell down on concrete path with her elbow down under her body. Somehow Ramesh and I helped her to stand up on her feet. She was having severe pain in her right elbow, we thought it might be broken, so we put her arm in an improvised sling and decided to take her to urgent care in the morning. Next day when we went to urgent care in Succasunna, the doctor on duty gave us a slip to get X-Ray done, for that we went to St. Claire's hospital in Dover where she used to work as volunteer. The X-Ray technician saw that elbow bones were broken, so she suggested that we should go to emergency and get proper sling, which we did. Third day we went to our orthopedic doctor Rozenzwieg, who had done her both knee surgeries. He looked at the X-Rays and said that elbow bones are broken in pieces, so he had to put artificial elbow and he fixed next week as surgery date. In the mean time he put more comfortable sling with cushion. After one week he performed the surgery and took 2½ hrs. He said that surgery went well and he put the same sling back on her arm, which has the soft cast, and then I brought her back home. After 6 weeks he took her cast off and she had to go for physical therapy for next 2 months.

Sharad Khemani's Destination wedding in Cancun Mexico (April 23, 2011): -

Sharad (Ratna's sister Maya's son) decided to wed Reia Balchan (Daughter of immigrants from Trinidad) in Cancun Mexico. Sharad and Reia made all the arrangements with hotel and transportation from airport to the hotel, food, décor etc. Ratna and I flew from NJ on April 21, 2011 and reached Cancun late in the night. Priya and Brinda with their families also flew from Boston. Next day we ate breakfast at the hotel and then hit the beach attached to the hotel. Khemani family took us for dinner to a restaurant in town. Next day was the wedding day. This was the beach wedding with ocean in the background and then cocktails on the beach. In the evening we had the reception at the restaurant of the hotel. Next day on 24th April we flew back to NJ.

4th Grand Child (3rd grand son) was born on May 28, 2011: -

We knew that Brinda (our daughter) was expecting a baby by end of June or July, but on May 28th we got a surprise call from John Tahiliani (our son-in-law) that baby boy was born 5 weeks premature and weighing only 5 lbs 13 oz. John's sister Sarah drew from PA, so John asked us to come after a week and Ratna should come prepared to stay for a month. That is what we did and I used to come to Boston every weekend. Brinda started nursing baby named James John Tahiliani (JJ) from the hospital, so in about 5 weeks he gained normal weight and was doing good. Brinda was lucky, being teacher in Boston school, after her maternity leave was over, she started her summer vacation till September, so that she can take care of the baby.

Ratna's back pain in 2011: -

Ratna's lower back pain started sometimes in 2007 and from MRI her rheumatologist Dr. Pare in NJ had said it is arthritis in the vertebrae of the spine. So she had prescribed 'Celebrex" and other medicines. By 2010 this pain became unbearable and at that time Dr. Pare said that it might be sciatic nerve in spine and she referred us to a pain management doctor, who sent us for MRI again. From that MRI report he said that vertebrae 7&8 of the spinal cord have severe arthritis and he programed for 3 epidural injections in the lower back, one every month from Feb. to May. After every shot Ratna was getting short time relief and then after a week or 10 days her pain was coming back. At her volunteer work at St. Clair's hospital in Dover, Ratna came to know of a Chinese doctor in Fair-lawns NJ, who does the pain management by Accu-Puncture. So we went to that doctor's office, where we found that there were two MD doctors, one male and one female. Both were partners and were practicing Accu-Puncture as alternate medicine. We liked the office, so we registered her for 3 times a week and a lady doctor was assigned to her. By this time Ratna's pain had gone down to her right thigh and right leg. Lady doctor said that it is the same nerve, which comes down from spinal cord to hip and then to leg. So she started putting needles on her right side from her lower back to leg and foot with some electric shock waves and then for last 10 mts after doc takes off the needles, a massage lady used to give her physical massage at the same area. I used to come from office at 6pm, Ratna used to be ready with my dinner and we used to rush to the doctor's office for her appointment at 6:30pm. While Ratna was getting the Accu-Puncture, I used to eat my dinner in car. Her session used to last for an hour and we used to reach home around 8:30pm. Ratna did this Accu-Puncture therapy for 3 months, but all in vain. Ratna did not get any relief from pain at all; on the contrary her pain went on increasing.

So in October 2011, we went to Dr. Rozenzwieg for check up of her leg because he had replaced her right knee in 2004. He took X-Rays and said that there is arthritis in her right hip, but we can wait because it is not so bad. For lower back pain he suggested that we see his partner Dr. Spielman who is spine surgeon. After a week we went to see him. He ordered the X-Rays of the spinal cord in the lower back area and from front in the pelvic area. From her spinal cord X-Rays he noticed arthritis in 7&8 vertebrae but from front pelvic view he noticed severe arthritis in her right hip, where cartilage has completely dried out. He would prefer that we should take care of the hip first and then spine, because after spine surgery she should be able to walk. Thus we were confused as to who is right.

November 2011 we went to Boston on Thanksgiving holidays, Drew (our son-in-law) suggested seeing a famous neurologist of his hospital, who is also a spine surgeon. So I extended my leave and went to see him. He took some X-Rays and confirmed that there is severe arthritis in vertebrae 7&8 and cartilage in between the vertebrae has also dried out. We thanked him for his opinion and took the CD of his X-Rays. In NJ we went back to Dr. Spielman and told him about the second opinion by doctor in MA and gave him CD to look at. We told him that we have finally decided to go for spine surgery. He did not agree with our decision and showed us on computer as to how bad was the hip compared to vertebrae, so he suggested going back to Dr. Rosenzwieg and getting hip replaced before he can do the spine surgery. I requested him to talk to Dr Rosenzwieg, being in same orthopedic group and in the same office, and then you both decide as to what we should do first. So in second week of December 2011 we went to see Dr. Rosenzwieg again, because he had discussed with Dr. Spielman and both had decided to get the hip replaced first. He finally planned for Ratna's right hip replacement surgery in February 2012.

Ratna's Right Hip surgery (Feb. 14, 2012): -
As explained before that orthopedic surgeon and spine surgeon decided among them that the hip surgery should be done first. So this Valentines Day was fixed for surgery. Hip surgery took 2 ½ hours and was successful. Ratna had

to stay in St. Clair's hospital in Denville NJ for 3 days and then she was transported in to Kessler Rehab Center in Chester NJ, near our home. I used to visit her everyday after work and then come home and have dinner. She stayed there for a week and then came home. Next day she continued outdoor therapy with Active Care Therapists in Roxbury mall. She did therapy for 3 months till her hip was healed and pain in the hip and leg was gone. But by God's grace her lower back pain was also gone. When we gave this good news to Dr. Rosenzwieg and thanked him for good surgery and told him to give our thanks to the spine surgeon Dr. Spielman, who had suggested to go for hip surgery first, and now there is no need for spine surgery. THANK GOD ALL HER PAINS WERE GONE. She became normal and started her volunteer work back in St. Claire's hospital in Dover NJ.

My Retirement from The Port Authority of NY & NJ (PA)-March 24, 2012: -

On May 28, 2011, when I completed 10 years with PA, I had decided to retire as soon as we sell our house. I had told this to all my family members, relatives, friends and colleagues. But in 2011 we were unable to sell our house, so we decided to completely renovate our kitchen in Dec.2011 and then try to sell it in 2012. In early January 2012, we came to know that newly elected Governor of NJ, Chris Christie, is going to cut some PA employees benefits. In first week of March, while we were having lunch, one of our colleagues said that Governor is asking all PA employees to pay share of medical insurance premium, which was being paid 100% by PA. I immediately called human resources to confirm that rumor. They said that yes it is coming but they did not know the effective date of that policy. I came home and discussed with Ratna and decided to retire immediately in order to get free medical insurance for life. Next day I called human resources and gave them 2 weeks notice with intention to retire. I sent them email to confirm in writing. Human resources sent me some forms to be filled in. In those forms I was surprised to see that PA wants commitment from me that I will pay the insurance premium after retirement from the date when policy becomes effective. I had no choice but to sign that agreement, because my retirement date was fixed as March 24, 2012. Finally when commission report was accepted by the NJ and NY Governors, it was decided that the portion of medical insurance premium shall be paid by all PA employees and retired employees with less than 25 years service, effective from Jan. 1, 2012. But my decision was final and March 24, 2012 was my last day at work, as senior Project Manager with The Port Authority of NY & NJ. Couples of parties and lunches were given in my honor and finally I said good-bye to all my friends and colleagues.

Ratna's Cataract Surgery (August 2012): -
On June 12 we went to our ophthalmologist for our regular six monthly checks up of eyes. Dr. Nayar had been warning us for last 5 years that Ratna has cataract developing in her both eyes. He was checking the growth every six months and this time he said it is time for surgery. Since I had retired, put the house on sale and we were planning to move to Boston, so we decided that it is good time that Dr. Nayar (who has been our ophthalmologist for last 30 years) to perform the surgery and remove the cataract. Doctor fixed the surgery dates as August 3 and August 17. Both surgeries were same day surgeries and went well. We asked doctor to give us all the prescription for one year till we move to Boston and find the good ophthalmologist. In November 2012, when we went back to NJ for my nephew's engagement, we went to Dr. Nayar for final check up of her eyes.

Sold our House at 104 Toby drive, Succasunna NJ 07876 and Moved to Boston (September 7, 2012): -
On May 28, 2011, I completed 10 years of regular service with the Port Authority of NY&NJ (PA), so I decided to retire as soon as we sell this house. So we listed this house for sale with Caldwell Bankers real estate agent. He was local guy and resident of Succasunna. We listed for $470k, but did not get much response, so from July 1st we reduced it to $450k, but still no response, so from Aug 1st we reduced it to $430k, but still no response. Lot of people used to come to see the house, but no one put any bid. Agent said that all houses below $400k are selling, but I was not ready for that low price. We decided to take it off the market, because our kitchen was obsolete, people were looking for granite countertop and stainless steel appliances and light colored cabinets. We gave contract to Sears for all above 3 items at the cost of $20k. They took whole month of Dec. 2011 to completely renovate the kitchen. Then I got the hallway and kitchen painted. Now the house was ready for sale in 2012.

We again put the house on the market with Wiechert Realtors in April 2012 for asking price of $420k. In May 2012 we reduced the price to $399k as per the recommendations of the realtors who were doing open house every other Sunday. In May after the open house visit one customer offered us the price of $370k, which we rejected. In June Brinda (our younger daughter) called from Boston that they have found a newly built 4 bed room colonial house in Dedham MA and they are going to buy it, closing will be in July and they will move by end of July 2012. She suggested that if we sell the house in NJ as soon as possible, move to Boston in August, and rent her 2-bed room condo, which she owns. This made us think, what a coincidence, so I called my realtor to follow up with the customer who offered us $370k, because we did not get any other offer till June end. Finally they came back in July (because they sold their condo in Succasunna) and started bargaining for the price. We finally agreed to median price of 387k. They wanted to close by mid August, because that is the time they are closing on their condo, but my niece Tina Tahiliani (daughter of my youngest brother Rajkumar) was getting married on August 31st in NJ. So we agreed to close on September 7,2012. For 2 weeks we agreed to keep POD (with all their belongings) on the front lawn. Priya and Brinda with their families came on August 27 to enjoy the pool & house for the last time and to attend Tina's wedding. They all left on Sept. 1, 2012 for Boston. Ratna and I finished the remaining packing of boxes. Movers came on Sept. 6 and took all boxes & furniture. Cleaning lady came in the evening and cleaned the whole house and sanitized bathrooms. Ratna & I went to a motel in Roxbury to sleep for the night. Next day morning on Friday Sept. 7, 2012, we came back to the house to pack the car and empty the refrigerator. We had only one car Lexus left to pack all remaining things, because Drew drove Camry to Boston, because Ratna was not able to drive due to her right hip surgery and she had pain in her left hip and right shoulder. When I started packing Lexus I found that big chest full of frozen food would not fit in trunk of the car. So Ratna called her friend Radmilla to come and take all the food, which she can use. We also gave her some plants and some clothes to keep in her condo, till we come back in Nov for my nephew's engagement.

After we packed Lexus and cleaned everything, at 2pm buyers came to inspect the house for the last time. They were satisfied and then we all left for their lawyer's office in Succasunna. There closing went well and after about 2 hrs when they received the bank check from their mortgage bank and handed over to us, we gave them the bunch of house keys. Ratna cried little bit because we lived in that house for last 32 years. We started for Boston at 5pm. We stopped for dinner on the way and reached Boston at Brinda's new home around 11pm. Next day on Saturday Sep 8, 2012, Movers came at Brinda's house to unload certain items which we were giving to them. After that John guided the mover's truck and we both went to Brinda's condo in our Lexus and unloaded all our furniture and boxes.

5th Grand Child (our fourth grand son) was born on November 23, 2012:
On Thursday Nov. 22nd we both and Priya with her family were all at Brinda's new home for Thanks-Giving dinner. John as usual was frying the Turkey. Brinda had invited some of their friends too. All ladies were preparing the food and setting up dinning table. Drew carved the Turkey and we all had dinner together. We all left Brinda's home at 11pm and came home and slept. Next day morning around 5am Brinda called that we should go to her house immediately because her contractions have started so she and John had to go to hospital and we had to take care of JJ (Brinda's first son who was 18 months old now). We reached her place at 6am on Nov 23,12, JJ was still sleeping and they both left for hospital. In the afternoon a baby boy named Ashram Tenzen Tahiliani was born, weighing about 7 lbs & 11.5ozs, delivery went normal and both were doing fine. In the evening John came home to take care of JJ, and Ratna & I went to the hospital. Brinda stayed in hospital for 3 days and then came home.

Taking Care of my dear wife Ratna (whole year of 2013): -
While we were still in NJ and before we reached Boston on Sept. 7, 2012, Ratna was complaining about pain in her Left Hip & Right Shoulder due to Rheumatoid Arthritis and she had stopped driving car. So here in Boston we asked Andrew Wagner (our son-in-law), who is urologist in Boston's best hospital 'Beth Israel Deacons Medical Center (BIDMC)', to recommend us the Orthopedic surgeon. He suggested Dr. Douglas Ayers for Hip and Dr. Zilberfarb for shoulder. Priya Wagner (our elder daughter), who is pediatrician, suggested Dr. Cathy Tong as our primary doctor. All these doctors were affiliated with BIDMC. At the same time we started looking for a condo close to Priya's and Brindas's house but away from the city. At present we were renting Brinda's condo in Roxbury, only 2 miles from downtown Boston.

First we visited Dr. Ayers on Nov. 5, 2012. He took X-Rays of her Left Hip and told us that her cartilage has dried out and only solution is to replace it with artificial hip. He sent us for hip surgery classes and fixed the hip surgery date as Jan. 10, 2013.

Next we went to Dr. Zilberfarb on Nov.28, 2012. He also took the X-Rays of her Right Shoulder and saw that cartilage has dried out and there was tear in rotator cup (which Ratna had torn about 8 years ago). For that purpose he sent us for MRI and suggested that we should get her hip replaced and then see him some times in March or April. Ratna asked him as to what shall we do in the mean time for her pain in that shoulder, which is unbearable. He suggested that we should go to pain management of BIDMC and get the Epidural Steroid injection before hip surgery. So we got her that injection on January 8th, 2013, so that she will not suffer from pain in shoulder during her hip surgery.

On January 10, 2013, Dr. Ayers performed the left hip surgery in BIDMC hospital, where Drew also performs his urological surgery, and so we were getting VIP treatment. That day Dr. Ayers had some complications during surgery of a patient before Ratna, so she had to wait for her turn till 4 pm. I had cough and cold that day, so Dr. ayers suggested that I should go home and after surgery he will call me home. After about 3 hrs. Dr. Ayers called me and gave me good news that surgery went well and she is in recovery room and in about an hour she will go into her private room. Next day morning I went up on 12th floor with flowers and met her in her private room. After 3 days she was transferred to Hebrew Rehab. Center in Roslindale, where she fully recovered in 10 days and on 24th January I brought her to our condo in Roxbury. For first two weeks, visiting nurse association of Boston sent physical therapist, occupational therapist and an aid to help her recover at home. After that I used to take her to Hebrew Rehab. Center for out patient therapy, 2 times a week till end of April 2013. During this therapy period Dr. Ayers checked her couple of times and declared her as fully recovered.

On April 18, 2013, we went to see Dr. Zilberfarb for her right shoulder, where her pain had become unbearable. He reviewed the X-Rays and MRI and said that the tear in rotator cuff has increased and the cartilage has also dried out, so this simple shoulder replacement prosthesis will not solve both problems and the only solution is **reverse prosthesis surgery** in which the ball from the upper part of the arm will have to be cut and artificial socket drilled into it and artificial ball will be drilled in to the torn rotator cuff. And he said that this is a specialized surgery, which he does not perform. He recommended Dr. Joseph De Angelis of BIDMC for this reverse shoulder surgery.

We immediately fixed appointment with Dr. De Angelis and visited him on 23rd April 2013. He looked at the X-Rays and MRI reports and agreed with

Dr. Zilberfarb that reverse prosthesis surgery is the only solution. After couple of more visits and more X-Rays, June 24th was fixed as the date for surgery. He wanted to give at least six months gap between her hip surgery and this surgery. Finally on 24 June 2013 @ 7:30 am this Reverse Prosthesis surgery was successfully performed and she was given a full arm cushioned sling to wear 24/7 for 6 weeks. Next day morning in the hospital, Ratna passed out for few moments, Dr. De Angelis was called in and he called me home and said 'not to worry, the nerve block which was given to her during surgery, sometimes reacts after 24 hours'. Ratna then complained to him that she did not have any feeling in her pinky and ring finger of the right hand. To that he replied that sometimes during surgery some nerves get compressed and it might take up to a year to come back. Ratna was supposed to stay in hospital for one night, but now Dr. De Angelis wanted her to stay for two nights to do some more tests, before releasing her. After two days Ratna came home and next day visiting nurse association of Boston sent the Occupational therapist and aid at home. Ratna continued this occupational therapy at home for 4 weeks.

While Ratna's therapy for right shoulder was still in progress, we had to pack our clothes and other belongings and move from Roxbury to Natick in Massachusetts (MA), where we have bought our newly built condo. Since Ratna was still in sling, I had to do all the packing. Luckily we had opened only the items we needed for living and rest of 150 boxes were in the storage room. Finally we moved in our condo on July 29, 2013 and started unpacking. Ratna's sling came off on August 8, 2013. From August 12,2013 we started her out patient therapy with Spaulding Rehabilitation center in Framingham, for 2 days in a week, every Tuesday and Thursday. This therapy continued till end of November 2013.

While her shoulder therapy was going on, Ratna started complaining about pain in left hip near the same area where cut was made. So we called Dr. Ayers, who gave us an appointment for November 1st, 2013 to see him. He took some more X-Rays, felt the spot where she was feeling pain and told us that the hip prosthesis is OK, but she is having pain in the muscle near surgery due to calcium built up. He prescribed oral medicine and said that it might take a year to dissolve this calcification and in the mean time she should do some physical therapy for the hip. Ratna decided to do this therapy in January 2014, after completing the shoulder therapy.

For her numbness in two fingers of right hand, Dr. De Angelis had suggested to go for EMG (electromyogram) test and then see the Hand Surgeon of BIDMC, Dr. Tamara Rozental. So we got the EMG test done at Spaulding rehab. Center and then met with Dr. Rozental on October 22,2013. From EMG test and X-Rays of right hand and elbow, she concluded that it is her right Ulnar nerve, which has been compressed due to 6 weeks in sling from hand to elbow. This will require a minor surgery to decompress this nerve.

Ratna was not happy to have surgery in her artificial right elbow and wanted to get 2nd opinion. One of her new friend in condo complex referred us to Dr. Mathew Liebman (hand surgeon who was not connected with BIDMC group), whom we visited on October 31, 2013. I gave him a disc of her hand and elbow X-Rays and a copy of EMG test report. He was not sure whether the Ulnar nerve was compressed at the elbow or the shoulder, so he sent us to Dr. Peter Warinner (Neurodiagnostic specialist). He basically performed the same EMG test but in a more refined way and he came to the positive conclusion that it is the right Ulnar nerve which is compressed at the elbow. After few days we went back to Dr. Leibman on November 12, 2013, who looked at the new EMG report and said that he has to perform the surgery at elbow to release the Ulnar nerve. Ratna and I discussed as to whom should we go for surgery, because both Dr. Rozental and Dr. Liebman are saying the same thing. We needed some time to think about it.

In the mean time we flew to Houston Texas to attend my niece's wedding and then we visited our relatives on the way to Dallas, from where we flew back to Boston. During this week of vacation to Texas, Ratna finally decided to go to Dr. Rozental, who is attached to BIDMC and she knows that we are Andrew Wagner's in-laws. So we visited Dr. Rozental on December 17, 2013 and she fixed the surgery date as January 21, 2014. After surgery Dr. Rozental came to see me in the waiting room and said that as soon as she made the cut in the elbow, her nerve just popped out and she relocated it properly. Surgery took only 20 minutes and she is doing fine. Once she recovers from Anesthesia, she will be ready to go home. After two weeks we visited her for post op. check up and everything looked normal. She prescribed some Occupational Therapy for few weeks and for nerve to get full strength might take about a year. By mid March 2014 all her therapies will be over and hopefully Ratna will be free of all pains.

Trip to Nova Scotia (July 20 to 29, 2014): -

Since Ratna started feeling better and her aches and pains were less, I suggested this trip in order to divert her mind and see this paradise of Canada. So on July 20th we flew to city of Nova Scotia. In the Hilton hotel near airport we met other tourists of Caravan Bus Tour Company. We were 46 tourists in a bus of 58-passenger capacity, and there was our tour guide Olive Murwin (a native of Halifax) and our bus driver Gelasius (Roman God) a native of Prince Edwards Island. On 21st we saw Flower pot rocks at Hopewell cape, Observed the gradual rise or fall of the bay of Fundy Tides, an average change of 6 to 8 feet per hour with astounding 50 feet throughout the day. Then we travelled over the 8-mile Confederation Bridge to the picturesque province of Prince Edwards Island (PEI). There we stayed at country inn in charlotte town for two nights.

On 23rd we took scenic route of Cape Breton Island and stayed in town of Cheticamp for two nights. Next day we all got ready and boarded a boat for Whale Watching, but unfortunately as soon as we reached the open sea, there were heavy wind and waves were high, so our tour guide decided to go back.

On 25th we started for Cabot Trail. We saw rugged cliffs and wonderful ocean views, till we reached a town of Baddeck where we stayed for 2 nights. From here we went to Alexander Graham Bell's house and museum, Fortress of Louisbourg and took a sail boat to take a round of bay and see the Graham Bell's house from ocean side. Tour guide said that this sailboat ride is in place of the Whale watching tour.

On 27th we drove to Peggy's Cove, a fishing village with Canada's oldest Light-house. There we had lunch and groups photograph and finally drove back to Halifax city, where we stayed for two nights. Next day we had a guided stroll along the historic waterfront and enjoyed a visit to the Maritime Museum of the Atlantic. On 29th we flew back to Boston.

This bus tour was too much for Ratna's shoulders, because every time while boarding the bus, she had to pull her body with her arms, this she had to do at least five times a day. She had surgery done on her Right shoulder about a year ago, so unconsciously she was putting more pressure on left shoulder, so for the last two days of tour she started feeling pain in her left shoulder. For one month after the tour she started putting ice on the left shoulder, thinking that sore pain will go away, but the pain kept on increasing. So on August 26th, 2014, we went to see Dr. Joseph De Angeles, who had done her right shoulder surgery. He examined the new X-rays of left shoulder and said everything is OK and there is no evidence of fracture or dislocation or advanced degenerative change due to arthritis, but there is slight inflammation of tissues called Tendonitis, for which he prescribed physical therapy for 8 weeks. So Ratna started her physical therapy in Spaulding Rehabilitation center with same therapist Tara, on September 2nd 2014.

STAGE 4 OF MY LIFE –(SANNYASA–THE WANDERING RECLUSE)

According to Hindu Vedas (about 3500 years old scriptures), Sannyasa is the state of dispassion and detachment from material life, denouncing worldly thoughts and desires in order to spend the remainder of life in spiritual contemplation.

In the modern world, it is difficult to follow the above ideals, but for my remaining life, I will try to control the five emotions (Desire, Anger, Greed, Attachments & Ego) to a lesser and lesser degree as the year's pass-by. This is my promise to myself at the age of 75 on November 19, 2014.

I am thankful to my wife Ratna, daughters Priya & Brinda, my grand daughter Genna, and my brothers & sisters, who all got together and gave me a surprise 75th Birthday party, in Scottsdale Arizona, during my nephew's wedding. They also showed a video of my life to everyone. I am really blessed to have such a loving nuclear family.

For me, my family comes first, then my GOD (Nature & Soul), and then the people of the world. At present my family is well settled in India & US, my SOUL is content and at peace, now I am going to spend rest of my life to the service of the needy and innocent people of the world.

I am going to live my life and forget my age. I have seen better days, but I have also seen worse. I don't have everything that I want, but I do have all I need. I wake up with some aches and pains, but I wake up and am conscious. My life may not be perfect, but I am blessed. I am so blessed to have lived long enough to have my hair turning grey, and to have my youthful laughs be forever etched in to deep grooves on my face. We have moved to Boston and bought a condo as our final residence, close to our five grandchildren. I will be watching them grow up step by step.

Success is very often confounded with making money – plenty of money and with gaining prestige and reputation. True success does not lie in these things. True success is in Freedom and Fulfillment.

As I have aged, I have become kinder to myself and less critical of myself. I have become my own friend. I know I am sometimes forgetful, but there again, some of the life is just as well forgotten. And, I eventually remember the important things. As you get older, it is easier to be positive. I care less about what other people think. I don't question myself anymore. I have even earned the right to be wrong.

So I like being old, it has set me Free and Fulfilled or Content.